B. Lee Cooper, PhD
Wayne S. Haney, MDiv

Rock Music in American Popular Culture III
More Rock 'n' Roll Resources

D1453467

*Pre-publication
REVIEWS,
COMMENTARIES,
EVALUATIONS . . .*

"**T**his volume is further evidence that Cooper and Haney are to rock 'n' roll resource research what FBI agents Scully and Mulder are to *The X-Files.* Rather than 'the truth is out there' mantra, it is 'the music is out there' for [thes]e two rock 'n' roll obsessives.

[The] dynamic duo engages readers [i]n endless round of rock 'n' roll [Jeop]*ardy!,* with musical categories [rang]ing from death, hoaxes, and [holi]days, to fools, tobacco, and [pub]lic schools.

[R]eaders can browse or bury [them]selves in this overwhelming [yet] orderly collage of song lists [and] lyrics, book and record re[view]s, bibliographies, discogra[phie]s, biographical sketches, and critical commentaries. The text is at once an archive, Web site, Walkman, and musical map of a pleasant journey through eras, styles, artists, and songs.

The amount of information here is truly staggering. Whether casual, curious, or compulsive, there is something in this collection for everyone. If there is a rock 'n' roll(ing) stone, nugget, gem, or relic left uncovered in this trilogy, be assured that it will be located, examined, and preserved by these two archival agents in the volumes to come. The only mystery that remains is: when do Cooper and Haney ever sleep?"

George Plasketes, PhD
*Associate Professor,
Radio/Television/Film,
Auburn University, AL*

"In a time of abstruse criticism of obscure texts, Cooper and Haney's work is a joy to read: lucid, practical, insightful, and erudite. Sometimes I read them for ideas; sometimes I read them just as a trip down memory lane. Their lists remind me time and again how saturated our lives are with popular music; their thematic excursions are day trips with an entertaining guide through the back forty. We know this landscape, we recognize this route. But this book teaches us to see familiar territory with new eyes, and to remember that popular music functions not only as a major component of our popular culture, but as a major public forum for debate *on* popular culture, and on issues political, moral, social, and personal.

I have spent a lot of time lately in Eastern and Central Europe. One thing has become obvious: when future generations ask, 'Just what was it America gave us in the American century?' the answer will not be poetry or fiction, postmodernism, or even consumerism, industrial capitalism, or environmental awareness. The answer will be 'hope . . . and McDonald's, cinema, television, and rock 'n' roll.' This is our cultural legacy, and any teacher or critic who fails to understand or chooses to ignore that fact merely exacerbates the split between school learning and the real world, and relegates himself or herself to cultural margins. This book, like its predecessors, helps all of us understand rock 'n' roll as a social force and a cultural commentary on issues as large as death, work, and education, and as small as tobacco and postal communication."

David R. Pichaske, PhD
Professor of English,
Southwest State University,
Marshall, MN

"Like the first two volumes, this third volume is a treasure trove of rock songs and perceptive commentary. It also features a current rock bibliography for those who wish to push deeper into specific lore. The simple topical and alphabetical arrangement makes it easy to use. I particularly recommend it for teachers thinking about using rock music in their classes. But, anyone who enjoys popular music will find it interesting. Of the all-new song areas, perhaps the most topical are those on death, military activities, patriotism, public schools, tobacco, and wartime."

Jerry Rodnitzky, PhD
Professor of History,
University of Texas at Arlington

More pre-publication
REVIEWS, COMMENTARIES, EVALUATIONS . . .

"**R**ock Music in American Popular Culture III: More Rock 'n' Roll Resources* demonstrates the strengths of B. Lee Cooper and Wayne S. Haney in guiding the reader through the constantly changing maze that is today's popular music. Cooper and Haney write that an understanding of today's rock 'n' roll comes from reading, singing, and analyzing the texts, not glancing at some platonic reflection in the clouds above the singers. As usual, they are right on target. This volume demonstrates the authors at their best, leading us through various types of popular music and providing sensible commentaries along with the finest bibliographies and listing of songs available. For singers and scholars alike, this volume is indispensable."

Ray Browne
Popular Culture Association,
Bowling Green State University,
Bowling Green, OH

"**C**ooper and Haney's 'Rock Music in American Popular Culture' series is the best effort of this sort since Dave Marsh and Kevin Stein's infamous 1971 *Book of Rock Lists.* From 'social commentary' to 'death' to 'foolish behavior,' Cooper and Haney define and trace thematic paths through the thick underbrush of rock 'n' roll, blazing valuable musical trails for educators who might wish to incorporate music in their classroom teaching, as well as rock junkies who are always looking for new rhythmic roads to run down. Especially important are the authors' incisive comments that put each topic in context, and their extensive bibliographies of further rock resources. If I were stranded on a desert isle, I'd want *Rock Music in American Popular Culture* with me, along with my desert discs. It's packed with intriguing and important information. Besides, it's big enough to use as a raft."

George H. Lewis, PhD
Professor of Sociology,
University of the Pacific,
Stockton, CA

"**W**ith this third volume in their 'Rock Music in American Popular Culture' series, Cooper and Haney continue to provide scholars and educators with an indispensable source for musical ideas and resources. The song lists and bibliographies should be a great boon to teachers in all grade levels."

Timothy E. Scheurer, PhD
Franklin University,
Columbus, OH

Rock Music in American Popular Culture III
More Rock 'n' Roll Resources

HAWORTH Popular Culture
Frank W. Hoffmann, PhD and B. Lee Cooper, PhD
Senior Editors

Rock Music in American Popular Culture III
More Rock 'n' Roll Resources

B. Lee Cooper, PhD
Wayne S. Haney, MDiv

The Haworth Press
New York • London • Oxford

The Haworth Press, Inc., 10 Alice Street, Binghamton, NY 13904-1580

Cover design by Jennifer M. Gaska.

Library of Congress Cataloging-in-Publication Data

Cooper, B. Lee.
  Rock music in American popular culture III : more rock 'n' roll resources / B. Lee Cooper, Wayne S. Haney.
        p.   cm.
  Includes bibliographical references, discographies, and index.
  ISBN 0-7890-0489-5 (hard : alk. paper).—ISBN 0-7890-0490-9 (pbk. : alk. paper).
    1. Rock music—United States—History and criticism. 2. Rock music—United States Bibliography. 3. Rock music—United States Discography. 4. Popular culture—United States—History—20th century. 5. Music and society—United States. I. Haney, Wayne S. II. Title.
ML3534.C665 1999
781.66'0973—dc21   99-10097
                                                                                                                    CIP

To
Jill, Michael, Laura, and Julie
and
Mary Catherine and Matthew James

ABOUT THE AUTHORS

B. Lee Cooper, PhD, is Provost and Vice President for Academic Affairs at the University of Great Falls in Montana. He is an internationally published expert in the area of lyric analysis, popular culture bibliography, discography, and teaching methods in social studies. His previous publications include *Rock Music in American Popular Culture: Rock 'n' Roll Resources; Images of American Society in Popular Music; The Popular Music Handbook; The Literature of Rock II* with Frank W. Hoffmann; and *Popular Music Perspectives: Ideas, Themes, and Patterns in Contemporary Lyrics.* He is a member of the American Association of Higher Education, the American Culture Association, and the Association of Recorded Sound Collections.

Wayne S. Haney, BME, MDiv, is a history teacher at North Branch High School, proprietor of The Stamp 'n' Grounds coffee shop, and former Rector of Grace Episcopal Church in Lapeer, Michigan. Formerly Associate Director of the Academic Resource Center at Olivet College, Mr. Haney is an organist and computer specialist who has co-authored *Rock Music in American Popular Culture: Rock 'n' Roll Resources; Response Recordings: An Answer Song Discography, 1950-1990;* and *Rockabilly: A Bibliographical Resource Guide.*

CONTENTS

Preface

This is the third volume in the Haworth "Rock Music in American Popular Culture" series. It continues the audio journey of the previous anthologies published in 1995 and 1997. Readers are invited to jog along selected paths of contemporary American life while listening to and analyzing tunes on their Sony Walkman headphones. Readers are also urged to explore thematic highways and byways depicted on television or in motion pictures, along with the ubiquitous soundtracks that enliven them. Finally, readers are encouraged to consider lyrical terminology, imagery, and direct illustrations of both human relations and geographical settings. The goals of *Rock Music in American Popular Culture III* are both to enlighten and to entertain.

The great chain of rock music, stretching from Chuck Berry to Hootie and the Blowfish, from The Flamingos to All-4-One, and from Wanda Jackson to Paula Abdul, offers fascinating opportunities for social analysis. Popular lyrics have always prompted both praise and criticism. Yet skillful researchers such as Mark Booth, Gary Burns, Mary Ellison, Jeff Green, John Grissim, Don J. Hibbard, Frank Hoffmann, Charles Keil, George H. Lewis, Bob Macken, Robert Palmer, David Pichaske, Robert G. Pielke, Ray Pratt, Lawrence N. Redd, Jerome L. Rodnitzky, William L. Schurk, Anne and Anthony Stecheson, and Larry Stidom have verified the broad impact and undeniable interaction of popular songs and American society. Contemporary music thrives. Variety remains the watchword. From Top 40 pop to gangsta rap, from urban country rock to classic oldies, listeners continue to be bombarded with ideas and images on a daily basis.

While the specific topics explored in the two previous Haworth volumes differ greatly from those examined here, the format of the entire series remains consistent (see Table A). Each chapter examines a specific theme. The body of the chapter may include an essay, an interview, a book review, or any combination of these short commentaries. In all instances, though, the focus is on lyrical involvement with key social and personal issues. Extensive lists of recordings and print references are provided. This emphasis on both discography and bibliography is another key element of this series. While functioning as entertainment for rock music fans and casual readers, the "Rock Music in American Popular Culture" series

TABLE A. Topics Covered in the Haworth "Rock Music in American Popular Culture" Series

Volume I	Volume II	Volume III
Baseball Songs	Answer Songs	Child Performers
Biographical Studies	Cars	Christmas Songs
Bootleg Records	Cigarettes	Death
Christmas Carols	City Life	Foolish Behavior
Commercial Catalogs	Disc Jockeys	Honoring Excellence
Dance Crazes	Doo-Wop Harmony	Jobs and Workplaces
Exported Recordings	Fads and Nostalgia	Novelty Recordings
Family Businesses	Halloween	Patriotism
Food Images	Horror Films	Popular Music
Games/Music Trivia	Humor	Postal Images
Hit Tunes	Legends	Public Schools
Imported Recordings	Marriage	Rock Songs
Journalists	Motion Pictures	Scholarship
and Critics	Multiculturalism	Social Commentary
Mass Media	Railroads	Song Revivals
Memorabilia/	Regional Music	Tobacco
Collectibles	Rock Journalism	Western Images
Nursery Rhymes	Science Fiction	
Radio Broadcasters	Sex	
Record Charts	Soul Music	
Rock 'n' Roll	War	
Legends	Women	
Sports Heroes		
Symptoms/Medical		
Imagery		
Work Experiences		

is clearly defined as an educational enterprise. Teachers, librarians, scholars, and students of contemporary society are strongly encouraged to listen and to read beyond this volume. The resources listed in each chapter constitute maps designed to generate greater exploration. The audio journey shouldn't end with the final page of this book.

Acknowledgments

This volume had its origin in the popular culture philosophies of Ray B. Browne and Russel B. Nye. Earlier writers championed vernacular investigation; later scholars have lauded the pursuit of the popular. But Browne and Nye are undeniably prime movers. They translated their ideas into programs and organizations. Browne remains preeminent as a planner, dreamer, and academic schemer. The radical ideas about popular culture that emanated from his Bowling Green State University pulpit in the late 1960s are currently so dominant in academia that they have become givens in the geometry of contemporary social research. Interdisciplinary exploration of censorship, Christmas songs, death, patriotism, and wartime letters is today the hallmark of popular culture study. Yet a collection of essays examining this strange variety of topics would have been unthinkable before Browne and Nye.

This volume pictures popular culture through an audio lens. Modern music provides lyric analysts, biographers, subject classification experts, and discographers with ample illustrations of commentaries on health care, holidays, jobs, monsters, and public schools. The essays presented here differ markedly in style, structure, and length. Book and record reviews are placed alongside footnoted historical investigations and brief biographical sketches. Both critical assessments and laudatory conclusions are mixed throughout the text. The alphabetical topic format permits readers to selectively peruse the text and to concentrate on particular items of interest. Extensive lists of literary resources and song titles within the chapters, along with a lengthy bibliography at the end of the volume, offer additional sources for future inquiries by teachers and scholars.

A writer relies upon friends and professional colleagues for ideas, assistance, stimulation, and criticism while pursuing scholarly production. We gratefully acknowledge the superb books, articles, and conference papers produced by the following exceptional thinkers: Mark Booth, Ray B. Browne, Gary Burns, George O. Carney, George Chilcoat, Norm Cohen, R. Serge Denisoff, Howard A. Dewitt, Philip H. Ennis, Colin Escott, Simon Frith, Reebee Garofalo, Archie Green, Charles Gritzner, Peter Hesbacher, Frank W. Hoffmann, David Horn, Hugo Keesing, Stephen Kneeshaw, John Litevich, J. Fred MacDonald, Hugh Mooney, Russel B. Nye,

David Pichaske, Lawrence Redd, Jerome Rodnitzky, Roger B. Rollin, Fred E. H. Schroeder, Larry Stidom, Warren Swindell, and Joel Whitburn. Through record collecting and correspondence concerning audiotapes, we have also established beneficial contacts with several shrewd, helpful persons: David A. Milberg, William L. Schurk, and Chas "Dr. Rock" White. Also of special note is the tremendous support and effort given by Ellen Elder with the compilation and layout of this work.

Finally, our activities as educators and administrators have enabled us to develop a cadre of professional friends who were sustaining and supportive during the inevitable research doldrums: Donna Brummett, Roger Buese, Dolores Chapman, Neil Clark, Colby Currier, Ron and Roberta Eckel, Charles and Jane Erickson, Shirley Erickson, Susan Gray, Elna Hensley, Una Koontz, Don and Zella Morris, Shirley Ryan, Mary Schroth, Linda Jo Scott, Audrey K. Thompson, Stewart Tubbs, Donald Walker, Dirk G. Wood, and especially library historian/popular culture scholar Wayne A. Weigand.

Authors also benefit from the loving, uncritical support of spouses, children, parents, and other loved ones. This indispensable sustenance was provided by Jill E. Cooper, Michael L. Cooper, Laura E. Cooper, Julie A. Cooper, Nicholas A. Cooper, Kathleen M. Cooper, Charles A. Cooper, Patty Jo Cooper, Larry W. Cooper, Dustin Cooper, Nicholas Cooper, Ellen Elder, Mary Catherine Haney, and Matthew James Haney.

The final type of support that made this study possible was financial. Two agencies provided direct economic assistance. We wish to thank the Division of Fellowships and Seminars of the National Endowment for the Humanities (NEH) for awarding B. Lee Cooper a "Travel to Collections" grant during 1985. We also acknowledge similar research funding provided by the Grants Committee and Board of Directors of the Association for Recorded Sound Collections (ARSC) in 1990 and again in 1992. This special financial support permitted lengthy periods of research access to both literary and audio materials housed in the Sound Recordings Archive of the William T. Jerome Library at Bowling Green State University.

B. Lee Cooper
Wayne S. Haney

Introduction

I earned my doctoral degree the same year Ron Denisoff launched *Popular Music and Society (PMS)*. While I had been a record collector since 1953, and had taught college-level courses in lyric analysis since 1968, I did not publish my initial music article until 1972. A decade later my first book—*Images of American Society in Popular Music*—was released by Nelson-Hall. Between 1984 and 1996, I produced ten more volumes, several of which were co-authored, on bibliographic music resources, thematic imagery in songs, discographic materials, and various topics of pedagogical and historical interest. Most of my books were derived from articles that have appeared in more than forty different scholarly journals, popular magazines, and educational periodicals. My two *Rock Music in American Popular Culture* volumes, compiled with Wayne Haney and released by The Haworth Press in 1995 and 1997, feature a variety of essays, book reviews, record commentaries, and reference compilations that typify my eclectic tastes in contemporary music. All of my writings stem from the conviction that modern music is a particularly revealing source of the human spirit. Poetic, profane, patriotic, pulsing, powerful, ponderous, and plagiaristic—music from the second half of the twentieth century merits serious investigation. This was an essential tenet of *Popular Music and Society*. It remains my guiding principle today.

Since the Rock Revolution predated the appearance of *PMS* by more than fifteen years, the following reflections on the journeys of music fans, critics, researchers, librarians, collectors, and artists span five decades. The conclusions I've reached are tentative. My observations remain subject to change. Yet, like Robert Frost's poetic traveler, I continue to find that selections of particular topics, bands, and recordings for study tend to define one's life. No music scholar can traverse all intellectual roads, follow all methodological paths, or tread all genre highways. Choosing

This essay by B. Lee Cooper was originally published as "It's Still Rock 'n' Roll to Me: Reflections on the Evolution of Popular Music and Rock Scholarship," *Popular Music and Society*, XXI (Spring 1997), pp. 101-108. Reprint permission has been granted by the author, editor Gary Burns, and The Bowling Green State University Popular Press.

subjects to research becomes a self-defining activity. The ability to move beyond narrow biographical or stylistic pathways and to perceive the virtues of other wanderers is a special gift. All good editors possess it. They revel in the travels of individuals who think, conjure, perceive, analyze, and write . . . differently. The value of an experimental journal such as *PMS,* whether under Ron Denisoff's founding leadership or Gary Burns's skillful editorial hand, is that it encourages scholars to envision music from a diversity of perspectives. The following pages contain the ruminations of a fifty-five-year-old teenager who is constantly reminded that Billy Joel was right. Bob Seger was too. Although public memory may fade, rock 'n' roll never forgets.

I

Despite HBO's video hoopla and Cleveland's commercial zeal for the Rock and Roll Hall of Fame, there will never be a mausoleum to authentically tout rock's rebellious roots. It isn't because there are no rebels left. There are plenty. But the 1990s society that warmly applauds Chuck Berry, that finds Jerry Lee Lewis enchanting, that marvels at Little Richard's antics, and that idealizes Fats Domino cannot begin to comprehend the glittering magic of their vibrant personas amid the 1950s pastel pop music scene. Energy, brilliance, pandemonium, experimentation, vitality, and danger lurked in the lyrics, licks, and leers from these seemingly tame, externally antique artists. I suspect their internal fires still burn. Fortunately, the music produced during their youth still belches forth over high-powered stadium speakers between innings, at halftimes, or during postgame celebrations. But so much of the rock music that followed was counterfeit. So many artists lost the "feel" while searching to reproduce the "sound." Authenticity still exists, though. The rockin' flame still burns in Delbert McClinton, Jimmy Vaughan, Lee Roy Parnell, Joe Ely, Bonnie Raitt, Hank Williams Jr., and George Thorogood. But we've lost so much with the passing of Stevie Ray Vaughan, Buddy Holly, Otis Redding, Jim Croce, Jimi Hendrix, Freddy King, Mike Bloomfield, Eddie Cochran, Phil Ochs, Lonnie Mack, Danny Gatton, Bobby Darin, Albert King, John Lennon, Sam Cooke, Jackie Wilson, Marvin Gaye, Duane Allman, and Nolan Strong. What might have been is tantalizing to consider. So is the specter of reconstructing the spirit of the early rock era.

II

Humor has always been a staple of rock 'n' roll. Regrettably, like adolescent rebellion, the comic nature of rock has been permitted to recede into the shadows. Along with Elvis, the early years of rock were spiced by the zaniness of disc jockeys and an array of lyrical lunatics. Screamin' Jay Hawkins bellowed, "I Put a Spell on You" (1956); Nervous Norvus shouted "Ape Call" (1956) and pleaded for a "Transfusion" (1956); and Buchanan and Goodman provided a free ride on a "Flying Saucer" (1956). Whether enjoying "The Ubangi Stomp" (1956) with Warren Smith or being "Stranded in the Jungle" (1956) with The Jayhawks, listeners were aware that the flaky spirit of Spike Jones had survived past the 1940s.

I'm always pleased to discover a new Pinkard and Bowden CD. Though occasionally profane, their irreverence toward contemporary social and political idiocy reminds me of the satirical roles played by Tom Lehrer and others. The mindless banter of Homer and Jethro, the marvelous situation comedies of Ray Stevens, the bizarre word play of Sheb Wooley, and the thousands of little-known and less-heralded answer song performers constituted the funny bone of modern music's mechanical monster. Weird Al Yankovic still makes money the old-fashioned way—with his tongue in his cheek. Long live Larry Verne! May Lonnie Donegan never discover the truth about the hardening of chewing gum! Let The Big Bopper and Sam the Sham be models for propriety at the next Rock and Roll Hall of Fame induction ceremony!

III

Popular music should never be categorized. (Sorry, Time-Life Music, Columbia House, BMG Music, and all other manipulative market niche merchandisers.) It deludes the variety, weakens the artistry, and (worst of all) segments listening audiences. Rhythm 'n' blues, rock 'n' roll, doo-wop, and all the magnificent musical variations of the 1950s were wildly integrating forces of black and white joy. Peter Guralnick, Stanley Booth, Michael Bane, and others have lauded varying uniting elements of inter-racial artistry that in tandem produced classic sounds. The Beatles and The Rolling Stones readily acknowledge their roots in mixed racial artistry. But race is less important than rhythm. Fast or slow, country or pop, jazz or blues—Louis Armstrong (or Duke Ellington) expressed the universal truth. There are only two kinds of music: good and bad. Roger Rollin and Simon Frith have added their own corollaries to that judgment. In matters of aesthetic decision, only the ear of the beholder is relevant.

IV

While technological change has doomed the 45 rpm record to extinction and has made vinyl LPs objects of collectability via garage sales, the emergence of compact disc retrospectives has increased the availability of many, many audio treasures. Time is being superseded by commercial culling. Generational gaps are filled with musical nostalgia. While my 1,800 little discs receive little attention and my LP collection gathers dust, I have gradually warmed to compact discs as reasonable replacements. The joy of discovering retrospective releases, especially flipside anthologies and answer song collections (thanks, Bear Family Records), is a heartening way to rediscover early rock gems.

V

Popular music scholarship remains a mixed bag. The demise of the critical generalist has led to conquest by the specialist. The advantages of a writer who knows an immense amount of songs, artists, and history of a particular genre is the backbone of academic scholarship in traditional disciplines. For music analysts, however, it is a disaster. For rock journalists, it is even worse. Breadth of listening experience and stylistic interest undergirds the quality of analysis. Without historical understanding, each new group seems like something springing from the head of Zeus. No roots. No predecessors. No context. No distinguishing characteristics. No points of comparison or contrast. So many of the manuscripts that I review on Madonna, Michael Jackson, Bruce Springsteen, Prince, or even Elvis Presley are devoid of perspective. Even if they are well-documented, the cramped vision of fandom is stifling.

Specialization is the bane of music analysis in general, not just in the realm of biographical studies. Too many theoreticians are sociological/ literary/ethnographic giants and musical pygmies. Their studies reflect their expertise. Page after page of jargon, arcane notations, methodological structures—but abysmally small samples of song lyrics or performer commentaries. Even those specialists with musical notation training tend to demonstrate little overview of popular music history while pouring forth grand theories about Chuck Berry's licks or Buddy Holly's vocalization. The viability of popular music observation rests in a deep, rich, broad conversation with popular music. The wonderful writings of David Pichaske, Jerome Rodnitzky, Peter Guralnick, Howard DeWitt, Simon Frith, Michael Bane, Stanley Booth, Colin Escott, Charles Keil, George H. Lewis, Dave Marsh, Nick Tosches, Stuart Colman, Paul Oliver, and Almost Slim stem from immersion in music. Nothing can substitute for that. It is the prerequisite for creative, analytical, critical thought.

VI

Record reviewing is a lost cause. The reasons for this phenomenon are related to the broadening of commercial interests and the narrowing perceptions of music critics. Recording companies readily supply review copies of new releases, but always with the tacit expectation of laudatory comments. Review editors yield to these expectations by assigning specific discs to specialists in heavy metal, rap, pop, rock, or whatever. The more zealous the specialist is, the less likely that critical objectivity will enter into the analysis. Too bad. As the rock era matures, it is increasingly possible to compare and contrast album themes, song lyrics, performer styles, and other aspects of particular discs. It is also reasonable to place artists in historical context and to note the repetition of designated ideas, riffs, or individual tunes. Yet the vast majority of contemporary reviews are parochial, noncritical, pandering, and largely unreliable as disc selection devices.

The early years of rock provide little guidance to resolve this reviewing quandary, though. Perhaps borrowing a technique initiated by Leonard Feather for jazz reviews might help. Invite articulate artists and broadly knowledgeable journalists to participate in "blind" critiques of soon-to-be-issued but as yet unreleased compact discs. Share reactions, thoughts, insights, and concerns among professionals. Let it all hang out—the good, the bad, the ugly. Then invite rock critics in pairs to react to these new releases from historical, creative, and quality of music perspectives. Put the Siskel and Ebert film review dynamic to work in the field of popular music. A journal such as *PMS* would be able to launch this kind of interaction more readily than fan-driven magazines such as *Kerrang!, Blue Suede News,* or even *Stereo Review.* Record reviewing ought to be a critical art with intellectual and educational aims. Presently, it is a self-congratulatory system of merchandising without any sense of balance, propriety, or history.

VII

"Writing about music is like dancing about architecture." Who said so? The works of Philip Ennis, Ron Denisoff, Simon Frith, Richard Peterson, Peter Hesbacher, and Charlie Gillett demonstrate how enlightening reasoned perspectives about the commercial recording industry can be. Moreover, selecting themes from lyrics can offer insight into the contemporary human condition. Ignoring music as a serious research field because Elvis Costello objects to literary analysis is like scrapping all historical study because Henry Ford declared history to be "bunk." The mature rock era (1955-1995) beckons authors with revisionist eyes and sharp wits, with thorough knowledge of contemporary performers and broad files of lyrics and melodies. This is no time to cease publishing.

VIII

Linking librarians and record collectors is the key to sustaining the scholarly study of twentieth century popular music. The Sound Recordings Archive at Bowling Green State University ought to become a model for the method of assembling, cataloging, and making available to serious music students the broadest realm of contemporary music. Certainly, jazz archives, country collections, blues archives, and other specialty areas remain invaluable. So are memorabilia palaces, whether as numerous as Hard Rock Cafes or as singular as Cleveland's Rock and Roll Hall of Fame. But the salvaging of private collections, a task lovingly pursued by Bowling Green's William L. Schurk, is a key task to be achieved over the next five decades.

It is humorous to recall how ephemeral even the most successful rock pioneers considered their 1950s recording efforts. No one could have predicted either the commercial longevity or the social impact of rock 'n' roll. But from the vantage point of the mid-1990s, it is obvious that scholarly investigation of the 1950s, 1960s, 1970s, and 1980s will depend upon liberating the much-loved private record collections from *Goldmine* readers and *DISCoveries* enthusiasts. Although the manufactured retrospectives of Time-Life Music afford truly enjoyable casual listening, research into rock history will require access to original audio sources. As today's private collectors age and die, librarians and sound recording archivists must convince their spouses, sons, daughters, and other family members to donate the cherished collections intact to archival facilities. Emotional attachment and greed will be staunch foes in this resource-accumulation pursuit. So will intransigence. The best bet for accomplishing this task is a firm commitment from the collectors themselves to carefully transfer their most treasured discs directly to a community of music scholars. Deferred giving via last will and testament bequests may sound outrageous as a means of assembling an academic archive. But it is the best way to assure that the heritage of American popular music won't be frittered away in the fashion that Gordon Stevenson described concerning "race records" of the 1920s and 1930s.

IX

God save us from postmodernists, British theoreticians, zealous ethnographers, and pompous twits. The study of popular music should be fun. It should be logical, documented, illustrated, and literate too. But over the past fifteen years the field of music analysis has been invaded by ideologues of many stripes. Perhaps I am too eclectic—or too dull to comprehend the genius lurking beneath so many convoluted articles appearing in Britain's *Popular Music* and other international journals. Granted, the slobbering silliness of American fanzine ravings are no better. But rock fans such as Marc Bristol of *Blue Suede News* and Jeff Tamarkin of *Goldmine* can be forgiven their naive excesses. The machinations of supposedly well-trained scholars are much more harmful, particularly when they elevate obtuse hypotheses above common sense.

X

My heroes have always been singers. Instrumental demons such as King Curtis, Bill Justis, Kenny G, David Sanborn, Bill Doggett, Sil Austin, and Gene Barge are wonderful, of course. But the lyrics of popular songs capture me. I am enamored of gifted writers. Wordsmiths fascinate me. But literary pages lack the soul-stealing rhythm of sound recordings. Despite the preaching of David Pichaske and Richard Goldstein, I am not convinced that traditional poetry and rock lyrics are interchangeable. Sound recordings as a total experience—words and music—are unique. The shamans of my life, the gatekeepers of ideas both visible and hidden, are singers. My involvement with popular music is immeasurably linked to Ray Charles, Paul Simon, Aretha Franklin, Carl Perkins, Bonnie Raitt, B. B. King, Linda Ronstadt, Burton Cummings, Marvin Gaye, Irma Thomas, Little Richard, Joan Baez, Sonny Til, and Carole King.

CONCLUDING OBSERVATIONS

Ron Denisoff functioned as a sociological scholar throughout his tenure as editor of *Popular Music and Society.* He was not adept as a manuscript manager; he was not timely in correspondence with contributors; he was neither helpful nor particularly visible to neophyte writers; and he exhausted the patience and goodwill of many of his Popular Press colleagues. But genius never fits a comfortable mold. His literary productivity remained high despite ill health. His critical and analytical skills were sharp to the end. The sadness for everyone who knew and appreciated his talent was how soon it was gone. The Denisoff legacy is his scholarship—books, articles, and a very special journal, *Popular Music and Society.* I am delighted that a competent, caring communicator such as Gary Burns has agreed to oversee the continuation of *PMS*. The editorial skills that were so shallow for so long will now deepen. The love of popular music will not lessen. Diversity of literary talent is the guideline that the new editor appears to be erecting. No more one-man operation. While both Denisoff and Burns cherish variety of opinion, I sense that the new editor will promote a stronger team approach to both reviewing and manuscript assessment. *PMS* is in good hands.

This study has surfed a variety of waves that continue to crash on the music scholarship shores. It is a rare opportunity for a lyric analyst to comment on the general state of rock research. The observations are tentative. They are subjective. But they are candid and, hopefully, helpful.

THE "HOT 100" POPULAR MUSIC BOOKS OF 1971-1995: KEY REFERENCES FOR ROCK RESEARCHERS

I own them. I use them. I recommend them. The following 100 texts are the most influential studies that I have encountered during my thirty years of popular music research and writing. Omission from this list does not indicate lack of value; inclusion does not certify superiority. The books featured below have been instrumental for me in locating audio resources, in fostering ideas, and in illustrating perspectives.

1. Michael Bane. 1982. *White Boy Singin' the Blues: The Roots of White Rock*. New York: Penguin Books.
2. Stephen Barnard. 1989. *On the Radio: Music Radio in Britain*. Milton Keynes, England: Open University Press.
3. Carl Belz. 1972. *The Story of Rock* (Second Edition). New York: Harper and Row.
4. Stanley Booth. 1991. *Rythm Oil: A Journey Through the Music of the American South*. New York: Pantheon Books.
5. John Broven. 1978. *Rhythm and Blues in New Orleans*. Gretna, LA: Pelican Publishing Company.
6. Harry Castleman and Walter J. Podrazik. 1975. *All Together Now: The First Complete Beatles Discography, 1961-1975*. New York: Ballantine Books.
7. Harry Castleman and Walter J. Podrazik. 1977. *The Beatles Again?* Ann Arbor, MI: Pierian Press.
8. Harry Castleman and Walter J. Podrazik. 1985. *The End of the Beatles?* Ann Arbor, MI: Pierian Press.
9. Steve Chapple and Reebee Garofalo. 1977. *Rock 'n' Roll Is Here to Pay: The History and Politics of the Music Industry*. Chicago: Nelson-Hall, Inc.

10. Donald Clarke (ed.). 1989. *The Penguin Encyclopedia of Popular Music.* New York: Viking Penguin, Inc.
11. Norm Cohen (with music edited by David Cohen). 1981. *Long Steel Rail: The Railroad in American Folksong.* Urbana, IL: University of Illinois Press.
12. Barbara Cohen-Stratyner (ed.). 1988. *Popular Music, 1900-1919: An Annotated Guide to American Popular Songs.* Detroit, MI: Gale Research, Inc.
13. Nik Cohn. 1989. *Ball the Wall: Nik Cohn in the Age of Rock.* London: Picador Books.
14. Stuart Colman. 1982. *They Kept on Rockin': The Giants of Rock 'n' Roll.* Poole, Dorset, England: Blandford Press.
15. B. Lee Cooper. 1991. *Popular Music Perspectives: Ideas, Themes, and Patterns in Contemporary Lyrics.* Bowling Green, OH: Bowling Green State University Popular Press.
16. B. Lee Cooper. 1986. *A Resource Guide to Themes in Contemporary American Song Lyrics, 1950-1985.* Westport, CT: Greenwood Press.
17. B. Lee Cooper and Wayne S. Haney. 1995. *Rock Music in American Popular Culture: Rock 'n' Roll Resources.* Binghamton, NY: Harrington Park Press.
18. Lee Cotten. 1995. *Reelin' and Rockin'—The Golden Age of American Rock 'n' Roll: Volume Two—1956-1959.* Ann Arbor, MI: Popular Culture, Ink.
19. Lee Cotten. 1989. *Shake, Rattle, and Roll—The Golden Age of American Rock 'n' Roll: Volume One—1952-1955.* Ann Arbor, MI: Pierian Press.
20. Anthony DeCurtis and James Henke, with Holly George-Warren (eds.). 1992. *The Rolling Stone Illustrated History of Rock and Roll* (fully revised and updated). New York: Random House.
21. R. Serge Denisoff. 1991. (c. 1988). *Inside MTV.* New Brunswick, NJ: Transaction Books.
22. R. Serge Denisoff. 1972. *Sing a Song of Social Significance.* Bowling Green, OH: Bowling Green State University Popular Press.
23. R. Serge Denisoff and Richard A. Peterson (eds.). 1972. *The Sounds of Social Change: Studies in Popular Culture.* Chicago, IL: Rand McNally.
24. R. Serge Denisoff and William D. Romanowski. 1991. *Risky Business: Rock in Film.* New Brunswick, NJ: Transaction Books.

25. R. Serge Denisoff, with the assistance of William L. Schurk. 1986. *Tarnished Gold: The Record Industry Revisited*. New Brunswick, NJ: Transaction Books.

26. Robin Denselow. 1990. (c. 1989). *When the Music's Over: The Story of Political Pop*. London: Faber and Faber.

27. Jonathan Eisen (ed.). 1969. *The Age of Rock: Sounds of the American Cultural Revolution*. New York: Vintage Books.

28. Jonathan Eisen (ed.). 1970. *The Age of Rock/2: Sights and Sounds of the American Cultural Revolution*. New York: Vintage Books.

29. Philip H. Ennis. 1993. *The Seventh Stream: The Emergence of Rock 'n' Roll in American Popular Music*. Hanover, NH: University Press of New England.

30. Colin Escott, with Martin Hawkins. 1991. *Good Rockin' Tonight: Sun Records and the Birth of Rock 'n' Roll*. New York: St. Martin's Press.

31. Bill Flanagan. 1987. *Written in My Soul: Conversations with Rock's Great Songwriters*. Chicago: Contemporary Books, Inc.

32. Simon Frith (ed.). 1988. *Facing the Music*. New York: Pantheon Books.

33. Simon Frith. 1981. *Sound Effects: Youth, Leisure, and the Politics of Rock 'n' Roll*. New York: Pantheon Books.

34. Simon Frith and Andrew Goodwin (eds.). 1990. *On Record: Rock, Pop, and the Written Word*. New York: Pantheon Books.

35. Jeffrey N. Gatten. 1995. *Rock Music Scholarship: An Interdisciplinary Bibliography*. Westport, CT: Greenwood Press.

36. Charlie Gillett. 1970. *The Sound of the City: The Rise of Rock and Roll*. New York: E.P. Dutton.

37. John Goldrosen and John Beecher. 1987. *Remembering Buddy: The Definitive Biography of Buddy Holly*. New York: Viking Penguin, Inc.

38. Fernando Gonzalez (comp.). 1977. *Disco-File: The Discographical Catalog of American Rock & Roll and Rhythm & Blues Vocal Harmony Groups, 1902 to 1976* (Second Edition). Flushing, NY: Gonzalez.

39. H. L. Goodall, Jr. 1991. *Living in the Rock 'n' Roll Mystery: Reading Context, Self, and Others As Clues*. Carbondale, IL: Southern Illinois University Press.

40. Michael H. Gray (comp.). 1983. *Bibliography of Discographies: Volume Three—Popular Music*. New York: R. R. Bowker Company.

41. Anthony J. Gribin and Matthew M. Schiff. 1992. *Doo-Wop: The Forgotten Third of Rock 'n' Roll*. Iola, WI: Krause Publications.

42. Peter Guralnick. 1971. *Feel Like Going Home: Portraits in Blues and Rock 'n' Roll*. New York: Outerbridge and Dienstfrey.
43. Peter Guralnick. 1979. *Lost Highway: Journeys and Arrivals of American Musicians*. Boston: David R. Godine.
44. Peter Guralnick. 1986. *Sweet Soul Music: Rhythm and Blues and the Southern Dream of Freedom*. New York: Harper and Row.
45. Jeff Hannusch (a.k.a. Almost Slim). 1985. *I Hear You Knockin': The Sound of New Orleans Rhythm and Blues*. Ville Platte, LA: Swallow Press.
46. Phil Hardy and Dave Laing. 1990. *The Faber Companion to 20th-Century Popular Music*. London: Faber and Faber.
47. Sheldon Harris (comp.). 1979. *Blues Who's Who: A Biographical Dictionary of Blues Singers*. New Rochelle, NY: Arlington House.
48. David Hatch and Stephen Millward. 1989. (c. 1987). *From Blues to Rock: An Analytical History of Pop Music*. Manchester, England: Manchester University Press.
49. Herb Hendler. 1983. *Year by Year in the Rock Era: Events and Conditions Shaping the Rock Generations That Reshaped America*. Westport, CT: Greenwood Press.
50. Gerri Hirshey. 1984. *Nowhere to Run: The Story of Soul Music*. New York: Penguin Books.
51. Ian Hoare, Tony Cummings, Clive Anderson, and Simon Frith. 1976. *The Soul Book*. New York: Dell Publishing Company, Inc.
52. Frank W. Hoffmann. 1981. *The Literature of Rock, 1954-1978*. Metuchen, NJ: Scarecrow Press, Inc.
53. Frank W. Hoffmann and B. Lee Cooper. 1986. *The Literature of Rock II, 1979-1983* (Two Volumes). Metuchen, NJ: Scarecrow Press, Inc.
54. Frank W. Hoffmann and B. Lee Cooper. 1995. *The Literature of Rock III, 1984-1990—With Additional Material for the Period 1954-1983*. Metuchen, NJ: Scarecrow Press, Inc.
55. David Horn (comp.) (1977). *The Literature of American Music in Books and Folk Music Collections: A Fully Annotated Bibliography*. Metuchen, NJ: Scarecrow Press, Inc.
56. Charles Keil. 1966. *Urban Blues*. Chicago: University Chicago Press.
57. Paul Kingsbury and the Country Music Foundation (eds.). 1994. *Country: The Music and the Musicians—From the Beginnings to the '90s* (Revised and Updated Edition). New York: Abbeville Publishing Group.

58. Donald W. Krummel. 1987. *Biographical Handbook of American Music*. Urbana, IL: University of Illinois Press.

59. Barry Lazell with Dafydd Rees and Luke Crampton (eds.). 1989. *Rock Movers and Shakers: An A to Z of the People Who Made Rock Happen*. New York: Billboard Publications, Inc.

60. George H. Lewis (ed.). 1993. *All That Glitters: Country Music in America*. Bowling Green, OH: Bowling Green State University Popular Press.

61. George H. Lewis (ed.). 1972. *Side-Saddle on the Golden Calf: Social Structure and Popular Culture in America*. Pacific Palisades, CA: Goodyear Publishing Co., Inc.

62. Brady J. Leyser, with additional research by Pol Gosset (comp.). 1994. *Rock Stars/Pop Stars: A Comprehensive Bibliography, 1955-1994*. Westport, CT: Greenwood Press.

63. Michael Lydon. 1974. *Boogie Lightning*. New York: Dial Press.

64. Michael Lydon. 1971. *Rock Folk: Portraits from the Rock 'n' Roll Pantheon*. New York: Dial Press.

65. Bob Macken, Peter Fornatale, and Bill Ayres (comps.). 1980. *The Rock Music Source Book*. Garden City, NY: Doubleday and Company, Inc.

66. Dave Marsh. 1985. *Fortunate Son*. New York: Random House.

67. Linda Martin and Kerry Segrave. 1988. *Anti-Rock: The Opposition to Rock 'n' Roll*. Hamden, CT: Archon Books.

68. Betty T. Miles, Daniel J. MIles, and Martin J. Miles. 1981. (c. 1971). *The Miles Chart Display of Popular Music—Volume I: Top 100, 1955-1970*. Boulder, CO: Convex Industries.

69. Jim Miller (ed.). 1976. *The Rolling Stone Illustrated History of Rock and Roll*. New York: Random House (Rolling Stone Press).

70. Michael Ochs. 1984. Rock Archives: *A Photographic Journal Through the First Two Decades of Rock and Roll*. New York: Doubleday and Company.

71. Paul Oliver (ed.). 1989. *The Blackwell Guide to Blues Records*. Cambridge, MA: Basil Blackwell.

72. Robert Palmer. 1981. *Deep Blues*. New York: Viking Press.

73. Big Al Pavlow. 1983. *Big Al Pavlow's the R & B Book: A Disc-History of Rhythm and Blues*. Providence, RI: Music House Publishing.

74. David Pichaske. 1979. *A Generation in Motion: Popular Music and Culture in the Sixties*. New York: Schirmer Books.

75. Robert Pruter. 1991. *Chicago Soul*. Champaign-Urbana, IL: University of Illinois Press.

76. Walter Rimler. 1984. *Not Fade Away: A Comparison of Jazz Age with Rock Era Pop Song Composers*. Ann Arbor, MI: Pierian Press.
77. Jerome L. Rodnitzky. 1976. *Minstrels of the Dawn: The Folk-Protest Singer As a Cultural Hero*. Chicago: Nelson-Hall, Inc.
78. Schaffner, Nicholas. 1982. *The British Invasion: From the First Wave to the New Wave*. New York: McGraw-Hill Book Company.
79. Timothy E. Scheurer. 1991. *Born in the U.S.A.: The Myth of America in Popular Music from Colonial Times to the Present*. Jackson, MS: University Press of Mississippi.
80. Quentin J. Schultze, Roy M. Anker, James D. Bratt, William D. Romanowski, John W. Worst, and Lambert Zuidervaart. 1991. *Dancing in the Dark: Youth, Popular Culture, and the Electronic Media*. Grand Rapids, MI: William B. Eerdmans Publishing Company.
81. Frank Scott and the Staff of *Down Home Music*. 1991. *The Down Home Guide to the Blues*. Pennington, NJ: A Cappella Books.
82. Frank Scott, Al Ennis, and The Staff of *Roots and Rhythm*. 1993. *The Roots and Rhythm Guide to Rock*. Pennington, NJ: A Cappella Books.
83. Nat Shapiro and Bruce Pollock (eds.). 1985. *Popular Music, 1920-1979—A Revised Cumulation* (Three Volumes). Detroit, MI: Gale Research.
84. Arnold Shaw. 1978. *Honkers and Shouters: The Golden Years of Rhythm and Blues*. New York: Collier Books.
85. Arnold Shaw. 1974. *The Rockin' '50s: The Decade That Transformed the Pop Music Scene*. New York: Hawthorn Books, Inc.
86. Wes Smith. 1989. *The Pied Pipers of Rock 'n' Roll: Radio DeeJays of the '50s and '60s*. Marietta, GA: Longstreet Press, Inc.
87. Irwin Stambler. 1989. *The Encyclopedia of Pop, Rock, and Soul* (revised edition). New York: St. Martin's Press.
88. Paul Taylor (comp.). 1985. *Popular Music Since 1955: A Critical Guide to the Literature*. New York: Mansell Publishing Limited.
89. Nick Tosches. 1977. *Country: The Biggest Music in America*. New York: Dell Publishing, Inc.
90. Nick Tosches. 1982. *Hellfire: The Jerry Lee Lewis Story*. New York: Dell Publishing, Inc.
91. Nick Tosches. 1984. *Unsung Heroes of Rock 'n' Roll: The Birth of Rock 'n' Roll in the Dark and Wild Years Before Elvis*. New York: Charles Scribner's Sons.
92. Jay Warner. 1992. *The Billboard Book of American Singing Groups: A History, 1940-1990*. New York: Billboard Books.

93. Pete Welding and Toby Byron (eds.). 1991. *Bluesland: Portraits of Twelve Major American Blues Masters.* New York: Dutton/Penguin Books.
94. Jerry Wexler and David Ritz. 1993. *Rhythm and the Blues: A Life in American Music.* New York: Alfred A. Knopf.
95. Joel Whitburn (comp.). 1994. *Pop Hits, 1940-1954.* Menomonee Falls, WI: Record Research, Inc.
96. Joel Whitburn (comp.). 1994. *Top Country Singles, 1944-1993.* Menomonee Falls, WI: Record Research, Inc.
97. Joel Whitburn (comp.). 1993. *Top Pop Album Tracks, 1955-1992.* Menomonee Falls, WI: Record Research, Inc.
98. Joel Whitburn (comp.). 1993. *Top Pop Albums, 1955-1992.* Menomonee Falls, WI: Record Research, Inc.
99. Joel Whitburn (comp.). 1994. *Top Pop Singles.* Menomonee Falls, WI: Record Research, Inc.
100. Joel Whitburn (comp.). 1988. *Top Rhythm and Blues Singles, 1942-1988.* Menomonee Falls, WI: Record Research, Inc.

Chapter 1

Child Performers

Brenda Lee, a Georgia-born country artist who began her professional singing career at age six, charted two Top 100 national hits before her thirteenth birthday. Her most noted holiday-related song—"Rockin' Around the Christmas Tree"—was recorded for Decca records prior to her fourteenth birthday. Before Brenda Lee's success, another thirteen-year-old youngster scored a No. 1 hit record with the Christmas novelty tune "I Saw Mommy Kissing Santa Claus." Little Jimmy Boyd followed this hit-making 1952 debut with three *Billboard*-charted songs during the next six months: "Tell Me a Story," "The Little Boy and the Old Man" (both duets with Frankie Laine), and "Dennis the Menace" (a duet with Rosemary Clooney). But even younger children have produced popular hit recordings. Seven-year-old Barry Gordon sang the 1955 holiday humor song "Nuttin' for Christmas" and Jo Ann Morse, a youngster of the same age in 1962, produced a Kennedy-ribbing recording titled "My Daddy Is President." Appearing with his father on the 1974 RCA recording "Daddy What If," five-year-old Bobby Bare Jr. is undeniably one of the youngest hit makers ever. Finally, numerous recordings such as Pink Floyd's "Another Brick in the Wall (Part II)," Buzz Clifford's "Baby Sittin' Boogie," and Tom Glazer's "On Top of Spaghetti" have featured children's choruses of wide-ranging ages.

The previous paragraph illustrates the roles of several young people as popular music performers. What is even more fascinating, though, is the variety of songs addressing children's interests, images, perspectives, and youthful culture that have achieved *Billboard* Top 100 ranking since 1945.

This chapter by B. Lee Cooper and William L. Schurk was originally published as "From 'I Saw Mommy Kissing Santa Claus' to 'Another Brick in the Wall': Popular Recordings Featuring Preteen Performers, Traditional Childhood Stories, and Contemporary Preadolescent Perspectives, 1945-1985," *International Journal of Instructional Media*, XVI, No. 1 (1989), pp. 83-90. Reprint permission granted by the authors, editor Phillip J. Sleeman, and the Westwood Press.

It is almost as though America's postwar baby boom helped launch a new genre of kiddie-oriented records that have become long-term cultural staples. If the early rock era (1954-1964) marked the emergence of teenage control of the radio airwaves, the decade before and the years since have featured many paeans to those carefree preteens.

What kind of music has attracted youthful attention? What type of recordings will parents gladly purchase for their youngsters? After a rigorous review of the 1945 to 1985 *Billboard* Top 100 charts, the answers are obvious. Over the past four decades parents and children have been especially attracted to popular recordings featuring: (a) familiar animated characters (Alley Oop, Cinderella, Sylvester the Cat and Tweety Bird, Snoopy, and Woody Woodpecker); (b) theme songs from Broadway shows, motion pictures, radio programs, and television series; (c) tunes with titles or lyrical content referring to toys, games, childhood chants, or slang terms; (d) references to major holidays, mythic characters, and comic situations ("Rudolph the Red-Nosed Reindeer," "The Purple People Eater," "The Little Drummer Boy," and "Peter Cottontail"); (e) depictions of family life ("Color Him Father," "1432 Franklin Pike Circle Hero," "Giddyup Go," "Hello Mudduh, Hello Fadduh (A Letter from Camp)," and "The Naughty Lady of Shady Lane"); (f) images from nursery rhymes, fairy tales, and other children's literature ("The Children's Marching Song," "Pop Goes the Weasel," "White Rabbit," and "Little Red Riding Hood"); plus (g) a variety of general topics relating to education, food, and religion.

The following discography presents more than 120 *Billboard*-charted 45 rpm or 78 rpm records featuring children's themes. These songs are divided into fifteen thematic topics.

A SELECTED DISCOGRAPHY OF POPULAR RECORDINGS FEATURING PRETEEN PERFORMERS, TRADITIONAL CHILDHOOD STORIES, AND CONTEMPORARY PREADOLESCENT PERSPECTIVES, 1945-1985

Animated Characters (from Comic Strips, Motion Pictures, and Television Programs)

- "Alley-Oop"
  (Lute 5905)
  The Hollywood Argyles (1960)

- "Bibbidi-Bobbidi-Boo (The Magic Song)"
  (RCA Victor 3113)
  Perry Como, with The Fontane Sisters (1950)

- "Boogie Bear"
  (Mercury 71479)
  Boyd Bennett (1959)

- "I Taut I Taw a Puddy Tat"
  (Capitol 1360)
  Mel Blanc (1951)

- "Snoopy for President"
  (Laurie 3451)
  The Royal Guardsmen (1968)

- "Snoopy vs. the Red Baron"
  (Laurie 3366)
  The Royal Guardsmen (1966)

- "Super-cali-fragil-istic-expiali-docious"
  (Buena Vista 434)
  Julie Andrews, Dick Van Dyke, and The Pearlies (1965)

- "When You Wish Upon a Star"
  (Laurie 3052)
  Dion and the Belmonts (1960)

- "The Woody Woodpecker"
  (Decca 24462)
  Danny Kaye and The Andrews Sisters (1948)

- "Zip-a-Dee Doo-Dah"
  (Philles 107)
  Bob B. Soxx and The Blue Jeans (1962)

Broadway Shows and Motion Pictures

- "The Candy Man"
  (MGM 14320)
  Sammy Davis Jr. (1972)

- "The Children's Marching Song"
  (Columbia 41317)
  Mitch Miller (1959)

- "Ding Dong! The Witch Is Dead"
  (Jubilee 5573)
  The Fifth Estate (1967)

- "Do-Re-Mi"
  (Columbia 41499)
  Mitch Miller (1959)

- "On the Good Ship Lollipop"
  (Philips 40380)
  Wonder Who? (1966)

- "One Tin Soldier (The Legend of Billy Jack)"
  (Warner Brothers 7509)
  Coven (1971)

- "Themes from The Wizard of Oz"
  (Millennium 620)
  Meco (1978)

Childhood Chants, Games, Sayings, and Slang Terms

- "ABC"
  (Motown 1163)
  Jackson Five (1970)

- "Double Dutch Bus"
  (WMOT 5356)
  Frankie Smith (1981)

- "Finders Keepers, Losers Weepers"
  (Wand 171)
  Nella Dodds (1965)

- "Hide and Go Seek"
  (Male 451)
  Bunker Hill (1962)

- "Hop Scotch"
  (Canadian American 124)
  Santo and Johnny (1961)

- "Leap Frog"
  (MGM 12449)
  The Chuck Alaimo Quartet (1957)

- "May I Take a Giant Step (into Your Heart)"
  (Buddha 39)
  1910 Fruitgum Co. (1968)

- "The Name Game"
  (Congress 230)
  Shirley Ellis (1964)

- "Pass the Dutchie"
  (MCA 52149)
  Musical Youth (1982)

- "Pin the Tail on the Donkey"
  (Columbia 43527)
  Paul Peek (1966)

- "Simon Says"
  (Buddha 24)
  1910 Fruitgum Company (1968)

- "Tic-Tac-Toe"
  (Stax)
  Booker T. and the MGs (1964)

Children and Family Life

- "Broomstick Cowboy"
  (United Artists 952)
  Bobby Goldsboro (1965)

- "Cats in the Cradle"
  (Elektra 45203)
  Harry Chapin (1974)

- "Color Him Father"
  (Metromedia 117)
  The Winstons (1969)

- "Daddy Sang Bass"
  (Columbia 44689)
  Johnny Cash (1968)

- "Feet Up (Pat Him on the Po-Po)"
  (Columbia 39822)
  Guy Mitchell (1952)

- "1432 Franklin Pike Circle Hero"
  (Elf 90020)
  Bobby Russell (1968)

- "Giddyup Go"
  (Starday 737)
  Red Sovine (1966)

- "Hello Mudduh, Hello Fadduh (A Letter from Camp)"
  (Warner Brothers 5378)
  Allan Sherman (1963)

- "Mother and Child Reunion"
  (Columbia 45547)
  Paul Simon (1972)

- "Nancy (with the Laughing Face)"
  (Columbia 36868)
  Frank Sinatra (1945)

- "The Naughty Lady of Shady Lane"
  (RCA 5897)
  Ames Brothers (1954)

- "Oh! My Pa-Pa"
  (RCA Victor 5552)
  Eddie Fisher (1953)

- "Papa Was a Rollin' Stone"
  (Gordy 7121)
  The Temptations (1972)

- "Patches"
  (Atlantic 2748)
  Clarence Carter (1970)

- "Playmates"
  (Dot 15370)
  The Fontane Sisters (1955)

- "Saturday Morning Confusion"
  (United Artists 50788)
  Bobby Russell (1971)

- "Teddy Bear"
  (Starday 142)
  Red Sovine (1976)

- "Teddy Bear's Last Ride"
  (Capitol 4317)
  Diana Williams (1976)

- "Watching Scotty Grow"
  (United Artists 50727)
  Bobby Goldsboro (1970)

- "Willie and the Hand Jive"
  (RSO 503)
  Eric Clapton (1974)

- "Yakety Yak"
  (Atco 6116)
  The Coasters (1958)

- "You Better Sit Down Kids"
  (Imperial 66261)
  Cher (1967)

Children As Recording Artists

- "Baby Sittin' Boogie"
  (Columbia 41876)
  Buzz Clifford (1961)

- "Daddy What If "
  (RCA 0197)
  Bobby Bare (1974)

- "Dennis the Menace"
  (Columbia 39988)
  Jimmy Boyd (1953)

- "I Saw Mommy Kissing Santa Claus"
  (Columbia 39871)
  Jimmy Boyd (1952)

- "The Little Boy and the Old Man"
  (Columbia 39945)
  Jimmy Boyd (1953)

- "My Daddy Is President"
  (Kapp 467)
  Little Jo Ann (1962)

- "Nuttin' for Christmas"
  (MGM 12092)
  Barry Gordon (1955)

- "One-zy Two-zy (I Love You-zy)"
  (ARA 136)
  Phil Harris (1946)

- "On Top of Spaghetti"
  (Kapp 526)
  Tom Glazer and The Do-Re-Mi Children's Chorus (1963)

- "Rock Around Mother Goose"
  (MGM 12166)
  Barry Gordon (1956)

- "Rockin' Around the Christmas Tree"
  (Decca 30776)
  Brenda Lee (1960)

- "Tell Me a Story"
  (Columbia 39945)
  Jimmy Boyd (1953)

Education

- "Another Brick in the Wall (Part II)"
  (Columbia 11187)
  Pink Floyd (1980)

- "The Free Electric Band"
  (Mums 6018)
  Albert Hammond (1973)

- "Harper Valley P.T.A."
  (Plantation 3)
  Jeannie C. Riley (1968)

- "The Logical Song"
  (A&M 2128)
  Supertramp (1979)

- "Swinging on a Star"
  (Dimension 1010)
  Big Dee Irwin (1963)

Fairy Tales, Nursery Rhymes, and Other Forms of Children's Literature

- "(Ain't That) Just Like Me"
  (Atco 6210)
  The Coasters (1961)

- "Beans in My Ears"
  (Philips 40198)
  The Serendipity Singers (1964)

- "The Children's Marching Song (Nick Nack Paddy Whack)"
  (London 1851)
  Cyril Stapleton and his Orchestra (1959)

- "Don't Let the Rain Come Down (Crooked Little Man)"
  (Phillips 40175)
  The Serendipity Singers (1964)

- "House at Pooh Corner"
  (United Artists 50769)
  Nitty Gritty Dirt Band (1971)

- "Inky Dinky Spider (The Spider Song)"
  (4 Corners 129)
  The Kids Next Door (1965)

- "Li'l Red Riding Hood"
  (MOM 13506)
  Sam the Sham and The Pharaohs (1966)

- "Pop Goes the Weasel"
  (London 9501)
  Anthony Newley (1961)

- "White Rabbit"
  (RCA 9248)
  Jefferson Airplane (1967)

Food

- "Eat It"
  (Rock 'n' Roll 04374)
  Weird Al Yankovic (1984)

- "Peanut Butter"
  (Arvee 5027)
  The Marathons (1961)

- "Shortnin' Bread"
  (Harper 100)
  Paul Chaplain and His Emeralds (1960)

Holidays

- "The Chipmunk Song"
  (Liberty 55168)
  The Chipmunks (1958)

- "Donde Esta Santa Claus?"
  (Metro 20010)
  Augie Rios (1958)

- "Frosty, the Snowman"
  (Columbia 38907)
  Gene Autry (1952)

- "Little Drummer Boy"
  (20th Century Fox 121)
  The Harry Simeone Chorale (1958)

- "Nuttin' for Christmas"
  (Dot 15434)
  The Fontane Sisters (1955)

- "Peter Cottontail"
  (Columbia 38750)
  Gene Autry (1951)

- "Rudolph the Red-Nosed Reindeer"
  (Columbia 38610)
  Gene Autry (1949)

- "Santa Claus Is Coming to Town"
  (Vee-Jay 478)
  The Four Seasons (1962)

New Stories About Childhood Experiences

- "Doggie in the Window"
  (Mercury 70070)
  Patti Page (1953)

- "He Ain't Heavy, He's My Brother"
  (Epic 10532)
  The Hollies (1969)

- "The Night Chicago Died"
  (Mercury 73492)
  Paper Lace (1974)

- "Puff, the Magic Dragon"
  (Warner Brothers 5348)
  Peter, Paul, and Mary (1963)

Nostalgia for Childhood

- "I Wish"
  (Tamla 54274)
  Stevie Wonder (1977)

- "My City Was Gone"
  (Sire 29840)
  The Pretenders (1982)

- "My Home Town"
  (Columbia 05728)
  Bruce Springsteen (1985)

- "Penny Lane"
  (Capitol 5810)
  The Beatles (1966)

Novelty Songs

- "All I Want for Christmas (Is My Two Front Teeth)"
  (RCA Victor 2963)
  Spike Jones (1949)

- "Alvin for President"
  (Liberty 55277)
  The Chipmunks, with David Seville (1960)

- "The Alvin Twist"
  (Liberty 55424)
  The Chipmunks, with David Seville (1962)

- "Baby Talk"
  (Dore 522)
  Jan and Dean (1959)

- "Bird's the Word"
  (Liberty 55553)
  The Rivingtons (1963)

- "In the Mood"
  (Warner Brothers 8301)
  The Henhouse Five Plus Two (1977)

- "Nee Nee Na Na Na Na Nu Nu"
  (Swan 4006)
  Dicky Doo and The Don'ts (1958)

- "Oh! Susanna"
  (RCA 6344)
  The Singing Dogs (1955)

- "Papa-Oom-Mow-Mow"
  (Liberty 55427)
  The Rivingtons (1962)

- "The Purple People Eater"
  (MGM 12651)
  Sheb Wooley (1958)

- "Real Wild Child"
  (Coral 62017)
  Ivan (1958)

- "Rudolph the Red-Nosed Reindeer"
  (Liberty 55289)
  The Chipmunks, with David Seville (1960)

- "They're Coming to Take Me Away, Ha-Haaa!"
  (Warner Brothers 5831)
  Napoleon XIV (1966)

- "Witch Doctor"
  (Liberty 55132)
  David Seville (1958)

Radio Programs and Television Shows

- "The Ballad of Davy Crockett"
  (Cadence 1256)
  Bill Hayes (1956)

- "Do You Know What Time It Is?"
  (Buddha 239)
  P-nut Gallery (1971)

- "The Jolly Green Giant"
  (Wand 172)
  The Kingsmen (1965)

- "Rubber Duckie"
  (Columbia 45207)
  Jim Henson (1970)

- "Up Your Nose"
  (Elektra 45369)
  Gabriel Kaplan (1977)

- "Western Movies"
  (Demon 1508)
  The Olympics (1958)

Religious Themes

- "The Bible Tells Me So"
  (Coral 61467)
  Don Cornwell (1955)

- "Little Altar Boy"
  (Dolton 48)
  Vic Dana (1961)

- "Open Up Your Heart (and Let the Sunshine In)"
  (Decca 29367)
  The Cowboy Church Sunday School (1955)

Toys

- "Computer Game"
  (Horizon 127)
  The Yellow Magic Orchestra (1980)

- "Hoopa Hoola"
  (Atlantic 2002)
  Betty Johnson (1958)

- "The Hula Hoop Song"
  (Roulette 4106)
  Georgia Gibbs (1958)

- "The Marvelous Toy"
  (Mercury 72197)
  The Chad Mitchell Trio (1963)

- "Pac-Man Fever"
  (Columbia 02673)
  Buckner and Garcia (1982)

- "Sidewalk Surfin"
  (Liberty 55727)
  Jan and Dean (1964)

- "Skip a Rope"
  (Monument 1041)
  Henson Cargill

BIBLIOGRAPHY

Butchart, Ronald E. and B. Lee Cooper. "Perceptions of Education in the Lyrics of American Popular Music, 1950-1980," *American Music,* V (Fall 1987), pp. 271-281.

Cooper, B. Lee. "Can Music Students Learn Anything of Value by Investigating Popular Recordings?" *International Journal of Instructional Media*, XX, No. 3 (1993), pp. 273-284.

Cooper, B. Lee. "Christmas Songs As American Cultural History: Audio Resources for Classroom Investigation, 1940-1990," *Social Education*, LIV (October 1990), pp. 374-379.

Cooper, B. Lee. Images of American Society in Popular Music: A Guide to Reflective Teaching. Chicago, IL: Nelson-Hall, Inc. 1982.

Cooper, B. Lee. "'It's a Wonder I Can Think at All': Vinyl Images of American Public Education, 1950-1980," *Popular Music and Society*, IX, No. 4 (1984), pp. 47-65.

Cooper, B. Lee. "Rhythm 'n' Rhymes: Character and Theme Images from Children's Literature in Contemporary Recordings, 1950-1985," *Popular Music and Society,* XIII (Spring 1989), pp. 53-17.

Cooper, B. Lee. "Terror Translated Into Comedy: the Popular Music Metamorphosis of Film and Television Horror, 1956-1991," *Journal of American Culture,* XX (Fall 1997) pp. 31-42.

Cooper, B. Lee. "Youth Culture," in *A Resource Guide to Themes in Contemporary American Song Lyrics, 1950-1985.* Westport, CT: Greenwood Press, 1996, pp. 265-337.

Epstein, Jonathan S. (ed.). *Adolescents and Their Music: If It's Too Loud, You're Too Old.* New York: Garland Publishing, 1994.

Frith, Simon. *Sound Effects: Youth, Leisure and the Politics of Rock 'n' Roll.* New York: Pantheon Books, 1981.

Frith, Simon, Andrew Goodwin, and Lawrence Grossberg (eds.). *Sound and Vision: The Music Video Reader.* New York: Routledge, 1993.

Hall, Stuart and Paddy Whannel. "The Young Audience," in *On Record: Rock, Pop, and the Written Word,* edited by Simon Frith and Andrew Goodwin. New York: Pantheon Books, 1990, pp. 27-37.

Kirschner, Tony. "The Lalapalooziation of American Youth," *Popular Music and Society,* XVIII (Spring 1994), pp. 69-90.

Leyser, Brady J. with additional research by Pol Gosset (comps.). *Rock Stars: Pop Stars: A Comprehensive Bibliography, 1955-1994*. Westport, CT: Greenwood Press, 1994.

Ross, Andrew and Tricia Rose (eds.). *Microphone Fiends: Youth Music and Youth Culture*. New York: Routledge, 1994.

Schultze, Quentin J., Roy M. Anker, James D. Bratt, William D. Romanowski, John W. Worst, and Lambert ZuiderVaart. *Dancing in the Dark: Youth, Popular Culture, and the Electronic Media*. Grand Rapids, MI: William B. Eerdmans Publishing Company, 1991.

Schurk, William L. "Beans in My Ears: Children's Songs on the Billboard Pop Charts, 1940-1980." Paper presented at the 15th Annual Midwest Popular Culture Association Conference on October 14, 1987.

Weinstein, Deena. "Rock Is Youth/Youth Is Rock," in *America's Musical Pulse: Popular Music in the Twentieth Century*, edited by Kenneth J. Bindas. Westport, CT: Greenwood Press, 1992, pp. 91-98.

Chapter 2

Christmas Songs

- *Alligator Stomp IV*
  (R2-71058 CD)

- *The Best of Cool Yule*!
  (R2-75767 CD)

- *Billboard Greatest Christmas Hits, 1935-1954*
  (R2-70637 CD)

- *Billboard Greatest Christmas Hits, 1955-Present*
  (R2-70636 CD)

- *Blue Yule*
  (R2-70568 CD)

- *Bummed Out Christmas*
  (R2-70912 CD)

- *Christmas Classics*
  (R2-701 92 CD)

- *Dr. Demento Presents the Greatest Christmas Novelty CD of All Time*
  (R2-75755 CD)

- *Doo Wop Christmas*
  (R2-71057 CD)

- *Hipster's Holiday*
  (R2-70910 CD)

This previously unpublished essay by B. Lee Cooper was developed as a review of several Yuletide compact discs released by Rhino Records.

Nowhere is American cultural diversity more clearly manifested than in the variety of annual commemorations of the birth of Jesus. Jews, Muslims, and other non-Christians cannot escape the post-Thanksgiving/pre-New Year's Day focus on Christmas. Public schools and colleges dismiss classes; newspapers and magazines are flooded with holiday sale advertisements; and businesses provide gala parties, special bonuses, and even paid vacations for employees late in December. Religion plays only one of many roles in America's championing of Christmas. The Yuletide season is a truly multicultural, pluralistic time when theology, economics, family relations, childhood dreams, and social mythology converge.

Commercial recording companies have issued Christmas songs for decades. Naturally, traditional Christian hymns were staples on early twentieth century 78 rpm discs. Other types of seasonal songs emerged during the 1940s and 1950s, though. It should not be forgotten that many landmark tunes—"White Christmas" by Bing Crosby, "Rudolph the Red-Nosed Reindeer" by Gene Autry, "The Christmas Song" by Nat King Cole, "All I Want for Christmas Is My Two Front Teeth" by Spike Jones and His City Slickers, "I Saw Mommy Kissing Santa Claus" by Jimmy Boyd, and "Here Comes Santa Claus (Down Santa Claus Lane)" by Gene Autry—emerged as national treasures less than sixty years ago. The rock era also contributed a variety of now widely celebrated Yuletide songs. These included "Jingle Bell Rock" by Bobby Helms, "Rockin' Around the Christmas Tree" by Brenda Lee, "The Chipmunk Song" by David Seville and The Chipmunks, and "The Little Drummer Boy" by The Harry Simeone Chorale. The divergence of themes featured in holiday recordings is obvious in this list of annual hits. Although the Bethlehem story is still present, Santa Claus is more and more dominant. So is comedy. Humor is found in children's perspectives on gifts and through various adult misbehaviors. It is also located in tales depicting imaginary creatures who help Kris Kringle or who contribute to a youngster's sense of sharing through their kindness and caring.

Rhino Records of Santa Monica, California, has chronicled the development of America's Christmas recording hit parade in two compact disc collections featuring major *Billboard*-charted tunes. This is a valuable contribution to exploring commercial vinyl culture. But Rhino has gone well beyond charted hits to assemble several other anthologies of less renowned Christmas tunes. Subcultures of race, region, age, and musical taste are amply represented in several splendid CD releases. For example, *Hipster's Holiday* features sassy jazz vocals and ribald R&B tunes by Louis Armstrong, Eartha Kitt, Miles Davis, Lionel Hampton, Pearl Bailey,

Lena Horne, and others. The songs presented are earthy, unconventional, and raucously funny. From "'Zat You, Santa Claus" to "Santa Done Got Hip," the Jolly Old Elf garners a series of new and imaginative portrayals. Materialism, a dominant trend at Yuletide, is unabashedly illustrated in "Santa Baby" and "Five Pound Box of Money." Social commentary is also featured in "Blue Xmas (To Whom It May Concern)."

Stylistic innovations of traditional Christmas songs ("White Christmas" by The Drifters) and magnificent group harmony versions of holiday love ballads ("What Are You Doing New Year's Eve" by The Orioles) are featured on *Doo Wop Christmas*. The Penguins, The Cadillacs, The Falcons, The Tuneweavers, The Moonglows, The Heartbeats, The Marcels, and other classic R&B groups demonstrate how "Rudolph the Red-Nosed Reindeer" can be rejuvenated and how nonholiday hits can be lyrically transformed into "Merry Merry Christmas Baby" (instead of the original "Happy Happy Birthday Baby"). Cajun song stylists Johnnie Allan, The Jambalaya Cajun Band, Michael Doucet, and Beausoleil perform creole vocal magic in *Alligator Stomp IV*. Fascinating medleys such as "Christmas Bayou/It Came Upon a Midnight Clear" and "Deck the Halls/ The Little Drummer Boy/Bonne Année/Auld Lang Syne" decorate the Crescent City-oriented disc. *Blue Yule* displays the rhythmic talents of Lightnin' Hopkins, Detroit Junior, John Lee Hooker, Louis Jordan, and Jimmy Liggins on tunes such as "Santa's Messin' With the Kid," "Merry Christmas Baby," and "Please Come Home for Christmas."

Off-the-wall, knee-slapping humor is the concern of all contributors to *Bummed Out Christmas* and *Dr. Demento Presents the Greatest Christmas Novelty CD of All Time*. The songs are iconoclastic and disjunctive in tone, theme, and lyric. The assumptions, values, and traditions of the holiday season are mutilated by Stan Freberg in "Green Chritma," by Cheech and Chong in "Santa Claus and His Old Lady," by Ron Holden and The Thunderbirds in "There Ain't No Santa Claus," and by Kip Adotta in "I Saw Daddy Kissing Santa Claus." Parodies of classic tunes such as "Jingle Bells" by The Singing Dogs and media-related spinoffs such as "Christmas Dragnet" by Stan Freberg and Daws Butler round out these wholly unholy discs.

The Rhino collections illustrate American cultural tolerance, self-criticism, and humor at their very best. Christianity and capitalism are juxtaposed with glee; holy figures and holy terrors are matched against talking snowmen, glowing reindeer, singing chipmunks, and barking canines, and traditional images of shepherds, stables, and stars are challenged by contemporary desires for wealth, wenches, and well-being. The Rhino collections proudly acknowledge the smooth, white-bread sounds of Bing

Crosby, Vaughn Monroe, The Andrews Sisters, and Gene Autry, but also feature more upbeat, sometimes offbeat, presentations of Huey Smith and The Clowns, James Brown, Bob and Doug McKenzie, The Pilgrim Travelers, Sonny Boy Williamson, Henry Fontenot, Frankie Lymon, and Wild Man Fischer. Ethnic jokes, dialects, and bizarre wishes ("I Want a Hippopotamus for Christmas" by Gayla Peevy) abound. Neither the Ku Klux Klan nor preachers of political correctness will understand the public's fascination with these marvelous howl-a-day collections. But the young at heart will genuinely appreciate this Rhino avalanche of Yuletide goodies. Let it snow! Let it snow! Let it snow!

BIBLIOGRAPHY

Almost Slim. "Christmas Classics," *Wavelength*, No. 26 (December 1982), pp. 21-22.

Almost Slim. "Christmas on Wax," *Wavelength*, No. 38 (December 1983), p. 17.

Almost Slim. "Rock 'n' Roll Banned for Christmas," *Wavelength*, No. 2 (December 1980), p. 14.

Barnett, James H. *The American Christmas: A Study in National Culture*. New York: Macmillan Company, 1954.

Belk, Russell W. "A Child's Christmas in America: Santa Claus As Deity, Consumption As Religion," *Journal of American Culture*, X (Spring 1987), pp. 87-100.

Butland, John. "A Semi-Exhausted and Opinionated Guide to Rock 'n' Roll and R&B Christmas Music . . . Or Stuff This in Your Stocking!" *DISCoveries*, No. 91 (December 1995), pp. 38-44.

Callahan, Mike. "Phil Spector, Christmas, and the Stereo Wall of Sound," *Goldmine*, No. 55 (December 1980), pp. 174-175.

Canale, Larry. "Christmas Compact Disc Reviews," in *Digital Audio's Guide to Compact Discs*. New York: Bantam Books, 1986, pp. 160-163.

Colby, J. M. and A. W. Purdue. *The Making of the Modern Christmas*. Athens, GA: University of Georgia Press, 1986.

Cooper, B. Lee. "Christmas," in *Popular Music Perspectives: Ideas, Themes, and Patterns in Contemporary Lyrics*. Bowling Green, OH: Bowling Green State University Popular Press, 1991, pp. 68-81.

Cooper, B. Lee. "Christmas Songs: Audio Barometers of Religious Tradition and Social Change in America, 1950-1987," *The Social Studies*, LXXIX (November/December 1988), pp. 278-280.

Cooper, B. Lee. "Do You Hear What I Hear? Christmas Recordings As Audio Symbols of Religious Tradition and Social Change in Contemporary America," *International Journal of Instruction Media*, XVI, No. 3 (1989), pp. 265-270.

Curtis, Bruce. "The Strange Birth of Santa Claus: From Artemis the Goddess to Nicholas the Saint," *Journal of American Culture*, XVIII (Winter 1995), pp. 17-32.

Dr. Demento. "Santa and the Hot 100: The History of Holiday Hit-Making," *Waxpaper*, 11 (October 28, 1977), pp. 18-20, 36.

Doggett, Peter. "Rockin' Around the Christmas Tree!" *Record Collector*, No. 28 (December 1981), pp. 44-51.

Elrod, Bruce. "In Country Music: A New Discovery and Some Holiday Chestnuts," *DISCoveries*, II (January 1989), pp. 94-95.

Fumar, Vincent. "Please Come Home for Christmas . . . And Bring the Turntable," *Wavelength*, No. 38 (December 1983), p. 16.

George, B. "Christmas in the Caribbean," *Goldmine*, No. 325 (December 25, 1992), pp. 26-30, 106.

Grein, Paul. "Grandma' Runs Over Bing in Holiday Race: Adams, Springsteen Join Ranks of Yule Chartmakers," *Billboard*, XLVII (December 21, 1985), p. 57.

Harker, Dave. "The Average Popular Song," in *One for the Money: Politics and the Popular Song*. London: Hutchinson and Company, Ltd., 1980), pp. 38-50.

Hoffmann, Frank. "The Utilization of Christmas Songs As a Learning Tool: An Essay and Discography," *Music Reference Services Quarterly*, No. 3 (1993), pp. 3-54.

Hoffmann, Frank W. and William G. Bailey, "White Christmas," in *Arts and Entertainment Fads* (New York: Haworth Press, 1990), pp. 355-357.

Koenig, John. "Christmas Releases for Collectors," *DISCoveries*, No. 79 (December 1994), p. 50.

Langstaff, Nancy and John Langstaff, *The Christmas Revel Songbook: Carols, Processionals, Rounds, Ritual, and Children's Songs*. Boston: Dr. R. Godine, 1985.

Lewisohn, Mark. "The Beatles' Christmas Records," *Record Collector*, No. 112 (December 1988), pp. 11-15.

Marsh, Dave and Steve Propes. "Jingle Bell Rock," *DISCoveries*, No. 67 (December 1993), pp. 35-37.

Marsh, Dave and Steve Propes. *Merry Christmas, Baby: Holiday Music from Bing to Sting*. Boston: Little, Brown and Company, 1993.

Mawhinney, Paul C. *MusicMaster: The 45 rpm Christmas Singles Directory—46 Years of Recorded Music from 1948 to 1994 Listed Alphabetically by Artist/Title* (Pittsburgh, Pennsylvania: Record-Rama Sound Archives, 1993), pp. 1-142.

McAuliffe, Jon. "Christmas Collectibles," *Music World*, No. 80 (December 1980), pp. 6-12.

Milberg, David A. "Christmas Collectibles on Disk in a CD World," *DISCoveries*, No. 67 (December 1993), pp. 38-39.

Milberg, David A. "Christmas Music," in *All Music Guide,* edited by Michael Erlewine and Scott Bultman. San Francisco, CA: Miller Freeman, Inc., 1992, pp. 610-620.

Milberg, David A. (comp.). *Radio/TV Dave's Greatest Christmas Hits of All Time: The Ultimate Collection of Christmas Hits and Novelty Tunes*. Chicago: D. A. Milberg, 1996.

Moonoogian, George. "Merry Christmas Baby," *Record Exchanger*, V (1978), pp. 12-19.

Moonoogian, George. "Remember When?" *Goldmine*, No. 31 (December 1978), p. 12.

Morthland, John. "Christmas," *Wavelength,* No. 62 (December 1985), p. 28.

Munn, Bob. "Popular Christmas Music: A Collector's Guide," *Goldmine,* No. 115 (December 21, 1984), pp. 60-62.

Nathanson, Paul. "You Can't Go Home Again . . . or Can You? Reflections on the Symbolism of TV Families at Christmastime," *Journal of Popular Culture,* XXVII (Fall 1973), pp. 149-161.

Neely, Tim. "Platter Chatter: Great Christmas Compilations," *Goldmine,* No. 429 (January 3, 1997), p. 28.

Oksanen, Dave. "The Elvis Presley Christmas Records," *Music World,* No. 80 (December 1980), pp. 39-43.

Osborne, Jerry P. "It's Beginning to Look a Lot Like Christmas," in *Our Best to You—From Record Digest.* Prescott, AZ: Record Digest, 1979), pp. 203-204.

Otnes, Cele, Young Chan Kim, and Kyungsevng. "All I Want for Christmas: An Analysis of Children's Brand Requests to Santa Claus," *Journal of Popular Culture,* XXVII (Spring 1994), pp. 183-194.

Otnes, Cele, Young Chan Kim, and Kyungsevng. "Yes, Virginia, There Is a Gender Difference: Analyzing Children's Requests to Santa Claus," *Journal of Popular Culture,* XXVIII (Summer 1994), pp. 17-29.

Pattillo, Ceaig W. *Christmas on Record: Best Selling Christmas Singles and Albums of the Past 40 Years.* Portland, OR: Braemer Books, 1983, pp. 1-208.

Pimper, Steve. "A Slix Pix Christmas!" *DISCoveries,* II (January 1989), pp. 100-101.

Radel, Cliff. "In Tune for Christmas," *Lansing [Michigan] State Journal* (December 13, 1992), pp. 1F, 3F.

Rosen, Mark. "Rockin' Around the Christmas Tree: A Rock and Roll Christmas Wrap-Up," *Goldmine,* No. 271 (December 14, 1990), pp. 56, 116, 118.

Russell, Wayne. "Rockin' Around the Christmas Tree," *Now Dig This,* No. 69 (December 1988), pp. 4-7.

Scaramuzzo, Gene. "Everywhere It's Christmas," *Wavelength,* No. 110 (December 1989), pp. 17-18.

Schurk, William L. "Santa Looked a Lot Like Daddy, and Daddy Looked a Lot Like Him: A 50-Year Perspective on Christmas Record Album Packaging and Artwork." Paper presented at the Eleventh National Convention of the American Culture Association in April 1989.

Scoppa, Jordon. "Picture This," *Music World,* No. 80 (December 1980), pp. 28-35.

Sherwood, Lydia. "The Chipmunks Chatter—A Talk with Ross Bagdasarian, Jr.," *Goldmine,* No. 79 (December 1982), pp. 16-18, 23.

Stidom, Larry. "Izatso?!" *Goldmine,* No. 31 (December 1978), p. 31.

Stierle, Wayne. "A Real Rock and Roll Christmas (or, How to Get Along Without Motown and Phil Spector and Still Have Some Super Holiday Music)," *DISCoveries,* No. 2 (December 1989), pp. 120-122.

Studwell, William E. *Christmas Carols: A Reference Guide.* New York: Garland Publishing, Inc., 1985.

Studwell, William E. *The Christmas Carol Reader.* Binghamton, NY: Haworth Press, 1995.

Studwell, William E. "From 'Jingle Bells' to 'Jingle Bell Rock': Sketches of Obscure or Fading American Popular Christmas Song Writers, 1857-1957 (And a Little Beyond)," *Music Reference Services Quarterly*, V, No. 2 (1996), pp. 11-22.

Whitburn, Joel. "Christmas," in *Top Pop Albums 1955-1992*, Menomonee Falls, WI: Record Research, Inc., 1993, pp. 924-931.

Whitburn, Joel. "Christmas Singles, 1955-1990," in *Pop Singles Annual 1955-1990*, Menomonee Falls, WI: Record Research, Inc., 1991, pp. 707-710.

Chapter 3

Death

The Death of Rock 'n' Roll: Untimely Demises, Morbid Preoccupations, and Premature Forecasts of Doom in Pop Music. By Jeff Pike. Boston: Faber and Faber, 1993. 289 pp.

Seattle freelance writer Jeff Pike presents a dark vision of the rock era. His 1993 book's subtitle—*Untimely Demises, Morbid Preoccupations, and Premature Forecasts of Doom*—defines his perspective. What a downer! In forty-two chapters, Pike highlights the haunted histories of Robert Johnson and Johnny Ace, the death-wish behaviors of Jerry Lee Lewis and Jim Morrison; the drug abuse lifestyles of Elvis Presley and Jimi Hendrix; the tragic airplane accidents of Jim Croce, Buddy Holly, Otis Redding, Rick Nelson, and Stevie Ray Vaughan; the violent murders of King Curtis and Marvin Gaye; and the drownings of Johnny Burnette, Brian Jones, and Dennis Wilson. The text also features twenty-three insert sections that further categorize musicians' deaths by electrocution, stabbing, poisoning, AIDS (e.g., Freddie Mercury), general diseases (Leadbelly and Woody Guthrie), pneumonia (Little Willie John and T-Bone Walker), tuberculosis (Jimmie Rodgers), heart failure (Bill Haley and Marty Robbins), lung cancer (Nat King Cole), brain tumors (Tammi Terrell), cancer (Mary Wells and Bob Marley), and even hanging (Phil Ochs). This book should not be read by anyone suffering from either mild depression or a personality disorder. Even those living artists cited by Pike—The Rolling Stones, Screamin' Jay Hawkins, Lou Reed, Leonard Cohen, Iggy Pop, Alice Cooper, and The Grateful Dead are depicted as walking dead men, singing zombies, or fellow conspirators in Johnson's mythical deal with the Devil.

The Death of Rock 'n' Roll is fact-filled, generally articulate, and occasionally intriguing. Yet it is fraught with serious flaws in both structure and

---

This chapter by B. Lee Cooper was originally published as "From Johnny Ace to Frank Zappa: Debating the Meaning of Death in Rock Music—A Review Essay," *Popular Culture in Libraries*, III, No. 1 (1995), pp. 51-75. Reprint permission granted by the author, editor Frank Hoffmann, and The Haworth Press.

perspective. The author teases readers with his leapfrog technique of randomly combining chapters and charts that bear no relation to each other. Casual
music fans and serious biographical researchers alike are going to be puzzled
when trying to locate Jesse Belvin (p. 34), The Big Bopper (p. 114), or Sam
Cooke (p. 164). No index is provided. This also negates the pursuit of
cross-references. For instance, Cooke is also listed under "Deaths Accompanied by Public Outpourings of Emotion" (p. 151). It is unexplainable, though,
why Cooke is omitted from the "Death at Another's Hand" section. Similarly
questionable is why James Dean is included while Marilyn Monroe is not
listed. One also wonders why the author briefly tips his hat to Barry Lazell,
Joel Whitburn, Norm N. Nite, Donald Clarke, and a few other reference
guide compilers in the acknowledgments section, but neglects to provide any
bibliography of studies dealing specifically with death themes in rock music.
These structural incongruities severely weaken the book. But even greater
problems plague Pike's pursuit.

The Death of Rock 'n' Roll is constructed on the assumption that the living
artists themselves sustain the success of rock music. Actually, once recordings are released, it is the record industry and the general public that collabo-
rate to create hits, myths, stereotypes, and ultimately rock legends. Music is
actually the lifeblood of the rock era. Even long-dead heroes—Jackie Wilson,
Elvis Presley, John Lennon, Buddy Holly, and Jim Morrison—continue to
yield hit after hit and to reign supreme on oldies-but-goodies airwaves, in
reissued CDs, and on motion picture soundtracks. Jeff Pike obviously prefers
obituary writing to marketing analysis. This robs his work of any real insight
into the meaning and impact of recorded death themes throughout the forty-
year rock era. Without paying much attention to the lyrical commentaries on
death and dying featured on so many post-1953 recordings, Pike unwittingly
ignores the pluralism of humor and horror that constitute the legacy of coffin
tunes. The remainder of this essay, plus the accompanying discography and
bibliography, illustrate the multitude of omissions in Pike's morbid volume.

"The Late Great Johnny Ace" was an especially thought-provoking song
featured on Paul Simon's 1983 *Hearts and Bones* album. This tune, reminis-
cent of such eulogy songs as "American Pie" and "Abraham, Martin, and
John," offers an individual's reflections on the frailty of human existence.
These three songs are more than just lyrical retrospectives. They assess the
psychological impact of death upon entire generations. This sounds extremely serious—and uncommon—for popular music fare. Yet Paul Simon, Don
McLean, and Dion DiMucci, along with a variety of other contemporary
singers and songwriters, have succeeded in delivering informed and informative visions concerning mortality.

The death theme is omnipresent in rock lyrics. Several scholars who have investigated this topic have elected to focus on the narrow topic of teenage coffin songs. These studies, emphasizing narrative ballads that explore youthful experiences with either suicide or accidental death, usually highlight recordings such as Mark Dinning's "Teen Angel," Jody Reynolds' "Endless Sleep," Ray Peterson's "Tell Laura I Love Her," The Shangri-Las' "Leader of the Pack," and Dickey Lee's "Patches." R. Serge Denisoff, a particularly perceptive popular music analyst, notes that the short-lived popularity of love-lost-through-death songs was due to the rapid cultural and political changes occurring during the mid-1960s. Specifically, Denisoff (1983) observes:

> Several death songs in the latter half of the 1960s—"Ode to Billy Joe" and "Honey"—sold quite well. Still, the teenage coffin song did not return after 1965. The demise of the coffin song correlates with the introduction of overt statements of social dissent as found in Barry McGuire's "Eve of Destruction," and Glen Campbell's version of "Universal Soldier." Conversely, the "He's a Rebel," "Tell Laura I Love Her," "Patches" oriented songs were *passe* with the advent of the counterculture and its disavowal of the social ethic of the 1950s. . . ." (p. 121)

Admittedly, the notion of courtly love diminished during the early 1960s, to be replaced by direct commentaries about overt physical attraction, freely spoken desires, and frequent nonmarital liaisons in the 1970s and 1980s. However, the death theme did not disappear. In fact, it became more visible and more broadly explored in popular lyrics *after* 1965. There were also many songs about death and dying that were *not* simply teenage laments that were popular throughout the 1950s. These tunes explored more than just dejected drownings or accidental auto tragedies. Premeditated homicides, spur-of-the-moment killings, and suicides are portrayed in numerous recordings from 1950 to the present. The next section continues this theme, beginning with an extensive list of death-related recordings.

A CHRONOLOGICAL DISCOGRAPHY OF DEATH THEME RECORDINGS, 1953-1993

1953

- "The Death of Hank Williams"
  (King 1172)
  Jack Cardell (1953)

1955

- "The Ballad of Davy Crockett"
  (Cadence 1256)
  Bill Hayes (1955)

- "Sixteen Tons"
  (Capitol 3262)
  Tennessee Ernie Ford (1955)

1956

- "John Henry"
  (London 1650)
  Lonnie Donegan and his Skiffle Group (1956)

1957

- "(There'll Be) Peace in the Valley (for Me)"
  (RCA EP 4054)
  Elvis Presley (1957)

1958

- "The Battle of New Orleans"
  (Columbia 41339)
  Johnny Horton (1958)

- "Endless Sleep"
  (Demo 1507)
  Jody Reynolds (1958)

- "Stagger Lee"
  (ABC-Paramount 9972)
  Lloyd Price (1958)

- "Tom Dooley"
  (Capitol 4049)
  The Kingston Trio (1958)

1959

- "Don't Take Your Guns to Town"
  (Columbia 41313)
  Johnny Cash (1959)

- "El Paso"
  (Columbia 41511)
  Marty Robbins (1959)

- "The Hanging Tree"
  (Columbia 41325)
  Marty Robbins (1959)

- "Mack the Knife"
  (Atco 6.147)
  Bobby Darin (1959)

- "Running Bear"
  (Mercury 71474)
  Johnny Preston (1959)

- "Three Stars"
  (Crest 1057)
  Tommy Dee with Carol Kay and The Teen-Aires (1959)

- "Tragedy"
  (Fernwood 109)
  Thomas Wayne (1959)

1960

- "The Ballad of the Alamo"
  (Columbia 41809)
  Marty Robbins (1960)

- "Big Iron"
  (Columbia 41589)
  Marty Robbins (1960)

- "Teen Angel"
  (MGM 12845)
  Mark Dinning (1960)

- "Tell Laura I Love Her"
  (RCA 7745)
  Ray Peterson (1960)

- "There's Something on Your Mind"
  (Fire 1022)
  Bobby Marchan (1960)

1961

- "Big Bad John"
  (Columbia 42175)
  Jimmy Dean (1961)

- "Ebony Eyes"
  (Warner Brothers 5199)
  The Everly Brothers (1961)

- "Frankie and Johnny"
  (Mercury 71859)
  Brook Benton (1961)

- "I Dreamed of a Hill-Billy Heaven"
  (Capitol 4567)
  Tex Ritter (1961)

- "Moody River"
  (Dot 16209)
  Pat Boone (1961)

1962

- "Patches"
  (Atlantic 2748)
  Clarence Carter (1962)

- "Where Have All the Flowers Gone?"
  (Capitol 4671)
  The Kingston Trio (1962)

1963

- "In the Summer of His Years"
  (MGM 13203)
  Connie Francis (1963)

1964

- "Dead Man's Curve"
  (Liberty 55672)
  Jan and Dean (1964)

- "Last Kiss"
  (Josie 923)
  Frank Wilson and The Cavaliers (1964)

- "Leader of the Pack"
  (Red Bird 014)
  The Shangri-Las (1964)

- "Ringo"
  (RCA 8444)
  Lorne Greene (1964)

1965

- "Eve of Destruction"
  (Dunhill 4009)
  Barry McGuire (1965)

- "Give Us Your Blessing"
  (Red Bird 030)
  The Shangri-Las (1965)

- "The Streets of Laredo"
  (Columbia 43313)
  Johnny Cash (1965)

- "Turn! Turn! Turn!"
  (Columbia 43424)
  The Byrds (1965)

- "The Universal Soldier"
  (Capitol 5504)
  Glen Campbell (1965)

- "A Well-Respected Man"
  (Reprise 0420)
  The Kinks (1965)

1966

- "The Ballad of the Green Berets"
  (RCA 8739)
  SSgt Barry Sadler (1966)

- "Billy and Sue"
  (Hickory 1395)
  B.J. Thomas (1966)

- "The Cruel War"
  (Warner Brothers 5809)
  Peter, Paul, and Mary (1966)

- "Eleanor Rigby"
  (Capitol 5715)
  The Beatles (1966)

- "Green, Green, Grass of Home"
  (Parrot 40009)
  Tom Jones (1966)

- "It Was a Very Good Year"
  (Reprise 0429)
  Frank Sinatra (1966)

- "That's Life"
  (Reprise 0531)
  Frank Sinatra (1966)

1967

- "Ode to Billy Joe"
  (Capitol 5950)
  Bobbie Gentry (1967)

1968

- "Abraham, Martin, and John"
  (Laurie 3464)
  Dion (1968)

- "Autumn of My Life"
  (United Artists 50318)
  Bobby Goldsboro (1968)

- "The Ballad of Bonnie and Clyde"
  (Epic 10283)
  Georgie Fame (1968)

- "Ballad of John Dillinger"
  (Mercury 72836)
  Billy Grammer (1968)

- "Delilah"
  (Parrot 40025)
  Tom Jones (1968)

- "Folsom Prison Blues"
  (Columbia 44513)
  Johnny Cash (1968)

- "Honey"
  (United Artists 50283)
  Bobby Goldsboro (1968)

- "The Snake"
  (Soul City 767)
  Al Wilson (1968)

- "A Tribute to a King"
  (Stax 248)
  William Bell (1968)

- "2 + 2 = ?"
  (Capitol 2143)
  The Bob Seger System (1968)

- "The Unknown Soldier"
  (Elektra 45628)
  The Doors (1968)

1969

- "And When I Die"
  (Columbia 45008)
  Blood, Sweat, and Tears (1969)

- "Don't Cry Daddy"
  (RCA 47-9768)
  Elvis Presley (1969)

- "Games People Play"
  (Capitol 2248)
  Joe South (1969)

- "In the Ghetto"
  (RCA 47-9741)
  Elvis Presley (1969)

- "In the Year 2525 (Exordium and Terminus)"
  (RCA 0174)
  Zager and Evans (1969)

- "My Way"
  (Reprise 0854)
  Frank Sinatra (1969)

- "Ruben James"
  (Reprise 0854)
  Kenny Rogers and The First Edition (1969)

- "Six White Horses"
  (Epic 10540)
  Tommy Cash (1969)

- "Yesterday, When I Was Young"
  (Dot 17246)
  Roy Clark (1969)

- "You Gave Me a Mountain"
  (ABC 11174)
  Frankie Laine (1969)

1970

- "Are You Ready?"
  (Columbia 45158)
  Pacific Gas and Electric (1970)

- "Fire and Rain"
  (Warner Brothers 7423)
  James Taylor (1970)

- "Indiana Wants Me"
  (Rare Earth 5013)
  R. Dean Taylor (1970)

- "Ohio"
  (Atlantic 2740)
  Crosby, Stills, Nash, and Young (1970)

- "Patches"
  (Atlantic 2748)
  Clarence Carter (1970)

- "Spirit in the Sky"
  (Reprise 0885)
  Norman Greenbaum (1970)

- "War"
  (Gordy 7101)
  Edwin Starr (1970)

1971

- "American Pie"
  (United Artists 50856)
  Don McLean (1971)

- "Battle Hymn of Lt. Calley"
  (Plantation 73)
  C. Company, featuring Terry Nelson (1971)

- "Done Too Soon"
  (Uni 55278)
  Neil Young (1971)

- "The Night They Drove Old Dixie Down"
  (Vanguard 35138)
  Joan Baez (1971)

- "One Tin Soldier (The Legend of Billy Jack)"
  (Warner Brothers 7509)
  Coven (1971)

- "Smackwater Jack"
  (Ode 66019)
  Carole King (1971)

- "Timothy"
  (Scepter 12275)
  The Buoys (1971)

- "When I'm Dead and Gone"
  (MGM 14206)
  Bob Summers (1971)

1972

- "Alone Again (Naturally)"
  (MAM 3619)
  Gilbert O'Sullivan (1972)

- "Conquistador"
  (A&M 1347)
  Procol Harum (1972)

- "Freddie's Dead"
  (Curtom 1975)
  Curtis Mayfield (1972)

- "Papa Was a Rollin' Stone"
  (Gordy 7121)
  The Temptations (1972)

- "Vincent"
  (United Artists 50887)
  Don McLean (1972)

1973

- "Daisy a Day"
  (MGM 14463)
  Jud Strunk (1973)

- "The Night the Lights Went Out in Georgia"
  (Bell 45303)
  Vicki Lawrence (1973)

- "Swamp Witch"
  (MGM 14496)
  Jim Stafford (1973)

1974

- "Billy, Don't Be a Hero"
  (ABC 11435)
  Bo Donaldson and The Heywoods (1974)

- "I Shot the Sheriff"
  (RSO 409)
  Eric Clapton (1974)

- "The Night Chicago Died"
  (Mercury 73492)
  Paper Lace (1974)

- "Rock and Roll Heaven"
  (Haven 7002)
  The Righteous Brothers (1974)

- "Seasons in the Sun"
  (Bell 45432)
  Terry Jacks (1974)

1975

- "Bohemian Rhapsody"
  (Elektra 45297)
  Queen (1975)

- "Emma"
  (Big Tree 16031)
  Hot Chocolate (1975)

- "Golden Years"
  (RCA 10441)
  David Bowie (1975)

- "The Last Game of the Season (Blind Man in the Bleachers)"
  (Big Tree 16052)
  David Geddes (1975)

- "Sixteen Tons"
  (Atlantic 3323)
  Don Harrison Band (1975)

- "Take the Money and Run"
  (Capitol 4260)
  The Steve Miller Band (1975)

- "The Wreck of the Edmund Fitzgerald"
  (Reprise 1369)
  Gordon Lightfoot (1975)

1977

- "From Graceland to the Promised Land"
  (MCA 40804)
  Merle Haggard and The Strangers (1977)

- "The King Is Gone"
  (Scorpion 135)
  Ronnie McDowell (1977)

- "My Way"
  (RCA PB-11165)
  Elvis Presley (1977)

1978

- "Copacabana (At the Copa)"
  (Arista 0339)
  Barry Manilow (1978)

- "The Gambler"
  (United Artists 1250)
  Kenny Rogers (1978)

- "Only the Good Die Young"
  (Columbia 10750)
  Billy Joel (1978)

1980

- "(Ghost) Riders in the Sky"
  (Arista 0582)
  The Outlaws (1980)

- "He Stopped Loving Her Today"
  (Epic 50867)
  George Jones (1980)

1981

- "Grandma's Song"
  (Warner Brothers 49790)
  Gail Davies (1981)

1982

- "Dirty Laundry"
  (Asylum 69894)
  Don Henley (1982)

1983

- "The Late, Great Johnny Ace"
  (Warner Brothers 23942-Album)
  Paul Simon (1983)

- "The Ride"
  (Columbia 03778)
  David Allan Coe (1983)

1984

- "Born in the U.S.A."
  (Columbia 04680)
  Bruce Springsteen (1984)

- "Do They Know It's Christmas?"
  (Columbia 04749)
  Band Aid (1984)

1985

- "All She Wants to Do Is Dance"
  (Geffen 29065)
  Don Henley (1985)

- "Leader of the Pack"
  (Atlantic 89478)
  Twisted Sister (1985)

- "Nightshift"
  (Motown 1773)
  The Commodores (1985)

- "Smuggler's Blues"
  (MCA 52546)
  Glenn Frey (1985)

1986

- "Spirit in the Sky"
  (I.R.S. 52880)
  Doctor and The Medics (1986)

- "That's Life"
  (Warner Brothers 28511)
  David Lee Roth (1986)

- "War"
  (Columbia 06432)
  Bruce Springsteen (1986)

1987

- "Kiss of Death"
  (Elektra 60735)
  Dokken (1987)

- "Smoking Gun"
  (Mercury 888343)
  The Robert Cray Band (1987)

1988

- "Candle in the Wind"
  (MCA 53196)
  Elton John (1988)

- "The Gift of Death"
  (Medusa 72278)
  Wasted Youth (1988)

1989

- "Death on Credit"
  (Cargo Car 05)
  Tupelo Chain Sex (1989)

- "They're Killing Us All (to Make the World Safe)"
  (Truetone TLP 792077)
  Celibate Rifles (1989)

1990

- "Death!"
  (Priority 57155)
  Ice Cube (1990)

- "Death Blow"
  (Jive 1388)
  Kool Moe Dee (1990)

- "Death Sentence"
  (Cold Chill 26715)
  Big Daddy Kane (1990)

- "Deathmarch"
  (Columbia 46142)
  Fishbone (1990)

- "Deathstyle"
  (In-Effect 3014)
  SPYZ (1990)

- "No Prayer for the Dying"
  (Epic 46905)
  Iron Maiden (1990)

1992

- "Cop Killer"
  (Sire 26878)
  Body Count (1992)

- "Wishing a Slow Death"
  (Blackjack Jack 009)
  Brainbombs (1992)

1993

- "Death to All Pigs"
  (Brokenskip 16)
  Naked Aggression (1993)

- "Teenage Suicide"
  (4AD Bad 3007)
  Unrest (1993)

As mentioned in the previous section, not all death-related tunes simply described accidental death. Even the gentle Beatles produced the delightfully sinister "Maxwell's Silver Hammer," a tune that rivals Alfred Hitchcock's "Psycho" for murderous insanity. What is more interesting, though, is the fact that the death theme appears in such a broad variety of visages over the past forty years. Among these different perspectives are: (a) aging and dying as natural life cycle events; (b) tragic airline disasters, train wrecks, and automobile crashes; (c) death as an acknowledged religious end or climactic existential event; (d) physical debilitation and demise from protracted drug abuse; (e) the passing of heroes or villains; (f) acts of murder and the lethal pursuit of murderers; (g) deaths of soldiers and other kinds of wartime casualties; and (h) suicide. As noted earlier, there are also a few epic hero songs that use either assassinations or accidental deaths of prominent political or musical figures as backdrops for generation-defining commentaries.

There is considerable discussion about aging in contemporary songs. From the tender side of thirty, Pete Townshend of The Who proclaimed that he hoped he would die before he grew old. But "My Generation" isn't typical of reflective songs about reaching maturity. Frank Sinatra offers two different assessments of fulfilled lives in "It Was a Very Good Year" and "My Way." The former tune chronicles the amorous evolution of an eminently successful womanizer. The latter song, authored by Canadian songsmith Paul Anka, is a classic paean to individual freedom and independence. Anticipating old age and hoping to establish a meaningful lifelong relationship is the theme of The Beatles' "When I'm Sixty-Four." For those who are much closer to retirement age, the image of unfulfilled expectations seems to be far more common. Roy Clark obviously longs for "Yesterday, When I Was Young," while Peggy Lee, in disillusioned fashion, sings "Is That All There Is?" The very frightening image of an aged male with shoddy clothes, greasy hands, and snot running down his nose is presented in Jethro Tull's grisly "Aqualung."

Death resulting from spectacular accidents constitutes the backbone of many heroic tales. Train wreck sagas about the brave engineer Casey Jones are legion in folk music. So are songs about John Henry. Within the popular song arena, automobile accidents and airline crashes are events that cause unexpected loss of life. The personal tragedy of losing a loved one to a flight disaster is reported by The Everly Brothers in "Ebony Eyes." James Taylor's "Fire and Rain" explores a reflective reaction to an airplane crash, too. In addition to the previously cited car death songs by Mark Dinning and Ray Peterson, the foremost examples of four-wheel disasters are J. Frank Wilson and The Cavaliers' "Last Kiss," The Shangri-Las' "Give Us Your Blessing," and Jan and Dean's "Dead Man's Curve."

Death interrupts anticipated continuity. It is usually a complete surprise, a bitter shock. Death fosters grief, revery, and a reminder of each person's mortality. Individual responses to life's finality vary in popular songs—just as they do in traditional poetry and classical literature. David Clayton Thomas of Blood, Sweat, and Tears confidently asserts that "There'll be one child born in this world to carry on . . ." after he passes away. The peace of mind found in "And When I Die" is totally absent in the short-term anguish over personal losses expressed in Thomas Wayne's "Tragedy," Bobby Goldsboro's "Honey," and Kenny Rogers and The First Edition's "Ruben James."

Several songs explore the death theme in an obscure or peculiar fashion. The 1960 Elvis Presley hit "Are You Lonesome Tonight?" was reissued after his death in 1977 and became a deep public eulogy rather than a simple individual hymn of lost love. David Geddes reiterates a son-performing-in-honor-of-his-deceased-dad tale in "The Game of the Season (A Blind Man in the Bleachers)." Paul McCartney and Wings salute the murderous inclinations of a daring secret agent in "Live and Let Die," while

Kenny Rogers secures wisdom from a dying "Gambler" as they travel together on a train reportedly bound for nowhere. Joe South sardonically observes that it doesn't matter what "Games People Play" in daily life because everyone eventually winds up riding to the cemetery in the back of a black limousine. Other recordings that focus on impending death include Blue Oyster Cult's "(Don't Fear) The Reaper," The Beatles' "Eleanor Rigby," Pacific Gas and Electric's "Are You Ready?," The Byrds' "Turn! Turn! Turn!," and Norman Greenbaum's "Spirit in the Sky."

Beyond references to the natural life cycle, beyond misfortunes of accidental demise, and beyond all other observations about inevitable mortality there are series of extremely violent lyrical perceptions. Death is not serene. it sometimes comes in a chemical disguise provided by Steppenwolf's dreaded "Pusher" and consumed by a "Snow Blind Friend." But drug abuse is most often a lonely form of victimization. In sharp contrast to solitary, debilitating deaths, the passing of figures that are larger than life—whether heroes or villains—is *always* noteworthy. In 1956 Lonnie Donegan resurrected the classic tale of the powerful, independent spike driver "John Henry." One year before, "The Ballad of Davy Crockett" had eulogized an authentic American hero of historic and mythic import. Fess Parker's tale of heroism was echoed by Marty Robbins' "Ballad of the Alamo." Death was also the focus of historical exploration concerning the fate of British soldiers in Johnny Horton's "The Battle of New Orleans" and Southern farmers in Joan Baez's "The Night They Drove Old Dixie Down." The police and National Guard are viewed as contemporary death merchants rather than protectors of local peace in "Ohio" by Crosby, Stills, Nash, and Young, in "Mad Dog" by Lee Michaels, and in "The Ballad of Bonnie and Clyde" by Georgie Fame. Heroes die, too. A soft-spoken giant of a man who saved his fellow miners from a cold dark grave by sacrificing his own life is lauded by Jimmy Dean in "Big Bad John." Gene Pitney praises the mysterious killer of a gunslinger who needed to be gunned down in "(The Man Who Shot) Liberty Valance." Jim Stafford even offers praise for the cruel, cunning, death-dealing "Swamp Witch" who, in a moment of uncharacteristic humanism, provided a life-saving potion to spare a small town from the plague.

Murder and mayhem seem miles away from teenage coffin songs. Yet homicide is a common feature in popular tunes throughout the past forty years. Traditional vengeance songs such as "Frankie and Johnny" and "Stagger Lee" have been successfully revived by Sam Cooke and Lloyd Price. Yet even more cold-blooded characters have found vinyl immortality since 1950. The wicked, killer-for-hire exploits of Bobby Darin's "Mack the Knife" were exceeded by the ungrateful, unprovoked, venomous attack of

Al Wilson's "The Snake"; and the bloody deeds of Marty Robbins' "Big Iron" and Lorne Greene's "Ringo" don't begin to match the psychotic bloodlust illustrated by Carole King's shotgun-wielding "Smackwater Jack" and The Beatles' mallet-carrying youth in "Maxwell's Silver Hammer."

The country music tradition continues to feed lyrical imagery of two-gun justice, violence, and death into the popular song arena. Johnny Cash is content to sing the "Folsom Prison Blues" because he shot a man in Reno, just to watch him die. Obviously, casual homicide doesn't pay. Despite a mother's warning—"Don't Take Your Guns to Town"—the "Streets of Laredo" death scene is reenacted in several tunes by Marty Robbins, in the Kingston Trio's "Tom Dooley," in Eric Clapton's "I Shot the Sheriff," and in scores of country ballads. Of course, there are other reasons for committing murder. Vicki Lawrence seeks personal vengeance in "The Night the Lights Went Out in Georgia"; Steve Miller describes a man killed during a robbery in "Take the Money and Run"; Bobby Marchan depicts a jealous suitor who shoots his lover when he finds her entertaining his friends in "There's Something on Your Mind"; and in a frightening example of cannibalism, The Buoys speculate on the unspeakable disappearance of their former friend "Timothy."

Death at an elderly age is regrettable; death by accident is shocking and unexpected, but also unpreventable; and murder is a singular event of individual violence motivated by greed, vengeance, fear, envy, anger, or insanity. But American society has reserved the most deliberate death-dealing activity for its young men. War is organized homicide. It is murder by carefully calculated plans, annihilation orchestrated by politicians, diplomats, generals, black marketeers, and the numerous "Masters of War" condemned by Bob Dylan. While Peter, Paul, and Mary chide "The Cruel War" and sadly ask, "How many times must a cannonball fly?" in "Blowing in the Wind," The Kingston Trio state an even harsher truth. They sing, "Where have all the soldiers gone? Gone to graveyards every one." The refrain to "Where Have All the Flowers Gone" indicts the military fighters, the politicians and diplomats, and the entire human race by asking, "When will they ever learn, when will they ever learn?" Victims of war include not only soldiers—as in "Billy, Don't Be a Hero" by Bo Donaldson and The Heywoods, "Billy and Sue" by Billy J. Kramer, and "2 + 2 = ?" by The Bob Seger System—but also their friends and loved ones who are left to mourn battlefield deaths. Although Terry Nelson and C. Company intend to defend trauma-motivated actions in Vietnam, "The Battle Hymn of Lt. Calley" is actually a grisly reminder of the brutality, the arbitrariness, and the universal pain and death inflicted by military madness. As Edwin Starr shouted in

1970, "War! What is it good for? Absolutely nothing!" His conclusion in "War" is that only the undertaker benefits from organized mass killing.

The ultimate act of cowardice or bravery, of defiance or lunacy, is suicide. An individual's decision to choose death over life is the ultimate existential act. Songs that recount self-inflicted death are numerous, generally melancholy, and sometimes mysterious. Most often, an act of suicide is described by a forlorn lover, by a remaining relative, or by a sad, confused friend. Don McLean eulogizes Van Gogh's misanthropic artistic genius in "Vincent"; unidentified lovers mourn the loss of mates in "Endless Sleep," "Emma," and "Moody River"; an Indian couple produce a watery Romeo and Juliet death scene in "Running Bear"; Bobbie Gentry is haunted by the tale of a young man who jumped off the Tallahachie Bridge in "Ode to Billy Joe"; and The Kinks and Simon and Garfunkel describe some very strange victims of society in "Richard Cory," "A Well-Respected Man," and "A Most Peculiar Man."

A postscript to the death theme in popular music is found in the coda of tributes to political and singing/songwriting heroes who have died since 1950. Although John Lennon and Elvis Presley have been praised on vinyl in every imaginable fashion, no single popular music artist has yet garnered a more well-crafted, skillfully performed, and positively received recorded eulogy than Buddy Holly. Don McLean's "American Pie" was not only a remembrance of the passing of a brilliant 1950s tunesmith, but also a metaphorical exploration of changes in American music from 1955 until the early 1970s. A song of similar historic scope, though totally political in nature and import, was Dion DiMucci's lament about the assassinated leaders Abraham Lincoln, Martin Luther King Jr., John Kennedy, and Robert Kennedy. The folkish "Abraham, Martin, and John" was also issued by Moms Mabley, Smokey Robinson and The Miracles, and Tom Clay to cover all of the record-purchasing public with versions of this sentimental hymn. The most inclusive tributes to contemporary musical artists are Tex Ritter's "I Dreamed of a Hill-Billy Heaven" and The Righteous Brothers' "Rock and Roll Heaven."

In "American Pie," Don McLean utilizes the death of an individual popular music figure to symbolize the end of American innocence. Since Buddy Holly was killed in 1959, the year that marked the termination of rock's "Golden Age," McLean's commentary actually focuses on the evolution of recorded music throughout the 1960s. As in most epic tales, there are references to a broad spectrum of historical characters. In this case, nearly all are musicians. The lyrical chronology includes references to The Monotones ("The Book of Love"), Marty Robbins ("A White Sport Coat and a Pink Carnation"), Elvis Presley, Bob Dylan, John Lennon, The Byrds,

The Beatles, Mick Jagger ("Jumpin' Jack Flash") and The Rolling Stones, and Janis Joplin. For McLean, the passing of Buddy Holly—along with J. P. "The Big Bopper" Richardson and Ritchie Valens—marked the ignition point for adolescent consciousness. A decade later the last vestiges of innocence were shredded by the horror of the Hell's Angels' murders during the Altamont Music Festival. The image of Mick Jagger as Satan, contrasted with Buddy Holly's angelic demeanor, is obvious. But mortality remains the central specter as the statement "The day the music died" is repeated again and again.

Paul Simon, master songsmith, perceptive social analyst, and self-proclaimed child of the rock generation, seized the same historic scope as Don McLean to comment on death as a shaper of social psyche. His song "The Late Great Johnny Ace" covers the period from 1954 to 1980. This melancholy tune focuses on three deaths. The strange Russian roulette, accidental suicide of rhythm and blues performer Johnny Ace is depicted as an unexplainably significant event in an adolescent's life. Ten years later the same music enthusiast labels 1964 as "The year of The Beatles . . . the year of The Stones." Yet the underlying event in the storyteller's image of the British musical invasion of America occurred in November 1963. Simon refers to 1964 as "a year after J.F.K." He and his girlfriend, obviously far removed from the Dallas assassination scene, are ". . . staying up all night and giving the days away" in mock Left Bank revelry. The concluding incident in this brief tune is a stranger's 1980 announcement that John Lennon has died. No details of the New York City murder are mentioned. The singer adjourns to a bar, pumps coins into a jukebox, and dedicates each song played to the late great Johnny Ace. The cycle of death is universal. It is complete from Ace to Lennon. This song updates Don McLean's meaning—"The day the music died"—too.

It should be clear that while Jeff Pike feels that the passing of rock era artists somehow marks the end of rock music, it is the music itself that sustains the era, defines death images, and even provides immortality to a small group of performers. Check 1994 CD sales. Elvis lives on RCA; Otis Redding thrives on Rhino; and Bobby Darin still swings on Atlantic. Even Frank Zappa grins from the grave via reissued recordings. Voices are no longer stilled by death.

BIBLIOGRAPHY

Armour, Robert A. and J. Carol Williams. "Death in Popular Culture," in *Handbook of American Popular Culture*, Volume Two, edited by M. Thomas Inge. Westport, CT: Greenwood Press, 1980, pp. 79-104.

Banney, Howard F. (comp.). *Return to Sender: The First Complete Discography of Elvis Tribute and Novelty Records.* Ann Arbor, MI: Pierian Press, 1987.

Barrett, Ruth, Kerry Cochrane, and Mary Anne Wolff. "On Being Involved," in *Give Peace a Chance: Music and the Struggle for Peace,* edited by Marianne Philbin. Chicago: Chicago Review Press, 1983, pp. 45-53.

Baucom, John Q. *The Elvis Syndrome: How to Avoid Death by Success.* Minneapolis, MN: Fairview Press, 1995.

Bird, Donald Allport, Stephen C. Holder, and Diane Sears. "Walrus Is Greek for Corpse: Rumor and the Death of Paul McCartney," *Journal of Popular Culture,* X (Summer, 1976), pp. 110-121.

Booth, Stanley. *Rythm Oil: A Journey Through the Music of the American South.* New York: Pantheon Books, 1991.

Burns, Gary. "Of Our Elaborate Plans, the End," *Popular Music and Society,* 11 (Winter 1987), pp. 47-60.

Cohen, Norm. *Long Steel Rail: The Railroad in American Folksong.* Urbana, IL: University of Illinois Press, 1981.

Colman, Stuart. *They Kept on Rockin': The Giants of Rock 'n' Roll.* Poole, Dorset, England: Blandford Press, 1982.

Cooper, B. Lee. "Death," in *A Resource Guide to Themes in Contemporary American Song Lyrics.* Westport, CT: Greenwood Press, 1986, pp. 49-63.

Cooper, B. Lee. "Death," in *Popular Music Perspectives: Ideas, Themes, and Patterns in Contemporary Lyrics.* Bowling Green, OH: Bowling Green State University Popular Press, 1991, pp. 82-93.

Cooper, B. Lee. "The Image of the Outsider in Contemporary Lyrics," *Journal of Popular Culture,* 12 (Summer 1978), pp. 168-178.

Cott, Jonathan and Christine Doudna (eds.). *The Ballad of John and Yoko.* Garden City, NY: Doubleday and Company, Inc., 1982.

Denisoff, R. Serge. "Death Songs and Teenage Roles," in *Sing a Song of Social Significance.* Bowling Green, OH: Bowling Green State University Popular Press, 1972, pp. 171-176.

Denisoff, R. Serge. "Teen Angel: Resistance, Rebellion, and Death—Revisited," *Journal of Popular Culture,* 16 (Spring 1983), pp. 116-122.

Dickinson, George E., Michael R. Leming, and Alan C. Merman (eds.). *Dying, Death, and Bereavement* (Second Edition). Guilford, CT: Dushkin Publishing Group, Inc., 1994.

Duncan, Robert. *Only the Good Die Young: The Rock 'n' Roll Book of the Dead* New York: Harmony Books, 1986.

Evans, Mike and Chet Flippo. *Graceland: The Living Legacy of Elvis Presley.* San Francisco, CA: Collins Publishers of San Francisco, 1993.

Fogo, Fred. *I Read the News Today: The Social Drama of John Lennon's Death.* Lanham, MD: Littlefield Adams Quality Paperbacks, 1994.

Fox, Aaron A. "The Jukebox of History: Narratives of Loss and Desire in the Discourse of Country Music," *Popular Music,* 11 (January 1992), pp. 53-72.

Fuller, John G. *Are the Kids All Right? The Rock Generation and Its Hidden Death Wish.* New York: Times Books, 1991.

Goddo, Teresa. "Bloody Daggers and Lonesome Graveyards: The Gothic and Country Music," in *Readin' Country Music: Steel Guitars, Opry Stars, and Honky Tonk Bars,* edited by Cecelia Tich. Durham, NC: Duke University Press, 1995, pp. 57-80.

"Gone but Not Forgotten," *Goldmine,* No. 246 (December 29, 1989), p. 99.

Grendysa, Peter. "Chuck Willis' Two-Sided Epitaph Still Haunts Studio Musicians Today," *Record Collector's Monthly,* No. 16 (January 1984): 1, 5.

Griggs, Bill. "Last Songs," *Rockin 50s,* No. 28 (February 1991), p. 24.

Harrell, Jack. "The Poetics of Destruction: Death Metal Rock," *Popular Music and Society,* XVIII (Spring 1994), pp. 91-103.

Harris, James F. *Philosophy at 33 $^1/_3$ R.P.M.: Themes of Classic Rock Music.* La Salle, IL: Open Court Publishing Company, 1993.

Hibbard, Don J. and Carol Kaleialoha. *The Role of Rock: A Guide to the Social and Political Consequences of Rock Music.* Englewood Cliffs, NJ: Prentice-Hall, Inc., 1983.

Hoffman, Paul Dennis. "Rock and Roll and JFK: A Study of Thematic Changes in Rock and Roll Lyrics Since the Assassination of John F. Kennedy," *Popular Music and Society,* 10 (Spring 1985), pp. 59-79.

Hoffmann, Frank W. and William G. Bailey. "Death Songs," in *Arts and Entertainment Fads.* Binghamton, NY: The Haworth Press, Inc., 1990, pp. 103-105.

Jackson, Laura. *Golden Stone: The Untold Life and Mysterious Death of Brian Jones.* London: Smith Gryphon, 1992.

Jacobs, Philip. *Rock 'n' Roll Heaven.* London: Apple Press, 1990.

Katz, Gary. *Death by Rock and Roll: The Untimely Deaths of the Legends of Rock.* Secaucus, NJ: Citadel Press, 1995.

Kinder, Bob. "Mark Dinning: Teen Angel Revisited," *Record Exchanger,* No. 30 (1982), pp. 26-27.

Kinder, Bob. "Rock and Roll Epitaphs," in the *Best of the First: The Early Days of Rock and Roll.* Chicago: Adams Press, 1986, pp. 24-40.

Kraft, Curt. "Till Death Do Us Part," *Story Untold,* No. 1 (1977), pp. 36-37.

Kübler-Ross, Elisabeth. *Death: The Final Stage of Growth.* Englewood Cliffs, NJ: Prentice Hall, Inc., 1975.

Kübler-Ross, Elisabeth. *On Death and Dying.* New York: Macmillan Company, 1969.

Langer, Lawrence. *The Age of Atrocity: Death in Modern Literature.* Boston: Beacon Press, 1978.

Lavey, Kathleen, Jacque Janssen, Don Ramsey, and Tom Jekel. "Immortal Message," *Lansing [Michigan] State Journal* (January 20, 1992), p. 1.

Lax, Roger and Frederick Smith. *The Great Song Thesaurus,* Second Edition, updated and expanded. New York: Oxford University Press, 1989.

Lazell, Barry with Dafydd Rees and Luke Crampton (eds.). *Rock Movers and Shakers: An A to Z of the People Who Made Rock Happen.* New York: Billboard Publications, Inc., 1989.

Lewis, George H. "A Tombstone Every Mile: Country Music in Maine," in *All That Glitters: Country Music in America*. Bowling Green, OH: Bowling Green State University Popular Press, 1993, pp. 102-115.

Lipsitz, George. *Time Passages: Collective Memory and American Popular Culture*. Minneapolis: University of Minnesota Press, 1990.

Loud, Lance. "End of the Line: Fave Graves of the Stars," *Exposure*, No. 3 (July 1990), pp. 79-81.

Lyle, Katie Letcher. *Scalded to Death by the Steam: Authentic Stories of Railroad Disasters and the Ballads That Were Written About Them*. Chapel Hill, NC: Algonquin Books of Chapel Hill, 1991.

Marcus, Greil. *Dead Elvis: A Chronicle of Cultural Obsession*. Garden City, NY: Doubleday and Company, Inc., 1991.

McDonald, James R. "Suicidal Rage: An Analysis of Hardcore Punk Lyrics," *Popular Music and Society*, 11 (Fall 1987), pp. 91-102.

McLaurin, Melton A. and Richard A. Peterson (eds.). *You Wrote My Life: Lyrical Themes in Country Music*. Philadelphia, PA: Gordon and Breach, 1992.

Murdoch, Brian. *Fighting Songs and Warring Words: Popular Lyrics of Two World Wars*. London: Routledge Publishing, Ltd., 1990.

Newlin, Jon. "Those Great Old Death Songs," *Wavelength*, No. 33 (July 1983), pp. 19-20.

Niemi, Robert. "JFK As Jesus: The Politics of Myth In Phil Ochs' 'Crucifixion,' " *Journal of American Culture*, 16 (Winter 1993), pp. 35-40.

Nolan, Alan. *Rock 'n' Roll Road Trip: The Ultimate Guide to the Sites, the Shrines, and the Legends Across America*. New York: Pharos Books, 1992.

Porterfield, Nolan. "The Day Hank Williams Died: Cultural Collisions in Country Music," in *America's Musical Pulse: Popular Music in Twentieth-Century Society*, edited by Kenneth J. Bindas. Westport, CT: Greenwood Press 1992, pp. 175-183.

Reeve, Andru J. *Turn Me On, Dead Man: The Complete Story of the Paul McCartney Death Hoax*. Ann Arbor, MI: Popular Culture, Ink, 1994.

Rodnitzky, Jerome L. *Minstrels of the Dawn: The Folk-Protest Singer As a Cultural Hero*. Chicago: Nelson-Hall, Inc., 1976.

Rogers, Jimmie N. *The Country Music Message: All About Lovin' and Livin.'* Englewood Cliffs, NJ: Prentice-Hall, Inc., 1983.

Rogers, Jimmie N. *The Country Music Message: Revisited*. Fayetteville, AR: University of Arkansas Press, 1989.

Roman, Shari. "Death As a Career Move," *Exposure*, No. 3 (July 1990), pp. 82-83.

Roos, Michael. "Fixin' to Die: The Death Theme in the Music of Bob Dylan," *Popular Music and Society*, No. 8 (1982): 103-116.

Rose, Cynthia. "Raves from the Grave: The Eternal Appeal of Rock's Death Songs," *History of Rock*, No. 29 (1982), pp. 574-575.

Ruitenbeek, H. M. (ed.). *Death: Interpretations*. New York: Dell Publishing Company, Inc., 1969.

Sammon, Paul M. (ed.). *The King Is Dead: Tales of Elvis Postmortem*. New York: Delta Books, 1994.

Schmidt-Joos, Siegfried. *Let It Bleed: The Rolling Stones in Altamont.* Frankfurt, Germany: Ulistein Press, 1984.

Somma, Robert (ed.). *No One Waved Goodbye: A Casualty Report on Rock and Roll.* New York: Outerbridge and Dienstfrey, 1971.

Spencer, Jon Michael. *Blues and Evil.* Knoxville, TN: University of Tennessee Press, 1993.

Stecheson, Anthony and Anne Stecheson (comps.). *The Stecheson Classified Song Directory.* Hollywood, CA: Music Industry Press, 1961.

Stecheson, Anthony and Anne Stecheson (comps.). *The Supplement to the Stecheson Classified Song Directory.* Hollywood, CA: Music Industry Press, 1978.

Stidom, Larry. "Necrology," in *Izatso? Larry Stidom's Rock 'n' Roll Trivia and Fact Book.* Indianapolis, IN: L. Stidom, 1986, pp. 100-106.

Stillion, Judith M. *Death and the Sexes: An Examination of Differential Longevity, Attitudes, Behaviors, and Coping Skills.* Washington, DC: Hemisphere Press, 1985.

Tamarkin, Jeff. "Pop Music Suicide Victims," *Goldmine,* No. 360 (May 13, 1994), pp. 10, 12.

Taylor, Rogan. *The Death and Resurrection Show.* London: Alond Press, Ltd., 1985.

Thomson, Elizabeth and David Gutman (eds.). *The Lennon Companion: Twenty-Five Years of Comment.* New York: Macmillan Books, 1988.

Thrush, John C. and George S. Paulus. "The Concept of Death in Popular Music: A Social Psychological Perspective," *Popular Music and Society,* No. 6 (1979), pp. 219-228.

Tosches, Nick. "Death in Hi-Fi, or First Tastes of Tombstone," *Waxpaper,* No. 3 (March 3, 1978), pp. 18-19, 39.

Tosches, Nick. *Unsung Heroes of Rock 'n' Roll: The Birth of Rock in the Wild Years Before Elvis,* Revised Edition. New York: Harmony Books, 1991.

Tunnell, Kenneth D. "Blood Marks the Spot Where Poor Ellen Was Found: Violent Crime in Bluegrass Music," *Popular Music and Society,* 15 (Fall 1991), pp. 95-115.

Tunnell, Kenneth D. "99 Years Is Almost for Life: Punishment for Violent Crime in Bluegrass Music," *Journal of Popular Culture,* No. 26 (Winter 1992), pp. 165-181.

"28 Stars Die Unnaturally in 21 Years," *Billboard,* 92 (December 20, 1980), p. 30.

Von Nordheim, DeLoris. "Visions of Death in Rock Music and Musicians," *Popular Music and Society,* XVII (Summer 1993), pp. 21-31.

Walser, Robert. *Running with the Devil: Power, Gender, and Madness in Heavy Metal Music.* Hanover, NH: University Press of New England, 1993.

West, John Foster. *Lift Up Your Head Tom Dooley: The True Story of the Appalachian Murder That Inspired One of America's Popular Ballads.* Asheboro, NC: Down Home Press, 1993.

Wiley, Mason. "It's a Wonderful Death: Our Magnificent Obsession with All-Star Stiffs," *Exposure,* III (July 1990), pp. 60-67.

Williams, Brett. *John Henry: A Bio-Bibliography.* Westport, CT: Greenwood Press, 1983.

Wilson, Charles Reagan. "Digging Up Bones: Death in Country Music," in *You Wrote My Life: Lyrical Themes in Country Music*, edited by Melton A. McLaurin and Richard A. Peterson. Philadelphia, PA: Gordon and Breach, 1992, pp. 113-129.

Chapter 4

Foolish Behavior

The fool theme is frequently explored in song lyrics. Personal analysis is pervasive. Self-referencing lyrics allow wayward voyagers on the seas of love to define their own personal dilemmas, to explain the complexity of romantic circumstances to others, or to lament situations in which cool rationality failed when hot emotion erupted. In song foolhardy behavior is usually related to momentary lapses of knowledge, experience, or sensibility. The fool in a romantic situation is the moral equivalent of Everyman (or Everywoman). The charm, satisfaction, and hubris of absolute trust, veneration, and pure love make fools of everyone. The human condition is invariably one of randomly demonstrated flaws rather than consistent perfection. The courtship scenario manifests absolute adulation that defies reason, reflection, assessment, and objectivity. Fool songs usually argue on behalf of retrospective balance. They are sources of self-learning. When shared as popular lyrics, they urge listeners to heed the transitory nature of all human relationships.

The fool concept is vague. The term is so prevalent in song titles and lyrics that its use defies conventional definition. Listening audiences may interpret a singer's situation as one that is overtly humorous, deserves pity, prompts outrage, or is simply unfathomable. The ambiguity of a fool's circumstance is fodder for a full spectrum of audience interpretation. There is seldom a gender-specific issue. Nor is the fool song limited by musical genre. Country, R&B, rock, blues, jazz, doowop, and even rap and heavy metal recordings feature fool themes. Since 1945, the realm of romantic irrationality has been thoroughly explored by singers and songwriters from a multitude of relationship perspectives. Whether falling for an irresistibly beautiful or handsome creature who is utterly unattainable

This chapter by B. Lee Cooper was originally published as "What Kind of Fool Am I? Audio Imagery, Personal Identity, and Social Relationships," *International Journal of Instructional Media*, XXIV, No. 3 (1997), pp. 253-267. Reprint permission granted by the author, editor Phillip J. Sleeman, and The Westwood Press.

or being rejected by a former lover, the fool usually assigns blame, swears never to make the same error again, and defines himself (or herself) as a better person for enduring the hurtful learning experience. But other conclusions are also afforded. Sometimes foolish behavior is viewed by an external observer with a cooler, more distant perspective. The fool then becomes the object of pity, ridicule, or humiliation. Still, the outside observer sometimes confesses personal foolishness as a source of understanding, sympathy, or recognition.

WHAT KIND OF FOOL AM I?

This question constitutes the rationale for this investigation. If fool status is indeed a universal experience, then what particular circumstances spark the realization for a victim of foolhardiness or for an observer of foolish actions? The fool trope, so ubiquitous in popular lyrics, is depicted and defined in a series of situations. Although prediction of individual susceptibility is impossible, foundation formulae in contemporary recordings offer clues to numerous human frailties during the onset or the demise of romantic relationships. Going out of one's head, falling head over heels, and losing control of rational thought may dismay scholarly analysts. However, it is a readily understandable phenomenon to the general populace. The essence of popular music's attraction is telling and retelling familiar tales of human experience. Stories from blues ballads and country laments translate readily into all forms of popular recordings. The fool label, though not an especially dignified sobriquet, is a reliable and accurate way to depict a condition that warrants sympathy, understanding, and a modicum of empathy.

The nontechnical nature of foolish behavior is both a strength and weakness in identifying with any precision exactly what a fool is. Yet certain attitudes and behaviors accumulate toward a general characterization. Fools manifest lack of common sense and sound judgment. They tend to disregard predictable consequences of their behaviors while articulating only desired (though unrealistic) ends. They may seem daring, reckless, or adventuresome—or just carefree and inconsiderate. Fools exercise limited self-control while being tricked, cheated, or manipulated by others.

In popular songs, a fool and his money can be readily parted. Big Al Downing discusses this circumstance in "I Ain't No Fool" (1979). But it is in the realm of passion-driven romance that otherwise reasonable creatures—both male and female—are transformed into silly, inconsistent, gullible, uncritical, obsessed beings. Love is too potent an elixir for most humans. Percy Sledge depicts such change in character in "When a Man

Loves a Woman" (1966). This same kind of critical amnesia is discussed in "Smoke Gets in Your Eyes" (1958). The universal nature of "A Fool in Love" (1960) is echoed in tunes such as "Everybody's Somebody's Fool" (1957) and "Everybody Plays the Fool" (1991). This is not a contagious disease; nor is it fatal. But it generates an emotional bashing that often leaves the fool loveless and friendless, though seldom speechless. In fact, a vast number of fool songs are soliloquies about personal flaws. Fools can learn. Fools can also teach. But fools cannot save either themselves or others from future bouts with romance or heartache.

MISUNDERSTANDING OF FEELINGS

Perception feeds emotions. The degree of attachment felt by one person for another is the basis for either a romantic interlude or heartbreak. Yet misperception and misunderstanding are common to the human condition. No simple equation can define the mutual magnitude of love between two independent beings. For instance, repeating the magic three words may be either a heartfelt pledge or an ornamental greeting. Bonnie Raitt captures the pain, if not the foolishness, of such a stressful problem in her ballad "I Can't Make You Love Me" (1991).

While many advice songs allude to the issue of misunderstanding, the situation being described is usually based upon painful hindsight. Hard-eyed, 20/20 hindsight is usually delivered in an emotion-free motif by a former lover, a distant friend, or a (temporarily) cured romantic. Illustrations of this perspective include "I Was Such a Fool (To Fall in Love with You)" (1962), "Foolish Fool" (1969), "I Pity the Fool" (1961), and "What a Fool I Was" (1951). A particularly poignant description of a major misunderstanding between a man and a woman is vocalized by Michael McDonald of The Doobie Brothers in "What A Fool Believes" (1979). This sparse tale involves an assumption of romantic interest by a "Sentimental fool" who discovers that although "She had a place in his life/ He never made her think twice." Rather than love lost, this is love never returned, acknowledged, or even recognized. The chorus of the song defines rationality. McDonald cautions, "But what a fool believes he sees/ No wise man has the power to reason away." What happens? The romantic fool elects to continue ignoring reality, choosing instead to fantasize that "Someday, somewhere, she will return."

EUPHORIA OF FALLING IN LOVE

Frankie Lymon and The Teenagers used a series of unanswered questions to illustrate romance as beyond the scope of human understanding.

"Why Do Fools Fall in Love?" (1956) is typical of songs that warn star-struck lovers that danger cannot be conceived in the midst of amour. "Fools Fall in Love" (1977), "Poor Little Fool" (1958), "Nobody Falls Like a Fool" (1985), and "Fools Rush In" (1963) echo the same sentiments. Beyond the direct use of the fool terminology, those bitten by the love bug are variously depicted as "All Shook Up" (1957), "Crazy" (1961), or "Dizzy" (1969). Perhaps the most insightful title is "There Should Be Rules (Protecting Fools Who Fall in Love)" (1955).

BLINDNESS TO FUTURE EVENTS

While not employing the fool terminology, "Smoke Gets in Your Eyes" (1958) constitutes the ideal illustration of a reverie concerning individual failure to predict an impending emotional letdown. A broken-hearted lover recalls the warnings of well-intentioned friends that were blithely ignored as a romance flourished, then floundered. The theme of failing to acknowledge cyclical romantic trends is often related to either immaturity or inexperience. "Fools Fall in Love" (1957) uses youth as a justification for errors. The Drifters describe young lovers as "blinded by rose-colored dreams." Tender age need not be the only element sparking foolhardy behavior, though. The trickiness of romantic involvement is captured in "Fooled Around and Fell in Love" (1976). Unexpected consequences are also highlighted in "Fools Rush In" (1960) and "You Were Only Fooling (While I Was Falling in Love)" (1948). Self-realization can be a prominent point of recognition, although it usually arrives only after the period of foolishness. Charlie Rich poses a significant postrelationship question in "Who Will the Next Fool Be" (1970).

SURRENDER OF SELF

When mutual respect and cooperative understanding are sacrificed within a loving relationship, the submissive partner is either viewed as, or depicts herself or himself as, a fool. This is common in popular lyrics. There is a peculiar irony in this circumstance since during most courtships there are promises of selflessness that bode well for future compromises. However, dominance is a corrupting factor that undermines trust, respect, and concern. The status of a "Seven Day Fool" (1961) is too painful to endure. The degree of dehumanization in "Touch Me (I'll Be Your Fool Once More)" (1983) is too high a price for mending a disintegrating relationship. The Elvis Presley pleas to treat me like a fool, treat me mean and cruel, but "Love Me" (1956) are too sacrificial. Other songs that illustrate helplessness and hopelessness in the midst of a crumbling partnership include: "Chain of Fools" (1968), "I'm a Fool to Want You" (1951), "(Now and Then There's) a Fool Such As I" (1953), and "Oh Me Oh My (I'm a Fool for You Baby)" (1972).

ACCEPTANCE OF PROLONGED ABUSE

Foolish commitments to relationships that are punctuated by physical mistreatment, psychological abuse, or even extended, unexplained absences are illustrated in songs such as "I Ain't Never" (1959), "Piece of My Heart" (1968), "Poor, Poor Pitiful Me" (1978), and "You Keep Me Hangin' On" (1966). The fool image is generally self-identified in these circumstances. The power to sustain the romantic relationship is conceded to the partner with pleas for either improved behavior or blessed release. The singer adopts a helpless role. One becomes readily convinced that a "Chain of Fools" (1968) has no independent links. Declarations such as "I'm a Fool to Care" (1961) and "If You Gotta Make a Fool of Somebody" (1965) are connected to being "A Fool in Love" (1960) and "A Fool for Your Stockings" (1979). Even the recognition that one's boyfriend or girlfriend might be "Runnin' Out of Fools" (1964) constitutes an incredibly self-degrading observation.

SOME SUGGESTIONS
FROM EXPERIENCED INDIVIDUALS

Experience may either harden hearts or broaden minds. It does not guarantee ultimate wisdom though. While Aaron Neville acknowledges that "Everybody Plays the Fool" (1991), some individuals gain much more insight than others from their bouts with fickle love. They invariably wish to share their tales. Such lyrical pedagogy is often preachy and usually ineffective. The about-to-become-a-fool listener is pursuing passion. This state of euphoria is least receptive to the pontification of a used-to-be fool. Nevertheless, suggestions for avoiding emotional trauma abound in popular music.

The Five Keys plead for unsuspecting romantics to listen to the "Wisdom of a Fool" (1956); Bobby Bland warns "I Pity the Fool" (1961) who falls in love with his former sweetheart; Charlie Rich ponders "Who Will the Next Fool Be?" (1970); and Connie Francis declares "Everybody's Somebody's Fool" (1960). The dimensions of misjudgment in romantic entanglements vary greatly. Some laments such as Sanford Clark's "The Fool" (1956) are vague about the circumstances that led to the premature, unwise decision to terminate a relationship. Others are more specific. A person blinded by love may be unaware that the significant other is without virtue, without scruples, or without loyalty. This kind of painful relationship is depicted in "Slippin' 'n' Slidin'" (1956), "Runnin' Out of Fools" (1964), "Fool #1" (1961), "Mary Lou" (1959), and "(Now and Then There's) a Fool Such As I" (1959).

OTHER FOOLS

Romance fosters more lyrical fools than all other human ventures combined. However, singers and songwriters are not adverse to applying the fool label to situations unrelated to courtship. First, showboating to gain attention, often described as acting the fool, is highlighted in recordings such as "Charlie Brown" (1959), "Dancin' Fool" (1975), and "Shoppin' for Clothes" (1960). Second, stupidity, ignorance, or overt irrationality are also depicted as foolish in "You Be Illin,'" (1986), "Swinging On a Star" (1963), and "D. W. Washburn" (1968). Third, random forgetfulness, laziness, or totally unproductive behavior also merit the fool image in songs such as "Daydream" (1966) and "Daydream Believer" (1967). Finally, political commentary such as "Won't Get Fooled Again" (1971) calls into question the ability of government officials to continually hoodwink the electorate. Similar images are found in "Fortunate Son" (1969) and dozens of other folk rock protest recordings of 1960s vintage.

CONCLUSION

The fool is the perfect image, the quintessential metaphor, for human frailty. It is a nonclinical, nonhistorical term. It is a self-diagnosis of situational recognition. Vagaries of psychoanalysis are replaced by certainty of self-perception. Pathos and humor meet. It is not a fatal condition. It is serious though. Remediation is available, but not necessarily pleasant nor permanent. Within the lyrics of songs, it constitutes a popular culture formula that exudes empathy no matter how often it is repeated. The Main Ingredient are correct in their assertion: "Everybody plays the fool . . . sometime!" The metamorphosis from foolishness to wisdom is never total either. The nature of romance and high emotional involvements foreordain the slippery slope of irrational behavior. The learning curve is unpredictable in each case.

The fact that popular music has so universally adopted fool nomenclature is easy to explain. First, rhyme scheme favors a brief and readily matchable word. Second, the genderless nature of the term allows both males and females to self-identify or to project the meaning to the opposite sex. Third, the concept of fool makes no reference to general intelligence, professional expertise, social or economic status, age, ethnicity, religion, or physical appearance. It is a circumstance of unanticipated origin and unspecified duration. Finally, the fool can become a source of advice or an illustration to protect others from similar amorous pitfalls.

SELECTED FOOL SONG DISCOGRAPHY, 1945-1995

- "Ain't It Funny What a Fool Will Do?"
  (United Artists 578)
  George Jones (1963)

- "All Shook Up"
  (RCA 47-6870)
  Elvis Presley (1957)

- "Any Fool Can See"
  (Atlantic 87180)
  Tracy Lawrence (1994)

- "Call Me a Fool"
  (EMI America 43017)
  Dana McVicker (1987)

- "Chain of Fools"
  (Atlantic 2464)
  Aretha Franklin (1968)

- "Charlie Brown"
  (Atco 6132)
  The Coasters (1959)

- "Crazy"
  (Decca 31317)
  Patsy Cline (1961)

- "D. W. Washburn"
  (Colgems 1023)
  The Monkees (1968)

- Dancin' Fool"
  (RCA 10075)
  The Guess Who (1975)

- "A Day in the Life of a Fool"
  (Kapp 781)
  Jack Jones (1966)

- "Daydream"
  (Kama Sutra 208)
  The Lovin' Spoonful (1966)

- "Daydream Believer"
  (Colgems 1012)
  The Monkees (1967)

- "Dizzy"
  (ABC 11164)
  Tommy Roe (1969)

- "Don't Be a Fool"
  (MCA 53880)
  Loose Ends (1990)

- "Don't Want to Be a Fool"
  (Epic 73879)
  Luther Vandross (1991)

- "Earth Angel (Will You Be Mine?)"
  (DooTone 348)
  The Penguins (1954)

- "Even a Fool Can See"
  (Warner Brothers 18561)
  Peter Cetera (1993)

- "Everybody Plays the Fool"
  (A&M 1563)
  Aaron Neville (1991)

- "Everybody Plays the Fool"
  (RCA 0731)
  The Main Ingredient (1972)

- "Everybody's Somebody's Fool"
  (Rama 231)
  The Heartbeats (1957)

- "Everybody's Somebody's Fool"
  (MOM 12899)
  Connie Francis (1960)

- "Famous Last Words of a Fool"
  (RCA 13628)
  Dean Dillon (1983)

- "Find Another Fool"
  (Geffen 50006)
  Quarterflash (1982)

- "The Fool"
  (Dot 15481)
  Sanford Clark (1956)

- "Fool, Fool"
  (MCA 51113)
  Brenda Lee (1981)

- "Fool, Fool, Fool"
  (Capitol 2151)
  Kay Starr (1952)

- "A Fool for You"
  (Atlantic 1063)
  Ray Charles (1955)

- "Fool for Your Love"
  (Epic 03783)
  Mickey Gilley (1983)

- "A Fool for Your Stockings"
  (Warner Brothers 3361)
  ZZ Top (1979)

- "A Fool in Love"
  (Sue 730)
  Ike and Tina Turner (1960)

- "A Fool Never Learns"
  (Columbia 42950)
  Andy Williams (1964)

- "Fool #1"
  (Decca 31309)
  Brenda Lee (1961)

- "Fool Such As I"
  (RCA 2641)
  Baillie and the Boys (1990)

- "Fool to Cry"
  (Rolling Stones 19304)
  Rolling Stones (1976)

- "A Fool Was I"
  (Capitol 2540)
  Nat King Cole (1953)

- "Fool's Paradise"
  (Mom 10562)
  Billy Eckstine (1949)

- "Fooled Around and Fell in Love"
  (Capricorn 0252)
  Elvin Bishop (1976)

- "Foolin' Around"
  (Capitol 4542)
  Kay Starr (1961)

- "Foolish Fool"
  (Mercury 72880)
  Dee Dee Warwick (1969)

- "Foolish Little Girl"
  (Scepter 1248)
  The Shirelles (1963)

- "Fools Fall in Love"
  (Atlantic 1123)
  The Drifters (1957)

- "Fools Fall in Love"
  (Mercury 55003)
  Jacky Ward (1977)

- "Fools for Each Other"
  (Warner 8714)
  Guy Clark (1979)

- "Fools Rush In"
  (Mercury 71722)
  Brook Benton (1960)

- "Fools Rush In"
  (Decca 31533)
  Ricky Nelson (1963)

- "Forgive This Fool"
  (Epic 9111)
  Roy Hamilton (1955)

- "Fortunate Son"
  (Fantasy 634)
  Creedence Clearwater Revival (1969)

- "From the Fool"
  (MCA 55054)
  Iv Xample (1995)

- "Go Back You Fool"
  (Capitol 3169)
  Faron Young (1955)

- "Go on Fool"
  (Avco Embassy 4559)
  Marion Black (1971)

- "Heartaches of a Fool"
  (Columbia 02558)
  Willie Nelson (1981)

- "Her Cheatin' Heart (Made a Drunken Fool Out of Me)"
  (El Dorado 156)
  Jerry Naill (1980)

- "Honky Tonkin' Fool"
  (BNA 62432)
  Doug Supernaw (1993)

- "I Ain't Never"
  (Decca 30923)
  Webb Pierce (1959)

- "I Ain't No Fool"
  (Warner Brothers 49141)
  Big Al Downing (1979)

- "I Can't Make You Love Me"
  (Capitol Cdp 96111)
  Bonnie Raitt (1991)

- "I Pity the Fool"
  (Duke 332)
  Bobby Bland (1961)

- "I Played the Fool"
  (Atlantic 977)
  The Clovers (1952)

- "I Was Such a Fool (to Fall in Love with You)"
  (Mom 13096)
  Connie Francis (1962)

- "I'd Rather Be an Old Man's Sweetheart (Than a Young Man's
    Fool)"
  (Fame 1456)
  Candi Staton (1969)

- "I'll Be Your Fool Tonight"
  (MCA 52619)
  Jim Glaser (1985)

- "I'm a Fool"
  (Imperial 66248)
  Slim Whitman (1967)

- "I'm a Fool for You"
  (Goldwax 328)
  James Carr (1967)

- "I'm a Fool to Care"
  (Capitol 2839)
  Les Paul and Mary Ford (1954)

- "I'm a Fool to Care"
  (Smash 1702)
  Joe Barry (1961)

- "I'm a Fool to Want You"
  (Columbia 39425)
  Frank Sinatra (1951)

- "I'm Her Fool"
  (Monument 8641)
  Billy Swan (1975)

- "(I'm Just a) Fool for You"
  (Constellation 167)
  Gene Chandler (1966)

- "I'm Just Your Fool"
  (Mercury 70251)
  Buddy Johnson and His Orchestra (1954)

- "I'm Not a Fool Anymore"
  (Smash 1830)
  T. K. Hulin (1963)

- "If I'm a Fool for Loving You"
  (Joy 285)
  Bob Wood (1964)

- "If You Gotta Make a Fool of Somebody"
  (Wand 1104)
  Maxine Brown (1965)

- "If You're Looking for a Fool"
  (ABC 12339)
  Freddy Fender (1978)

- "Love Me"
  (RCA EPA 992)
  Elvis Presley (1956)

- "Love's Made a Fool of You"
  (United Artists 50756)
  Cochise (1971)

- "M.m.d.r.n.f. (My Mamma Didn't Raise No Fool)"
  (Zoo 14073)
  Voices (1992)

- "Mary Lou"
  (Roulette 4177)
  Ronnie Hawkins and The Hawks (1959)

- "Maybe I'm a Fool"
  (Columbia 10900)
  Eddie Money (1979)

- "New Fool at an Old Game"
  (MCA 53473)
  Reba McEntire (1988)

- "Nobody but a Fool (Would Love You)"
  (RCA 8746)
  Connie Smith (1966)

- "Nobody Falls Like a Fool"
  (RCA 14172)
  Earl Thomas Conley (1985)

- "Nobody's Fool but Yours"
  (Capitol 4679)
  Buck Owens (1962)

- "Nothin' but a Fool"
  (Capitol 5053)
  Natalie Cole (1981)

- "(Now and Then There's) a Fool Such As I"
  (Columbia 39930)
  Jo Stafford (1953)

- "(Now and Then There's) a Fool Such As I"
  (RCA 47-7506)
  Elvis Presley (1959)

- "Oh Me Oh My (I'm a Fool)"
  (Atlantic 2838)
  Aretha Franklin (1972)

- "Oh, What a Fool"
  (Cub 9033)
  The Impalas (1959)

- "Once a Fool"
  (Rocket 40506)
  Kiki Dee (1976)

- "One of Her Fools"
  (Duke 107)
  Paul Davis (1960)

- "Only a Fool Would Say That"
  (MCA 2617)
  Steely Dan (1973)

- "Piece of My Heart"
  (Columbia 44626)
  Big Brother and The Holding Company (1968)

- "Poor Fool"
  (Sue 753)
  Ike and Tina Turner (1961)

- "Poor Little Fool"
  (Imperial 5528)
  Ricky Nelson (1958)

- "Poor, Poor Pitiful Me"
  (Asylum 45462)
  Linda Ronstadt (1978)

- "Portrait of a Fool"
  (Mom 13050)
  Conway Twitty (1962)

- "Runnin' Out of Fools"
  (Columbia 43113)
  Aretha Franklin (1964)

- "Seven Day Fool"
  (Argo 5402)
  Etta James (1961)

- "She's a Fool"
  (Mercury 72180)
  Lesley Gore (1963)

- "Shoppin' for Clothes"
  (Atco 6178)
  The Coasters (1960)

- "Silly, Silly Fool"
  (Atlantic 2705)
  Dusty Springfield (1970)

- "Slippin' and Slidin' (Peepin' and Hidin')"
  (Specialty 572)
  Little Richard (1956)

- "Smoke Gets in Your Eyes"
  (Mercury 71383)
  The Platters (1958)

- "Some Enchanted Evening"
  (Columbia 4559)
  Ezio Pinza (1949)

- "Some Fools Never Learn"
  (MCA 52644)
  Steve Wariner (1985)

- "Statue of a Fool"
  (Columbia 73077)
  Ricky Van Shelton (1989)

- "Still a Fool"
  (Chess 1480)
  Muddy Waters (1951)

- "Story of a Fool"
  (Atlantic 987)
  The Blue Bells (1953)

- "Swinging on a Star"
  (Dimension 1010)
  Big Dee Irwin (with Little Eva) (1963)

- "Take a Fool's Advice"
  (Capitol 4582)
  Nat King Cole (1961)

- "Takes a Fool to Love a Fool"
  (Portrait 70024)
  Burton Cummings (1979)

- "There Should Be Rules (Protecting Fools Who Fall in Love)"
  (Mom 12094)
  Betty Madigan (1955)

- "There's No Fool Like a Young Fool"
  (Warner Brothers 5051)
  Tab Hunter (1959)

- "They All Say I'm the Biggest Fool"
  (Decca 11000)
  Buddy Johnson (1946)

- "Thoughts of a Fool"
  (Decca 31241)
  Ernest Tubb (1961)

- "Through the Eyes of a Fool"
  (Capitol 5099)
  Roy Clark (1964)

- "Toast to the Fool"
  (Volt 4082)
  The Dramatics (1972)

- "Touch Me (I'll Be Your Fool Once More)"
  (Mercury 810455)
  Tom Jones (1983)

- "Twentieth-Century Fool"
  (Liberty 1525)
  Kenny Rogers (1985)

- "Victim or a Fool"
  (Warner Brothers 50008)
  Rodney Crowell (1982)

- "What a Fool"
  (Ronn 72)
  Ted Taylor (1973)

- "What a Fool Believes"
  (Warner Brothers 8725)
  The Doobie Brothers (1979)

- "What a Fool I've Been"
  (Atlantic 2189)
  Carla Thomas (1963)

- "What a Fool I Was"
  (RCA Victor 2700)
  Eddy Arnold (1948)

- "What a Fool I Was"
  (Specialty 400)
  Percy Mayfield (1951)

- "What Are You Doing with a Fool Like Me"
  (Capitol 44543)
  Joe Cocker (1990)

- "What Kind of Fool"
  (Columbia 11430)
  Barbra Streisand and Barry Gibb (1981)

- "What Kind of Fool"
  (MCA 54237)
  Lionel Cartwright (1991)

- "What Kind of Fool Am I"
  (Reprise 20048)
  Sammy Davis, Jr. (1962)

- "What Kind of Fool (Do You Think I Am)"
  (ABC-Paramount 10502)
  The Tams (1963)

- 'What Kind of Fool Do You Think I Am"
  (Arista 12431)
  Lee Roy Parnell (1992)

- "When a Man Loves a Woman"
  (Atlantic 2326)
  Percy Sledge (1966)

- "Who Will the Next Fool Be"
  (Sun 1110)
  Charlie Rich (1970)

- "Who'll Be the Fool Tonight"
  (Warner Brothers 49282)
  The Larsen-Feiten Band (1980)

- "Why Do Fools Fall in Love"
  (Gee 1002)
  Frankie Lymon and The Teenagers (1956)

- "Wisdom of a Fool"
  (Capitol 3597)
  The Five Keys (1956)

- "Won't Get Fooled Again"
  (Decca 32846)
  The Who (1971)

- "You Be Illin' "
  (Profile 5119)
  Run-D.M.C. (1986)

- "You Keep Me Hangin' On"
  (Motown 1101)
  The Supremes (1966)

- "You Were Only Foolin' (While I Was Falling in Love)"
  (Capitol 15226)
  Kay Starr (1948)

- "You're Makin' a Fool Out of Me"
  (MGM 12707)
  Jimmy Newman (1958)

- "Your Fool Still Loves You"
  (Top and Bottom 402)
  Oscar Weathers (1970)

BIBLIOGRAPHY

Cawelti, John G. *Adventure, Mystery, and Romance: Formula Stories As Art and Popular Culture.* Chicago: University of Chicago Press, 1976.

Cooper, B. Lee. *Popular Music Perspectives: Ideas, Themes, and Patterns in Contemporary Lyrics.* Bowling Green, OH: Bowling Green State University Popular Press, 1991.

Cooper, B. Lee. *A Resource Guide to Themes in Contemporary American Song Lyrics.* Westport, CT: Greenwood Press, 1986.

Cooper, B. Lee. "Wise Men Never Try: A Discography of Fool Songs, 1945-1955," *Popular Music and Society,* XXI, No. 2 (Summer 1997), pp. 115-131.

Cooper, B. Lee and Wayne S. Haney. *Rock Music in American Culture: Rock 'n' Roll Resources,* Binghamton, NY: Haworth Press, 1995.

Dunne, Michael. *Metapop: Self-Referentiality in Contemporary American Popular Culture.* Jackson, MS: University Press of Mississippi, 1992.

Ferguson, Gary Lynn (comp). *Song Finder: A Title Index to 32,000 Popular Songs in Collections, 1854-1992.* Westport, CT: Greenwood Press, 1995.

Green, Jeff (comp.). *The Green Book of Songs Subject: The Thematic Guide to Popular Music* (Fourth Edition, updated and expanded). Nashville, TN: Professional Desk Services, 1995.

Harris, James F. *Philosophy at $33^{1}/3$ R.P.M.: Themes of Classic Rock Music.* La Salle, IL: Open Court Publishing, 1993.

Kawin, Bruce F. *Telling It Again and Again: Repetition in Literature and Film.* Ithaca, NY: Cornell University Press, 1972.

Orrin E. Klapp. *Heroes, Villains, and Fools: The Changing American Character.* Englewood Cliffs, NJ: Prentice-Hall, Inc., 1962.

Lax, Roger and Frederick Smith. *The Great Song Thesaurus* (Second Edition, updated and expanded). New York: Oxford University Press, 1989.

Macken, Bob, Peter Fornatale, and Bill Ayres (comps.). *The Rock Music Source Book.* Garden City, NY: Doubleday and Company, Inc., 1980.

Rimler, Walter. *Not Fade Away: A Comparison of Jazz Age with Rock Era Pop Song Composers.* Ann Arbor, MI: Pierian Press, 1984.

Rogers, Jimmie N. *The Country Music Message: All About Lovin' and Livin'.* Englewood Cliffs, NJ: Prentice-Hall, 1983.

Rogers, Jimmie N. *The Country Music Message: Revisited.* Fayetteville, AR: University of Arkansas Press, 1989.

Stecheson, Anthony and Anne Stecheson. *Stecheson Classified Song Directory.* Hollywood, CA: Music Industry Press, 1961.

Stecheson, Anthony and Anne Stecheson. *The Supplement to the Stecheson Classified Song Directory.* Hollywood, CA: Music Industry Press, 1978.

Whitburn, Joel (comp.). *Pop Hits, 1940-1954*. Menomonee Falls, WI: Record Research, 1994.

Whitburn, Joel (comp.). *Top Country Singles, 1944-1993*. Menomonee Falls, WI: Record Research, 1994.

Whitburn, Joel (comp.). *Top Pop Singles, 1955-1993*. Menomonee Falls, WI: Record Research, 1994.

Whitburn, Joel (comp.). *Top R & B Singles, 1942-1995*. Menomonee Falls, WI: Record Research, 1996.

Willeford, William. *The Fool and His Scepter: A Study of Clowns and Jesters and Their Audience*. Evanston, IL: Northwestern University Press, 1969.

Chapter 5

Honoring Excellence

The advent of the compact disc has prompted more than merely technological change. It has promoted the reissuing, repackaging, and regeneration of several decades of popular music. Tunes originally released in other formats, on 78 rpm records, in $33^1/_3$ rpm albums, or as 45 rpm discs have been compiled and recycled on high-tech CDs. Tribute records constitute a particularly interesting subset of the total spectrum of recordings produced as CD releases. Even a discographer with the intellectual fortitude of Swedish botanist Linnaeus would have a difficult time establishing a thematic nomenclature that would adequately designate all types of tribute approaches. However, the challenge of systematic categorization is too fascinating to avoid. The following pages suggest a typology for organizing tribute records and provide selected illustrations from the current compact disc market.

BIZARRE RECOGNITIONS

While most tribute recordings contain serious explorations of an artist's songbook, there are a few illustrations of comic interpretations of classic songs or off-the-wall, unconventional commentaries concerning a particular performer's influence:

- Big Daddy, *Sgt. Pepper's* (Santa Monica, California: Rhino, 1992).
- *Elvis Mania: A Total Collection of 52 Elvis Presley Novelty and Tribute Songs* (Prague, Czechoslovakia, Live Gold, 1991), featuring

The material in this chapter by B. Lee Cooper was originally published as "A Taxonomy of Tributes on Compact Disc," *Popular Music and Society,* XX, No. 2 (Summer 1996), pp. 204-217, and "Saluting Stevie Ray Vaughan," *Popular Music and Society,* XX, No. 3 (Fall 1996), pp. 125-127. Reprint permission granted by the author, editor Gary Burns, and the Bowling Green State University Popular Press.

Roy Hall, Audrey, Stan Freberg, Janis Martin, Lou Monte, Bill Parsons, Felton Jarvis, Lavern Baker, Jerry Reed, Carl Perkins, and others.
- *Elvis Mania 2: A Total Collection of 27 More Elvis Presley Novelty and Tribute Songs* (Prague, Czechoslovakia, Live Gold, 1992), featuring Link Davis, Rob Robbins, Billy Adams, Titus Turner, Rick Dees and His Cast of Idiots, Steven Bays, and others.

COLLABORATIVE EFFORTS

A rarity among tribute recordings is a compilation of signature songs where the original artists join a new group in reprise performances of classic hits:

- Manhattan Transfer, *Tonin'* (New York: Atlantic, 1994), featuring Frankie Valli on "Let's Hang On," Smokey Robinson on "I Second That Emotion," B.B. King on "The Thrill Is Gone," Felix Cavaliere on "Groovin'," Ben E. King on "Save the Last Dance for Me," and others.
- George Jones, *Bradley's Barn Sessions* (Universal City, California, MCA, 1994), featuring Keith Richards on "Say It's Not You," Mark Knopfler on "White Lightin'," Travis Tritt on "The Race Is On," Tricia Yearwood on "Bartender Blues," and others.

EULOGY RELEASES

The death of a particular performer or songwriter often prompts the release of two types of tribute recordings. First, there may be a gathering of "greatest hits" from earlier albums or single releases. Then, there can be an anthology of signature songs recorded by a variety of other artists who either knew, had played along with, had previously recorded, or just admired the work of the deceased person:

- Arthur Alexander, *The Greatest* (London: Ace, 1989).
- *Adios Amigo: A Tribute to Arthur Alexander* (New York: Razor and Tie, 1994), featuring Roger McGuinn, Elvis Costello, Robert Plant, Graham Parker, Chuck Jackson, Mark Knopfler, Marshall Crenshaw, Gary U.S. Bonds, and others.
- *Hats Off to Stevie Ray: L. A. Blues Authority—Volume Three.* (Blues Bureau BB 2009-27.) By Pat Travers, Rick Derringer, Leslie West,

Frank Marino, Ricky Medlocke, Jon Butcher, Steve Hunter, Kevin Russell, Craig Erickson, and Tony Spinner. (Novato, California: Blues Bureau International/Scrapnel Records, 1993).
- *Greatest Hits* (Epic EK 66217). By Stevie Ray Vaughan and Double Trouble. (New York: Epic/Sony Music Entertainment, 1995).
- *A Tribute to Stevie Ray Vaughan* (Epic EK 67599). By Bonnie Raitt, Jimmy Vaughan, B.B. King, Buddy Guy, Eric Clapton, Robert Cray, Dr. John, and Art Neville. (New York: Epic/Sony Music Entertainment, 1996).

Rarely does a popular music legend have no legacy of *Billboard* Hot 100 success. Nevertheless, such was the case with Dallas-born blues giant Stevie Ray Vaughan. Not a single tune from his first five commercial albums, *Texas Flood* (1983), *Couldn't Stand the Weather* (1984), *Soul to Soul* (1985), *Live Alive*, (1986), or *In Step* (1989), achieved pop hit status. Yet these five collections of blues/R&B/rock magic sold well enough to build lasting reputations for Stevie Ray and his Double Trouble cronies; bassist Tommy Shannon, drummer Chris Layton, and keyboardist Reese Wynans.

The helicopter crash that claimed Stevie Ray's life on August 27, 1990 generated an ironic flash of national attention. The Vaughan brothers' *Family Style* (1990) duet album charted for thirty-eight weeks, peaked higher than any previous Stevie Ray album and yielded the first Hot 100 hit, titled "Tick Tock." This CD was followed by a compilation of 1984-1989 recordings titled *The Sky Is Crying* (1991), which charted for forty-six weeks. Far less successful, though, was the release of a live Austin performance of April 1, 1980 vintage under the quasi-biblical title *In the Beginning* (1992).

Recent tributes to the performing genius of Stevie Ray Vaughan have pursued three distinct formats. First, Pat Travers, Rick Derringer, and several less well-known session artists compiled retrospective covers of ten Stevie Ray songs, including "Cold Shot," "Empty Arms," "Telephone Song," "Lenny," "The Things (That) I Used to Do," "Pride and Joy," "Crossfire," "Tell Me," "Texas Flood," and "Look at Little Sister." The session concluded with a guitar jam labeled "Blues for Stevie." This concoction, called *Hats Off to Stevie Ray* (1993), is pedestrian. Only Frank Marino and Ricky Medlocke seem capable of conjuring fire and feeling for Texas blues.

Epic Records showed a more traditional approach to acknowledging a fallen recording idol by reprising ten of Stevie Ray's best cuts on a *Greatest Hits* (1995) disc. Tunes included were "Texas Flood," "The House Is

Rockin'," "Pride and Joy," "Tightrope," "Little Wing," "Crossfire," "Change It," "Cold Shot," "Couldn't Stand the Weather," and "Life Without You." A strange rendition of the Beatles' song "Taxman" is also included. This exceptional compilation provides a fascinating overview of Stevie Ray's eclectic song selections, playing styles, and vocal skills. The only reasonable fan complaint would be . . . too few selections and omission of such signature numbers as "Hard to Be," "Tick Tock," "Telephone Song," "Leave My Girl Alone," "Lookin' Out the Window," "Voodoo Chile," "Honey Bee," and "Love Struck Baby." One suspects that a more epic Epic box set may be on the drawing board, though.

A Tribute to Stevie Ray Vaughan (1996) constitutes an authentic all-star salute to the man and his music. Jimmie Vaughan, rockin' big brother and Fabulous Thunderbirds guitarist, gathered the four artists—B. B. King, Buddy Guy, Eric Clapton, and Robert Cray—who had played alongside Stevie Ray at the Alpine Valley, Wisconsin, concert on the day before the helicopter accident. Jimmie also added Bonnie Raitt, Dr. John, and Art Neville, plus Double Trouble, to complete the distinguished tribute band. The live set was recorded at the Austin City Limits Studio on May 11, 1995. Songs featured included eight Stevie Ray tunes—"Pride and Joy," "Texas Flood," "Telephone Song," "Long Way from Home," "Ain't Gone 'n Give Up on Your Love," "Love Struck Baby," "Cold Shot," and "Tick Tock." The full ensemble also performed Jimmy's personal eulogy to his brother titled "Six Strings Down," plus a rousing version of the "SRV Shuffle." The only serious omission from this exceptional salute is the absence of Stevie Ray's close friend and songwriting collaborator, Doyle Bramhall.

For most deceased artists, it is reasonable to engage a number of current stars performing a montage of hit recordings. This is not the case for Stevie Ray Vaughan, though. His sound, his energy, and his distinctive style defies replication. *Greatest Hits* is ideal. *Hats Off to Stevie Ray* is a poor copy. But *A Tribute to Stevie Ray Vaughan* works because the individual artists involved are so strong in their own interpretative agenda that the Stevie Ray songs gain new vibrance rather than mere repetition.

GREATEST HITS COMPILATIONS

The most prevalent form of tribute recording is the compilation of an artist's most popular hits. This is often accomplished in dual formats—studio renditions of hit songs and live recordings of a public concert performance:

- *Rhythm and Blues—Ray Charles, 1954-1966* (Burbank, California: Time-Life Music/Warner Special Products, 1991).

- Ray Charles, *Ray Charles Live* (New York: Atlantic, 1987).
- Foreigner, *Foreigner Records* (New York: Atlantic Records, 1982).
- Foreigner, *Classic Hits Live* (New York: Atlantic Records, 1993).
- Jerry Lee Lewis, *Original Sun Greatest Hits* (Santa Monica, California: Rhino, 1984).
- Jerry Lee Lewis, *The Greatest Live Shows on Earth* (Hamburg, West Germany: Bear Family, 1991).

HOLIDAY HITS

Seasonal songs that have achieved extended years of popularity have become fodder for CD compilations. While "Easter Parade" and "My Funny Valentine" remain singular nostalgia favorites, tributes to hit songs depicting wacky Halloween antics and joyous Christmas expectations are dominant:

- *Elvira Presents Haunted Hits* (Santa Monica, California: Rhino, 1988), featuring Bobby "Boris" Pickett and The Crypt-Kickers, Jumpin' Gene Simmons, Ray Parker Jr., Screamin' Jay Hawkins, The Jayhawks, The Cramps, and others.
- *Elvira Presents Revenge of the Monster Hits* (Los Angeles, California: Rhino, 1995), featuring Warren Zevon, Elvira, Charles Sheffield, The Tubes, Bobby "Boris" Pickett, and Oingo Boingo.
- *Home for Christmas*—Two Volumes (Santa Monica, California: Rhino, 1992), featuring Burl Ives, Bobby Helms, Gene Autry, Brenda Lee, Eartha Kitt, Charles Brown, Mel Torme, Bing Crosby, Harry Simeone Chorale, Vaughn Monroe, Jimmy Boyd, Spike Jones, Perry Como, Mahalia Jackson, and others.
- *The Ultimate Christmas Album* (Narberth, Pennsylvania: Collectibles, 1994), featuring Brook Benton, The Drifters, Chuck Berry, Alvin and The Chipmunks, Bobby Darin, and others.
- *The Ultimate Christmas Album*—Volume Two (Narberth, Pennsylvania: Collectibles, 1995), featuring The Beach Boys, Dean Martin, Andy Williams, Gene Autry, Johnny Mathis, Elmo and Patsy, Augie Rios, Barry Gordon, Roy Orbison, Bing Crosby, and others.

INSTRUMENTAL ACKNOWLEDGMENTS

Virtuoso instrumentalists occasionally assemble discs honoring acclaimed vocal standards or traditional holiday favorites:

- David Sanborn, *Pearls* (New York: Elektra, 1995), featuring "Try a Little Tenderness," "Smoke Gets in Your Eyes," "For All We Know," "Come Rain or Come Shine," and others.
- Kenny G., *Miracles: The Holiday Album* (New York: Arista, 1994), featuring "Winter Wonderland," "White Christmas," "Silent Night," "Away in a Manger," and others.

MUSICAL LOCATIONS

The legendary creativity attributed to specific recording studios or American cities has generated the compilation of tribute discs that salute artists and songs associated with particular geographical locations:

- *Memphis Soul Classics* (Burbank, California: Warner Special Products, 1987), featuring The Staple Singers, The Mar-Keys, Rufus Thomas, King Curtis, Sam and Dave, Carla Thomas, Booker T. and The MGs, Eddie Floyd, and others.
- *The Muscle Shoals Sound* (Los Angeles, California: Rhino, 1993), featuring Arthur Alexander, Jimmy Hughes, Percy Sledge, Otis Redding, Wilson Pickett, Aretha Franklin, Arthur Conley, Etta James, Clarence Carter, and others.
- *The New Orleans Hit Story: Twenty Years of Big Easy Hits, 1950-1970* (London: Instant/Charly, 1993), featuring Fats Domino, Clarence Henry, Paul Gayten, Jessie Hill, Bobby Marchan, Aaron Neville, Ernie K-Doe, Chris Kenner, The Showmen, Lee Dorsey, Benny Spellman, Dixie Cups, The Meters, Johnny Adams, Irma Thomas, Eddie Bo, and others.
- *Highlights from Crescent City Soul: The Sound of New Orleans, 1947-1974* (New York: EMI Records, 1996), featuring Jewel King, Archibald, The Bees, Smiley Lewis, Fats Domino, Chris Kenner, Earl King, and others.

PARTICULAR SONGS

Although rare, there are a few tribute recordings that illustrate the diversity of styles and performers that have released a single classic tune:

- *Best of Kansas City: Great Versions of Leiber and Stoller's Classic Rock Song* (Plymouth, Minnesota: K-tel International, 1994), featur-

ing Little Willie Littlefield, Joe Williams, The Everly Brothers, Peggy Lee, Trini Lopez, Wilbert Harrison, Little Milton, Lou Rawls, Bill Haley and The Comets, and The Leiber-Stoller Big Band.
- *The Best of "Louie Louie"*—Two Volumes (Santa Monica, California: Rhino, 1989), featuring Richard Berry, The Kingsmen, The Rice University Marching Band, and many, many others.

PASSING THE TORCH

A new generation of performing artists sometimes pays tribute to an earlier generation of recording stars by recording an anthology of signature songs by the veteran singers:

- *The New Tradition Sings the Old Tradition* (Burbank, California: Warner Brothers, 1989), featuring Hank Williams Jr., k.d. lang, Dwight Yoakam, Highway 101, Michael Martin Murphy, Emmylou Harris, Rodney Crowell, and others.
- Natalie Cole, *Unforgettable* (New York: Elektra, 1991).
- *Come Together: America Salutes the Beatles* (Nashville, Tennessee: Liberty, 1995), featuring Tanya Tucker, Willie Nelson, Delbert McClinton, Collin Raye, Billy Dean, Randy Travis, Huey Lewis, Little Texas, Suzy Bogguss and Chet Atkins, and others.
- *Fit for a King: L.A. Blues Authority—Volume Four* (Novato, California: Blues Bureau International, 1993), featuring Leslie West, Craig Erickson, Steve Hunter, Kevin Russell, Pat Travers, Frank Marino, Rick Derringer, and others.
- *Hats Off to Stevie Ray: L.A. Blues Authority—Volume Three* (Novato, California: Blues Bureau International, 1993), featuring Pat Travers, Tony Spinner, Craig Erickson, Leslie West, Ricky Medlocke, Rick Derringer, Frank Marino, and others.
- *Not Fade Away: Remembering Buddy Holly* (Universal City, California: Decca, 1996), featuring The Mavericks, Nanci Griffith, Los Lobos, Mary Chapin Carpenter, Waylon Jennings, Mark Knopfler, Dave Edmunds, Marty Stuart, Stevie Earle, and others.

RECORD COMPANIES

Bigger than specific songs, individual artists, or even musical genres are those tribute box sets assembled to herald the commercial success and popular recognition achieved by specific recording corporations:

- *The Buddha Box: A History of Buddha Records on Three CDs* (Englewood Cliffs, New Jersey: Essex, 1993).
- *Chess Rhythm and Roll* (Universal City, California: Chess/MCA, 1994).
- *Rock Around the Clock: The Decca Rock 'n' Roll Collection* (Universal City, California: Decca/MCA, 1994).
- *Stardust: The Classic Decca Hits and Standards Collection* (Universal City, California: Decca/MCA, 1994).
- *The Fire/Fury Records Story* (Nashville, Tennessee: Capricorn, 1992).
- *The King R & B Box Set* (Nashville, Tennessee: King, 1995).
- *Hitsville USA: The Motown Singles Collection* (Los Angeles, California: Motown, 1992).
- *The Specialty Story* (Berkeley, California: Specialty/Fantasy, 1994).
- *The Sun Records Collection* (Los Angeles, California: Rhino, 1994).

RECORDINGS THAT INSPIRED SUPERSTARS

As successful rock performers reveal those recordings and specific artists that influenced their vocal styles, lyrical patterns, and instrumental techniques, CD anthologies of retrospective tributes appear:

- *Love 'Em Do! 24 Hits That Inspired the Beatles* (London: Instant/ Charly, 1992), featuring Carl Perkins, Chuck Berry, The Shirelles, The Isley Brothers, Little Richard, Wilbert Harrison, Lee Dorsey, The Teddy Bears, and others.
- *Under the Influence: The Original Versions of the Songs the Beatles Covered* (London: Sequel, 1992), featuring Arthur Alexander, The Cookies, Lenny Welch, Peggy Lee, The Marvellettes, Smokey Robinson and The Miracles, The Donays, Barrett Strong, Larry Williams, Buck Owens, Buddy Holly, and others.
- *Stone Rock Blues: The Original Recordings of Songs Covered by the Rolling Stones* (Universal City, California: Chess/MCA, 1994), featuring Chuck Berry, Muddy Waters, Bo Diddley, Arthur Alexander, Howlin' Wolf, Buddy Holly, and Dale Hawkins.
- *Stoned Alchemy: 27 Original Blues and R & B Hits That Inspired the Rolling Stones* (London: Instant/Charly, 1989), featuring Benny Spellman, Alvin Robinson, Jimmy Reed, Irma Thomas, Bobby Womack, Gene Allison, Buster Brown, Chuck Berry, Bo Diddley, and others.

ROCK 'N' ROLL HEAVEN

Tribute recordings often capitalize on the signature songs of prominent artists who died at the peak of their careers or on the lyrical reflections of other popular singers about the continuing influence of deceased performers:

- *Gone but Not Forgotten: A Tribute to Those Who Rocked* (New York: Risky Business/Sony, 1995), featuring Eddie Cochran, Mike Berry and The Outlaws, Johnny Cymbal, Ronnie McDowell, The Righteous Brothers, The Commodores, Charlie Daniels, and others.
- *Hillbilly Heaven: A Tribute to Country's Late Great Stars* (New York: Sony Music, 1995), featuring Tex Ritter, Conway Twitty, Roger Miller, Roy Orbison, Patsy Cline, Marty Robbins, Johnny Horton, Hank Williams, Bob Wills and His Texas Playboys, and others.

SALUTING COMPOSERS

Just as performers merit acknowledgments for their stylistic excellence, songwriters earn tributes for creating tunes that have achieved public praise and commercial success:

- *Puttin' On the Ritz: Capitol Sings Irving Berlin* (Hollywood, California: Capitol, 1992).
- *Brace Yourself: A Tribute to Otis Blackwell* (Newton, New Jersey: Shanachie, 1993).
- *The Brill Building Sound: Singers and Songwriters Who Rocked the 60's* (Plymouth, Minnesota: Era, 1993).
- *Back to the Street: Celebrating the Music of Don Covay* (Newton, New Jersey: Shanachie, 1993).
- *Mood Indigo: Capitol Sings Duke Ellington* (Hollywood, California: Capitol, 1994).
- *The Song Is You: Capitol Sings Jerome Kern* (Hollywood, California: Capitol, 1992)
- *There's a Riot Goin' On! The Rock 'n' Roll Classics of Leiber and Stoller* (Santa Monica, California: Rhino, 1991).
- *People Get Ready: A Tribute to Curtis Mayfield* (Newton, New Jersey: Shanachie, 1993).
- *A Tribute to Curtis Mayfield* (Burbank, California: Warner Brothers, 1994).
- *Till the Night Is Gone: A Tribute to Doc Pomus* (Los Angeles, California: Forward, 1995).

SIGNIFICANT MUSICAL STYLES

From rhythm and blues to doo-wop, record companies scramble to assemble CD compilations that illustrate the artists and songs that helped to define distinctive genres of popular music:

- *Red-Hot Rockabilly* (Burbank, California: Time-Life Music/Warner Special Products, 1990), featuring Billy Lee Riley, Wanda Jackson, Jack Scott, The Johnny Burnette Trio, Gene Vincent, Buddy Holly, Charlie Feathers, and others.
- *Rock This Town: Rockabilly Hits*—Two Volumes (Santa Monica, California: Rhino, 1991), featuring Bill Haley, Roy Orbison, Brenda Lee, Sanford Clark, Janis Martin, Dale Hawkins, Sonnee West, Buddy Knox, The Cricketts, Eddie Cochran, Johnny Horton, The Collins Kids, The Blasters, Ray Campi, Jerry Lee Lewis, and others.
- *Rock-a-Billy Rock* (New York: Sony Music Special Products, 1991), featuring Sleepy LaBeef, Dave Edmunds, Carl Perkins, Marty Stuart, Shakin' Stevens, Bob Luman, Stevie Earle, Rick Nelson, and others.
- *Rites of Rhythm and Blues: Rhythm and Blues Foundation 1993 Pioneer Awards* (Hollywood, California: Capitol, 1993), featuring James Brown, Lowell Fulson, Wilson Pickett, Solomon Burke, Carla Thomas, Big Joe Turner, Jimmy Witherspoon, and others.
- *Rites of Rhythm and Blues—Volume Two: Rhythm and Blues Foundation 1994 Pioneer Awards* (Los Angeles, California: Motown, 1994), featuring Little Richard, Fats Domino, Bill Doggett, Ron Covay, Clarence Carter, Irma Thomas, The Coasters, Johnny Otis, and others.
- *The King R & B Box Set* (Nashville, Tennessee: King, 1995), featuring Bull Moose Jackson, The Ravens, Ivory Joe Hunter, Hank Ballard, Little Willie John, James Brown, Freddy King, The Charms, and others.
- *The R & B Box: 30 Years of Rhythm and Blues* (Los Angeles, California: Rhino, 1994), featuring Louis Jordan and His Tympany Five, Amos Milburn, Percy Mayfield, Jackie Brenston, Willie Mae "Big Mama" Thornton, The Chords, Ray Charles, Johnny Ace, Jesse Belvin, Jackie Wilson, Clyde McPhatter, Aaron Neville, and others.

SONG HITS OF A SPECIFIC ARTIST

The repertoire of a particular performer will sometimes be attractive as a tribute recording within a variety of contexts: as a collection of tunes designed for children, as a soundtrack anthology for a particular motion picture, or as a vehicle to introduce new artists' styles in performing traditional hit songs:

- *Blue Suede Sneakers* (New York: Lightyear, 1995), featuring Suzy Bogguss, Ann Wilson, Shari Lewis, Rodney Crowell, Brian Setzer, Shawn Colvin, Ronnie McDowell, Ronnie Milsap, and others.
- *Honeymoon in Vegas* (New York: Epic Records, 1992), featuring Billy Joel, Ricky Van Shelton, Amy Grant, Travis Tritt, Bryan Ferry, Dwight Yoakam, Trisha Yearwood, Jeff Beck, Vince Gill, John Mellencamp, Willie Nelson, and Bono.
- *It's Now or Never: The Tribute to Elvis* (New York: Mercury, 1994), featuring Travis Tritt, Tanya Tucker, Tony Bennett, Bryan Adams, Michael Bolton, Carl Perkins, Chris Isaak, Billy Ray Cyrus, Marty Stuart, Aaron Neville, Melissa Ethridge, and others.
- *A Tribute to Elvis* (Paris, France: Charly, 1993), featuring Little Junior Parker, Johnny Cash, Jerry Lee Lewis, Sleepy LaBeef, Dave Dudley, Jimmy Ellis, and others.

SOUNDTRACK SALUTES

Motion picture soundtracks often utilize the distinctive recording artists or classic songs from a particular era to create an audio montage that will validate the historical setting or the special mood of films. For Disney films of course, the music, not the artist, is the message:

- *41 Original Hits from the Soundtrack of American Graffiti* (Universal City, California: MCA, 1973), featuring Bill Haley and The Comets, The Crests, Buddy Holly, Chuck Berry, The Platters, Fats Domino, The Flamingos, and others.
- *Music from the Motion Picture Soundtrack of Malcolm X* (Burbank, California: Quest/Warner Brothers, 1992), featuring Joe Turner, Lionel Hampton, Billie Holiday, Erskine Hawkins, Louis Jordan, Ella Fitzgerald, John Coltrane, Ray Charles, Duke Ellington, and others.
- *Original Motion Picture Soundtrack from Sleepless In Seattle* (New York: Epic, 1993), featuring Jimmy Durante, Louis Armstrong, Nat King Cole, Joe Cocker, Carly Simon, Harry Connick Jr., and others.
- *Classic Disney: 60 Years of Musical Magic* (Burbank, California: Walt Disney Records, 1995).

SPECIFIC DANCES

Tribute recordings are sometimes compiled to illustrate songs that motivated or sustained particular dance styles:

- *Let's Twist* (Plymouth, Minnesota: K-tel International, 1994), featuring Chubby Checker, The Isley Brothers, Joey Dee and The Starliters, The Ventures, The Marvelettes, King Curtis, and Gary U.S. Bonds.
- Joe Carr and The Texas Lone Star Band, *Line Dance Party* (Compose, 1993).

STYLISTIC ACKNOWLEDGMENTS

In some cases, tribute recordings reveal not only the passive acknowledgment of song borrowing or of stylistic influence, but also an active, direct genuflection to historical artists who inspired a present-day performer:

- *From Ripley to Chicago: 26 Original Cuts That Inspired Eric Clapton* (London: Instant/Charly, 1993), featuring Chuck Berry, Ernie K. Doe, Billy Boy Arnold, Bo Diddley, Robert Johnson, Memphis Slim, Little Walter, Howlin' Wolf, Buddy Guy, Elmore James, Otis Rush, Jimmy Reed, and others.
- Eric Clapton, *From the Cradle* (Burbank, California: Reprise, 1994).
- John Hammond, *Found True Love* (Beverly Hills, California: Point Blank/Virgin, 1995).
- John Hammond, *Got Love If You Want It* (Beverly Hills, California: Point Blank/Virgin, 1992.
- John Hammond, *Trouble No More* (New York: Charisma, 1993).
- John Hammond, *You Can't Judge a Book by the Cover: The Electric Side of John Hammond* (Santa Monica, California: Vanguard Recording Society, 1993).
- *The Commitments* (Universal City, California: MCA, 1991).
- *The Commitments—Volume Two* (Universal City, California: MCA, 1992).
- *Classic Recordings by the Original Artists of the Music Featured in the Motion Picture "The Commitments"* (New York: ATCO/Atlantic, 1991), featuring Wilson Pickett, Aretha Franklin, Otis Redding, Clarence Carter, James Brown, Percy Sledge, and Isaac Hayes.

- The Jeff Healey Band, *Cover to Cover* (New York: Arista, 1995).
- Jeff Beck and The Big Town Playboys, *Crazy Legs* (New York: Sony, 1993).
- Paul Rodgers, *Muddy Water Blues: A Tribute to Muddy Waters* (Los Angeles, California: Victory, 1993).

TIMELESS TUNES

The remaking of classic hit songs constitutes the foremost illustration of paying tribute to both the composers and the original recording artists:

- Michael Bolton, *Timeless: The Classics* (New York: Columbia, 1992), featuring "Since I Fell for You," "To Love Somebody," "You Send Me," "Yesterday," "Bring It on Home to Me," "Knock on Wood," "Drift Away," "White Christmas," and others.
- *Cover Me Soul* (Los Angeles, California: Hi, 1993), featuring "My Girl," "I Pity the Fool," "People Get Ready," "Soul Man," "Hideaway," "Memphis, Tennessee," "Shop Around," "I Say a Little Prayer," "Respect," and others.
- *Rhythm, Country and Blues* (Universal City, California: MCA, 1994), featuring "Funny How Time Slips Away," "I Fall to Pieces," "Somethin' Else," "Chain of Fools," "Since I Fell for You," "Southern Nights," "The Weight," and others.

TOTAL TRIBUTE PACKAGES

Very few performers or groups merit tribute packages that include double greatest hits releases, a live performance of their most popular tunes, a reunion release, plus a tribute disc by an all-star ensemble. Beyond the single illustration below, such attention has been focused on The Beatles, Elvis Presley, The Everly Brothers, and very few others:

- The Eagles, *Their Greatest Hits, 1971-1975* (New York: Elektra/Asylum, 1976).
- The Eagles, *Eagles Greatest Hits—Volume Two* (New York: Elektra/Asylum, 1982).
- The Eagles, *Eagles Live* (New York: Elektra/Asylum, 1980).
- The Eagles, *Hell Freezes Over* (Los Angeles, California: Geffen, 1994).

- *Common Thread: The Songs of the Eagles* (Nashville, Tennessee: Giant, 1993), featuring Travis Tritt, Little Texas, Clint Black, John Anderson, Alan Jackson, Suzy Bogguss, Diamond Rio, Trisha Yearwood, Billy Dean, Tanya Tucker, Brooks and Dunn, and Lorrie Morgan.

WILD KARAOKE

The audience participation format of karaoke singing constitutes a popular tribute to tunes familiar to broad numbers of want-to-be performers and their indulgent friends:

- *Sing the Hits of the Beach Boys* (Pioneer, 1996).
- *Sing Like Elton John* (Priddis, 1994).
- *Sing Like Madonna* (Priddis, 1994).

Chapter 6

Jobs and Workplaces

It is difficult to imagine a more stinging indictment of the unethical, impersonal, materialistic practices of many of America's corporate managers than Ray Stevens' statements in "Mr. Businessman" (1968). The goals identified in Stevens' song are without lasting value—bigger cars, bigger houses, term insurance for the spouses—and the personal sacrifices are staggering—ignoring the children growing up and missing the music of their laughter as they play. Many other popular songs challenge the morality of business leaders. Among these recordings are Bob Dylan's "Masters of War" (n.d.) and "Only a Pawn in Their Game" (n.d.). Other tunes criticize the harshness of personnel managers—"9 to 5" (1980) and "Take This Job and Shove It" (1977)—and the failure of middle managers or foremen to acknowledge the humanity of their workers—"Sunshine" (1971), "Big Boss Man" (1961), and "Workin' for the Man" (1962). But none of these songs can match the intensity, hostility and sense of ethical depravity voiced in "Mr. Businessman."

In the business world there are few managers and numerous workers. Thus, most songs portray the world of work from the vantage point of the employee. Upward mobility appeals to many employees who are "Working in the Coal Mine" (1966) or scrubbing at the "Car Wash" (1976), but most people seem to "Feel Like a Number" (1981) in stagnant job situations. For Billy Joel, the big lie of unattainable future success was implanted by hypocritical teachers in "Allentown" (1982). It is hard enough just to "Get a Job" (1958), according to The Silhouettes, let alone to become wealthy and successful. But even though "She Works Hard for the Money" (1983), Donna Summer notes for most employees there are no rainbows at the end of each day. Dolly Parton asserts that workin' "9 to 5" (1980) "ain't no way to make a livin'." The typical employee eyes the

---

The material in this chapter by B. Lee Cooper was originally published as "Occupations, Materialism, and Workplaces" and "Poverty and Unemployment" in *A Resource Guide to Themes in Contemporary American Song Lyrics, 1956-1985.* Westport, CT: Greenwood Press, 1986, pp. 111-129 and 201-212. Reprint permission granted by the author and the Greenwood Press Publishing Group, Inc.

factory clock and listens for the plant whistle with eager anticipation. Freedom arrives in the "Five O'Clock World" (1965) after the workplace has been abandoned. Individual pursuits dominate weekend activities when secretaries, car wash attendants, miners, stock boys, and assembly line workers can "Rip It Up" (1956), "Dance to the Music" (1968), and (symbolically, if not literally) "Take This Job and Shove It" (1977).

Not unexpectedly, numerous recording industry occupations are mentioned in popular song lyrics. The plight of unsuccessful performers and songwriters is the central message in "Please Come to Boston" (1974), "Rock 'n' Roll (I Gave You the Best Years of My Life)" (1974), "Tulsa Time" (1980), and "I'm Comin' Home" (1974). The boredom of itinerant rock 'n' roll bands is capsulized in "Homeward Bound" (1966); the exhilaration of stardom (real or imagined) is communicated in "Travelin' Band" (1970), "Guitar Man" (1981), "Keep Playin' That Rock 'n' Roll" (1971), and "Takin' Care of Business" (1974). While "The Under Assistant West Coast Promotion Man" (1965) continues to hunt for musical talent and many agents tell auditioning bands "Don't Call Us, We'll Call You" (1974), the carrot of fame keeps drawing would-be recording artists. They all dream of seeing their faces on "The Cover of the 'Rolling Stone'" (1972).

In contrast to the numerous victims of the economic system, a few individuals challenge and defeat the materialistic world. This does not necessarily mean that they gain success, fame, and wealth though. The young man who runs away from his parents and teachers to join "The Free Electric Band" (1973) is obviously marching to Henry David Thoreau's different drummer. Likewise, the young woman who isn't ready to be tied down in monogamy also hears a "Different Drum" (1968). But Lou Rawls outdoes both Albert Hammond and Linda Ronstadt in making his case against mindless, meaningless employment. The challenge in "A Natural Man" (1971) is antiauthority, antimaterialistic, and prohumanistic.

A cornerstone of individual development in American society is the expectation of personal success. This goal may be achieved through hard work, formal educational training, luck, or careful professional networking. Whatever the route, the assumptions of equal opportunity for advancement and open access to channels of economic development are fundamental to promoting social mobility. The soggy-shoed, would-be executive depicted in Jim Croce's "Workin' at the Car Wash Blues" (1974) epitomizes the plans of many young men who long to be "smokin' big cigars and talkin' trash to the secretaries."

Dreams can spawn achievement. So can frustration. Billy Joel provides a vignette about an urban dweller who has to move out of his parent's home in order to move up in society. This departure from the nest in search of wider spaces, more opportunities, bigger challenges, and the achievement of individual identity is not limited to "Movin' Out (Anthony's Song)" (1978). This theme has been a staple of rock lyrics since Chuck Berry's guitar-strumming "Johnny B. Goode" (1958) hit the road, since Elvis Presley's young hero caught a flight to the West Coast's "Promised Land" (1974), and since Lou Rawls abandoned his Chicago area "Dead End Street" (1967) and denounced his "Tobacco Road" (n.d.) roots.

Physical shifts of location by themselves aren't usually sufficient to produce success for either a self-made man or an upwardly mobile woman. Curtis Mayfield capsuled the essence of individual spirit and personal motivation among a minority group when The Impressions urged young blacks to "Keep on Pushin' " (1964). On the distaff side, Helen Reddy offered the same challenge to young and old alike in her 1972 anthem "I Am Woman." The sentiments expressed in Sly Stone's "You Can Make It if You Try" (n.d.), in David Naughton's "Makin' It" (1979), and in Jim Croce's "I Got a Name" (1973) laud strength of character across the boundaries of race, sex, and social class to entice individuals to improve themselves. If there are logical subsets to the general theme of social mobility, they include varying elements of freedom, ingenuity, enthusiasm, determination, incentive, and access. But there is also risk to setting high goals; the reality of failure is the flipside of success. Not all dreams come true. Jobs that once appeared to be brief, exciting employment steps on an occupational ladder toward financial self-sufficiency can become boring, dead-end emotional traps. Persistence alone may not be sufficient to keep an individual at the top of his or her field forever. What then? The answer lies in maintaining personal integrity, at least for Frank Sinatra's "My Way" (1969), for Sammy Davis Jr.'s "I've Gotta Be Me" (1969), and for Lou Rawls' "A Natural Man" (1971). There is no quantitative way to measure the value of character against the goal of mobility.

Although sociologists and psychologists may draw fine distinctions between occupations and vocations or between jobs and professions, few clear work-related boundaries are found in popular lyrics. Human labor is rarely viewed as ennobling. In fact, work is generally depicted as drudgery performed out of inescapable financial necessity. Craftsmanship and the concern for high-quality on-the-job performance is rarely mentioned. The money paid for a day's work, a week's work, or even a month's hard labor is never enough. And the five o'clock whistle can never blow soon enough. Although singers may laud their unions, their fellow workers, or the boss's pretty daughter, it is undeniable that the work environment represents a form of wage slavery that denies men and women opportunities for freedom, self-development, leisure, travel, and other forms of personal enjoyment.

Betty Hutton outlined several occupational options in "Doctor, Lawyer, Indian Chief" (1945), while Frank Sinatra preached the lifelong volatility of job-related success and failure in "That's Life" (1966). The Silhouettes note the hostile domestic environment of a man who needs to "Get a Job" (1958), while The Who bemoaned the loss of personal freedom due to work obligations in "Summertime Blues" (1970). The variety of occupations mentioned in popular songs is staggering. Among the positions described are school teachers—"Abigail Beecher" (1964), "Mr. Lee" (1957), "To Sir with Love" (1967), and "Don't Stand So Close to Me" (1981); secretaries—"Take a Letter, Maria" (1969) and "9 to 5" (1980); disc jockeys and broadcast journalists—"Agent Double-O-Soul" (1965), "Kansas City Star" (1965), "Dirty Laundry" (1982), and "Clap for the Wolfman" (1974); bartenders—"Smokey Joe's Cafe" (1955) and "Come a Little Bit Closer" (1964); trainmen—"Rock Island Line" (1970) and "The City of New Orleans" (1972); miners—"Big Bad John" (1961), "Sixteen Tons" (1976), and "Working in the Coal Mine" (1966); truckers—"Convoy" (1975), "Drivin' My Life Away" (1980), and "Phantom 309" (1967); telephone operators—"Memphis" (1964) and "Operator (That's Not the Way It Feels)" (1972); and dozens of other jobs. Not unexpectedly, movie stars and popular music personalities are focal points for job interests. Among the songs examining various motion picture and recording industry occupations are: "Act Naturally" (1965), "Albert Flasher" (1971), "The All American Boy" (1958). "The Cover of the 'Rolling Stone'" (1972), "The Entertainer" (1974), "Jazzman" (1974), "Keep Playin' That Rock 'n' Roll" (1971), "On the Road Again" (1980), "Piano Man" (1974), "So You Want to be a Rock 'n' Roll Star" (1967), "Star Baby" (1974), "Travelin' Band" (1970), "The Under Assistant West Coast Promotion Man" (n.d.), and "We're an American Band" (1973).

Unsavory occupations and illegal activities are also surveyed in contemporary lyrics. Men who make their livings with cards, fortune wheels, and dice are featured in "The Gambler" (1978), "Go Down Gamblin'" (1971), "Ramblin' Gamblin' Man" (1969), and "Stagger Lee" (1971). Drug dealers, rum runners, and murderers are also described in "Freddie's Dead" (1972), "Superfly" (1972), "The Ballad of Thunder Road" (1957), and "Mack the Knife" (1959). The world of striptease, pornography, and prostitution is examined in "Bad Girls" (1979), "Backstreet Ballet" (1983), "Blue Money" (1971), "Lady Marmalade" (1975), "The House of the Rising Sun" (1981), "Painted Ladies" (1973), "Shake Your Money Maker" (n.d.), and "Sweet Cream Ladies, Forward March" (1968). In 1933 Ginger Rogers proclaimed "We're in the Money (The Gold Digger's Song)." Although the impact of the Great Depression made this lyric highly ironic, the linkage of material wealth with physical and psychological well-being has been a longtime American assumption. As Joel Grey and Liza Minnelli asserted in "The Money Song" from the 1972 film *Cabaret*, it's money that makes the world go around. Who could refute their claim? Even chronic misfortune can supposedly be resolved by "Pennies from Heaven" (1960).

Not everyone feels that money is the solution to all problems, though Ray Charles expresses the pain of being "Busted" (1963), while The Beatles assert that money "Can't Buy Me Love" (1964). Even though Bobby Hebb claims that there isn't one rich man in ten with "A Satisfied Mind" (1966), the power of wealth continues to allure. Barrett Strong's unequivocal statement—"Money (That's What I Want)" (1960)—finds varying adherents. Roy Orbison wants to be a woman's "Candy Man" (1961); B. B. King demands respect and obedience because he's working and thereby "Paying the Cost to Be the Boss" (1968); and Gene Watson condemns the selfish materialism of women who contemplate clothes, jewelry, and cash with a "Fourteen Carat Mind" (1981).

The majority of contemporary lyrics are critical of material ends that emphasize the cost of everything while finding lasting value in nothing. Pleas for personal freedom as a better life than dwelling in lonely mansions are heard from Taxxi in "Gold and Chains" (1983) and from Linda Ronstadt in "Silver Threads and Golden Needles" (1974). The Temptations attack the materialistic pillaging of ghetto life in "Masterpiece" (1973), while the O'Jays denounce the act of a woman selling her precious body "For the Love of Money" (1974). The predatory skills of such dollar-driven ladies are also depicted in "She Only Meant to Use Him" (1982), "Maneater" (1982), and "Fancy" (1969).

Other criticisms focus on the problems of remaining emotionally sensitive to others while living in a materialistic society. These commentaries are often symbolic in tone. Attacks on money-grubbing television evangelists and overzealous church collections are featured in "The American Dream" (1982) and "Signs" (1971). Stan Freberg even denounces hedonistic Yuletide sales campaigns in "Green Chritma" (1958). The materialistic sameness of suburban life is parodied in Pete Seeger's "Little Boxes" (1964) and The Monkees' "Pleasant Valley Sunday" (1967). This critical trend is also notable in "Fortunate Son" (1969), "American Woman" (1970), and "Cheeseburger in Paradise" (1978). Attacks on the immorality or lost innocence of dollar-seeking individuals also illustrates the antimaterialism theme. These recordings include "Goldfinger" (1965) by Shirley Bassey, "Conquistador" (1972) by Procol Harum, and "Rhinestone Cowboy" (1975) by Glen Campbell. Perhaps the best example of a song that encapsules the lost feeling of someone who has gained fame and fortune but lost all direction and meaning in life is Joe Walsh's "Life's Been Good" (1978).

Little Richard lauded both payday and the weekend in his 1956 recording of "Rip It Up." The notion of leaving a frustrating workplace is as popular in work-related tunes as Chuck Berry's descriptions of students joyfully escaping from classes in his school songs. The necessity of daily labor is largely unquestioned; but the love of work—unless it's related to playing in a band, performing as a disc jockey, or serving as a lifeguard—is nonexistent in popular lyrics. Loverboy freely admits to "Working for the Weekend" (1982), while both The Easybeats and The Vogues announce they have "Friday on My Mind" (1967) while looking toward a "Five O'Clock World" (1965). Bobby Smith combines staccato audio images of being stuck in traffic, of facing a screaming boss, of getting a headache, and of being indicted on his job for doing everything wrong. His conclusion is "It's Been One of Those Days" (1982).

Continuing job frustration is even more difficult to resolve than the understandable longing for a regular weekend break. Bob Seger complains that his boss can't even recall his name in "Feel Like a Number" (1981). For Dolly Parton it's not anonymity but lack of formal recognition and thoughtful praise that makes her "9 to 5" (1980) service so upsetting. Bobby Bare views his assembly line job as crushing monotony. He longs to leave "Detroit City" (1963) for a warmer climate, more friendly neighbors, and the cotton fields back home. Reverie and fantasy in the form of "Dreams of the Everyday Housewife" (1968) also mark a form of dissatisfaction with a domestic job situation.

Work without sufficient time for human pleasure, leisure, and social amenities is truly drudgery. Even top managers need to "Stop and Smell the Roses" (1974) says Mac Davis. But Lou Rawls equates continuous self-sacrifice to job requirements over an entire lifetime with pure foolishness. This is particularly true if the boss can control his own life and leisure at the expense of his workers. Stated succinctly in "A Natural Man" (1971), Rawls says that he doesn't want a gold watch for working forty years from nine to five. One senses that he would prefer to be "Takin' Care of Business" (1974) on the beach with Bachman-Turner Overdrive. Billy Joel blames the entire community of "Allentown" (1982) for lying to its youth about the occupational future. Even the frustration of repetitive steel production is preferable to stagnating unemployment brought on by poor planning, inadequate schooling, misleading national myths, and industrial pullouts. The cynicism of this song is matched only by Albert King's personal feelings of isolation in "Angel of Mercy" (1972). The late nineteenth and early twentieth century tunes of working-class anger do have a continuing presence during the 1950-1985 period. Ironically, they are sung by highly successful musicians who are far removed from California waitresses who work hard for their money or blue-collar factory employees who languish in Pennsylvania.

POVERTY AND UNEMPLOYMENT

All poor people are not unemployed and all unemployed people are not poor. Earning a salary does not guarantee suitable living conditions, personal satisfaction, hope for the future, or many other desirable goals. The continuing existence of ghettos, both urban and rural, based on either race or nationality demonstrates that securing employment alone cannot alleviate all social problems. It is ironic that being unemployed is not necessarily a sign of poverty. Short-term layoffs and wildcat strikes may take workers off assembly lines for abbreviated periods of time, but their incomes may be maintained through union fund support or by federal unemployment insurance. The retired also constitute a growing class of unemployed but not necessarily impoverished Americans. Whether from the military with healthy federal pensions, from industry with a package of union benefits, from teaching with long-term TIAA-CREF investment support, or from private business with personal nest eggs, many nonworking folks today who are still financially stable.

Most contemporary songs that address themes of poverty and unemployment ignore the complexities of the American economic environment. Lyrical commentary is inevitably simplified and personalized. Although there are a few notable exceptions—"Masterpiece" (1973), "For the Love of Money" (1974), and "Living for the City" (1975)—most songs survey the impact of poverty and unemployment on individuals rather than groups. For example, Jim Croce's would-be business executive is totally discontented while singing the "Workin' at the Car Wash Blues" (1974); Albert King pleads for an "Angel of Mercy" (1972) to help him maintain his job so that his children can eat properly and his family won't be evicted from their apartment; and Ray Charles enumerates dozens of needs that he can't meet because he's "Busted" (1963). Elvis Presley notes that both landlords and female companions express the same kind of materialistic concern—you've got to have "Money Honey" (1956) if you want to get along with them. This individualizing tendency, so typical of most popular media, frequently disguises broader social implications of serious financial problems.

The most caustic commentary about the contemporary American economy is contained in Billy Joel's "Allentown" (1982). Some might feel this song echoes the anticapitalistic sentiments of folk singers from the 1930s and 1940s; others might view the tune as a logical extension of the criticism of the company store system found in Tennessee Ernie Ford's "Sixteen Tons" (1955); and a few might contend that Joel's statements merely echo ideas contained in other "anti-bossism" songs recorded by Jimmy Reed, Johnny Cash, Bobby Bare, Roy Orbison, and Johnny Paycheck. Whatever the motivation, Billy Joel strikes numerous chords of social discontent in "Allentown." He identifies the immediate impact of declining levels of mining activities and the termination of steel production in a particular Pennsylvania city. As the factories close, former workers simply kill time by standing in lines and filling out unemployment forms. Next, he shifts his commentary to the upward mobility desired by Americans who participated in World War II. Joel's sympathies rest with the men and women, former soldiers, and USO volunteers who settled in Allentown to raise families, mine coal, and make steel. The real target in this lyrical diatribe of lost dreams and found hypocrisy is the American social and economic system as misrepresented by public school educators. Teachers emphasized, according to the singer, the values of hard work, good behavior, and general learning. They omitted what was real: iron and coke, chromium steel. That is, neither industrial automation nor energy obsolescence were discussed; neither job insecurity nor the probability of geographical dislocation were considered. Middle-class myths of eternal upward mobility and unquestioned patriotism masked the cruel reality of plant conversions and mine closings, of times when all of the coal would be taken from the ground and the union people would crawl away. The song concludes with a statement mixing dream and reality. Joel says that he's still living in Allentown. He declares that it's hard to keep a good man down; but he regrets that he won't be getting up today.

Poverty results from a variety of circumstances. Sometimes lack of interest in contributing to the family income, failure to follow the work ethic, or just individual laziness, ignorance, or nonmotivation render people financially poor. Although they may not be particularly unhappy—as in the instances of the "Good-Hearted Woman" (1976) by Waylon Jennings and Willie Nelson, the "King of the Road" (1965) by Roger Miller, and "Mr. Bojangles" (1968) by Jerry Jeff Walker—they tend to envy the workless, irresponsible way of "That Lucky Old Sun" (1963). Ray Charles is frequently a spokesman for the poor, but his messages are often delivered with humor in his lyric and a twinkle in his tone. "If you ain't got no money, you just ain't no good," he theorizes in "Hit the Road Jack" (1961). He also contributes images of moneyless predicaments in "Busted" (1963) and "Them That Got" (1961). Additional examples of poverty depicted in humorous situations include The Goose Creek Symphony's "(Oh Lord Won't You Buy Me a) Mercedes

Benz" (1972), Leo Sayer's "Long Tall Glasses (I Can Dance)" (1975), and Guy Drake's "Welfare Cadillac" (1970).

Too often it is forgotten that poverty is generally a problem that exceeds individual ability to explain or to overcome. Circumstances of race, nationality, religion, sex, and social class both create and prolong personal financial strife. Contemporary lyrics address these issues. Desires to escape from areas of rural and urban poverty are common as expressed in The Nashville Teens' "Tobacco Road" (1964), Chuck Berry's "Johnny B. Goode" (1958), and Lou Rawls' "Dead End Street" (1967). There is a force at work in the ghetto, however, that seems to undermine efforts to escape. This undertow exists in the form of poor education, lack of peer support for upward mobility, few constructive mentors for economic success, and the mixed negative elements of crime, racism, and sexism. Recordings that identify the social class conflicts and economic depression found in isolated pockets of poverty include Billy Joe Royal's "Down in the Boondocks" (1965), B. B. King's "Ghetto Woman" (1971), The McCoys' "Hang On Sloopy" (1965), Ray Charles' "Living for the City" (1975), The Temptations' "Masterpiece" (1973), Johnny Rivers' "Poor Side of Town" (1966), The Four Seasons' "Rag Doll" (1964), The Animals' "We Gotta Get Out of This Place" (1965), and B. B. King's "Why I Sing the Blues" (1969).

It is understandable that the frustration of living in a closed social system, in an unforgiving, harsh economic environment could spark strong responses for independence. One such reaction is criminal activity. This approach to acquiring money without any scruples includes a wide gamut of undertakings. Robbery and murder, chicanery and trickery, drug dealing, pornography, rum running, gambling, and prostitution are among the roads to fast money depicted in Robert Mitchum's "The Ballad of Thunder Road" (1962), Donna Summer's "Bad Girls" (1979), Van Morrison's "Blue Money" (1971), The O'Jays' "For the Love of Money" (1974), Curtis Mayfield's "Freddie's Dead" (1972), Cher's "Gypsys, Tramps, and Thieves" (1971), Tony Joe White's "Polk Salad Annie" (1969), Tommy Roe's "Stagger Lee" (1971), and The Steve Miller Band's "Take the Money and Run" (1976). The second response to escaping from poverty is to heighten one's self-image and to raise one's self-esteem as the principle for personal behavior. This does not necessarily rule out illegal activity, as described by Bobbie Gentry's "Fancy" (1969) and O. C. Smith's "The Son of Hickory Holler's Tramp" (1968). There is also overt recognition that one's level of income directly affects the behavior of others in Nina Simone's "Nobody Knows You When You're Down and Out" (1960) and Richard Fields' "People Treat You Funky (When Ya Ain't Got No Money)" (1982). Whether portrayed humorously by The

Big Bopper in "Chantilly Lace" (1958) or more defensively by John Anderson in "Black Sheep" (1983) and Sammy Johns in "Common Man" (1981), there are several songs that decry using money as the only barometer of individual success. Aggressive stances by less-than-wealthy individuals who value self-esteem and integrity more than selling out to others for cash are featured in Creedence Clearwater Revival's "Fortunate Son" (1969), Tom Jones' "I (Who Have Nothing)" (1970), Marty Robbins' "Ruby Ann" (1962), Donna Summer's "She Works Hard for the Money" (1983), Linda Ronstadt's "Silver Threads and Golden Needles" (1974), and Otis Redding and Carla Thomas's "Tramp" (1967).

Unemployment is often the result of an accumulating process of job dissatisfaction. An individual may be earning a decent wage but still be upset with his or her day-to-day workplace. Hatred of the boss, feelings of anonymity in the hourly operation of a plant, disagreements with fellow workers, and other job-related problems may create an unhappy employee. The drag of the required Monday-through-Friday, nine-to-five presence is chronicled in Fats Domino's "Blue Monday" (1957), Albert King's "Cadillac Assembly Line" (1976), Bobby Bare's "Detroit City" (1963), The Vogues' "Five O'clock World" (1965), The Easybeats' "Friday on My Mind" (1967), Bobby Bland's "Stormy Monday Blues" (1962), and Mel McDaniel's "Take Me to the Country" (1982). Anger with the boss, the foreman, or some other supervisor is expressed in Elvis Presley's "Big Boss Man" (1967), Billy Joe Royal's "Down in the Boondocks" (1965), Dolly Parton's "9 to 5" (1980), Roy Orbison's "Workin' for the Man" (1962), and Johnny Paycheck's "Take This Job and Shove It" (1977). Other forms of personal alienation and frustration are illustrated in Bob Seger's "Feel Like a Number" (1981), McGuffey Lane's "Making a Living's Been Killing Me" (1982), Eddie Cochran's "Summertime Blues" (1958), The Coasters' "Wake Me, Shake Me" (1960), Huey Lewis and The News' "Workin' for a Livin'" (1982), and Devo's "Working in a Coal Mine" (1981).

Unemployment means that an individual must search for a new workplace. Rodney Lay's "I Wish I Had a Job to Shove" (1982) and The Silhouettes' "Get a Job" (1958) illustrate the personal and family-related tensions involved in an ongoing job search. The action of being released from even an unwanted work position is embarrassing and frustrating. Heatwave's "Lettin' It Loose" (1982) and Bill Anderson's "Laid Off" (1982) illustrate this feeling. Although Billy Joel's "Allentown" (1982) speaks more broadly to industrial change and worker relocation as reasons for reducing workforces, Albert King's impending dismissal described in "Angel of Mercy" (1972) is much more demoralizing. Of course, the ultimate commentary of suspended hiring judgment to a would-be employee is found in the title of Sugarloaf's 1974 hit, "Don't Call Us, We'll Call You."

All job terminations are not unhappy. Retirements, shifts from one company to another, and decisions of employees not to continue in dead-end positions are self-determined acts of workplace change. Taking advantage of opportunities for new jobs are the central themes of Billy Joel's "Movin' Out (Anthony's Song)" (1978), The Lovin' Spoonful's "Nashville Cats" (1966), Jay and The Americans' "Only in America" (1963), Irene Cara's "Out Here on My Own" (1980), Dave Loggins' "Please Come to Boston" (1974), Chuck Berry's "Promised Land" (1965), and Don Williams' "Tulsa Time" (1978). Although Mac Davis expresses some frustration about his career in "Rock 'n' Roll (I Gave You the Best Years of My Life)" (1974), it is Lou Rawls who states the ultimate position of independence in "A Natural Man" (1971). Rawls encapsules the feeling of many workers in saying that his commitment to forty-hour-per-week employment is not total and that unequal pay and opportunities among employees and supervisors make him seek genuine freedom beyond the nine-to-five existence. The natural man works only for the convenience of an income and reserves his personal life for his ultimate enjoyment.

BIBLIOGRAPHY

Allmendinger, Blake. *The Cowboy: Representations of Labor in an American Work Culture.* New York: Oxford University Press, 1992.

Black, Sharon. "Checking Out the Librarian: The Depiction of Librarians and Libraries on Prime Time Television," *Popular Culture in Libraries*, I, No. 4 (1993), pp. 35-62.

Butchart, Ronald E. and B. Lee Cooper. "Perceptions of Education in the Lyrics of American Popular Music, 1950-1980," *American Music*, V (Fall 1987), pp. 271-281.

Cantor, Louis. *Wheelin' on Beale: How WDIA-Memphis Became the Nation's First All-Black Radio Station and Created the Sound That Changed America.* New York: Pharos Books, 1992.

Cohen, Norm (with music edited by David Cohen). *Long Steel: The Railroad in American Folksong.* Urbana, IL: University of Illinois Press, 1981.

Cooper, B. Lee. "From Anonymous Announcer to Radio Personality, from Pied Piper to Payola: The American Disc Jockey, 1950-1970," *Popular Music and Society*, XIV (Winter 1990), pp. 89-95.

Cooper, B. Lee. *The Popular Music Handbook: A Resource Guide.* Littleton, CO: Libraries Unlimited, 1984.

Cooper, B. Lee. *Popular Music Perspective: Ideas, Themes, and Patterns in Contemporary Lyrics.* Bowling Green, OH: Bowling Green State University Popular Press, 1991.

Cooper, B. Lee. *A Resource Guide to Themes in Contemporary Song Lyrics, 1950-1985.* Westport, CT: Greenwood Press, 1986.

Cooper, B. Lee. "Review of *Work's Many Voices* (JEMF 110/1 11) Compiled by Archie Green (1986)," *Popular Music and Society,* XII (Spring 1998), pp. 77-79.

Cooper, B. Lee and Donald E. Walker. "Baseball, Popular Music, and Twentieth-Century American History, *Social Studies,* LXXXI (May-June 1990), pp. 120-124.

Cooper, B. Lee and Donald E. Walker with assistance from William L. Schurk. "The Decline of Contemporary Baseball Heroes in American Popular Recordings," *Popular Music and Society,* XV (Summer 1991), pp. 49-58.

Dannen, Frederic. *Hit Men* (Updated Edition). New York: Vintage Books, 1991.

Denisoff, R. Serge with the assistance of William L. Schurk. *Tarnished Gold: The Record Industry Revisited.* New Brunswick, NJ: Transaction Books, 1986.

Dorf, Michael and Robert Appel (eds.), *Gigging: The Musician's Underground Touring Directory.* Cincinnati, OH: Writer's Digest Books, 1989.

Foner, Philip S. *American Labor Songs of the Nineteenth Century.* Urbana, IL: University of Illinois Press, 1975.

Glatt, John. *Rage and Roll: Bill Graham and the Selling of Rock.* New York: Birch Lane Press, 1993.

Good, Howard. *Outcasts: The Image of Journalists in Contemporary Film.* Metuchen, NJ: Scarecrow Press, 1989.

Goodall, H. L. Jr. *Living in the Rock 'n' Roll Mystery: Reading Context, Self and Others As Clues.* Carbondale, IL: Southern Illinois University Press, 1991.

Graham, Bill and Robert Greenfield. *Bill Graham Presents: My Life Inside Rock and Out.* Garden City, NY: Doubleday and Company, Inc., 1992.

Grant, Judith. "Prime Time Crime: Television Portrayals of Law Enforcement," *Journal of American Culture,* XV (Spring 1992), pp. 57-68.

Green, Archie. "A Discography (LP) of American Labor Union Songs," *New York Folklore Quarterly,* I (Autumn 1961), pp. 1-18.

Green, Archie. *Only a Miner: Studies in Recorded Coal-Mining Songs.* Urbana, IL: University of Illinois Press, 1972.

Guralnick, Peter. *Lost Highway: Journeys and Arrivals of American Musicians.* New York: Harper and Row, 1989.

Harker, Dave. *One for the Money: Politics and the Popular Song.* London: Hutchinson and Company, Ltd., 1980.

Hendler, Herb. *Year by Year in the Rock Era: Events and Conditions Shaping the Rock Generations That Reshaped America.* Westport, CT: Greenwood Press, 1983.

Hugill, Stan. *Shanties from the Seven Seas: Shipyard Work-Songs and Songs Used as Work-Songs from the Great Days of Sail* (Revised Edition). London: Routledge and Kegan Paul, 1984.

Huntington, Gale. *Songs That the Whalemen Sang.* Barre, MA: Barre Gazette, 1964.

Inciardi, James A. and Juliet L. Dee, "From Keystone Cops to Miami Vice: Images of Policing in American Popular Culture," *Journal of Popular Culture*, XXI (Fall 1987), pp. 84-102.

Jackson, Bruce. *Wake Up Dead Man: Afro-American Worksongs from Texas Prisons.* Cambridge, MA: Harvard University Press, 1972.

Lyle, Katie Letcher. *Scalded to Death by the Steam: Authentic Stories of Railroad Disasters and Ballads That Were Written About Them.* Chapel Hill, NC: Algonquin Books of Chapel Hill, 1991.

MacLeod, Bruce A. *Club Date Musicians: Playing the New York Party Circuit.* Urbana, IL: University of Illinois Press, 1993.

Negus, Keith. *Producing Pop: Culture and Conflict in the Popular Music Industry.* New York: Edward Arnold, 1992.

Newman, Mark. *Entrepreneurs of Profit and Pride: From Black Appeal to Radio Soul.* New York: Praeger Books, 1988.

Owens, Joe. *Welcome to the Jungle: A Practical Guide to Today's Music Business.* New York: Harper Collins, 1992.

Passman, Arnold. *The Dee Jays.* New York: Macmillan Company, 1971.

Peterson, Richard A. "Five Constraints on the Production of Culture: Law, Technology, Market, Organizational Structure, and Occupational Careers," *Journal of Popular Culture*, XVI (Fall 1982), pp. 143-153.

Ruess, Richard A. (ed.). *Songs of American Labor, Industrialization, and the Urban Work Experience: A Discography.* Ann Arbor, MI: Labor Studies Center in the Institute of Labor and Industrial Relations at the University of Michigan, 1983.

Sanjek, Russell and David Sanjek. *The American Popular Music Business in the 20th Century.* New York: Oxford University Press, 1991.

Seeger, Pete and Bob Reiser. *Carry It On: A History in Song and Pictures of the Working Men and Women of America.* New York: Simon and Schuster, 1985.

Smith, Joe (edited by Mitchell Fink). *Off the Record: An Oral History of Popular Music.* New York: Warner Books, 1988.

Smith, Wes. *The Pied Pipers of Rock 'n' Roll: Radio Deejays of the 50s and 60s.* Marietta, GA: Longstreet Press, Inc., 1989.

Walker, Donald E. and B. Lee Cooper. *Baseball and American Culture: A Bibliographic Guide for Teachers and Libraries*, Jefferson, NC: McFarland and Company, Inc., 1995.

Walker, Donald E. and B. Lee Cooper. "Black Players and Baseball Cards: Exploring Racial Integration with Popular Culture Resources," *Social Education*, LV (March 1991), pp. 169-173, 204.

Chapter 7

Novelty Recordings

The Wacky Top 40 by Bruce Nash and Allan Zullo. Holbrook, MA: Bob Adams, Inc., 1993. Illustrated. 206 pp.

Bruce and Allan (obviously unrelated to Burns and Allen) have assembled a slim volume saluting their candidates for "the most outrageous, hilarious, and unforgettable" recordings in contemporary pop music history. No selection criteria are revealed. Some songs are sexy ("Telephone Man"); some are absurd ("Surfin' Bird"); some songs are topical ("Junk Food Junkie"); some songs are parodies ("Eat It"); some songs are boring ("Mac-Arthur Park"); some are sophomoric ("Yummy, Yummy, Yummy"); and some are . . . just wacky ("They're Coming to Take Me Away, Ha-Haa!"). Each of the forty entries includes a black-and-white photograph of the performing artist, the complete song lyrics, and random trivia notes about the tune's origin, the artist's background, or initial public reaction to the recording.

Identification of wacky discs has been a preoccupation of many post-World War II record collectors. Rock-era lyric lunatics learned their trade from 1940s favorites such as Spike Jones, Jimmy Durante, Louis Jordan, and Yogi Yorgesson. During the 1950s manic disc jockeys such as Cleveland's Pete "Mad Daddy" Meyers linked madcap melodies and bizarre lyrics with his own warped platter chatter to dazzle Lake Erie listeners. Most recently, Dr. Demento (a.k.a. Barry Hansen) has occupied the role of chief chronicler of crazy commentaries on CD. The extent of the novelty recording mania is amazing. From Pinkard and Bowden in country music to Weird Al Yankovic in rock, the beat goes on. Of course, without Homer and Jethro, Buchanan and Goodman, Nervous Norvus, The Coasters, Ray

---

This chapter by B. Lee Cooper and William L. Schurk was originally published as "Review of the *Wacky Top 40* by Bruce Nash and Allan Zullo," *Popular Music and Society,* XVIII (Fall 1994), pp. 91-96. Reprint permission granted by the authors, managing editor Pat Browne, and the Bowling Green State University Popular Press.

Stevens, Jerry Reed, and hundreds of other off-the-wall audio tricksters, the funny bone of popular music would have atrophied.

Nash and Zullo extend the challenge to readers who don't find their favorite wacky song in this text to send suggestions to them for a "second collection of zany tunes." Bruce and Allan don't offer to share any future royalties with generous contributors. Nevertheless, I contacted Sound Recordings Archivist Bill Schurk at Bowling Green State University to seek his advice and consultation on the following two lists (see Table 7.1). First, we sought to develop a "More Wacky Top 40" chart to out-silly, out-laugh,

TABLE 7.1. Comparative Wacky Top 40

The Nash and Zullo "Wacky Top 40"	The Cooper and Schurk "More Wacky Top 40"
1. "They're Coming to Take Me Away, Ha-Haa!" Napoleon XIV (1966)	1. "Assholes on Parade" Pat McDonald (1981)
2. "Yummy, Yummy, Yummy" Ohio Express (1968)	2. "Nee Nee Na Na Na Na Nu Nu" Dicky Doo and the Don'ts (1958)
3. "MacArthur Park" Richard Harris (1968)	3. "It's Money That I Love" Randy Newman (1979)
4. "Disco Duck" Rick Dees (1976)	4. "I Love Them Nasty Cigarettes" Jim Nesbitt (1971)
5. "You Know My Name" The Beatles (1970)	5. "Don't Wake Up the Kids" Otis Williams and the Charms (1958)
6. "Pac-Man Fever" Jerry Buckner and Gary Garcia (1982)	6. "Three Mile Island" Pinkard and Bowden (1984)
7. "(You're) Having My Baby" Paul Anka with Odia Coates (1975)	7. "Bruce" Rick Springfield (1984)
8. "Telephone Man" Meri Wilson (1977)	8. "My Ding-a-Ling" Chuck Berry (1972)
9. "The Purple People Eater" Sheb Wooley (1958)	9. "The Flying Saucer" Buchanan and Goodman (1956)
10. "Short People" Randy Newman (1977)	10. "Would Jesus Wear a Rolex?" Ray Stevens (1987)
11. "Billy, Don't Be a Hero" Bo Donaldson and the Heywoods (1974)	11. "Guns Made America Great" Pinkard and Bowden (1984)
12. "Itsy Bitsy Teenie Weenie Yellow Polka Dot Bikini" Brian Hyland (1960)	12. "Dang Me" Roger Miller (1964)

The Nash and Zullo "Wacky Top 40"

13. "Shaddap You Face"
    Joe Dolce (1981)
14. "Louie Louie"
    Kingsmen (1963)
15. "Tie Me Kangaroo Down, Sport"
    Rolf Harris (1963)
16. "Alley Oop"
    Hollywood Argyles (1960)
17. "Convoy"
    C. W. McCall (1975)
18. "Surfin' Bird"
    Trashmen (1964)
19. "Mr. Custer"
    Larry Verne (1960)
20. "The Homecoming Queen's
    Got a Gun"
    Julie Brown (1984)
21. "Junk Food Junkie"
    Larry Groce (1976)
22. "Bohemian Rhapsody"
    Queen (1975)
23. "Playground in My Mind"
    Clint Holmes (1972)
24. "Sugar, Sugar"
    Archies (1969)
25. "Y.M.C.A."
    Village People (1978)
26. "Eat It"
    Weird Al Yankovic
    (1986)
27. "Chug-a-Lug"
    Roger Miller
    (1964)
28. "Yakety Yak"
    The Coasters (1958)
29. "Kookie, Kookie (Lend Me Your
    Comb)"
    Edd Byrnes and Connie Stevens (1969)
30. "I'm Henry VIII, I Am"
    Herman's Hermits (1965)

The Cooper and Schurk "More Wacky Top 40"

13. "Transfusion"
    Nervous Norvus (1956)
14. "The Jolly Green Giant"
    Kingsmen (1965)
15. "The Naughty Lady of Shady Lane"
    Ames Brothers (1954)
16. "Ape Call"
    Nervous Norvus (1956)
17. "Beep Beep"
    Playmates (1958)
18. "Papa-Oom-Mow-Mow"
    Rivingtons (1962)
19. "Draft Dodger Rag"
    Phil Ochs (1965)
20. "Little Red Riding Hood"
    Big Bopper
    (1958)
21. "Oreo Cookie Blues"
    Lonnie Mack (1985)
22. "Mah-Na-Mah-Na"
    Piero Umilini (1960)
23. "A Boy Named Sue"
    Johnny Cash (1969)
24. "Baby Sittin' Boogie"
    Buzz Clifford (1961)
25. "Shoppin' for Clothes"
    The Coasters (1960)
26. "The Eggplant That Ate Chicago"
    Dr. West's Medicine Show and
    Junk Band (1966)
27. "Cocktails for Two"
    Spike Jones and His City Slickers,
    featuring Carl Grayson (1945)
28. "Mr. Bass Man"
    Johnny Cymbal (1963)
29. "Valley Girl"
    Frank and Moon Unit Zappa
    (1982)
30. "Two Hearts, Two Kisses"
    Frank Sinatra (1955)

TABLE 7.1 *(continued)*

The Nash and Zullo "Wacky Top 40"	The Cooper and Schurk "More Wacky Top 40"
31. "The Monster Mash" Bobby "Boris" Pickett and the Crypt-Kickers (1962)	31. "I Put a Spell on You" Screamin' Jay Hawkins (1956)
32. "Wooly Bully" Sam the Sham and The Pharaohs (1965)	32. "Uneasy Rider" Charlie Daniels Band (1973)
33. "Witch Doctor" David Seville (1958)	33. "Like a Surgeon" Weird Al Yankovic (1985)
34. "Escape (The Piña Colada Song)" Rupert Holmes (1979)	34. "Teenie Weenie Meanie" Rev. Billy C. Wirtz (1988)
35. "More, More, More" Andrea True Connection (1976)	35. "The Streak" Ray Stevens (1974)
36. "Paradise by the Dashboard Light" Meat Loaf (1978)	36. "A Dying Cub Fan's Last Request" Steve Goodman (1981)
37. "Timothy" Buoys (1971)	37. "Stranded in the Jungle" Jayhawks (1956)
38. "Shannon" Henry Gross (1976)	38. "The Trouble with Harry" Alfi and Harry (1956)
39. "Afternoon Delight" Starland Vocal Band (1976)	39. "Headaches" Allan Sherman (1963)
40. "Tie a Yellow Ribbon Round the Ole Oak Tree" Dawn, featuring Tony Orlando (1973)	40. "Does Your Chewing Gum Lose Its Flavor (On the Bedpost Overnight?)" Lonnie Donegan (1961)

out-gross, and (probably) outrage Nash and Zullo. The result of our comparative "Wacky Top 40" challenge is provided in Table 7.1.

Beyond this general comparison to Top 40 insanity, it is perhaps more entertaining and challenging to consider other wacky record lists related to specific themes. Certainly, the subject of outrageous food songs ("Jolly Green Giant," "The Eggplant That Ate Chicago," "Who Stole the Keeshka!," and "Rubber Biscuit") would be fun. Similarly, zany telephone tunes ("Beep a Freak," "Chantilly Lace," "Don't Call Us, We'll Call You," and "Obscene Phone Caller") could make a terrific book. But Bill Schurk and I elected to illustrate our theme-driven wacky Top 40 by compiling a list of songs with sexually suggestive tones. The following is an alphabetical list of the songs that we assembled.

THE COOPER AND SCHURK WACKY TOP 40
OF SEXUALLY SUGGESTIVE RECORDINGS

1. "Baby Got Back"
   Sir Mix-a-Lot (1992)
2. "Baby Scratch My Back"
   Slim Harpo (1966)
3. "Big Ten-Inch Record"
   Bull Moose Jackson (1953)
4. "Chantilly Lace"
   The Big Bopper (1958)
5. "Funky Cold Medina"
   Tone Lōc (1989)
6. "Hard to Handle"
   The Black Crowes (1991)
7. "The Horizontal BOD"
   Bob Seger and The Silver Bullet Band (1980)
8. "I Love Traci Lords"
   Ronnie Mack (1986)
9. "Jumper Cable Man"
   Marty Robbins (1981)
10. "Keep Your Hands to Yourself"
    Georgia Satellites (1986)
11. "Lady Marmalade"
    LaBelle (1975)
12. "Love Potion No. 9"
    Clovers (1959)
13. "Makin' Whoopee"
    Ray Charles (1965)
14. "Maneater"
    Daryl Hall and John Oates (1982)
15. "Midnight at the Oasis"
    Maria Muldaur (1974)
16. "My Ding-a-Ling"
    Dave Bartholomew (1952)
17. "(Night Time Is) the Right Time"
    Ray Charles (1959)
18. "No"
    Bulldog (1972)

19. "Obscene Phone Call"
    Johnny Russell (1977)

20. "One Mint Julep"
    Clovers (1952)

21. "One Night"
    Smiley Lewis (1967)

22. "Pop That Coochie"
    2 Live Crew (1991)

23. "Pull Up to the Bumper"
    Grace Jones (1981)

24. "Pump It (Nice an' Hard)"
    Icy Blu (1991)

25. "Push It"
    Salt-N-Pepa (1987)

26. "Reelin' and Rockin' "
    Chuck Berry (1972)

27. "Ring My Bell"
    Anita Ward (1979)

28. "Sixty-Minute Man"
    Dominoes (1951)

29. "Skinny Legs and All"
    Joe Tex (1967)

30. "Start Me Up"
    Rolling Stones (1981)

31. "Stoop Down Baby"
    Chick Willis (1972)

32. "Sweet Rhode Island Red"
    Ike and Tina Turner (1974)

33. "39-21-46"
    Showmen (1966)

34. "What'd I Say?"
    Ray Charles (1959)

35. "Whip It"
    Devo (1980)

36. "Wild Thing"
    Tone Lōc (1988)

37. "Work with Me Annie"
    Midnighters (1954)

38. "You Ain't Seen Nothing Yet"
    Bachman-Turner Overdrive (1974)
39. "You Can Leave Your Hat On"
    Joe Cocker (1986)
40. "You Never Done It Like That"
    Captain and Tennille (1978)

Nash and Zullo have created an interesting study on novelty recordings. They have also sparked a nationwide debate that will have pop music pundits screaming with laughter over off-the-wall recordings by Nervous Norvus, Stan Freberg, Pinkard and Borden, and Ray Stevens. What fun!

BIBLIOGRAPHY

Baker, Glenn A. "Pop Schlock: A Guide to Tasteless Records," *Goldmine*, No. 163 (October 24, 1986), pp. 32, 64.

Barnes, Ken. "The Weird World of Beatle Novelties," *Who Put the Bomp!* No. 13 (Spring 1975), pp. 13-15 (continued listing in No. 14 (Fall 1975), p. 45).

Big Bopper Bill. "Discography of 'High School U.S.A.'" *Paul's Record Magazine*, III (February 1976), p. 23.

Clark, Alan. *The Big Bopper (1930-1959): Chantilly Lace—Number Three.* West Covina, CA: Alan Lungstrum/National Rock and Roll Archives, 1989.

Cusic, Don. "Comedy and Humor in Country Music," *Journal of American Culture*, XVI (Summer 1993), pp. 45-50.

Dillingham, Mick. "Collecting Exotica," *Record Collector*, No. 174 (February 1994), pp. 90-95.

Dr. Demento. "Allan Sherman: Profile in Dementia," *Waxpaper*, III (July 7, 1978), pp. 29-32.

Duxbury, Janell R. (comp.). *Rockin' the Classics and Classicizin' the Rock: A Selectively Annotated Discography—First Supplement.* Westport, CT: Greenwood Press, 1991.

Firminger, John. "Stan Freberg," *Now Dig This*, No. 94 (January 1991), pp. 22-23.

Girmarc, George and Pat Reeder. *Hollywood Hi-Fi: Over 100 of the Most Outrageous Celebrity Recordings Ever!* New York: St. Martin's Griffin, 1995.

Gonzalez, John D. "Records Meant to Be Broken," *Lansing [Michigan] State Journal* (September 10, 1988), pp. 1D, 2D.

Guterman, Jimmy and Owen O'Donnell. *The Worst Rock 'n' Roll Records of All Time: A Fan's Guide to the Stuff You Love to Hate.* New York: Citadel Press, 1991.

Hoftede, David. "Singing TV Stars," *DISCoveries*, No. 88 (September 1995), pp. 47-51.

Lemlich, Jeffrey M. "Twistin' with Tricky: A Richard Nixon Dickography," *Goldmine*, No. 361 (May 27, 1994), p. 15.

Levy, Lester S. *Flashes of Merriment: A Century of Humorous Songs in America, 1805-1905*. Norman, OK: University of Oklahoma Press, 1971.

Lofman, Ron. *Goldmine's Celebrity Vocals: Surprising, Unexpected, and Obscure Recordings by Actors, Sports Heroes, and Celebrities*. Iola, WI: Krause Publications, 1994.

Magahern, Jim. "They're Bad, Really Really Bad," *The Detroit [Michigan] News*, (August 25, 1988), p. 2C.

Marsden, Michael T. "Da Yoopers: Business Poets of Michigan's Upper Peninsula," *Popular Music and Society*, XVIII (Winter 1994), pp. 1-6.

Mirtle, Jack, with the Assistance of Ted Hering (comps.). *Thank You Music Lovers: A Bio-Discography of Spike Jones and His City Slickers, 1941-1965*. Westport, CT: Greenwood Press, 1986.

Montgomery, Scott, with Gary Norris and Kevin Walsh. "The Invisible Randy Newman: The Metric Music to Reprise Years, 1960-1995," *Goldmine*, No. 394 (September 1, 1995), pp. 16-42, 56-75, 135-146, 152 ff.

"Outbreak of Oddball Song Hits," *Life*, XLVI (June 29, 1959), pp. 47-50.

Rowland, Mark. "He's the Kind of Guy Who Knows When Something Sounds Absurd! It's Beautiful," *Musician*, No. 123 (January 1989), pp. 28-32.

Sandmel, Ben. "Whose Toot-Toot?" *Wavelength*, No. 56 (June 1985), pp. 24-28.

Skurzewski, Bob. "Slipped Discs: Musical Oddities," *Record Collector's Monthly*, No. 6 (February 1983), p. 8.

Stidom, Larry (comp.). *Izatso?! Larry Stidom's Rock 'n' Roll Trivia and Fact Book*. Indianapolis, IN: L. Stidom, 1986.

Stidom, Larry. "Sheb Wooley a.k.a. Ben Colder: The Purple People Eater Revisited," *Goldmine,* No. 65 (October 1981), pp. 178-179.

Tamarkin, Jeff. "White House Funnies: Presidential Satire Records," *Goldmine,* No. 217 (November 18, 1988), pp. 26-27, 83-85.

Warner, Jay. "Big Daddy: Making Music for Laughs," *DISCoveries*, No. 72 (May 1994), pp. 33-35.

Woodford, Chris. "Don't Mess with My Toot Toot!" *Now Dig This*, No. 31 (October 1985), p. 25.

Young, Jordan R. *Spike Jones Off the Record: The Man Who Murdered Music*. Beverly Hills, CA: Past Times Publishing Company, 1994.

Chapter 8

Patriotism

Born in the U.S.A.: The Myth of America in Popular Music from Colonial Times to the Present. By Timothy E. Scheurer. Jackson, MS: University Press of Mississippi, 1991. 280 pp.

Born in the U.S.A. defines in broad historical perspective the influence of popular lyrics as myth-perpetuating texts. The contrasting roles of songs as contributors to cultural continuity as well as fuel for the fires of political dissent are examined via oral tradition, sheet music, and audio recordings over the past 300 years. Drawing heavily upon the social theories of Clifford Geertz, Antonio Gramsci, and Joseph Campbell, the author traces lyrical symbols relating to land, freedom and liberty, opportunity, pilgrims and patriots, and manifest destiny as defining factors in American culture. From ancient Puritan hymns to contemporary Living Color rock tunes, from Stephen Foster's regionalism to Irving Berlin's nationalism, and from Tin Pan Alley tunesmiths to Bruce Springsteen and John Mellencamp, Timothy Scheurer compares, contrasts, and offers cogent commentaries on the myths of America.

The strengths of Scheurer's study are numerous. First, the author's ability to link historical events, literary imagery, and anthropological theory with lyrical commentary generates an invaluable interdisciplinary analysis. Second, the text's chronological organization and the clarity of the author's writing style make *Born in the U.S.A.* a reasonable volume for numerous college courses. Third, the generous use of quoted or para-

The material in this chapter by B. Lee Cooper was originally published as "Review of *Born in the U.S.A.* by Timothy E. Scheurer," *Journal of American Culture*, XV (Summer 1992), pp. 91-92; and "I'll Fight for God, Country, and My Baby: Persistent Themes in American Wartime Songs," *Popular Music and Society*, XVI (Summer 1992), pp. 95-111. Reprint permission granted by the author, editor R. Serge Denisoff, managing editor Pat Browne, and the Bowling Green State University Popular Press.

phrased song lyrics throughout the work provides even novice readers with helpful examples of the imagery undergirding Scheurer's commentary. Finally, the ten-page bibliography contains a goldmine of musicological resources.

Omissions, many by design, constitute the Achilles' heel of *Born in the U.S.A.* Despite the fact that American music has been an internationally influential phenomenon since World War II, Scheurer elects to ignore all foreign singer/songwriter observations about the nature and meaning of U.S. society. Bad decision. Failing to include lyrical statements by Pete Townshend, John Lennon, Elton John, Burton Cummings, Supertramp, The Rolling Stones, and Pink Floyd is tantamount to ignoring abolitionist writers when describing the nineteenth-century political debate on American slavery. The absence of observations by such domestic performers as John Fogerty and Billy Joel is also mysterious. Beyond the specific patriotic themes and designated mythic symbols identified by Scheurer, more mundane elements of employment, public education, transportation options, and leisure images also create the essence of modern America. Perhaps a chapter on such distinctive twentieth-century features as hamburgers, telephones, blue jeans, and automobiles would enhance this fine study.

Born in the U.S.A. rivals Greil Marcus' *Mystery Train* (1975) as a longitudinal assessment of music's impact on American thought. David Pichaske's *A Generation in Motion: Popular Music and Culture in the Sixties* (1979) presents a more striking, thorough linkage between the lyrics and lifestyles during a single decade. The best analysis of the role of contemporary lyrics and popular performers on international politics as well as in American society is Robin Denselow's *When the Music's Over: The Story of Political Pop* (1989). Scheurer's informative volume should be required reading for any student of American culture, popular music, or U.S. history.

PERSISTENT THEMES IN WARTIME SONGS

International warfare has been a central concern of the American public since 1914. Whether trying to avoid involvement in conflicts among other belligerents, attempting to rationalize brief invasions of South American countries, planning and executing major European or Asian military efforts, expressing fear about diminishing national security or dread over proliferating international nuclear capability, or conducting negotiations to end specific battlefield stalemates, the United States has participated in many, many armed conflicts over the past nine decades. Popular music has both reflected and influenced most of these military adventures. In fact, twentieth-century song lyrics are replete with themes that echo public images of World War I, World War II, the Vietnam War, and the Persian Gulf War. Not surprisingly, these themes overlap in numerous instances. And even where distinctive ideas or perspectives emerge in lyrics, traditional American belief patterns or behavioral expectations march alongside the new words.

Persistent War-Related Themes

> I've a letter from my sweetheart,
> And he writes me in this way:
> "Somewhere, dear, in France we're fighting,
> But just where we dare not say.
> Be brave and do not sigh,
> And I will come back by and by.
>
> "My Sweetheart Is Somewhere in France" (1917)

> Yes, leers the universal soldier,
> And he really is to blame.
>
> "The Universal Soldier" (1965)

> Peace, love, and understanding!
> Tell me, is there no place for them today?
>
> "War" (1970)

It would be inaccurate to assume that war-related songs are only produced, marketed, or played during wartime. The ideas of isolationism, neutrality, pacifism, and general disinterest in any form of military intervention are most prevalent prior to the onset of major armed conflict. From the World War I pleas of "Don't Take My Darling Boy Away" (1915) and "I Didn't Raise My Boy to Be a Soldier" (1915) to the pre-Vietnam perspectives expressed in "Where Have All the Flowers Gone" (1962) and "Blowin' in the Wind" (1963), appeals for nonbelligerency are common during peacetime. While American troops were preparing to launch the massive aerial attack on Iraqi forces, a slightly revised version of John Lennon's Vietnam-era tune "Give Peace a Chance" (1991) achieved popularity. It is also significant to note that postwar periods are frequently filled with songs that praise the bravery of American GIs and U.S. generals, herald traditional symbols of national unity, and remind younger generations of previous battles for freedom. Recordings following World War II that featured such reflective themes included "P.T. 109" (1962), "Old Soldiers Never Die" (1951), "Stars and Stripes Forever" (1950), "Battle Hymn of the Republic" (1959), "The Battle of New Orleans" (1959), and "Ballad of the Alamo" (1960).

During wartime a variety of persistent themes appear in popular songs that reflect both political and personal concerns. Justifications for military service, whether by the voluntary route or through the draft system, are key elements in lauding the sacrifices of America's soldiers. Songs play a unique role in this difficult socialization realm. For many, the challenge, excitement and honor of service in uniform is an unquestioned citizenship obligation. Tunes such as "America, Here's My Boy" (1917), "Goodbye Dear, I'll Be Back in a Year" (1941), "The All-American Boy" (1958), and "God, Country, and My Baby" (1961) illustrate this absolute conviction. There are also several patriotic stories and historic images repeated again and again in lyrics that spark individual zeal for military commitment. "You're a Grand Old Flag" (1917), "Lafayette (We Hear You Calling)" (1918), "Yankee Doodle Boy" (1943), "Remember Pearl Harbor" (1942), and "We Did It Before (And We Can Do It Again)" (1942) are songs designed to incite support for successful war efforts. Of course, recordings that denigrate the enemy, or poke fun at rival political and military figures, also function to arouse popular support. World War II tunes were often comical, full of saber-rattling bluster, negative caricatures, and derogatory ethnic slurs. Such derisive songs included "Der Fuehrer's Face" (1942), "You're a Sap, Mr. Jap" (1942), and "Put the Heat on Hitler, Muss Up Mussolini, and Tie a Can to Japan" (1943). The Persian Gulf War, focusing public attention on the invasion to rape Kuwait ordered by the implacable Iraqi dictator, featured even more lyrically uncomplimentary songs such as "The Beast in the Middle East" (1990), "Mr. Saddam Hussein (You Must Be Insane)" (1991), and "Who'll Put a Bomb on Saddam Saddam Saddam" (1990).

Personal communications of caring and concern invariably dominate American airwaves during overseas military conflicts. Whether in the form of "Three Wonderful Letters from Home" (1918) or tape-recorded expressions of love "From a Distance" (1990), U.S. soldiers resonate to heartfelt contacts from loved ones on the home front. Naturally, letters from stateside sweethearts sometimes contain ominous warnings about personal safety during battle or unwanted direct statements about terminations of romantic relationships. "Billy, Don't Be a Hero" (1974) illustrates the fear of losing a loved one during a skirmish; "Billy and Sue" (1966) provides an example of a soldier's deadly reaction to receiving a "Dear John" message by military mail. Wartime recordings also frequently allude to the protective mantle of a Supreme Being guarding U.S. troops from harm as they pursue their God-ordained frightening missions. These songs do not label enemy soldiers as either atheistic or beyond prayerful concern. They simply highlight the ideals of liberty, honor, justice, truth, and equality around which American war aims are invariably crafted. Songs of religious support include: "God Be with Our Boys Tonight" (1918), "Say a Prayer for the Boys Over There" (1918), "God Bless America" (1942), "Praise the Lord and Pass the Ammunition" (1942), "The Battle Hymn of the Republic" (1959), and "God Bless the U.S.A." (1991). Certain popular singers such as John McCormack, Kate Smith, and Lee Greenwood have become synonymous with tunes of spiritual support for American war efforts.

Recordings containing lyrics related to the battlefield perspectives of U.S. troops tend to emphasize two issues: the dreary nature of military existence away from home and apart from loved ones; and the universal desire for an immediate, victorious end to current hostilities. The initial idealism expressed in "God, Country, and My Baby" (1961) is countered by the stark realism of battlefield fear, fatigue, and boredom. The latter two issues are particularly well illustrated in "Pack Up Your Troubles in Your Old Kit Bag and Smile, Smile, Smile" (1917), "Oh, How I Hate to Get Up in the Morning" (1918), "Life in a Trench in Belgium" (1918), "(Lights Out) 'Til Reveille" (1941), and "This Is the Army, Mr. Jones" (1942). Postwar normalcy beckons. Peace is the much-desired goal. Soldiers, their families, and their sweethearts long for lyrics that eulogize a peaceful existence after war even as the battles rage. Songs full of hopeful postwar imagery are: "Keep the Home Fires Burning" (1917), "Some Day They're Coming Home Again" (1918), "(There'll Be Bluebirds Over) The White Cliffs of Dover" (1942), "When the Lights Go On Again (All Over the World)" (1942), "I'll Be Coming Home" (1991), "My Baby's Coming Home" (1991), and "When Johnny Comes Marchin' Home Again" (1991).

Wartime Themes Representing Different Perspectives

Every day I kiss his picture,
And I tell him I'll be true.
Just as he is to his country,
And the old red, white, and blue.
Both day and night I yearn,
I pray and pray for his return.

"My Sweetheart Is Somewhere in France" (1917)

Well come on all of you big, strong men,
Uncle Sam needs your help again.
He's got himself in a terrible jam,
Away off yonder in Viet-Nam.

"I-Feel-Like-I'm-Fixin'-to-Die Rag" (1969)

By the time we got to Woodstock,
We were half a million strong.
And everywhere was a song and a celebration.

"Woodstock" (1970)

War is an enemy to all mankind.
The thought of war blows my mind.

"War" (1986)

Although both World War I and World War II spawned songs that challenged the practice of universal military conscription, that questioned the appropriateness of military intervention, and that championed U.S. neutrality, the lengthy American military involvement in Southeast Asia produced the most hostile barrage of antiwar songs during the twentieth century. Echoes of recordings from the late 1960s and the early 1970s are still heard during the early 1990s. Such prominent and influential song-writers as Bob Dylan, John Lennon, Phil Ochs, and John Fogerty spawned the audio attack against military actions being perpetrated in Vietnam, Cambodia, and elsewhere. Prior U.S. war efforts against Germany, Japan, Mexico, Cuba, and elsewhere were examined and condemned in "Masters of War" (1967), "With God on Our Side" (1962), and "I Ain't Marchin' Anymore" (1969); the practice of forced conscription was ridiculed in "The Draft Dodger Rag" (1966) and "I Feel-Like-I'm-Fixin'-to-Die Rag" (1969); the belligerent behavior of politicians, generals, and superpatriotic citizens was cynically condemned in "Fortunate Son" (1969) and "Eve of Destruction" (1965), and the skeptical attitude of an alienated youth culture was captured in the tune "War" (1970), which featured the repetitious chant: "War! What is it good for? Absolutely nothing!" As might be expected, there were frequent patriotic responses to this troubadour tirade against U.S. military activity in Southeast Asia. Many Americans churned with nationalistic anger at the antiwar manifestos, protest marches, and draft resistance meetings that used popular lyrics to support their positions. "Gallant Men" (1966), "Okie from Muskogee" (1969), and "The Fightin' Side of Me" (1970) contained typical recorded responses.

Themes unleashed in the antiwar songs of the Vietnam era were more often more theoretical, more personalized, and more idealistic than statements found in tunes from World War I, World War II, or the later Persian Gulf War. "2+2=?" (1968) questioned the meaning of losing a close friend to a bullet in a foreign jungle land; "Who Will Answer?" (1967) pondered the reason for the senseless death of a young father; "Woodstock" (1970) dreamed of deadly bombers being miraculously transformed into harmless butterflies; and "Won't Get Fooled Again" (1971) promised that look-alike, sound-alike politicians would not be able to trick the next generation into any fruitless, glory-hunting military excursions. The idealism of international peace spurred numerous 1960s singers and 1970s songwriters. Rather than either prewar warning or postwar mourning, there was a tremendous outpouring of pacificist emotions and world-without-war imagery between 1967 and 1975. Specifically, these songs included: "The Ballad of John and Yoko" (1969), "Give Peace a Chance" (1969), "Lay Down (Candles in the Rain)" (1970), "Imagine" (1971), "Love Train" (1973), and "There Will Never Be Peace (Until God Is Seated at the Conference Table)" (1974).

The Continuing Battle of Wartime Themes

"Viva Pershing" is the cry across the sea,
We're united in this fight for liberty.
France sent us a soldier, brave Lafayette,
Whose deeds and fame we cannot forget.
Now that we have the chance,
We'll pay our debt to France.

"Goodbye Broadway, Hello France" (1917)

Looking backward through the ages,
We can read on history's pages,
Deeds that famous men have done . . .
Take our own great Revolution,
That began our evolution,
Washington then won his fame.
Today across the sea,
They're making history,
The Yankee spirit still remains the same.

"Just Like Washington Crossed the Delaware,
General Pershing Will Cross the Rhine" (1918)

For I marched to the battles of the German trench,
In a war that was bound to end all wars.
Oh, I must have killed a million men,
And now they want me back again.

"I Ain't Marchin' Anymore" (1969)

Now come on Generals, let's move fast,
Your big chance is here at last.
Now you can go out and get those Reds,
'Cause the only good Commie is one that's dead.

"I-Feel-Like-I'm-Fixin'-to-Die Rag" (1969)

The Persian Gulf War, the amazingly brief, almost clinical military annihilation of the Iraqi army, featured a return to more traditional war-time themes. Yet in the years between the hasty American withdrawal from Saigon in 1975 and the deadly air barrage over Baghdad in 1991, the lyrical battles over war aims and objectives continued. The radio airwave battlefield featured performers of high stature and sincere commitment, including Bruce Springsteen, Don Henley, The Charlie Daniels Band, Billy Joel, and Lee Greenwood. Songs that carried forth the debate included: "In America" (1980), "Still in Saigon" (1982), "Goodnight Saigon" (1983), "Born in the U.S.A." (1984), and "War" (1986). The final shot of the pacificist argument prior to the devastating outbreak of Operation Desert Storm was "Give Peace a Chance" (1991).

Concluding Comments

It's time for every boy to be a soldier,
To put his strength and courage to the test.
It's time to place a musket on his shoulder,
And wrap the stars and stripes around his breast.

It's Time for Every Boy to Be a Soldier" (1917)

Goodbye Mama, I'm off to Yokohama,
For the red, white, and blue,
My country and you.
Goodbye Mama, I'm off to Yokohama,
Just to teach all those Japs,
That the Yanks are no saps.

"Goodbye Mama (I'm Off to Yokohama)" (1942)

When I saw the cities burning,
I knew that I was learning,
That I ain't a-marchin' anymore.

"I Ain't Marchin' Anymore" (1969)

The preceding pages offer a brief illustration of the most persistent lyrical themes related to American military activity between 1914 and 1991. The consistency of these recorded perspectives is intriguing. The unanticipated pluralism of pro-war and antiwar commentaries that emerged during the Vietnam War is also fascinating. This preliminary analysis will hopefully stimulate students of oral history, popular culture, propaganda, communication studies, military history, American studies, journalism, and musicology to probe more deeply into the meaning and influence of war-related recordings. Clearly, an expanded perspective is required to comprehend the adaptations of songs such as "Tie a Yellow Ribbon Round the Ole Oak Tree" (1973), "Rock the Casbah" (1982), "God Bless the U.S.A." (1984), and "Somewhere Out There" (1986) as pro-military anthems during the Persian Gulf War. Similarly, the recycling of particular songs such as "War" (first by Edwin Starr in 1970, and then by Bruce Springsteen in 1986), "Give Peace a Chance" (first by John Lennon in 1969, and then by The Peace Choir in 1991) and "The Battle of New Orleans" (first by Johnny Horton in 1959, then by Harpers Bizarre in 1968, and finally by The Nitty Gritty Dirt Band in 1974) deserves investigation. Finally, the issue of whether particular American musical genres—blues, country, folk, pop, and rock—tend to produce more patriotic or more ideologically consistent sets of war songs is a subject awaiting conclusive scholarly treatment.

The final portion of this essay presents a theme-defined listing of war-related songs. Titles and release dates of illustrative recordings are listed below each theme. Most of these records can be obtained for either instructional use or research purposes by contacting Sound Recordings Archivist William L. Schurk at The Jerome Library of Bowling Green State University in Bowling Green State University in Bowling Green, Ohio 43403.

Hear them calling you and me,
Every son of liberty.
Hurry right away, no delay, go today.
Make your daddy glad to have had such a lad.
Tell your sweetheart not to pine,
To be proud her boy's in line.

"Over There" (1917)

Goodbye dear, I'll be back in a year,
'Cause I'm in the Army now.
They picked my number out of a hat,
There's nothing a guy can do about that . . .

"Goodbye Dear, I'll Be Back in a Year" (1941)

Come on fathers, don't hesitate,
Send your sons off before it's too late.
Be the first one on your block
To have your boy come home in a box.

"I Feel-Like-I'm-Fixin'-to-Die Rag" (1969)

War, I despise,
'Cause it means destruction of innocent lives.
War means tears to thousands of mothers' eyes,
When their sons go off to fight and lose their lives.

"War" (1986)

DISCOGRAPHY OF WARTIME SONGS
AND THEIR THEMES

Admiration for the Valor of U.S. Soldiers

- "Over There" (1917)
- "The Yanks Are at It Again" (1918)
- "Tell That to the Marines" (1919)
- "There'll Be a Hot Time in the Town of Berlin (When the Yanks Go Marching In)" (1943)
- "She Wore a Yellow Ribbon" (1949)
- "The Ballad of the Green Berets" (1966)
- "Gallant Men" (1966)
- "He Wore a Green Beret" (1966)
- "The Battle Hymn of Lt. Calley" (1971)
- "Another Old Soldier" (1990)
- "Desert Storm" (1991)
- "The Eagle" (1991)
- "Voices That Care" (1991)

Anticipation of Soldiers Returning to Civilian Life

- "Keep the Home Fires Burning" (1917)
- "Somewhere in France Is Daddy" (1917)
- "Bring Back My Soldier Boy to Me" (1918)
- "Just a Baby's Prayer at Twilight (For Her Daddy Over There)" (1918)
- "Some Day They're Coming Home Again" (1918)
- "Baby's Prayer Will Soon Be Answered" (1919)
- "Dreaming of Home, Sweet Home" (1919)
- "Oh, How I Wish I Could Sleep Until My Daddy Comes Home" (1919)
- "When the Boys Come Home" (1919)
- "Don't Sit Under the Apple Tree (With Anyone Else But Me)" (1942)
- "(There'll Be Bluebirds Over) The White Cliffs of Dover" (1942)
- "When the Lights Go On Again" (1942)
- "They're Either Too Young or Too Old" (1943)
- "Bring the Boys Home" (1971)
- "Billy, Don't Be a Hero" (1974)
- "Welcome Home Soldier" (1990)
- "Dear Little Soldier" (1991)
- "I'll Be Coming Home" (1991)
- "My Baby's Coming Home" (1991)
- "When Johnny Comes Marchin' Home Again" (1991)

Antiwar Statements and Indictments of Weapons Dealers

- "Only a Pawn in Their Game" (1969)
- "The Universal Soldier" (1965)
- "The Cruel War" (1966)
- "I Ain't Marchin' Anymore" (1969)
- "Kill for Peace" (1966)
- "Masters of War" (1967)
- "The War Drags On" (1967)
- "2 + 2 = ?" (1968)
- "The Ballad of John and Yoko" (1969)
- "Fortunate Son" (1969)
- "Give Peace a Chance" (1969)
- "Stop the War Now" (1970)
- "War" (1970)
- "Military Madness" (1971)

- "War Song" (1972)
- "Undercover (Of the Night)" (1983)
- "War Games" (1983)
- "War" (1986)

Communications Between U.S. Soldiers and the American Home Front

- "Hello Central, Give Me No Man's Land" (1918)
- "Three Wonderful Letters from Home" (1918)
- "V-Mail from a Female" (1943)
- "Soldier's Last Letter" (1944)
- "To a Soldier Boy" (1959)
- "Billy and Sue" (1966)
- "To Susan on the West Coast Waiting" (1969)
- "Soldier's Last Letter" (1971)
- "Billy, Don't Be a Hero" (1974)
- "Somewhere Out There" (1986)
- "From a Distance" (1990)
- "Dear Little Soldier" (1991)
- "I'll Be Coming Home" (1991)

Death on the Battlefield

- "Eve of Destruction" (1965)
- "Billy and Sue" (1966)
- "The Draft Dodger Rag" (1966)
- "Who Will Answer?" (1967)
- "2 + 2 = ?" (1968)
- "The Unknown Soldier" (1968)
- "I Feel-Like-I'm-Fixin'-to-Die Rag" (1969)
- "War" (1970)
- "War" (1986)

Domestic Unrest Related to Military Involvement

- "The Times They Are a-Changin' " (1964)
- "Eve of Destruction" (1965)
- "Home of the Brave" (1965)
- "The Universal Soldier" (1965)
- "Seven O'Clock News/Silent Night" (1966)

- "For What It's Worth (Stop, Hey What's That Sound)" (1967)
- "Who Will Answer?" (1967)
- "Outside of a Small Circle of Friends" (1968)
- "2 + 2 = ?" (1968)
- "Fortunate Son" (1969)
- "America, Communicate with Me" (1970)
- "Ball of Confusion (That's What the World Is Today)" (1970)
- "Ohio" (1970)
- "War" (1970)
- "Chicago" (1971)
- "(For God's Sake) Give More Power to the People" (1971)
- "What's Going On" (1971)
- "Won't Get Fooled Again" (1971)
- "Born in the U.S.A." (1984)
- "War" (1986)

Idealism Seeking a World Without War

- "Friendship Train" (1969)
- "Lay Down (Candles in the Rain)" (1970)
- "Woodstock" (1970)
- "Imagine" (1971)
- "Peace Train" (1971)
- "Love Train" (1973)

Mocking Enemy Soldiers, Their Countrymen, and Their Political Leaders

- "Der Fuehrer's Face" (1942)
- "Let's Take a Rap at the Jap" (1942)
- "Mussolini's Letter to Hitler" (1942)
- "Put the Heat on Hitler, Muss Up Mussolini, and Tie a Can to Japan" (1943)
- "Slap the Jap Right Off the Map" (1943)
- "They're Going to Be Playing Taps on the Japs" (1943)
- "We've Got a Job to Do on the Japs, Baby" (1943)
- "You're a Sap, Mr. Jap" (1942)
- "On the Day of Hitler's Funeral" (1943)
- "A Message to Khomeini" (1979)
- "Bomb Iran" (1980)
- "Rock the Casbah" (1982)

- "Welcome to the Jungle" (1988)
- "The Beast in the Middle East" (1990)
- "Iraq Is Robbin' " (1990)
- "The Ballad of Saddam Hussein" (1991)
- "Letter to Saddam Hussein" (1991)
- "Mr. Saddam Hussein (You Must Be Insane)" (1991)

Mundane Nature of Noncombative Military Life

- "Pack Up Your Troubles in Your Old Kit Bag and Smile, Smile, Smile" (1917)
- "Life in a Trench in Belgium" (1918)
- "Oh, How I Hate to Get Up in the Morning" (1918)
- "Boogie Woogie Bugle Boy" (1941)
- "(Lights Out) 'Til Reveille" (1941)
- "He Wears a Pair of Silver Wings" (1942)
- "This Is the Army, Mr. Jones" (1942)
- "A Fellow on Furlough" (1944)
- "Dogface Soldier" (1955)

Patriotic Reactions to Antiwar Statements, Protest Marches, and Draft Evasions

- "For Your Country and My Country" (1917)
- "Dawn of Correction" (1965)
- "An Open Letter to My Teenage Son" (1967)
- "This Is My Country" (1968)
- "Okie from Muskogee" (1969)
- "The Fightin' Side of Me" (1970)
- "In America" (1980)
- "Still in Saigon" (1982)
- "The Flags Fly High" (1990)
- "Proud to Be an American for Freedom" (1991)

Prewar Pleas for Isolationism, Neutrality, or Peace

- "I Didn't Raise My Boy to Be a Soldier" (1915)
- "I Think We've Got Another Washington (Wilson Is His Name)" (1916)
- "Where Have All the Flowers Gone" (1962)
- "Blowin' in the Wind" (1963)

- "The Universal Soldier" (1963)
- "Give Peace a Chance" (1991)

Promoting Public Support for the War Effort

- "Let's All Be American Now" (1917)
- "Over There" (1917)
- "God Be with Our Boys Tonight" (1918)
- "Lafayette (We Hear You Calling)" (1918)
- "Liberty Loan March" (1918)
- "The Yanks Are at It Again" (1918)
- "Any Bonds Today?" (1941)
- "Arms for the Love of America" (1941)
- "Remember Pearl Harbor" (1942)
- "We Did It Before (And We Can Do It Again)" (1942)

Reactions to the Draft System and Voluntary Military Service

- "Don't Take My Darling Boy Away" (1915)
- "I Didn't Raise My Boy to Be a Soldier" (1915)
- "America, Here's My Boy" (1917)
- "(Goodbye, and Luck Be with You) Laddie Boy" (1917)
- "Goodbye Dear, I'll Be Back in a Year" (1941)
- "Twenty-One Dollars a Day—Once a Month" (1941)
- "Goodbye, Mama (I'm Off to Yokohama)" (1942)
- "The All-American Boy" (1958)
- "God, Country, and My Baby" (1961)
- "The Universal Soldier" (1965)
- "Draft Dodger Rag" (1966)
- "Greetings (This Is Uncle Sam)" (1966)
- "I Ain't Marchin' Anymore" (1969)
- "Draft Resister" (1969)
- "Fortunate Son" (1969)
- "I Feel-Like-I'm-Fixin'-to-Die Rag" (1969)
- "It's for God, Country and You, Mom" (1969)

Religious Imagery Supporting Military Activities

- "The Battle Hymn of the Republic" (1917)
- "God Be with Our Boys Tonight" (1918)
- "Say a Prayer for the Boys Over There" (1918)

- "God Bless America" (1942)
- "Praise the Lord and Pass the Ammunition" (1942)
- "Comin' in on a Wing and a Prayer" (1943)
- "I Had a Little Talk with the Lord" (1944)
- "The Battle Hymn of the Republic" (1968)
- "It's for God, Country and You, Mom" (1969)
- "God Bless the U.S.A." (1991)

Romantic Involvements of U.S. Soldiers

- "If He Can Fight Like He Can Love (Good Night Germany)" (1918)
- "My Belgian Rose" (1918)
- "The Soldier's Sweetheart" (1927)
- "Don't Sit Under the Apple Tree (With Anyone Else but Me)" (1942)
- "Johnny Doughboy Found a Rose in Ireland" (1942)
- "Cleanin' My Rifle (And Dreamin' of You)" (1944)
- "Shoo-Shoo Baby" (1944)
- "She Wore a Yellow Ribbon" (1949)
- "To a Soldier Boy" (1959)
- "Soldier Boy" (1962)
- "Kiss Me Sailor" (1964)
- "Navy Blue" (1964)
- "He Wore a Green Beret" (1966)
- "Ruby, Don't Take Your Love to Town" (1969)
- "To Susan on the West Coast Waiting" (1969)
- "Somewhere Out There" (1986)
- "From a Distance" (1990)

Support for Pacifism and Peace Negotiations

- "Where Have All the Flowers Gone" (1962)
- "Blowing' in the Wind" (1963)
- "The Cruel War" (1966)
- "Peace Brother Peace" (1968)
- "Give Peace a Chance" (1969)
- "Peace Will Come (According to Plan)" (1970)
- "Peace Train" (1971)
- "We Got to Have Peace" (1971)
- "There Will Never Be Peace (Until God Is Seated at the Conference Table)" (1974)
- "Give Peace a Chance" (1991)

Symbols of Military Honor and National Unity

- "For Dixie and Uncle Sam" (1916)
- "Star-Spangled Banner" (1917)
- "Stars and Stripes Forever March" (1917)
- "You're a Grand Old Flag" (1917)
- "Just Like Washington Crossed the Delaware, General Pershing Will Cross the Rhine" (1918)
- "LaFayette (We Hear You Calling)" (1918)
- "Liberty Bell (It's Time to Ring Again)" (1918)
- "Patriotic March Medley" (1929)
- "The Son-of-a-Gun Who Picks On Uncle Sam" (1942)
- "Stars and Stripes Forever" (1942)
- "There's a Star-Spangled Banner Waving Somewhere" (1943)
- "Yankee Doodle Boy" (1943)
- "Battle of New Orleans" (1959)
- "The Declaration" (1970)
- "The Battle of New Orleans" (1974)
- "Star-Spangled Banner" (1991)
- "These Colors Never Run" (1991)

BIBLIOGRAPHY

Austlander, Ben H. "If Ya Wanna End War and Stuff, You Gotta Sing Loud: A Survey of Vietnam-Related Protest Music," in *American Popular Music—Volume Two: The Age of Rock,* edited by Timothy E. Scheurer. Bowling Green, OH: Bowling Green State University Popular Press, 1989, pp. 179-184.

Ballard-Reisch, Deborah. "China Beach and Tour of Duty: American Television and Revisionist History of the Vietnam War," *Journal of Popular Culture,* XXV (Winter 1991), pp. 135-149.

Bindas, Kenneth J. and Craig Houston. "Takin' Care of Business: Rock Music, Vietnam, and the Protest Myth," *The Historian,* LII (November 1989), pp. 1-23.

Braubard, Stephen R. *Mr. Bush's War: Adventures in the Politics of Illusion.* New York: Hill and Wang, 1991.

Chilcoat, George W. "The Images of Vietnam: A Popular Music Approach," *Social Education,* XLIX (October 1985), pp. 601-603.

Cleveland, Les. "When We Send the Last Yank Home: Wartime Images of Popular Culture," *Journal of Popular Culture,* XVIII (Winter 1984), pp. 31-36.

Cooper, B. Lee. "Military Conflicts," in *A Resource Guide to Themes in Contemporary American Song Lyrics, 1950-1985.* Westport, CT: Greenwood Press, 1986, pp. 101-109.

Cooper, B. Lee. "Popular Songs, Military Conflicts, and Pubic Perceptions of the United States at War," *Social Education,* LVI (March 1992), pp. 150-158.

Denisoff, R. Serge. "Fighting Prophecy with Napalm: 'The Ballad of the Green Berets,' " *Journal of American Culture,* XIII (Spring 1990), pp. 81-93.

Denisoff, R. Serge and William D. Romanowski. "The Pentagon's Top Guns: Movies and Music," *Journal of American Culture,* XII (Fall 1989), pp. 67-78.

Ellison, Mary. "War—It's Nothing But a Heartbreak: Attitudes to War in Black Lyrics," *Popular Music and Society,* X (Fall 1986), pp. 29-42.

Herring, George C. *America's Longest War: The U.S. and Viet-Nam, 1950-1975* (Second Edition). New York: Alfred A. Knopf, Inc., 1986.

Hesbacher, Peter and Les Waffen. "War Recordings: Incidence and Change, 1940-1980," *Popular Music and Society,* VIII (Summer/Fall 1982), pp. 77-101.

Landon, Philip J. "From Cowboy to Organization Man: The Hollywood War Hero, 1940-1955," *Studies in Popular Culture,* XII (Winter 1989), pp. 28-41.

Lees, Gene. "1918-1968: From Over There to Kill for Peace," *High Fidelity,* XVIII (November 1968), pp. 56-60.

Lingeman, Richard A. *Don't You Know There's a War On?* New York: G.P. Putnam's Sons, 1970.

Litoff, Judy Barrett and David C. Smith. " 'Will He Get My Letter?': Popular Portrayals of Mail and Morale During World War II," *Journal of Popular Culture,* 23 (Spring 1990), pp. 21-43.

Marsh, Dave. "Life During Wartime," *Rock and Roll Confidential*, No. 86 (March 1991), pp. 1-4.

Mohnnann, G.P. and F. Eugene Scott. "Popular Music and World War II. The Rhetoric of Continuation," *Quarterly Journal of Speech*, XLII (February 1976), pp. 145-156.

Murdoch, Brian. *Fighting Songs and Warring Words: Popular Lyrics of Two World Wars.* London: Routledge, 1990.

O'Brien, Tim. *The Things They Carried.* New York: Houghton-Mifflin Company, 1990.

Philbin, Marianne (ed.). *Give Peace a Chance: Music and the Struggle for Peace.* Chicago: Chicago Review Press, 1983.

Ridgeway, James (ed.). *The March to War: From Day One to War's End and Beyond.* New York: Four Walls Eight Windows Press, 1991.

Rodnitzky, Jerome. *Minstrels of the Dawn: The Folk-Protest Singer As a Cultural Hero.* Chicago: Nelson-Hall, Inc., 1976.

Scheurer, Timothy E. *Born in the U.S.A.: The Myth of America in Popular Music from Colonial Times to the Present.* Jackson, MS: University Press of Mississippi, 1991.

Shain, Russell Earl. *An Analysis of Motion Pictures About War Released by the American Film Industry 1939-1970.* New York: Arno Press, 1976.

Shindler, Colin. *Hollywood Goes to War: Films and American Society, 1939-1952.* Boston: Routledge Books, 1979.

Strada, Michael J. "Kaleidoscopic Nuclear Images of the Fifties," *Journal of Popular Culture,* XX (Winter 1986), pp. 179-198.

Suid, Lawrence. *Guts and Glory: Great American War Movies.* Reading, MA: Addison-Wesley Publishing Company, 1978.

Tischler, Barbara L. "One Hundred Percent Americanism and Music in Boston During World War I," *American Music*, IV (Summer 1986), pp. 164-176.

Titus, Constandina A. and Jerry L. Simich. "From 'Atomic Bomb Baby to Nuclear Funeral': Atomic Music Comes of Age, 1945-1990," *Popular Music and Society*, XII (Winter 1990), pp. 11-37.

VanDevanter, Lynda and Joan Furey (eds.). *Visions of War, Dreams of Peace: Writings of Women in the Vietnam War*. New York: Warner Books, 1991.

Waffen, Less and Peter Hesbacher. "War Songs: Hit Recordings During the Vietnam Period," *ARSC Journal*, XIII (Spring 1981), pp. 4-18.

Woll, Allen L. *The Hollywood Musical Goes to War*. Chicago: Nelson-Hall, Inc., 1983.

Young, Marilyn B. *The Vietnam Wars, 1945-1990*. New York: Harper Perennial Books, 1991.

Chapter 9

Popular Music

The Seventh Stream: The Emergence of Rocknroll in American Popular Music. By Phillip H. Ennis. Hanover, NH: Wesleyan University Press, 1992. Illustrated. 445 pp.

Using the single word "rocknroll" to define a specific type of music that developed in the United States after World War II, Phillip Ennis argues that the American recording industry was significantly altered artistically, politically, and economically by the advent of this new sound. Actually, the author's primary metaphor is liquid rather than auditory. Ennis contends that before 1945 American popular music was a broad river of sound flowing in six homogeneous streams—white pop, country, black pop (rhythm and blues), gospel, jazz, and folk. However, during the twenty years after Hiroshima a dynamic, independent, and heterogeneous seventh stream emerged. This radical rocknroll rivulet owed its origins to the artistry of composers and performers from the other six tributaries of modern American music, although it originally appeared to emerge solely from the melding of country and R&B in the persona of Elvis Presley. Ennis eschews such a simplistic explanation. The multiple causation approach that he elucidates is so thorough, so complex, and yet so reasonable that it staggers the imagination. This is twentieth-century musical history at its best.

The Seventh Stream is a distinctive, defining contribution to the study of American popular music. The author joins the ranks of Charlie Gillett (*The Sound of the City: The Rise of Rock and Roll,* Rev. ed. 1983), R. Serge Denisoff (*Tarnished Gold: The Record Industry Revisited,* 1986), and Simon Frith (*Sound Effects: Youth, Leisure, and the Politics of Rock*

The book and record reviews in this chapter by B. Lee Cooper have appeared in several issues of *Popular Music and Society.* Reprint permission granted by the author, managing editor Pat Browne, and the Bowling Green State University Popular Press.

'n' Roll, 1981) as the foremost sociological commentators on recording industry policies, practices, and results. In addition to being a compelling, cogent academic writer, though, Phillip Ennis is also an ethnomusicologist, geographer, statistician, demographer, storyteller, and sage. These traits and interests translate into knowledgeable perceptions about the rock era that are fascinating, fruitful, funny, and intellectually stimulating.

The foundation idea for this study was undoubtedly born in 1953 when Ennis worked with William N. McPhee and Rolf Meyersohn on a commercial project for the Bureau of Applied Social Research at Columbia University. This study was titled "The Disk Jockey: A Study of the Emergence of a New Occupation and Its Influence on Popular Music in America." Four decades later Ennis presents a rigorously researched, carefully argued collage of conclusions not only about key radio gatekeepers (Bill Randle, Alan Freed, the WDIA jocks, and others), but also concerning musical property rights, impacts of new technologies, social movements, business shifts (Nashville, Hollywood, and Detroit), expanding audiences, new performance venues (festivals, rock concerts, and MTV), and revolutionary performers (from Little Richard, Connie Francis, and Jerry Lee Lewis to Hammer, Madonna, and Bruce Springsteen) that launched, sustained and continue to maintain unpredictable rocknroll's vitality.

The Seventh Stream is an invigorating, yet exhausting volume. The author is a relentless thinker and a superb illustrator of each and every hypothesis or generalization he offers. Charts and tables abound. Footnotes are both historically supportive and wonderfully explanatory. Each page contains a new insight that sparks further thought. This is not a volume to be taken lightly. On the other hand, it is not a dry, technical, overly verbose scholarly tome. Ennis is eminently readable, and because of his sly humor, he is capable of investing criticism and praise, heroes and villains with marvelous and mirthful descriptions. For instance, the comparisons of Mitch Miller and Phil Spector (pp. 270-275), Pat Boone and Elvis Presley (pp. 243-252), and Bill Anson and Bill Randle (pp. 148-159) demonstrate tremendous insight into both flamboyant personalities and the public perceptions they produced.

Many authors are adept at assembling the details of a particular musical period and then reporting them in a clear, well-organized fashion. Other writers abandon such detail in favor of constructing a theory. They sketch in only the broadest strokes the overarching ideas and philosophies of a specific era. Phillip Ennis assumes both literary responsibilities. *The Seventh Stream* weaves facts, figures, and dates into a seamless historical web of aesthetic, business, and sociopolitical trends. The birth of rocknroll is depicted so wisely and so well by Ennis that no future investigation of this topic will be able to avoid reference to Ennis's interpretations.

* * *

Reelin' and Rockin'—The Golden Age of American Rock 'n' Roll: Volume Two, 1956-1959. By Lee Cotten. Ann Arbor, MI: Popular Culture, Ink., 1995. Illustrated. 506 pp.

This hefty volume chronicles the roots of the rock era in three distinct formats: in chronological events (touring activities, recording sessions, and concert appearances of Louis Jordan, Chuck Berry, Elvis Presley, and others), through monthly hit song charts (featuring "The Great Pretender," "Wake Up Little Susie," "Mack the Knife," and others), and with biographies (profiling Paul Anka, Frankie Lymon, Larry Williams, and others). The detail is spectacular. The organization is clear. Best of all, the historical hindsight is twenty-twenty in respect to the diversity, perversity, and complexity of rock's raucous, joyous birth.

Lee Cotten initiated his "Golden Age of Rock 'n' Roll" series for Popular Culture, Ink. in 1989. The initial volume, *Shake, Rattle and Roll,* covered the transitional rhythm and blues period of 1952-1955. This study, rivaled only by Galen Gart's magnificent annual explorations of R&B music for Big Nickel Publications, constitutes a landmark linkage of gospel, country, pop, blues, jump, swing, and the other pesky musical streams that fed the rock 'n' roll flood of the mid-1950s. Cotten's study doesn't eclipse prior analyses by Charlie Gillett, Phillip Ennis, Nick Tosches, Peter Guralnick, and other music history scholars; however, his thorough, consistent chronological explication of dates, names, songs, and events puts colorful flesh on the skeletal theories of many previous writers. *Reelin' and Rockin'* continues the marvelous process of unearthing the richness of rock.

The genius of Cotten's achievement is found in the stylistic balance he maintains. As a Presley-oriented researcher (author of *The Elvis Catalog*—1987, *Did Elvis Sing in Your Hometown?*—1995, *All Shook Up*—1985, and *Jailhouse Rock*—1983), the temptation to overwhelm readers with Elvis minutiae could have been a tragic flaw in this text. At the other extreme, as illustrated in the shallow biographical work of Norm N. Nite and the populist overview of rock espoused by Dick Clark, Cotten could have randomly listed names and dates without supplying either context or priority. The author skillfully avoids both errors. His aim is true. What is especially tantalizing about his perspective, though, is the breadth and depth of his rock 'n' roll definition. America's youth culture adopted a vast array of recording heroes and heroines because they provided a multiplicity of images in their lyrics: heartbreak and romance, rebellion and obedience, failure and success, cheating and loyalty. The musical genres of the late 1950s were as diverse as the song themes, featuring doo-wop, rockabilly, R&B, pop ballads, folk, calypso, and numerous novelty tunes. *Reelin' and Rockin'* rekindles this vitality. Cotten names names (Buchanan and Goodman, Dell-Vikings, Sanford Clark, Connie Francis, Little Richard, Gene Vincent, Jimmy Reed, Marty Robbins, and others) that will initially mean little to members of Generation X, to most rap enthusiasts, or to many Garth Brooks fans. Yet contemporary music of all genres was nurtured in the rich soil of 1950s rhythm 'n' rock.

This study, along with Volume One, deserves a place on the bookshelf of every baby boomer who wants to revel in the real roots of rock. More significantly, though, music librarians, popular culture researchers, students of pre-Beatles recording practices, and teachers of twentieth-century American history can glean a tremendous amount of worthwhile information from *Reelin' and Rockin'*. This is no . . . Trivial Pursuit.

* * *

Doowop: The Chicago Scene. By Robert Pruter. Champaign, IL: University of Illinois Press, 1996. Illustrated. 304 pp.

This well-researched, richly detailed historical study examines the emergence, success, and subsequent decline of close-harmony singing by African American recording artists in Chicago between 1945 and the late 1960s. Using a combination of direct telephone interviews with doo-wop singers, personal discussions with record industry personnel and prominent disc collectors, and research drawn from local newspapers (*Chicago Defender* and *Chicago Tribune*), classic music magazines (*Record Exchanger, Story Untold*, and *Bim Bam Boom*), and noteworthy book-length studies, Robert Pruter has assembled a perceptive, fact-filled overview of the vocal bridge between 1940s rhythm and blues and 1960s soul. Actually, his thesis is even more succinct. Doo-wop provided the transitional sound between R&B and rock 'n' roll.

Doowop: The Chicago Scene is structured to reveal how black folk art/street singing was translated into an immensely popular commercial enterprise. Tales related by Pruter involve South Side entrepreneurial thrusts by talent scouts, disc jockeys, and independent record company owners as they navigated the swift currents of musical change in post-World War II America. For Chicago, an ethnically rich city that had experienced a marked influx of black workers and their families since 1920, the stories of blue-collar leisure music are too rich to be limited to blues, jazz, or any other single genre. Yet the attraction of a capella harmony defied reason. Neither lyric nor melody could explain the sense of feeling, emotion, and freedom that encouraged young men of color to soar beyond the universal pain of poverty, segregation, and personal employment disasters. The flickering goal of financial gain offered by recording for the Chance, Parrot, Chess, United, or Vee Jay labels was directly connected to the possibility of individual celebrity. And celebrity was related to recognition, honor, and prestige. Doo-wop singing became verbal jousting to establish claims to audio knighthood. Pruter recounts story after story of young black men seeking personal recognition through their group's creativity, discipline, and enthusiasm. The myth of an NBA contract is far less reasonable today than the goal of a hit single in the 1950s, when gold could be garnered by harmonizing on "See Saw," "Sincerely," or "I'll Be Home."

Pruter's *Doowop* is riddled with group titles and individual participants, club names and locations, radio stations and disc jockeys, and recording companies and their management teams. Unlike current corporate America, the 1950s music scene in Chicago was largely unorchestrated and painfully unpredictable. Pruter not only shares a wealth of facts; he also explodes several myths, urging new ways of viewing old performers. Specifically, the author rejects the proposition that black and white musical acts of the 1950s rarely shared the same concert stage. He notes that The Everly Brothers, Buddy Holly, Jerry Lee Lewis, The Diamonds, or Danny and The Juniors were often booked at the same concert appearance with Frankie Lymon, Sam Cooke, Jackie Wilson, or Larry Williams (p. 239). Another intriguing insight by Pruter concerns the fact that rhythmic rocker Bo Diddley was fascinated by doo-wop harmony and incorporated much vocal group styling complexity into his rambling, rolling repertoire (pp. 71-78).

The only complaint that seems reasonable after reading and analyzing this superb piece of regional scholarship relates to the failure of the author to provide sufficient national perspective. Pruter waits until he has completed his entire volume to engage the reader in a provocative discussion concerning the historical image of doo-wop throughout America. This is an error. What Pruter has to say about stylistic validation, critical judgment, nostalgia patterns, and the ignorance of current music critics concerning 1940s, 1950s, and 1960s musical trends is too valuable to be consigned to "Afterword" status (pp. 245-252). The cultural dialogue that the author seeks needs to be pressed through a full-scale reevaluation of 1950s music. Although the shoulders of the giants (Charlie Gillett, Galen

Gart, Peter Grendysa, Phil Groia, Anthony J. Gribin, Matthew M. Schiff, and Jay Warner) remain available in print to glimpse beyond the musical horizon, the creative revision of rock's birth decade still remains to be drafted. The richness of doo-wop, country, R&B, rock 'n' roll, blues, and pop that bombarded the Eisenhower-era airwaves demands more attention. Nostalgia isn't sufficient. The paradigm shift from big band/pop music was much more than an Elvis sneer, a Pat Boone shoe, or the teacher hollering at Chuck Berry. Rediscovering doo-wop's vitality is a significant but humble beginning. Much more digging, thinking, and writing is still required.

With the publication of *Doowop* (1996) as a follow-up to *Chicago Soul* (1991), Robert Pruter has established his reputation as the preeminent commentator on Windy City music of the 1950s, 1960s, and 1970s. Of course, a larger challenge still beckons. Will Pruter's next volume focus on Chicago's most vibrant, vociferous musical mode—the electric blues? From Chess/Checker to Alligator Records, the raunchy sounds that influenced The Rolling Stones and Eric Clapton deserve the kind of historical perspective and analytical clarity that are the benchmarks set by Pruter's two University of Illinois Press volumes.

* * *

Go Cat Go! Rockabilly Music and Its Makers, by Craig Morrison. Urbana, IL: University of Illinois Press, 1996. Illustrated. 326 pp.

Canadian ethnomusicologist Craig Morrison has deftly transformed his 1984 York University master's thesis into a definitive study of rockabilly music. This book is a gem! Unlike most rockabilly mavens, Morrison is a professionally trained musician, a lucid writer, a savvy sociologist, and a critical yet balanced evaluator of singers, songwriters, and songs. The blending of such theoretical strength and musical knowledge is rare among popular music commentators.

The genius of this investigation resides in the author's pursuit of cultural meaning rather than just stylistic definition. Morrison explores the rockabilly phenomenon as musical integration—(country and western performers tackling rhythm and blues tunes), youthful rebellion, sexual exploration, and regional recording experimentation. From the Memphis-based explosion of Elvis Presley, Carl Perkins, and Jerry Lee Lewis to the worldwide revivalism of Robert Gordon, The Stray Cats, Matchbox, and The Cramps, Morrison probes gender patterns, instrumentation structures, lyric themes, vocalization techniques, dress codes, and personal idiosyncrasies that connote and denote rockabilly. Biographical sketches constitute more than half of the volume. These vignettes are masterfully concise yet revealing, although not especially well documented.

The most challenging issue addressed in this volume concerns genre vitality and continuity. Is rockabilly music a truly distinctive stylistic form of American audio artistry, or was it simply a brief historical phenomenon (1954-1960) that has since spawned several copycat performers who are merely guitar-strumming caricatures of their earlier recording heroes? Morrison argues both cases admirably. Yet it is apparent that while twentieth-century blues stylists have moved from their early roots (Robert Johnson, Muddy Waters, and Elmore James) to reverence toward classic living artists (John Lee Hooker and B. B. King) to the emergence of new superstars (Robert Cray, Eric Clapton, Son Seals, and Joe Louis Walker), the rockabilly path from the 1950s to the musical present is much more artistically tortured and commercially narrow. Could rockabilly be only a brief transitional phase of modern rock? For that matter, was rock 'n' roll only a momentary precursor of the more lethal rock performed by The Rolling Stones, Black Sabbath, and Metallica? *Go Cat Go! Rockabilly Music and Its Makers* ponders many significant questions and proposes a variety of plausible answers.

While *Go Cat Go!* features an exemplary song title index and selected discography, the chapter notes are sparse and the bibliography section is surprisingly weak. Morrison may have decided that his personal interviews with rockabilly artists and his own theoretical insights were more valuable than previous rockabilly publications by others. Yet in a work of this scholarly caliber, it is mandatory to acknowledge literary trails forged by earlier critics, journalists and historians. Among the works omitted from Morrison's resource listing are:

Bane, Michael. *White Boy Singin' the Blues: The Black Roots of White Rock*. New York: Da Capo Press, 1992 (c. 1982).

Becker, Bart. *'Til the Cows Come Home: Rock 'n' Roll Nebraska*. Seattle, WA: Real Gone Books, 1985.

Blackburn, Richard (comp.). *Rockabilly: A Comprehensive Discography of Reissues*. No location noted: R. Blackburn, 1975.

Booth, Stanley. *Rythm Oil: A Journey Through the Music of the American South*. New York: Pantheon Books, 1991.

Clark, Alan (comp.) *Legends of Sun Records*. West Covina, CA: Alan C. Lungstrum/National Rock and Roll Archives, 1986.

Clark, Alan (comp.) *Legends of Sun Records—Number Two*. West Covina, CA: Alan C. Lungstrum/National Rock and Roll Archives, 1992.

Clark, Alan (comp.). *Rock-a-Billy and Country Legends—Number Two*. West Covina, CA: Alan C. Lungstrum/National Rock and Roll Archives, 1989.

Clark, Alan (comp.) *Rock-a-Billy and Country Legends—Number Three.* West Covina, CA: Alan C. Lungitrum/National Rock and Roll Archives, 1990.

Colman, Stuart. *They Kept on Rockin': The Giants of Rock 'n' Roll.* Poole, Dorset, England: Blandford Press, 1982.

Cooper, B. Lee and Wayne S. Haney. *Rockabilly: A Bibliographic Resource Guide.* Metuchen, NJ: Scarecrow Press, 1990.

Cotten, Lee. *Shake, Rattle, and Roll—The Golden Age of American Rock 'n' Roll: Volume One, 1952-1955.* Ann Arbor, MI: Pierian Press, 1989.

Cotten, Lee. *Reelin and Rockin': The Golden Age of American Rock 'n' Roll: Volume Two, 1956-1959.* Ann Arbor, MI: Popular Culture, Ink., 1995.

Dawson, Jim and Steve Propes. *What Was the First Rock 'n' Roll Record?* Boston: Faber and Faber, 1992.

DeWitt, Howard A. *Elvis: The Sun Years—The Story of Elvis Presley in the Fifties.* Ann Arbor, MI: Popular Culture, Ink., 1993.

Escott, Colin. *Tattooed on Their Tongues: A Journey Through the Backrooms of American Music.* New York: Schirmer Books, 1996.

Forte, Dan. "The Roots of Rockabilly," *Guitar Player*, XVII (December 1983), 67-70, 96-98.

Frew, Timothy. *Rockabilly: The Life, Times, and Music Series.* New York: Friedman/Fairfax Publishers, 1996.

Fumar, Vincent. "Rockabilly: The Differences Between Rockabilly Then and Now Range from Slight to Vast, *Wavelength*, No. 18 (April, 1982), 19-20.

Garland, Phyl. "Basic Library of Rhythm-and-Blues," *Stereo Review*, XLII (May 1979), pp. 72-77.

Gordon, Mike. "Rockabilly," *Record Collector*, No. 13 (September 1980), 29-32.

Guralnick, Peter. "The Million Dollar Quartet," *New York Times Magazine* (March 25, 1979), 28-30 ff.

Guralnick, Peter. "Rockabilly," in *The Rolling Stone Illustrated History of Rock and Roll* (Revised Edition), edited by Anthony DeCurtis and James Henke, with Holly George-Warren. New York: Random House, 1992, pp. 67-72.

Hull, Robert A. and J. Sasfy. "B-I Bickey-Bi, Bo-Bo-Go: Rockabilly's Radio Moment," *Creem*, XI (February, 1980), 30-31 ff.

Isler, Scott. "Rockabilly: A Historical Overview," *Country Style*, No. 63 (August 1981), pp. 10-12.

Kiefer, Kit. "Rockabilly Boogie," in *They Called It Rock: The Goldmine Oral History of Rock 'n' Roll,* Iola, WI: Krause Publications, 1991, pp. 38-57.

Kinder, Bob. *The Best of the First: The Early Days of Rock and Roll.* Chicago: Adams Press, 1986.

Kirsch, Don. "Rockabilly Roots of Major Country Stars," *Goldmine*, No. 120 (March 1, 1985), pp. 32, 80.

Kirsch, Don. "Those Rockabilly Ladies and Their Collectibility," *Goldmine*, No. 124 (April 26, 1985), 75.

Millar, Bill. "In the Farms and on the Forecourts: The Short-Lived Heyday of Rockabilly," *History of Rock*, No. 6 (1982), pp. 112-113.

Millar, Bill. "Rockabilly: Was His the Purist Style of Rock?" *History of Rock*, No. 6 (1982), pp. 101-103.

Morthland, John. "Rockabilly," in *The Best of Country Music: A Critical and Historical Guide to the 750 Greatest Albums.* Garden City, NY: Dolphin/Doubleday, 1984, pp. 239-279.

Norman, Philip. *Rave On: The Biography of Buddy Holly.* New York: Simon and Schuster, 1996.

North, Chris. "From Blue Caps to Stray Cats: How Rockabilly Came Back in the Seventies," *History of Rock*, No. 6 (1982), pp. 118-120.

Oermann, Robert K. "Those Wild, Wild Women," *Country Style*, No. 69 (August, 1981), pp. 38-40.

Osborne, Jerry. "DISCoveries Mailbox," *DISCoveries*, II (December, 1989), pp. 8-12. [Reactions to Wayne Stierle's article of October 1989.]

Palmer, Robert. "C'mon Everybody: Rockabilly Outside Memphis," in *Country: The Music and the Musicians*, edited by Paul Kingsbury and Alan Axelrod. New York, Abbeville Press, 1988, pp. 296-297.

Palmer, Robert. "Get Rhythm: Elvis Presley, Johnny Cash, and the Rockabillies," in *Country: The Music and the Musicians* (revised and updated editions), edited by Paul Kingsbury and The Country Music Foundation. New York: Abbeville Press, 1994, pp. 193-211.

Perkins, Carl and David McGee. *Go, Cat, Go! The Life and Times of Carl Perkins.* New York: Hyperion Press, 1996.

Raper, Jim. "Fifties Rockabilly in the United Kingdom," *Record Collector,* No. 139 (March 1991), pp. 84-87.

Redd, Lawrence N. *Rock Is Rhythm and Blues: The Impact of Mass Media.* East Lansing, MI: Michigan State University Press, 1974.

Rockabilly! Milwaukee, WI: Hal Leonard Publishing Corporation, 1993.

"Rockabilly: A Fusion of Country and Rock 'n' Roll," *Billboard,* LXXV (November 2, 1963), pp. 1-40.

"Rockabilly in the Compact Disc Age . . ." *Goldmine*, No. 273 (January 11, 1991), pp. 126-128.

Schoemer, Karen. "Rockabilly Music: Far from Dead and Not for Misfits, *The New York Times* (May 11, 1990), pp. 1C, 22C.

Scott, Frank, Al Ennis, and the Staff of Roots and Rhythm. *The Roots and Rhythm Guide to Rock*. Pennington, NJ: A Capella Books, 1993.

Stierle, Wayne. "Rockabilly Music? There's No Such Thing!" *DISCoveries*, II (October, 1989), p. 144.

Sumrall, Harry. *Pioneers of Rock and Roll: 100 Artists Who Changed the Face of Rock*. New York: Billboard Books, 1994.

Tosches, Nick. "The Rise of Rockabilly," *Country Music*, VIII (January-February, 1980), pp. 32-35.

Tosches, Nick. *Unsung Heroes of Rock 'n' Roll: The Birth of Rock 'n' Roll in the Dark and Wild Years Before Elvis*. New York: Charles Scribner's Sons, 1984.

Executive editor Judith McCulloch continues to attract marvelous manuscripts for the University of Illinois Press "Music in American Life" Series. Recent contributions by Robert Pruter, Burton Peretti, Steven Loza, and others have provided spectacular insights into the crazy quilt artistry of twentieth-century music. *Go Cat Go! Rockabilly Music and Its Makers* is a sterling contribution to the advancement of knowledge about a much-maligned, little-understood, but absolutely key transitional element in American popular music and culture.

* * *

From Blues to Rock: An Analytical History of Pop Music. By David Hatch and Stephen Millward. Manchester, England: Manchester University Press, 1987. 217 pp.

This fascinating volume lives up to its title. David Hatch and Stephen Millward present a well-illustrated, carefully argued analysis of the transmission of country/folk blues into popular music vernacular. The authors employ both song texts and musical transcriptions to explain their thesis. The links that they assemble between Blind Lemon Jefferson and Carl Perkins ("Matchbox Blues"), Robert Johnson and Cream ("Crossroads Blues"), Joe Turner and Elvis Costello ("Honey Hush"), and Buddy Holly and The Rolling Stones ("Not Fade Away") firmly establish a continuing chain of contemporary music from 1920 through the 1980s. Clearly, sources and styles of music beyond the blues evolved simultaneously—and were influenced similarly by twentieth-century changes in social environment, technology, political climate and individual artistry. But Hatch and Willward note that the tap root of America's multimillion-dollar recording industry is found in black-and-white song interchanges over the past seventy years.

Unlike many earlier blues-to-rock diatribes, this study neither glorifies *all* black artists nor condemns *all* white followers. Ideology, commercialism, and racism are downplayed in this volume in favor of historical accuracy, artistic evolution, and theoretical analysis. While the creative genius of performers such as Robert Johnson and Jimmie Rodgers is readily acknowledged, similar acclaim is also provided for Eric Clapton and Mick Jagger. Early in *From Blues to Rock* the authors sketch out a three-stage musical learning curve. This device enables them to demonstrate elements of song-family extensions through direct copying (initial stage), through improvisation on given lyrics or notation systems (second stage), and through the creation of new material within the blues family format. This oversimplified description hardly does justice to the complex, thoughtful scheme of analysis that permeates this exceptional work.

Like the best works of Charlie Gillett (*The Sound of the City*) and Peter Guralnick (*Sweet Soul Music*), this volume bristles with sociological and ethnomusicological perceptions that may startle the reader. Comments about Hank Williams' live performances being much more blues-oriented than his historic studio cuts, about the decline of rock 'n' roll occurring not in the traditionally accepted 1959-1963 period but during the so-called rock opera period of 1967-1973, and about the evolution of Bruce Springsteen's lyrics are worthy of reflection and debate. Similarly, assertions about the key roles of Chuck Berry, Bo Diddley, and other blacks in the rise of rock 'n' roll are perceptive and provocative.

This brief volume deserves to be read and discussed by popular music fans and scholars alike. It should spark both thinking and rethinking about modern music in America.

* * *

Come Go with Me: The History of Dot Records—Volume Two (Varese Sarabande VSD 5687). By The Dell-Vikings, Tab Hunter, Carol Jarvis, Sanford Clark, Travis and Bob, Dodie Stevens, Pat Boone, Nick Todd, The Shields, Jim Lowe, Jimmy Dee, Jimmy Gilmer, Ronnie Love, and Arthur Alexander. Studio City, CA: Varese Sarabande Records, 1996. Fourteen songs.

Randy Wood's Dot label, founded in 1950 by the owner of Randy's Record Shop in Gallatin, Tennessee, benefitted from a strong stable of vocalists (Pat Boone, Gale Storm, The Fontane Sisters, and The Hilltoppers) and intense promotion from Nashville radio station WLAC. Producing cover versions of hit recordings by other artists was the label's trademark. However, this anthology highlights Dot's most original releases between 1956 and 1963. From chart-topping novelties ("The Green Door" by Jim Lowe and "Sugar Shack" by Jimmy Gilmer and The Fireballs) through classic period pieces ("Come Go with Me" by The Dell-Vikings, "The Fool" by Sanford Clark, and "Tell Him No" by Travis and Bob), to obscure rockers ("Henrietta" by Jimmy Dee and "Chills and Fever" by Ronnie Love), the original achievements of Dot are proudly paraded. Beatle fans should especially enjoy Arthur Alexander's 1962 rendition of his own composition "Anna (Go to Him)" that The Fab Four recorded and released in 1963.

While Volume One (VSD 5686) of this series features Dot's more productive, more famous artists, this disc is much more fascinating as an illustration of the diversity of songs, styles, and artists that populated popular music charts during rock's first decade.

* * *

Chess Rhythm and Roll (MCA/Chess CHD 4-9352). Universal City, CA: Chess/MCA Records, 1994.

The King R&B Box Set (King KBSCD 7002). Nashville, TN: King Records, 1995.

The R&B Box: 30 Years of Rhythm and Blues (Rhino R2-71806). Los Angeles: Rhino Records, 1994. Six discs.

No single term can accurately describe the dynamic, rhythmic, rocking music that pervaded black American communities from 1945 through 1975. Still, rhythm and blues (R&B) is the most commonly applied descriptor. The difficulty ethnomusicologists experience in deciphering the roots and branches of early R&B (blues, jazz, gospel, big band, and so on) and then in explaining their transformation into middle and late R&B (doo-wop, rock 'n' roll, soul, and so on) is understandable. The magnitude of the recorded music produced, the diversity of artists who composed, played, and sang R&B tunes, and the inability of music critics, journalists, or record companies to categorize either performers or performed material sustains the mythic nature of the R&B flood. The three box sets reviewed here provide valuable insights tell the whole story. No collection ever will.

Chess Rhythm and Roll highlights ninety-nine songs. This retrospective of rock 'n' roll and R&B traces the vinyl progeny of Leonard and Philip Chess's Chicago-based label (originally "Aristocrat") from 1947 to 1967. Coverage ranges from the ridiculous—The Five Blazes, Clarence Samuels, and The Dozier Boys—to the sublime—Chuck Berry, The Dells, and

Etta James. The collection taps numerous classic tunes ("Rocket 88," "Sincerely," "I'll Be Home," "Ain't Got No Home," and "Suzie Q") and various rockin' dudes (Bo Diddley, Jimmy McCracklin, Little Milton, and The Moonglows). It features pathos, humor, social commentary, instrumental wizardry, and group harmony. The key player for the company *and* for the multifaceted R&B transition is clearly singer/songwriter/guitarist Chuck Berry.

The King R&B Box Set, with extensive notes by Colin Escott, features eighty-five songs. This compilation constitutes an ostensible tribute to King Records founder Syd Nathan. But the Cincinnati entrepreneur is upstaged by the raucous stable of R&B stars that parade their audio wares in this 1945 through 1965 revue. Early hits by Bull Moose Jackson, Wynonie Harris, Roy Brown, Lonnie Johnson, and Ivory Joe Hunter were followed by later smashes by Little Willie John, Bill Doggett, Hank Ballard, Freddy King, and James Brown. Signature selections include "Honky Tonk," "Fever," "The Twist," "Hideaway," and "Hearts of Stone." The transitional characters among the King artists were many, but The Dominoes, The Platters, Little Willie John, and James Brown constitute the most gifted interpreters.

The R&B Box is a magnificently far-reaching, inclusive collection of recording artists and hit songs from 1943 through 1972. Obviously, the focus of the 108-song review is rhythm and blues. But unlike either the Chess or the King sets, the Rhino compilation spans several prominent recording companies and thus illustrates more broadly the popular trends reflecting the evolution of black music. The six discs cover a variety of classic artists: first, Louis Jordan, Joe Liggins, Roy Milton, and Percy Mayfield; second, Jackie Brenston, The Orioles, Joe Turner, and The Penguins; third, Ray Charles, Smiley Lewis, The Five Satins, and Jesse Belvin; fourth, The Coasters, Jerry Butler, Clyde McPhatter, and The Marcels; fifth, Gene Chandler, Marvin Gaye, Little Milton, and The Four Tops; and sixth, The Isley Brothers, Aaron Neville, Otis Redding, and The Spinners. The song selections are as noteworthy as the artists featured on this nationwide R&B tour. (The Rhino compilers even apologize for licensing restrictions that forced them to omit selections by Sam Cooke, Stevie Wonder, Cecil Gant, Hank Ballard, Little Willie John, and a few others.)

Although several other box sets of R&B tunes are currently on the market (Atlantic, Stax/Volt, Fire/Fury, Motown, Specialty, and Sue), one can glean a tremendous amount of information and understanding from these three releases. The lessons are sometimes surprising. First, R&B is a misnomer. The sounds of Chess, King, and the six-disc Rhino box are the essence of twentieth-century American popular music, not simply an amusing ethnic subset. As Rhino booklet contributor Billy Vera so wisely confesses, this music is designed to be universal entertainment. It is functional, for dancing or courtship. Specially, Vera notes that ". . . a high-minded concept such as art was not the foremost consideration, but an occasional by-product." Wouldn't it be pleasant to have such candor and honesty come from analysts of 1920s, 1930s, and 1940s pop tunes as well? Second, (with very few exceptions) women were generally relegated to song subject status rather than song performer recognition during the 1945-1965 period. Although some fascinating R&B mamas are included in each of the three sets (Mitzi Mars, Sugar Pie DeSanto, Etta James, Lulu Reed, Little Esther, Annie Laurie, Nellie Lutcher, Faye Adams, LaVern Baker, Ruth Brown, and Doris Troy) along with a few notable female groups (Martha and The Vandellas, The Chantels, and Patti LaBelle and The Bluebelles), it is apparent that only the dawning of gospel/pop/soul diva Aretha Franklin brought black R&B women to center stage. Third, booklet authors Peter Grendysa, Billy Vera, and Colin Escott are too politically correct to attempt to rate the influence of particular R&B performers. Too bad. Stylists such as Ray Charles, Solomon Burke, Clyde McPhatter, Sam Cooke, James Brown, Jackie Wilson, and Chuck Berry are remarkably heroic figures in the musical integration of post-World War II America. Like The Beatles, these gifted artists were at once eclectic and distinctive. They owed their styles to an amalgamation of borrowed traits as well as to their own individual talents. They were gutsy, glamorous, and gifted. Being black in a white society added mystery, personal pressure, and charisma. Bing and Frank pale by comparison.

Fourth, the three box sets reveal the synergistic commercial connections of businessmen (Syd Nathan, The Chess Brothers, Sam Phillips, and others), local radio station owners and disc jockeys, and club and theater proprietors in seeking, promoting, displaying, and garnering revenue from a new product—namely, popular music. The mysticism of record company moguls is largely reduced to greed; the love of melodies and lyrics is strictly a union between performers and record buyers. So it is. So it always shall be. Finally, the diversity of tunes (comedy, balladry, and rhythmic rock), singing styles, and instrumentation screams vitality, freedom, and enjoyment. *The R&B Box* in particular lends ample testimony to the truth that good music knows no color, no age, and no audio boundaries.

Is there anything dramatically wrong with any of these collections? Yes. They all lack balance. The Chess set opts too often for historical obscurity and fails to provide sufficient samples of superior R&B performances by Chess's more well-known artists (with the single exception of Chuck Berry). The King Box focuses so heavily on Syd Nathan's toughguy image and his early 1950s speeches that it largely ignores— gulp!—James Brown. The Rhino set is (in Mercer lingo) too marvelous for words. However, in showcasing *everyone* only once, there is little way to comprehend the immense and broad contributions of those stars whose careers spanned several decades. Mary Wells doesn't equate to Marvin Gaye; Eddie Floyd can't match The Isley Brothers; The Spinners aren't The Temptations; and *nobody* can beat Ray Charles, Joe Turner, Fats Domino, Solomon Burke, Otis Redding, or Aretha Franklin.

BIBLIOGRAPHY

Broven, John. "The Rhythm and Blues Explosion, 1943-1949—Part One," *Juke Blues*, No. 3 (December, 1985), pp. 19-22.

Broven, John. *Rhythm and Blues in New Orleans*. Gretna, LA: Pelican Publishing, 1978.

Brown, Ashley. "The Roots of Soul," *The History of Rock,* No. 17 (1982), pp. 321-322.

Callahan, Mike. "The Vee-Jay Story—Part One: Scenes from a Family Owned Company," *Goldmine*, No. 60 (May 1981), pp. 6-18 and 163.

Callahan, Mike. "The Vee-Jay Story—Part Two: Vee-Jay Is Alive and Living in Burbank," *Goldmine*, No. 60 (May 1981), pp. 161-163.

Cantor, Louis. *Wheelin' on Beale: How WDIA-Memphis Became the Nation's First All-Black Radio Station and Created the Sound That Changed America.* New York: Pharos Books, 1992.

Clark, Chris. "Chicago to London: Pye International R&B." *Record Collector*, No. 166 (June 1993), pp. 109-113.

Cotten, Lee. *Reelin' and Rockin': The Golden Age of American Rock 'n' Roll— Volume Two: 1956-1959*. Ann Arbor, MI: Popular Culture, Ink., 1995.

Cotten, Lee. *Shake, Rattle, and Roll—The Golden Age of American Rock 'n' Roll: Volume One—1952-1955*. Ann Arbor, MI: Pierian Press, 1989.

Cummings, Tony. "Roots, Forerunners, and Originators," in *The Soul Book*, edited by Ian Hoare, Tony Cummings, Clive Anderson, and Simon Frith. New York: Dell Publishing, 1976, pp. 1-38.

Dawson, Jim and Steve Propes. *What Was the First Rock 'n' Roll Record?* Boston: Faber and Faber, 1992.

Doggett, Peter. "Rhythm Boxes," *Record Collector*, No. 170 (July 1994), pp. 116-118.

Ennis, Philip H. *The Seventh Stream: The Emergence of Rocknroll in American Popular Music*. Hanover, NH: Wesleyan University Press, 1992.

Escott, Colin. *Tattooed on Their Tongues: A Journey Through the Backrooms of American Music*. New York: Schirmer Books, 1996.

Fancourt, Les (comp.) *Chess R&B: A Discography of the R&B Artists on the Chess Labels, 1947-1975* (Second Edition). Faversham Kent, England: Les Fancourt, 1991.

Ferlingere, Robert D. (comp.) *A Discography of Rhythm & Blues and Rock 'n' Roll Vocal Groups 1945 to 1965.* Hayward, CA: California Trade School, 1976.

Garland, Phyl. "Basic Library of Rhythm-and-Blues," *Stereo Review,* XLII (May 1979), pp. 72-77.

Gart, Galen (comp.) *First Pressings—Volume One 1948-1950: Rock History As Chronicled in Billboard Magazine.* Milford, NH: Big Nickel Publications, 1986.

Gart, Galen (comp.) *First Pressings—Volume Two 1951-1952: Rock History As Chronicled in Billboard Magazine.* Milford, NH: Big Nickel Publications, 1986.

Gart, Galen (comp.) *First Pressings: The History of Rhythm and Blues—Special 1950 Volume.* Milford, NH: Big Nickel Publications, 1993.

Gart, Galen (comp.) *First Pressings—The History of Rhythm and Blues: Volume One—1951.* Milford, NH: Big Nickel Publications, 1991.

Gart, Galen (comp.). *First Pressings—The History of Rhythm and Blues: Volume Two—1952.* Milford, NH: Big Nickel Publications, 1992.

Gart, Galen (comp.). *First Pressings—The History of Rhythm and Blues: Volume Three—1953.* Milford, NH: Big Nickel Publications, 1989.

Gart, Galen (comp.). *First Pressings—The History of Rhythm and Blues: Volume Four—1954.* Milford, NH: Big Nickel Publications, 1989.

Gart, Galen (comp.). *First Pressings—The History of Rhythm and Blues: Volume Five—1955.* Milford, NH: Big Nickel Publications, 1990.

Gart, Galen (comp.) *First Pressings—The History of Rhythm and Blues: Volume Six—1956.* Milford, NH: Big Nickel Publications, 1991.

Gart, Galen (comp.). *First Pressings—The History of Rhythm and Blues: Volume Seven—1957.* Milford, NH: Big Nickel Publications, 1993.

Gart, Galen (comp.). *First Pressings—The History of Rhythm and Blues: Volume Eight—1958.* Milford, NH: Big Nickel Publications, 1995.

Gart, Galen and Roy C. Ames, with contributions from Ray Funk, Rob Bowman, and David Booth. *Duke/Peacock Records: An Illustrated History with Discography.* Milford, NH: Big Nickel Publications, 1990.

Gillett, Charlie. *Making Tracks: Atlantic Records and the Growth of a Multi-Billion-Dollar Industry.* New York: E.P. Dutton and Co., 1974.

Gillett, Charlie. *The Sound of the City: The Rise of Rock and Roll* (Second Edition, newly illustrated and expanded). New York: Da Capo Press, 1996 (c. 1983).

Gonzalez, Fernando (comp.). *Disco-File: The Discographical Catalog of American Rock & Roll and Rhythm & Blues Vocal Harmony Groups, 1902 to 1976* (Second Edition). Flushing, NY: F. L. Gonzalez, 1977.

Grendysa, Peter A. "The Okeh Label, 1951-1958," *DISCoveries,* No. 58 (March 1993), pp. 31-37.

Gribin, Anthony J. and Matthew M. Schiff. *Doo-Wop: The Forgotten Third of Rock 'n' Roll.* Iola, WI: Krause Publications, 1992.

Groia, Philip. *They All Sang on the Corner: A Second Look at New York City's Rhythm and Blues Vocal Groups* (Revised Edition). West Hempstead, NY: Phillie Dee Enterprises, Inc., 1984.

Guralnick, Peter. *Sweet Soul Music: Rhythm and Blues and the Southern Dream of Freedom.* New York: Harper and Row, 1986.

Hannusch, Jeff (a.k.a. Almost Slim). *I Hear You Knockin': The Sound of New Orleans Rhythm and Blues.* Ville Platte, LA: Swallow Press, 1985.

Hansen, Barry. "Doo-Wop" and "Rhythm and Gospel," in *The Rolling Stone Illustrated History of Rock and Roll* (fully revised and updated), edited by Anthony DeCurtis and James Henke, with Holly George-Warren. New York: Random House, 1992, pp. 17-20 and 92-101.

Haralambos, Michael. *Right On: From Blues to Soul in Black America.* New York: Drake Publishers, 1975.

Hildebrand, Lee. *Stars of Soul and Rhythm and Blues.* New York: Billboard Books, 1994.

Hirshey, Gerri. *Nowhere to Run: The Story of Soul Music.* New York: Da Capo Press, 1994 (c. 1984).

Jancik, Wayne. "Fire-Fury Records," *Goldmine*, No. 315 (August 1992), p. 2022.

Jones, LeRoi (a.k.a. Imamu Amiri Baraka). *Blues Peoples: Negro Music in White America.* New York: William Morrow, 1963.

Kamin, Jonathan. "Taking the Roll Out of Rock 'n' Roll: Reverse Acculturation," *Popular Music and Society,* II (Fall 1972), pp. 1-17.

Kamin, Jonathan. "The White R&B Audience and the Music Industry, 1952-1956," *Popular Music and Society,* No. 4 (Fall 1975), 170-187.

Karp, Kitty. "R&B Pioneer Awards," *DISCoveries,* No. 96 (May 1996), 2023.

Kiefer, Kit (ed.). *They Called It Rock: The Goldmine Oral History of Rock 'n' Roll, 1950-1970.* Iola, WI: Krause Publications, 1991.

King, Woodie Jr. "Searching for Brothers Kindred: Rhythm & Blues of the 1950's," *The Black Scholar,* VI (November 1974), pp. 19-30.

Koppel, Martin. "Introduction to a Label: The Chicago Sound of Okeh," *Soul Survivor,* No. 5 (Summer 1986), pp. 24-26.

Kreiter, Jeff. *45 R.P.M. Group Collector's Record Guide: A Guide to Valuable Recordings of Rhythm & Blues/Doowops/Vocal Group Sounds from 1950-1992.* Wheeling, WV: Boyd Press, 1993.

Leichter, Albert. *Discography of Rhythm & Blues and Rock & Roll, Circa 1946-1964: A Reference Manual.* Staunton, VA: A. Leichter, 1975.

Lepri, Paul. *The New Haven Sound, 1946-1976.* New Haven, CT: Paul Lepri, 1977.

Levine, Lawrence W. *Highbrow/Lowbrow: The Emergence of Cultural Hierarchy in America.* Cambridge, MA: Harvard University Press, 1988.

Lichtenstein, Grace and Laura Dankner. *Musical Gumbo: The Music of New Orleans.* New York: W. W. Norton, 1993.

Martin, Linda and Kerry Segrave. *Anti-Rock: The Opposition to Rock 'n' Roll.* New York: Da Capo Press, 1993 (c. 1988).

Marsh, Dave. "The Okeh Series: An American Treasure," *Rolling Stone,* No. 368 (April 1982), pp. 53-54.

Maultsby, Portia K. "Rhythm and Blues, 1945-1955: A Survey of Styles," in *Black American Popular Music: Rhythm and Blues 1945-1955*, compiled by B. J. Reagon. Washington, DC: National Museum of American History and The Smithsonian Institution, 1986, pp. 6-23.

McCourt, Tom. "Bright Lights, Big City: A Brief History of Rhythm and Blues, 1945-1957," in *American Popular Music—Volume Two: The Age of Rock,* edited by Timothy E. Scheurer. Bowling Green, OH: Bowling Green State University Popular Press, 1989, pp. 46-62.

McCutcheon, Lynn Ellis. *Rhythm and Blues: An Experience and Adventure in Its Origin and Development.* Arlington, VA: Beatty Publications, 1971.

McEwen, Joe. "The Sound of Chicago," in *The Rolling Stone Illustrated History of Rock and Roll* (fully revised and updated), edited by Anthony DeCurtis and James Henke, with Holly George-Warren. New York: Random House, 1992, pp. 171-176.

McKee, Margaret and Fred Chisenhall. *Beale Black and Blue: Life and Music on Black America's Main Street.* Baton Rouge, LA: Louisiana State University Press, 1981.

Millar, Bill. "Rhythm and Blues," *The History of Rock,* No. 2 (1982), pp. 29-32.

Nelson, George. *The Death of Rhythm and Blues.* New York: Pantheon Books, 1988.

O'Gorman, Pete. "King Records: The Early Years of the Mid-West Monarch," *Now Dig This,* No. 93 (December 1990), pp. 4-7.

Pavlow, Al (comp.) *Big Al Pavlow's the R&B Book: A Disc-History of Rhythm and Blues.* Providence, RI: Music House Publishing, 1983.

Pearson, Barry. "Jump Steady: The Roots of R&B." In *Nothing But the Blues: The Music and the Musicians,* compiled by Lawrence Cohn. New York: Arbeville Press, 1993, pp. 313-345.

Pruter, Robert (ed.). *The Blackwell Guide to Soul Recordings.* Oxford, England: Basil Blackwell, Ltd., 1993.

Pruter, Robert. *Chicago Soul.* Champaign-Urbana, IL: University of Illinois Press, 1991.

Pruter, Robert. *Doowop: The Chicano Scene.* Urbana: University of Illinois Press, 1996.

Redd, Lawrence N. *Rock Is Rhythm and Blues: The Impact of Mass Media.* East Lansing, MI: Michigan State University Press, 1974.

Redd, Lawrence N. "Rock! It's Still Rhythm and Blues," *Black Perspective in Popular Music,* XIII, No. 1 (Spring 1985), pp. 31-47.

Rowe, Mike. *Chicago Breakdown.* New York: Drake Publishers, 1975.

Rowland, Mark. "Review of Atlantic Rhythm and Blues, 1947-1974 (Vol. 1-7)," *Musician,* No. 89 (March 1986), pp. 86, 88.

Rumble, John. "Roots of Rock and Roll: Henry Glover at King Records," *Journal of Country Music,* XIV, No. 2 (1992), pp. 30-42.

Ruppli, Michel (comp.) *The Aladdin/Imperial Labels: A Discography.* Westport, Connecticut: Greenwood Press, 1991.

Ruppli, Michel (comp.) *Atlantic Records: A Discography (Four Volumes).* Westport, CT: Greenwood Press, 1979.

Ruppli, Michel (comp.). *The Chess Labels: Discography (Two Volumes).* Westport, CT: Greenwood Press, 1983.

Ruppli, Michel, with the assistance of Bill Daniels (comps.). *The King Labels: A Discography (Two Volumes).* Westport, CT: Greenwood Press, 1985.

Ruppli, Michel, with assistance from Bob Porter (comps.). *The Savoy Label: A Discography*. Westport, CT: Greenwood Press, 1980.

Scott, Frank, Al Ennis, and the Staff of Roots and Rhythm. *The Roots and Rhythm Guide to Rock*. Pennington, NJ: A Cappella Books, 1993.

Shawl, Arnold. *Honkers and Shouters: The Golden Years of Rhythm and Blues*. New York: Collier Books, 1978.

Shawl, Arnold. *The Rockin' 50s: The Decade That Transformed the Pop Music Scene*. New York: Hawthorn Books, Inc., 1974.

Silvani, Lou. *Collecting Rare Records: A Guide to Take You Through the World of Rare Records*. Bronx: Times Square Records, 1992.

Smith, Wes. *The Pied Pipers of Rock 'n' Roll: Radio Deejays of the '50s and '60s*. Marietta, GA: Longstreet Press, Inc., 1989.

Sumrall, Harry. *Pioneers of Rock and Roll: 100 Artists Who Changed the Face of Rock*. New York: Billboard Books, 1994.

Tosches, Nick. *Unsung Heroes of Rock 'n' Roll: The Birth of Rock in the Wild Years Before Elvis* (Revised Edition). New York: Harmony Books, 1991.

Wade, Dorothy and Justine Picardie. *Music Man: Ahmet Ertegun, Atlantic Records, and the Triumph of Rock 'n' Roll*. New York: W.W. Norton and Company, 1990.

Warner, Jay. *The Billboard Book of American Singing Groups: A History, 1940-1990*. New York: Billboard Books, 1992.

Wexler, Jerry and David Ritz. *Rhythm and the Blues: A Life in American Music*. New York: Alfred A. Knopf, 1993.

Whitburn, Joel (comp.) *The Billboard Pop Chart, 1955-1959*. Menomonee Falls, WI: Record Research, Inc., 1992.

Whitburn, Joel (comp.) *Pop Hits, 1940-1954*. Menomonee Falls, WI: Record Research, Inc., 1994.

Whitburn, Joel (comp.) *Top Pop Singles, 1955-1993*. Menomonee Falls, WI: Record Research, Inc., 1994.

Whitburn, Joel (comp.) *Top R&B Singles, 1942-1995*. Menomonee Falls, WI: Record Research, Inc., 1996.

White, Timothy. "Jerry Wexler: The Godfather of Rhythm and Blues," *Rolling Stone*, No. 331 (November 1980), pp. 48-52, 74-81.

Zucker, Mark J. "The Saga of Lovin' Dan: A Study in the Iconography of Rhythm and Blues Music of the 1950's," *Journal of Popular Culture*, 16 (Fall 1987), pp. 43-51.

Chapter 10

Postal Images

Popular culture pervades American society. It is neither good nor evil, neither beneficial nor detrimental. It is omnipresent. For English students and educators, the texture of contemporary language, the descriptions of modern institutions, and the quality of human relations cannot be explored apart from the jargon and imagery found in popular culture. Baseball metaphors, extending from recent governmental policy toward criminals ("Three strikes and you're out") to romantic entanglements ("He can't get to first base with her") and from business boardrooms ("Make a strong pitch so the client will feel safe at home with our product") to street corners ("I'll pinch hit for you if necessary"). The melding of institutional language, symbols, and tasks with popular culture media illustrates the spongelike nature of popular culture. It not only circulates new terms but also absorbs and revitalizes descriptions of the most mundane human actions. One need only reflect on the lyrical adaptation of children's nursery rhymes ("Lil' Red Riding Hood"), formal schooling ("Another Brick in the Wall-Part II"), or unemployment ("Allentown") to note oral art reflecting life.

I memorize every line,
And I kiss the name that you sign.

Dick Haymes
"Love Letters" (1945)

I'm not alone in the night,
When I can have all the love you write.

Ketty Lester
"Love Letters" (1962)

This chapter by B. Lee Cooper was originally published as "Please Mr. Postman: Images of Written Communication in Contemporary Lyrics," *International Journal of Instructional Media*, XXIII, No. 1 (1996), pp. 79-89. Reprint permission granted by the author, editor Phillip J. Sleeman, and The Westwood Press.

Conventional wisdom dictates that personal letters have very little in common with sound recordings. Letters are produced privately for individual enlightenment; recordings are commercially manufactured according to industry standards for public entertainment. Letters are either handwritten or typed and feature specific details about personal concerns; recordings are mass produced in vinyl, tape, and compact disc formats and relate general social situations or conventional relationship themes. Other characteristics of letters as opposed to recordings include prior knowledge held by the receiving audience, lack of required rhyme scheme, anticipation of a written response (interactive expectation), and the integrated nature of a communication exchange. It seems obvious that the personal letter, as one portion of a written dialogue, is the absolute antithesis of the oral monologue of a sound recording.

Yet despite the previous evidence, letters and recordings share more similarities than differences. All letters are not the same of course. A love letter, for instance, is markedly dissimilar from an office memo, a military dispatch, a travel journal account, or a scholarly note to an editor. Recordings differ greatly as well. Although the lyrics of some songs relate stories about raising children, tales of railroad history, criticisms of governmental policies, or humorous adaptations of nursery rhymes, the dominant topic in popular music is courtship—the exploration of various stages of romantic entanglement. As in most love letters, the point of view of the audio communicator is usually first person. Thousands of male and female recording artists sing, "I love you," echoing identical literary sentiments penned by thousands of letter-writing counterparts. But letters are *real* and song lyrics aren't, some might protest. Yet hundreds of singer-songwriters readily acknowledge that their own personal experiences fuel much of their lyrical commentaries. What would country music be without "cheatin' " songs? What would pop music be without lost love tunes? Hank Williams, Joni Mitchell, Billy Joel, Jim Croce, Smokey Robinson, Dolly Parton, Paul McCartney, Bonnie Raitt, Gordon Lightfoot, and scores of other composer/performers are either directly or indirectly autobiographical in many of their compositions. As for personal letters, the popularity of epistolary novels in Western literature demonstrates that fictional letter exchanges have traditionally been an especially potent source of both social commentary and romantic titillation. Letters and recordings dealing with courtship themes are often fascinating and unbalanced blends of fact, fiction, experience, illusion, and desire. Although not all personal letters are love letters, the lines of demarcation between personal letters and sound recordings blur significantly in respect to love themes.

Further exploration illustrates that in regard to romantic communication, letters and recordings are not only strangely similar, but nearly identical. Both use relatively brief texts to communicate personalized perspectives on facts and feelings; both permit the receiver to read and reread an original text for greater meaning or to yield a deeper emotional response; both direct their words toward an individual, even though broader audiences might intercept and understand the private messages being communicated; both use common, nontechnical language that is usually more precise than oral speech, but far less philosophical than a formal treatise; and both are immensely self-revealing, relying on a combination of personal imagination, common phrases, and familiar illustrations drawn from the popular culture regarding personal heartbreak, pledges of lasting love, pleas for marriage or marital fidelity, and dreams or schemes of future sexual liaisons. Love letters and sound recordings dealing with romantic involvements are emotionally volatile. They explore vulnerabilities and strengths in personal relationships, tearful times, and triumphs of love. The broad, public audiences for fictional letters (i.e., epistolary novels such as *Abelard and Héloise*) and for popular love songs ("I Heard It Through the Grapevine") will recognize little thematic difference in the emotional and physical territories traversed by both authors and lyricists. Complexity of storyline notwithstanding, love letters and love songs constitute an overlapping popular culture phenomenon.

The following pages explore *only* the audio dimension of the love letter/love song continuum. Ignoring script material (written epistles and novels), this study examines the overt manifestations of postal imagery within general lyrics. Specifically, the focus of this chapter is on direct references to letter exchanges, physical interactions with specific postal authorities, and personal reactions to written communications as they are formulated, mailed, sought after, received, and read. Illustrations of postal imagery are provided throughout this chapter and a discographic table.

> I gave a letter to the postman,
> He put it in his sack.
> Bright and early next morning,
> He brought my letter back.

Elvis Presley
"Return to Sender" (1962)

> Here comes the mailman, bringin' me tears.

Gladys Knight and The Pips
"Letters Full of Tears" (1962)

Popular songs are chock-full of social imagery. Lyric analysts have investigated metaphors, allegories, and other forms of symbolism in recorded tunes related to automobiles, baseball, Christmas, food, and even medicine. One particularly interesting lyrical realm that has not been explored, though, is the pervasive influence of postal exchanges on human relationships. Written communication obviously preceded the advent of sound recording technology by many centuries. However, the combining of lyric messages and melodies during the twentieth century has served to reinforce memories of various romantic scenarios. Within lyric lines, composers often create letter-related tales that communicate the eternal verities of love: attraction, jealousy, endearment, heartache, adoration, ambivalence, physical longing, absence, fidelity, infidelity, comfort, discomfort, sexual desire, enchantment, disenchantment, and so on. Though the tales may vary, the listening audience clearly understands the differences between a "Dear John Letter" and a saucy invitation to a romantic interlude.

Although the volume of personal letters may be declining today due to excessive postage rate hikes, frequent e-mail transmissions, and increased telephone use, the cultural presence of written correspondence remains ubiquitous in contemporary lyrics. Even when personal letters themselves are mentioned only obliquely by a recording artist, postal terminology is still common. Postal employees are directly mentioned in "Letter Full of Tears" (1962), "Please Mr. Postman" (1961), and "Twistin' Postman" (1962). Various classes of mail are noted in "Special Delivery" (1948), "Postcard from Jamaica" (1967), and "Airmail to Heaven" (1962). Other general postal terms utilized in song titles include "Address Unknown" (1939), "Return to Sender" (1962), and "Zip Code" (1967). Humorous adaptations of letter-related jargon are also visible—with obvious gender connotations—in "U.S. Male" (1968) and "Overnight Male" (1992).

Letters themselves are central features in many lyrical tales. On the positive side, declarations pledging continuing attachments, enduring emotions, and strong romantic feelings are staples for courtship missives and private notes between lovers. "Love Letters" (1962) straight from the heart are genuinely powerful. The two different songs titled "P.S. I Love You" (1953, 1964) share the common theme of communicating deep emotional involvement to an absent mate. "Teardrops on Your Letter" (1959) also inspires the singer to pledge to return to his sweetheart as soon as possible. The notion of reuniting with a distant lover is also a recurring theme of literary joy. "My baby's coming home tomorrow. Ain't that good news?" sings Sam Cooke. His sentiments upon receiving a letter in "(Ain't That) Good News" (1964) are echoed by The Box Tops in "The Letter" (1967) and also by Rusty York in "Sugaree" (1959).

SELECTED POPULAR RECORDINGS CONTAINING
LYRICAL REFERENCES TO LETTER WRITING
OR FEATURING POSTAL SERVICE TERMINOLOGY

- "Address Unknown"
  (Decca 2707)
  Ink Spots (1939)

- "(Ain't That) Good News"
  (RCA 8299)
  Sam Cooke (1964)

- "Air Mail to Heaven"
  (Columbia 42222)
  Carl Smith (1962)

- "At Mail Call Today"
  (Okeh 6737)
  Gene Autry (1945)

- "Because I Love You (The Postman Song)"
  (LMR 2724)
  Stevie B (1990)

- "Billy and Sue"
  (Hickory 1395)
  B. J. Thomas and The Triumphs (1966)

- "Check in the Mail"
  (Ichiban 1501-2)
  Millie Jackson (1994)

- "Cry"
  (Okeh 6840)
  Johnnie Ray (1951)

- "Dear Elvis"
  (Plus 104)
  Audrey (1956)

- "Dear John"
  (MGM 10904)
  Hank Williams (1951)

- "Dear John Letter"
  (Capitol 2502)
  Jean Shepard and Ferlin Huskey (1953)

- "Dear Mr. President"
  (Ovation 1139)
  Max D. Barnes (1980)

- "Dear Uncle Sam"
  (Decca 31893)
  Loretta Lynn (1966)

- "Detroit City"
  (RCA 8183)
  Bobby Bare (1963)

- "Greetings (This Is Uncle Sam)"
  (Miracle 6)
  Valadiers (1961)

- "Happy, Happy Birthday Baby"
  (Checker 872)
  Tune Weavers (1957)

- "Hey, Western Union Man"
  (Mercury 72850)
  Jerry Butler (1968)

- "(How Can I Put on Paper) What I Feel in My Heart"
  (RCA 7950)
  Jim Reeves (1961)

- "I Wish I'd Never Learned to Read"
  (Capitol 3185)
  Five Keys (1955)

- "I'll Be Home"
  (Checker 830)
  Flamingos (1956)

- "I'm Gonna Sit Right Down and Write Myself a Letter"
  (Columbia 02187)
  Willie Nelson (1981)

- "Kiddio"
  (Mercury 71652)
  Brook Benton (1960)

- "The Letter"
  (Male 565)
  Box Tops (1957)

- "The Letter"
  (Vault 916)
  Sonny and Cher (1965)

- "The Letter Edged in Black"
  (Brunswick 2900)
  Vernon Dalhart (1929)

- "Letter from a Soldier (Dear Mama)"
  (MGM 13545)
  Connie Francis (1966)

- "A Letter from a Teenage Son"
  (Philips 40503)
  Brandon Wade (1967)

- "A Letter from Betty"
  (Liberty 55581)
  Bobby Vee (1963)

- "Letter from Elaina"
  (Warner Brothers 5474)
  Casey Kasem (1964)

- "Letter from My Darling"
  (King 4935)
  Little Willie John (1956)

- "Letter Full of Tears"
  (Fury 1054)
  Gladys Knight and The Pips (1962)

- "Letter Home"
  (Warner Brothers 27839)
  Forester Sisters (1988)

- "A Letter to an Angel"
  (Ace 551)
  Jimmy Clanton (1958)

- "Letter to Dad"
  (Buddha 25)
  Every Father's Teenage Son (1967)

- "Letter to Lucille"
  (Parrot 40074)
  Tom Jones (1973)

- "A Letter to Myself"
  (Brunswick 55491)
  Chi-Lites (1973)

- "Letter to Saddam Hussein"
  (Desert Storm 1161791)
  Jerry Martin (1991)

- "A Letter to The Beatles"
  (Capitol 5143)
  Four Preps (1964)

- "Letters Have No Arms"
  (Decca 46207)
  Ernest Tubb (1950)

- "Lonely Blue Boy"
  (MOM 12857)
  Conway Twitty (1959)

- "Lonesome for a Letter"
  (Dot 15481)
  Sanford Clark (1956)

- "(Love Always) Letter to Home"
  (Atlantic American 99647)
  Glen Campbell (1985)

- "Love Letter"
  (Atlantic 87835)
  Robin Lee (1990)

- "Love Letters"
  (Capitol 79127)
  Bonnie Raitt (1990)

- "Love Letters"
  (Era 3068)
  Ketty Lester (1962)

- "Love Letters in the Sand"
  (Dot 15570)
  Pat Boone (1957)

- "An Open Letter to My Teenage Son"
  (Liberty 55996)
  Victor Lundberg (1967)

- "P.S. I Love You"
  (Dot 45-15085)
  Hilltoppers (1953)

- "P.S. I Love You"
  (Tollie 9008)
  The Beatles (1964)

- "Please Mr. Postman"
  (Tamla 54046)
  Marvelettes (1961)

- "Return to Sender"
  (RCA 47-8100)
  Elvis Presley (1962)

- "Rock and Roll Love Letter"
  (Arista 0185)
  Bay City Rollers (1976)

- "Send Me Some Lovin'"
  (Specialty 598)
  Little Richard (1957)

- "Soldier's Last Letter"
  (Decca 6098)
  Ernest Tubb (1944)

- "Strawberry Letter 23"
  (Quest 18919)
  Tewin Campbell (1992)

- "Sugaree"
  (Chess 1730)
  Rusty York (1959)

- "Take a Letter Maria"
  (Atco 6714)
  R. B. Greaves (1969)

- "Take a Letter, Miss Brown"
  (Decca 3626)
  Ink Spots (1941)

- "Teardrops on Your Letter"
  (King 5171)
  Hank Ballard and The Midnighters (1959)

- "Twistin' Postman"
  (Tamla 54054)
  Marvelettes (1962)

- "Western Union"
  (Abnak 120)
  Five Americans (1967)

- "Why Don't You Write Me?"
  (RPM 428)
  Jacks (1955)

- "Words by Heart"
  (Mercury 314-514758-2)
  Billy Ray Cyrus (1993)

- "Write Me a Letter"
  (20th Century 2128)
  DeFranco Family Featuring Tony DeFranco (1974)

- "Write Me a Letter"
  (National 9038)
  Ravens (1947)

- "Write Me Sweetheart"
  (Okeh 6723)
  Roy Acuff (1944)

- "Yesterday's Letters"
  (Decca 32431)
  Bobby Lord (1969)

- "Yesterday's Mail"
  (Capitol 15132)
  Hank Thompson (1948)

- "Zip Code"
  (Abnak 123)
  Five Americans (1967)

Letters also function in songs to communicate deep caring and concern for loved ones—especially sons and husbands—trapped abroad in life-threatening military activities. From the offbeat reaction of The Valadiers to reading an induction letter in "Greetings (This Is Uncle Sam)" (1961) to Loretta Lynn's more serious "Dear Uncle Sam" (1966), the issue of involuntary separation from friends, family, and loved ones is frequently explored in lyrics. Correspondence during wartime flies both ways, of course. While loved ones on the home front produce literary items to be shared "At Mail Call Today" (1945), G.I. writers respond with "I'll Be Home" (1956), "Letter from a Soldier (Dear Mama)" (1966), and "Soldier's Last Letter" (1944). And while some overseas correspondence is humorous, such as the audio letter to Private Elvis Presley titled "Dear 53310761" (1958), other mail of the Dear John ilk is brutally lethal, as illustrated dramatically in the recording "Billy and Sue" (1966).

Poignant pleas for a second chance at love, for better communication with a romantic partner, for an end to marital conflict, or for the rekindling of romance dominate the so-called lost love theme. Letters are often provocative. They allow very difficult items of personal communication to be exchanged under non-face-to-face circumstances. Tears flow freely; painful memories parade openly. The death-producing "Billy and Sue" (1966) letter is significantly toned down in "Dear John" (1951), "Dear John Letter" (1953), and "Dear John Letter Lounge" (1976). Emotional distress is unmistakable, though. While some "Cry" (1951) upon receiving the letter of goodbye, others assert in vain that "I Wish I'd Never Learned to Read" (1955). Rejecting a "Letter Full of Tears" (1962) is just as difficult as receiving unopened apologies marked with the cold postal message

"Return to Sender" (1962). Long after romantic ties are broken, lyrical correspondence imagery can still depict lingering pain. Two excellent illustrations of such long-term disillusionment are "Love Letters in the Sand" (1957) and "Happy, Happy Birthday Baby" (1957). The lost love theme, as communicated by letter, is perhaps best capsuled in Little Willie John's "My Baby's in Love with Another Guy" (1958).

While love themes and letter imagery are commonly linked in lyrics, other reasons for writing are also illustrated in sound recordings. The generation gap, replete with strong disagreements over religious values, clothing styles, political commitments and behavioral norms can be found in "An Open Letter to My Teenage Son" (1967), "Letter to Dad" (1967), and "A Letter from a Teenage Son" (1967). There is also a limited amount of literary deceit to be found in lyrics. Bobby Bare fools the folks back home by writing that he's doing fine in "Detroit City" (1963). Billy Williams fools himself when he creates a warm, caring epistle in "I'm Gonna Sit Right Down and Write Myself a Letter" (1957). And The Newbeats are infuriated by a "Poison Pen" (1965) letter sent to a loved one by a trouble-making, lying romantic competitor. Finally, lyrical correspondence with famous and infamous figures is a frequently featured audio activity. As one might guess, Elvis Presley and The Beatles are objects of affection in several tunes, including "Dear Elvis" (1956), "Dear 5331076" (1958), and "A Letter to The Beatles" (1964). But a much more diverse population of political leaders and popular journalists are also addressed on record. Songs of strong opinion and humorous advice include "Dear Mr. President" (1980), "Dear Abby" (1963), and "Letter to Saddam Hussein" (1991).

BIBLIOGRAPHY

Altman, Janet Gurkin. *Epistolarity: Approaches to a Form.* Columbus, OH: Ohio State University Press, 1982.

Carroll, Peter N. *Keeping Time, Memory, Nostalgia and the Art of History.* Athens, GA: University of Georgia Press, 1990.

Cawelti, John G. *Adventure, Mystery, and Romance: Formula Stories As Art and Popular Culture.* Chicago, IL: University of Chicago Press, 1976.

Cooper, B. Lee. *Images of American Society in Popular Music: A Guide to Reflective Teaching.* Chicago, IL: Nelson-Hall, Inc., 1982.

Cooper, B. Lee. *Popular Music Perspectives: Ideas, Themes, and Patterns in Contemporary Lyrics.* Bowling Green, OH: Bowling Green State University Popular Press, 1991.

Cooper, B. Lee. *A Resource Guide to Themes in Contemporary American Song Lyrics, 1950-1985.* Westport, CT: Greenwood Press, 1986.

Cooper, B. Lee and Wayne S. Haney. *Rock Music in American Popular Culture: Rock 'n' Roll Resources.* New York: The Haworth Press, 1995.

Ennis, Philip H. *The Seventh Stream: The Emergence of Rocknroll in American Popular Music*. Hanover, NH: University Press of New England, 1993.

Frith, Simon. *Sound Effects: Youth, Leisure and the Politics of Rock 'n' Roll*. New York: Pantheon Books, 1981.

Goodall, H. L. Jr. *Living in the Rock 'n' Roll Mystery: Reading Context, Self and Others As Clues*. Carbondale, IL: Southern Illinois University Press, 1991.

Kauffman, Linda S. *Special Delivery: Epistolary Modes in Modern in Modern Fiction*. Chicago: University of Chicago Press, 1992.

Kawin, Bruce F. *Telling It Again and Again: Repetition in Literature and Film*. Ithaca, NY: Cornell University Press, 1972.

Lipsitz, George. *Time Passages: Collective Memory and American Popular Culture*. Minneapolis, MN: University of Minnesota Press, 1990.

Lull, James (ed.). *Popular Music and Communication* (Second Edition). Newbury Park, CA: Sage Publications, 1992.

Macken, Bob, Peter Fornatale, and Bill Ayres (comps.). *The Rock Music Source Book*. Garden City, NY: Anchor Press/Doubleday, 1980.

McLavrin, Melton A. and Richard A. Peterson (eds.). *You Wrote My Life: Lyrical Themes in Country Music*. Philadelphia: Gordon and Breach, 1992.

Rogers, Jimmie N. *The Country Music Message: All About Lovin' and Livin'*. Englewood Cliffs, NJ: Prentice-Hall, Inc., 1993.

Schultze, Quentin J., Roy M. Anker, James D. Bratt, William D. Romanowski, John W. Worst, and Lambert Zuidervaart. *Dancing in the Dark: Youth, Popular Culture, and the Electronic Media*. Grand Rapids, MI: William B. Eerman, 1991.

Whitburn, Joel (comp.). *Pop Memories 1890-1954: The History of American Popular Music*. Menomonee Falls, WI: Record Research, 1986.

Whitburn, Joel (comp.). *Top Pop Singles, 1955-1993*. Menomonee Falls, WI: Record Research, Inc., 1994.

Chapter 11

Public Schools

Formal education constitutes a key foe for angry rap chanters and aggressive heavy metal headbangers. Their words depicting school experiences are invariably harsh. But 1990s lyrical indictments of teachers, principals, and curricula as unresponsive, unintelligible, and irrelevant can be traced to the earliest rock performers. In fact, throughout the first quarter century of the post-big band era (1955-1980), audio portrayals of junior and senior high school experiences ranged from mockery to rage. With ancestral roots as deep as Chuck Berry and images as vitriolic as those vocalized by Pink Floyd, it is little wonder that through present-day singers and songwriters, adolescent American society continues to deride public schooling. The following commentary provides a detailed analysis of recordings from the early rock era that illustrates young America's disenchantment with institutionalized learning.

Despite the cacophony of criticisms from many reform-minded pressure groups, observations from one key group—students, the subject of the whole educational enterprise—are generally ignored. But youth has not remained mute. Scholars simply have not applied their critical skills to a wide enough variety of resources on this issue. Popular music, a principal artifact of youth culture, gives voice to a broad range of concerns, values, and priorities of young people. A thorough analysis of scores of popular songs demonstrates that lyrics consistently depict formal schooling as dehumanizing, irrelevant, alienating, laughable, isolating, and totally unworthy of any link with the Socratic tradition. Some might argue, of course, that popular music does not actually reflect student perceptions *per se*. Most hit tunes, after all, are not written by students. Pop recordings are simply products of market devices. But lyricists and singers are clearly the troubadours of contemporary young people. To claim that they do not

This revised and updated chapter by B. Lee Cooper was originally published as "Sounds of Schooling in Modern America: Recorded Images of Public Education, 1950-1980," *International Journal of Instructional Media,* XI, No. 3 (1983/1984), pp. 255-271. Reprint permission granted by the author, editor Phillip J. Sleeman, and The Westwood Press.

179

represent student perceptions because they are no longer students them-selves is equivalent to arguing that balladeers of medieval Europe did not reflect the culture of courtly society because they were not part of the aristocracy. Troubadours in any age are honored precisely because their musical messages resound with the perceptions and emotions of their audience. Indeed, modern troubadours are probably better mirrors of the culture in whose name they sing than their feudal antecedents. Unlike minstrels of old, modern rock musicians, though generally no longer stu-dents when they write or perform their music, have actually been in the classroom; their medieval counterparts were never aristocrats.

Popular music has not always portrayed schooling in a negative way. Education appeared less frequently as a theme in the prerock era, but when it did, lyrics were usually nostalgic as in "School Days" or "In the Little Red School House." In addition, earlier education themes were generally ori-ented toward college students, despite the fact that only a small proportion of young people attended universities prior to 1950. From the 1906 record-ing of "College Life," through "Collegiate," (1925) "The Varsity Drag," (1927) "Betty Co-Ed," (1930) and "The Sweetheart of Sigma Chi" (1927) to "The Whiffenpoof Song" in 1936, early popular music dealing with education emphasized the carefree joys of campus social life. Ironically, in an age when university attendance has become the norm, very few rock songs deal with college life. Most focus exclusively on public school expe-riences, particularly on secondary schooling. And with very few excep-tions—The Arbors' "Graduation Day" and The Beach Boys' "Be True to Your School"—the sentiments communicated are anything but nostalgic.

> School days, school days,
> Dear old golden rule days,
> Readin' and writin' and 'rithmatic,
> Taught to the tune of a hickory stick.

Sentiments of good times, firm discipline, and inculcation of basic com-munication and computation skills featured in the traditional tune "School Days" represent learning perceptions from another era. Whether accurate or inaccurate, realistic or idealistic, this song came to symbolize formal educa-tion during the early twentieth century. But as Bob Dylan noted during the 1960s, "the times they are a-changin." In 1954, the U.S. Supreme Court ordered American education to cease the practice of utilizing racially segre-gated, "separate but equal" learning arenas. But the integration of public schools wasn't the only revolution occurring in mid-1950s America. Cur-rents of popular music were also beginning to flow more swiftly. The rock 'n' roll floodtide emerged when country music tunes and rhythm and blues songs found synthesizing spokesmen in Bill Haley, Otis Williams, Elvis Presley, Chuck Berry, Carl Perkins, and Jerry Lee Lewis. This popular music rampage, aided by influential disc jockeys, several technological recording inventions, motion picture hype ("Blackboard Jungle"), and improved record company promotional techniques, launched a fundamental change in America's musical tastes as well as in lyrical imagery.

As the rock era evolved, it enlisted more and more singers and songwriters who were drawn from and remained committed to youthful values. Observations, ideals, and images contained in their songs were uncompromisingly student-oriented. This meant that public schools, the physical setting for so much teenage activity, were scrutinized, analyzed, and depicted in numerous song lyrics. The impact of this audio examination of American schooling is eminently clear—and staggering. Internal verification of current educational practices replaced external expectations and historic ideals concerning the nature of the learning enterprise. Neither truth nor reality could be guaranteed by this change in perspective and commentators. However, viewpoints drawn from actual student experience were undeniably sharper in assessing the behavior of principals, teachers, PTOs, student groups, and individual learners than the more theoretical observations offered by educational philosophers or other public school analysts.

No systematic, comprehensive statement of public school criticism can be found in the grooves of popular recordings. Nevertheless, several key ideas *are* present. Between 1955 and 1980 previously dominant preachment and pretense images of schooling were directly challenged. Lyrical idealism was not totally absent, of course. Admiration for teachers who were bright, deeply committed to learning, concerned about pupils, and engaged in a constant battle to overcome ignorance was eulogized in tunes such as "To Sir with Love" and "Welcome Back." But a much more critical tone dominates the majority of lyrical commentaries about schooling. Teachers are generally condemned for being ignorant of student feelings ("Bird Dog"), for pursuing irrelevant classroom topics ("Wonderful World"), for corrupting student idealism ("The Logical Song"), and for intentionally stifling the development of pupils' social and political awareness ("Another Brick in the Wall-Part II"). It is difficult to imagine a more blatant denunciation of the entire educational system than Paul Simon's introductory phrases in "Kodachrome":

> When I think back on all the crap I learned in high school,
> It's a wonder I can think at all.
> And though my lack of education hasn't hurt me none,
> I can see the writing on the wall.

To illustrate the image of American public education present in popular music lyrics during the first quarter century of the rock era, it is necessary to isolate and define several key elements directly related to the formal schooling process. The following definitions govern the use of terminology in this study:

School—the physical building (classrooms, hallways, cafeteria, restrooms, library, administrative offices, and teacher lounges) and the total potential learning environment available to students (special meetings and annual ceremonies, organization of school personnel, and institutional heritage).

Students—a group of young people ranging from fourteen to eighteen years old, both male and female, predominantly American, in all physical shapes, sizes, and psychological dimensions, from different ethnic, religious, and socioeconomic groups.

Teachers—a group of adults ranging in age from twenty-two to sixty-five years, both male and female, predominantly American, in all physical shapes and sizes, and psychological dimensions; primarily middle class, mostly white and Protestant, possessing at least four years of college education.

Principals—the chief administrative officers in the schools possessing at least five years of college education and several years of classroom teaching experience; a group of adults ranging in age from thirty to sixty-five years, predominantly white, male, middle class, Protestant, and American; in all physical shapes, sizes, and psychological dimensions.

Parents—adult men and women responsible for one or more children, mostly married, ranging in age from thirty-two to fifty-five or older, of different ethnic backgrounds, religions, and social and economic conditions, political persuasions, and personal interests.

Community—the geographic area that constitutes the primary dwelling place for parents and students and for the vast majority of teachers and principals; it is also the site of the school.

Education—the primary goals of public education are transmitting factual knowledge, fostering socialization, and preparing students for democratic citizenship; teachers conduct a variety of learning activities under the administrative supervision of principals, with community involvement by individual parents and parent-teacher organizations.

Beyond defining these seven elements of American public education, it is also necessary to identify three perceptual perspectives in order to assess activities within the formal schooling environment:

> *Preachment*—the ideals or highest goals of a social organization or of any person associated with that organization.

> *Pretense*—justifications for specific actions within a social organization which are not functionally appropriate to furthering the ideals of that organization; a shadowy dimension of shifting personal attitudes and physical behaviors located between the zones of idealized preachment and actual practice.

> *Practice*—activities that constitute the hour-by-hour, day-to-day operations of a social organization.

All seven elements within the formal schooling process—schools, students, teachers, principals, parents, the community, and education—are frequently depicted in early rock-era songs. As might be predicted, most lyrical comments are directly related to personal involvement in real (practice) rather than ideal (preachment) school situations. Although practice may be more visible and more individually identifiable, many songs do contain lyrical segments that allude to all three dimensions. Based upon an impressionistic lyrical review, Table 11.1 illustrates the broad perspectives of formal education that exist in the analyzed popular recordings. The radical divergence between preachment/pretense and practice was so sharp, according to most 1955-1980 lyrical commentaries, that one wonders if the American public school system might be malfunctioning.

Lyrical images of American public education are lively, colorful, direct, and generally critical. A brief review of recorded commentaries on each of the seven elements of the formal schooling process follows.

IMAGES OF SCHOOL

"School" is dually depicted as a state of mind as well as a physical entity. A few songs beckon students to "(Remember the days of the) Old School Yard." Cat Stevens' nostalgic reverie is echoed by the eighteen spirited versions of "High School U.S.A." recorded by Tommy Faceda, by The Beach Boys' loyalty hymn "Be True to Your School," and by The Arbors' nostalgic "Graduation Day." But these tunes are atypical of the genre. The majority of lyrics describing school life portray the buildings and grounds as a series of sinister, segregated compartments that dictate varying kinds of student behavior.

TABLE 11.1. Terms Illustrating Preachment, Pretense, and Practice Imagery About American Public Education in the Lyrics of Popular Songs, 1955-1980

Area of Lyrical Commentary	Preachment Images	Pretense Images	Practice Images
1. School	human development cultural repository knowledge resource civic center	alma mater school loyalty commencement honor code	separation from life isolation from peers irrelevance social interaction
2. Students	inquiry reflection rationality	questioning participation investigating	friends, dancers clowns, romancers victims, gangs
3. Teachers	mentors, models	friends, counselors	baby-sitters fools arbitrary actors
4. Principals	learning leader experienced educator	chief administrator responsibility	authoritarian irresponsible
5. Parents	loving concern family stability	guiding hands mature guides	misunderstanding interference
6. Community	democracy participation	due process socialization	conformity hypocrisy
7. Education	wisdom knowledge diversity understanding freedom	information citizenship decision making communication stability	regimentation indoctrination illiteracy cynicism fear

The classroom is generally depicted as the dictatorial domain of a teaching tyrant. "Gee, she don't know how mean she looks," snorts Chuck Berry in "School Day." Activities that occur in classrooms are conducted in lockstep, intimidating, teacher-directed fashion. A student such as The Coasters' "Charlie Brown" may walk into the classroom cool and slow, but then he'd better become quiet, orderly, and without guile. By contrast, the hallways are always alive with noise. Rigidly enforced classroom silence and cerebral irrelevance give way to cacophonous peer chatter and delirious social interaction. Discussions of cars, sex, smokes, food, films, and immediate wants and needs occur in the jostling, locker-slamming hallway atmosphere. School corridors also lead to freedom—". . . down the hall and into the street" ("School Day"); to a secret cigarette break in the restroom ("Smokin' in the Boys Room"); to a luncheon record hop ("High School Dance"); to more private activities in outdoor recreation areas ("Me and Julio Down by the Schoolyard"); and to the parking lot filled with decorated cars and vans. The key word to describe most lyrical observations about the school building is escape. Even those songs that laud memories of bygone secondary school experiences—such as Adrian Kimberly's "Pomp and Circumstance"—praise commencement as the eternal relief of alma mater status felt by all alumni. This escapist theme is also clearly delineated in songs that depict the annual freedom period from June through August: Gary "U.S." Bonds' "School Is Out" and Alice Cooper's "School's Out."

IMAGES OF STUDENTS

Lyrical images of students vary greatly. Clear recognition of peer pressures and special interest groups within each school is illustrated in The Beach Boys' "I Get Around," Dobie Gray's "In Crowd," and Connie Frances' "Where the Boys Are." The isolation of non-conforming individuals and out-groups is depicted in The Crystals' "He's a Rebel," The Dixie Cups' "Leader of the Pack," and Janis Ian's "At Seventeen" and "Society's Child." Although they make up the most heterogeneous group within the public educational system, students are lyrically characterized as the least franchised ("Summertime Blues"), most harassed ("Yackety Yak"), most regimented ("Another Brick in the Wall-Part II"), least trusted ("Smokin' in the Boy's Room"), most humorous ("Charlie Brown" and "My Boy Flat Top"), most victimized ("My Generation" and "Society's Child"), and least understood ("It Hurts to Be Sixteen" and "You and Me Against the World").

Students are usually described as physically active and singularly non-contemplative. In fact, as Sam Cooke declared in his 1960 hit, "Wonderful World," the typical romantic high school youth:

> Don't know nothin' 'bout a science book
> Don't remember the French I took.

Nearly two decades later, Art Garfunkel, Paul Simon, and James Taylor revived Cooke's "(What A) Wonderful World" with an additional anti-intellectual refrain:

> Don't know nothin' 'bout no Rise and Fall,
> Don't know nothin' 'bout nothin' at all.

This sense of educational futility is a dominant element in popular lyrics. Paul Simon's 1973 song "Kodachrome," which begins with a stunning indictment of academic irrelevance, was followed three years later by an even more negative analysis of post-high school life in "Still Crazy After All These Years." This self-assessment was shared with a former high school girlfriend. Several other songs also capture poignant vignettes of post-high school reflections. Tunes such as Bob Seger's "2 + 2 = ?" explore the meaning of a school friend's senseless death in Vietnam; Alice Cooper's "Eighteen" examines the "I'm a boy, but I'm a man" predicament of a recent high school graduate; and Bob Dylan's "Subterranean Homesick Blues" presents an image of an illogical, mean-spirited society that awaits formally educated, but nonstreetwise youngsters.

IMAGES OF TEACHERS AND PRINCIPALS

Adults who control the environment within public schools are neither admired nor respected. Even those few songs which praise individual teachers—"Mr. Lee" by The Bobbettes, "To Sir with Love" by Lulu, and "Abigail Beechert" by Freddie Cannon—offer sharp, derogatory contrasts between the caring behavior and independent actions of their *favored* instructors and the general demeanor of the *majority* of teachers who are boobs, bumpkins, and boors. Chuck Berry, The Coasters, The Who, Janis Ian, Paul Simon, and dozens of other singers reinforce the simple message chanted by Pink Floyd: "Teacher, leave them kids alone!"

If teachers are fools, antiquarians, babysitters, arbitrary actors, and persons generally out of touch with reality, principals are outright villains with malevolent motives and totalitarian instincts. Although very few lyrical commentaries are addressed directly to the chief administrative officers in schools, the implications of managerial rule-making authority and the harsh methods of discipline enforcement abound. The jangling bell system, a lock-step, class-to-class routine, depersonalized hall passes, regimented class changes, overly brief lunch periods ("School Days"), and dozens of other system-defining annoyances are passively attributed to the principal, though they are actively enforced by teachers.

Most distressing is the fact that teachers are universally defined as antithetical to their students. They lack common sense ("Bird Dog"), are cynical ("The Logical Song"), humorless ("School Days" and "Charlie Brown"), out of touch with personal problems, and represent a system of thought and action that hides from rather than confronts genuine social problems ("Another Brick in the Wall-Part II"). Even John Sebastian's laudatory "Welcome Back" tribute to a single teacher's devotion and responsibility carefully notes the exception to the norm.

IMAGES OF PARENTS AND THE COMMUNITY

Students generally regard the school system as an extension of the policymaking power and educational goals of parents and other members of the local community. Lyrics in many recordings depict the parental/principal/community nexus as the primary source of conformity, authoritarianism, hypocrisy, and frustration. At best, students dwell in a world where they are "Almost Grown." But parents and community leaders seem unwilling to accept occasional mistakes that are normal aspects of personal maturation and social development. Schools do not function as experimental stages for reflective consideration of alternative social, political, economic, and personal ideas and behaviors; instead, they are cloisters, cells, and societal buffers. Deviant behavior is harshly labeled ("The Rebel" and "Leader of the Pack") by a unified adult population ("Town without Pity," "Sticks and Stones," and "Society's Child"). Insensitivity to growing pains ("At Seventeen") is compounded by intense social pressure to conform in thought, word, and deed ("Fortunate Son" and "The Free Electric Band"). Despite occasional public lapses between preachment and practice among community members ("Harper Valley P.T.A.") and parents ("That's the Way I've Always Heard It Should Be"), schools remain bastions of patriotic, loyal ("Be True to Your School"), and moral ("Me and Julio Down By the Schoolyard") direction. Such a strong parental/community stance obviously renders democratic processes, instructional independence, intellectual objectivity, and open communication among students and teachers impossible. The smothering hand of community control is lyrically chided in the Simon and Garfunkel ballad "My Little Town."

IMAGES OF EDUCATION

"Please tell me who I am." This request paraphrases Socrates' more positively stated dictum, "Know thyself." But it is central to the lyrical criticism of formal education posed by Supertramp in their 1979 hit "The Logical Song." Echoing Rousseau's naturalistic educational premise, the lyric depicts an untutored youngster who views life as wonderful, beautiful, and magical. Then he is sent away to school where he learns to be clinical, logical, cynical, sensible, responsible, and practical. Pink Floyd's "Another Brick in the Wall-Part II" challenged the formal educational system with a a more direct, stinging, chanting attack:

> We don't need no education.
> We don't need no thought control.

The Supertramp/Pink Floyd assertions seem far more deep-rooted and radical than the humorous, exasperated tales of Chuck Berry and The Coasters. Yet they are logical extensions of lyrical critiques presented by Janis Ian, Paul Simon, and others who are understandably appalled by the failure of American education to meet or even to approach in practice its oft-repeated ideals. The laudable goals of fostering human dignity, creativity, freedom, individualism, knowledge, diversity, and objectivity are submerged in public schools beneath a miasma of regimentation, indoctrination, cynicism, arbitrariness, authoritarianism, local morality, and cultural bias. The disembodied voice of American youth—popular recordings— chants a consistent, sad refrain.

It might be easy to argue, in defense of enlightened teaching, that few popular songs could appropriately detail the virtues of an inspired history lecture, the potential delight of analyzing Shakespeare's sonnets, or the feeling of confidence gained by conducting a successful chemistry experiment. However, the weight of contemporary lyrical evidence is conclusive. Good teaching is an exception; inept classroom performance is expected and received. Similarly, belittling ridicule rather than reinforcing praise is the norm for dealing with students—from principals, from parents, from instructors, and (not infrequently) from insensitive, conforming peers as well. The public school arena is a polity that Aristotle would probably label an "unjust society" where the "just" person (logical, creative, sensitive, democratic) will either become or be perceived as alienated and rebellious. What is even more regrettable, though, is the apparent success of this system in sustaining itself.

If public schools are such ineffective sources of learning, then how do young people gain knowledge? Although tunesmiths provide a spectacular variety of options, they seem to concur on one point. Most valuable ideas, information, social contacts, feelings, beliefs, and personal values are secured through individual experience *outside* of the classroom. Recorded commentaries argue "I Gotta Be Me," "My Way," "Just the Way You Are," and "You May Be Right." The individualistic road through life is not necessarily solipsistic, alienating, or narcissistic. Once again, lyrical images of community pressures ("Town Without Pity"), peer criticisms ("Sticks and Stones"), parental restraints ("Yackety Yak" and "Summertime Blues"), church irrelevance ("Only the Good Die Young"), political skul- duggery ("Won't Get Fooled Again"), and wage labor meaninglessness ("Wake Me, Shake Me," "Get a Job," "Take This Job and Shove It," and "Workin' at the Carwash Blues") tend to hinder personal development through outside-of-school contacts.

This study does not intend to suggest that 1955-1980 recordings are devoid of paeans to the joy of intellectual growth and self-discovery. Abundant examples illustrate constructive personal experiences. Some are humorous, such as "Spiders and Snakes," "Mr. Businessman," and "Dead End Street"; some are serious, such as "Question," "Who Will Answer," and "Eve of Destruction"; and some are poignant, such as "Color Him Father," "Son of Hickory Holler's Tramp," and "Patches." In each of these instances, of course, the learning is directly connected to individual per- ceptions of personally meaningful life events. No organized, administered, routinized system can replace authentic human experience. Rousseau may not be correct about a person's natural bent toward goodness; however, Thoreau's concept of simplifying in order to enrich each person's life might serve as a guiding principle to revise and reshape formal education. Real learning, if those messages communicated in popular songs are to be believed, is intrinsically personal. Therefore, the bureaucratic public edu- cational system of the United States is antithetical to the process of indi- vidual growth (Johnson, 1993). Is it any wonder that school consolidation, classroom and curriculum regimentation, computerization, teacher union- ization, and other facets of mass education have further alienated so many students? Images of schools as minimum security detention centers ("Smokin' in the Boy's Room" "School Day," and "Charlie Brown") are more depressing than comic. The hard work of good principals, creative and caring teachers, and concerned parents to improve community schools may be futile because their efforts fail to take into account several funda- mental educational prerequisites. For some people, learning is intrinsically personal. The needs and experiences of such American students defy the factory-like organizational patterns that may have worked well during the post-World War I period. The shifting technology of American society—a car culture, a television culture, a computer culture—is dramatically alter- ing the lives of young and old alike. Similarly, events of the past forty years ranging from the launching of Sputnik and the prolonged Vietnam conflict to the attempted assassination of Ronald Reagan and the rise of Japanese economic dominance have altered the collective psyche of stu- dents. But the primary audio barometer of America's youth culture—popular music—continues to illustrate the expectations, observations, assumptions, and goals of school-age people.

The observations in this study are undeniably as impressionistic and subjective as the lyrical evidence compiled to support it. Formal education is clearly not respected in contemporary lyrics. Worse than that, it is openly ridiculed and condemned. Singers and songwriters openly attack the narrowness of hypocritical community norms and praise the survival of individuals beyond the classroom. Contemporary performers are, to no small extent, minstrels and balladeers for America's youth. This indicates that they offer sprightly, rhythmic entertainment as well as admittedly fictionalized, sometimes overdramatized ("Subterranean Homesick Blues") pictures of life in a complex, confusing, highly industrialized, urbanized nation. Their messages should be heeded. Current problems of student illiteracy and school violence are indicative of chronic mismatches of persons and place.

Rock music expresses youthful disenchantment, at least with efforts to socialize young people to a world in contradiction and crisis. But nowhere in the music can one find attempts to understand this disenchantment. No genuine analysis is ventured. Unlike the spate of politically oriented music that emerged during the late 1960s, rock music is devoid of authentic, constructive ideological comment. Rock lyricists are content to demand, "Teachers, leave them kids alone!" Rock music, then, reflects contemporary youth's fatalistic, uncritical view of the future. That view, with its lack of perspective or sense of options, should give pause. There is, ultimately, a beguiling nihilism in the observation contained in Sam Cooke's oft-recorded, "Don't know nothin' 'bout nothin' at all."

The conclusions reached in this study are not invigorating. What is particularly sad, though, is that changes are unlikely to occur in a system dedicated to socialization rather than education, to increasing patriotism rather than civic action, to establishing order rather than fomenting creativity, and to molding passive citizens rather than enlivening renaissance thinkers. The antischool legacy of early rock lyrics continues to echo in the verbal hostilities of Twisted Sister, in the taunting cynicism of Billy Joel, and in the general anti-institutional indictments of many gangsta rappers. Adolescent views of formal education remain stridently negative. The startling revelation for contemporary adults is that the persistent problems being identified on recordings actually exist. Formal learning is too significant to be stifled by an unresponsive and ever-burgeoning educational bureaucracy. While lyrics may be imperfect reflections of reality, they constitute a legitimate cry for revision and renewal of the entire American schooling system. Is anyone listening?

SELECTED DISCOGRAPHY OF EDUCATION-RELATED
RECORDINGS, 1955-1980

- "Abigail Beecher"
  (Warner Brothers 5409)
  Freddy Cannon (1964)

- "After School"
  (Decca 29946)
  Tommy Charles (1956)

- "After School"
  (Dale 100)
  Randy Staff (1957)

- "Almost Grown"
  (Chess 1722)
  Chuck Berry (1959)

- "Another Brick in the Wall-Part II"
  (Columbia 11187)
  Pink Floyd (1979)

- "At Seventeen"
  (Columbia 10154)
  Janis Ian (1975)

- "Back to School"
  (Checker 1158)
  Bo Diddley (1967)

- "Back to School Again"
  (Cameo 116)
  Timmie Rogers (1957)

- "Be True to Your School"
  (Capitol 5069)
  The Beach Boys (1963)

- "Bennie and the Jets"
  (MCA 40198)
  Elton John

- "Bird Dog"
  (Cadence 1350)
  The Everly Brothers (1958)

- "Cat's in the Cradle"
  (Elektra 45203)
  Harry Chapin (1974)

- "Charlie Brown"
  (Atco 6132)
  The Coasters (1959)

- "The Class"
  (Parkway 804)
  Chubby Checker (1959)

- "Class Cutter (Yeah Yeah)"
  (Checker 916)
  Dale Hawkins (1959)

- "Class of '57"
  (Mercury 73315)
  Statler Brothers (1972)

- "Class of '49"
  (Starday 779)
  Red Sovine (1966)

- "Color Him Father"
  (Metromedia 117)
  The Winstons (1969)

- "Dead End Street"
  (Capitol 5869)
  Lou Rawls (1967)

- "Department of Youth"
  (Atlantic 3280)
  Alice Cooper (1975)

- "Dialogue (Part I and II)"
  (Columbia 45717)
  Chicago (1972)

- "Don't Be a Drop-Out"
  (King 6056)
  James Brown (1966)

- "Don't Drop Out of School"
  (ABC 10944)
  Trends (1967)

- "Don't Stand So Close to Me"
  (A&M 2301)
  The Police (1980)

- "Eighteen"
  (Warner Brothers 7449)
  Alice Cooper (1971)

- "Eve of Destruction"
  (Dunhill 4009)
  Barry McGuire (1965)

- "Everybody's Talking"
  (RCA 0161)
  Harry Nilsson (1969)

- "Fortunate Son"
  (Fantasy 634)
  Creedence Clearwater Revival (1969)

- "The Free Electric Band"
  (Mums 6018)
  Albert Hammond (1973)

- "From a School Ring to a Wedding Ring"
  (ABC-Paramount 9732)
  Rover Boys (1956)

- "From the Teacher to the Preacher"
  (Brunswick 55387)
  Gene Chandler and Barbara Acklin (1968)

- "Got a Job"
  (Ember 1029)
  The Silhouettes (1958)

- "Graduation Day"
  (ABC-Paramount 9700)
  Rover Boys (1956)

- "Graduation Day"
  (Capitol 3410)
  Four Freshmen (1956)

- "Graduation Day"
  (Garpax 44175)
  Bobby Pickett (1963)

- "Graduation Day"
  (Date 1561)
  The Arbors (1967)

- "Graduation's Here"
  (Dolton 3)
  The Fleetwoods (1959)

- "Harper Valley P.T.A."
  (Plantation 3)
  Jeannie C. Riley (1968)

- "Harper Valley P.T.A. (Later That Same Day)"
  (MOM 13997)
  Ben Colder (1968)

- "He's a Rebel"
  (Philles 106)
  The Crystals (1962)

- "Hey Little Girl"
  (Abner 1029)
  Dee Clark (1959)

- "Hey, School Girl"
  (Big 613)
  Tom & Jerry (1958)

- "High School Confidential"
  (Sun 296)
  Jerry Lee Lewis (1958)

- "High School Dance"
  (Capitol 4405)
  Sylvers (1977)

- "High School Dance"
  (Specialty 608)
  Larry Williams (1957)

- "High School Days"
  (Fairlane 21020)
  Bill Erwin and The Four Jacks (1962)

- "High School Hero"
  (Tower St 5127)
  Jake Hohnes (1970)

- "High School Romance"
  (ABC-Paramount 9838)
  George Hamilton IV (1957)

- "High School U.S.A."
  (Atlantic 51-78)
  Tommy Facenda (1959)

- "High School Yearbook"
  (Liberty 1389)
  Nitty Gritty Dirt Band (1980)

- "I Am a Rock"
  (Columbia 43617)
  Simon and Garfunkel (1966)

- "I Am, I Said"
  (Uni 55278)
  Neil Diamond (1971)

- "I Get Around"
  (Capitol 5174)
  Beach Boys (1964)

- "I Think We're Alone Now"
  (Roulette 4720)
  Tommy James and The Shondells (1967)

- "(I Wanna) Dance with the Teacher"
  (Demon 1512)
  The Olympics (1959)

- "I Wish"
  (Tamla 54274)
  Stevie Wonder (1977)

- "I'm Going Back to School"
  (Vee Jay 462)
  Dee Clark (1962)

- "The 'In' Crowd"
  (Charger 105)
  Dobie Gray (1965)

- "I've Got a Name"
  (ABC 11389)
  Jim Croce (1973)

- "I've Gotta Be Me"
  (Reprise 0779)
  Sammy Davis Jr. (1968)

- "It Hurts to Be Sixteen"
  (Big Top 3156)
  Andrea Carroll (1963)

- "It's Your Thing"
  (T-Neck 901)
  Isley Brothers (1969)

- "Just the Way You Are"
  (Columbia 10646)
  Billy Joel (1977)

- "Kodachrome"
  (Columbia 45859)
  Paul Simon (1973)

- "The Last Game of the Season (A Blind Man in the Bleachers)"
  (Big Tree 16052)
  David Geddes (1975)

- "The Leader of the Pack"
  (Red Bird 014)
  The Shangri-Las (1964)

- "The Logical Song"
  (A&M 2128)
  Supertramp (1979)

- "Lonely School Year"
  (Rocket 40464)
  Hudson Brothers (1975)

- "Mama Told Me (Not to Come)"
  (Dunhill 4239)
  Three Dog Night (1970)

- "Mammas Don't Let Your Babies Grow Up to Be Cowboys"
  (RCA 11198)
  Willie Nelson (1978)

- "Me and Julio Down by the Schoolyard"
  (Columbia 45585)
  Paul Simon (1972)

- "Mr. Businessman"
  (Monument 1083)
  Ray Stevens (1968)

- "Mr. Leet"
  (Atlantic 1144)
  Bobbettes (1957)

- "My Back Pages"
  (Columbia 44054)
  The Byrds (1967)

- "My Boy-Flat Top"
  (King 1494)
  Boyd Bennett and His Rockets (1955)

- "My Generation"
  (Decca 31877)
  The Who (1966)

- "My Little Town"
  (Columbia 10230)
  Simon & Garfunkel (1975)

- "My Old School"
  (ABC 11396)
  Steely Dan (1973)

- "My Way"
  (Reprise 0817)
  Frank Sinatra (1969)

- "New Girl in School"
  (Liberty 55672)
  Jan and Dean (1964)

- "New Kid in Town"
  (Asylum 45373)
  Eagles (1977)

- "Night Moves"
  (Capitol 4369)
  Bob Seger and The Silver Bullet Band (1977)

- "Ohio"
  (Atlantic 2740)
  Crosby, Stills, Nash, and Young (1970)

- "Okie from Muskogee"
  (Capitol 2626)
  Merle Haggard and The Strangers (1969)

- "Only Sixteen"
  (Keen 2022)
  Sam Cooke (1959)

- "Only Sixteen"
  (Capitol 4171)
  Dr. Hook (1976)

- "Only the Good Die Young"
  (Columbia 10750)
  Billy Joel (1978)

- "Open Letter to My Teenage Son"
  (Liberty 55996)
  Victor Lundberg (1967)

- "Patches"
  (Atlantic 2748)
  Clarence Carter (1970)

- "A Place in the Sun"
  (A&M 1976)
  Pablo Cruise (1977)

- "Please Come to Boston"
  (Epic 11115)
  Dave Loggins (1974)

- "Pomp and Circumstance (The Graduation Song)"
  (Calliope 6501)
  Adrian Kimberly (1961)

- "(Remember the Days of the) Old Schoolyard"
  (A&M 1948)
  Cat Stevens (1977)

- "Queen of the Senior Prom"
  (Decca 30299)
  The Mills Brothers (1957)

- "Question"
  (Threshold 67004)
  The Moody Blues (1970)

- "Rebel"
  (Dot 15586)
  Carol Jarvis (1957)

- "Respect Yourself"
  (Stax 0104)
  Staple Singers (1971)

- "The Right Thing to Do"
  (Elektra 45843)
  Carly Simon (1973)

- "Rock and Roll (I Gave You the Best Years of My Life)"
  (Columbia 10070)
  Mac Davis (1975)

- "Rose and a Baby Ruth"
  (ABC-Paramount 9765)
  George Hamilton IV (1956)

- "Roses Are Red (My Love)"
  (Epic 9509)
  Bobby Vinton (1962)

- "School Bell Rock"
  (King 5247)
  Roy Brown (1959)

- "School Bells Are Ringing"
  (Dimension 1004)
  Carole King (1962)

- "School Boy Crush"
  (Atlantic 3304)
  Average White Band (1975)

- "School Boy Romance"
  (ABC-Paramount 9888)
  Danny and The Juniors (1958)

- "School Bus"
  (Leader 808)
  Kris Jensen (1960)

- "School Day"
  (Chess 1653)
  Chuck Berry (1957)

- "School Dance"
  (ABC-Paramount 9908)
  Dwayne Hickman (1958)

- "School Day Crush"
  (Gone 5039)
  Nicky and The Nobels (1959)

- "School Days Are Back Again"
  (Imperial 5478)
  Smiley Lewis (1957)

- "School Daze"
  (Magic 93000)
  Funn (1981)

- "School Fool"
  (Mam 12553)
  Mark Dinning (1957)

- "School Is In"
  (LeGrand 1012)
  Gary "U.S." Bonds (1961)

- "School Is Out"
  (LeGrand 1009)
  Gary "U.S." Bonds (1961)

- "School of Love"
  (KoKo 2112)
  Tommy Tate (1972)

- "School Teacher"
  (Reprise 1069)
  Kenny Rogers and The First Edition (1972)

- "School's All Over"
  (World 10)
  Adorables (1964)

- "School's Out"
  (Warner Brothers 7596)
  Alice Cooper (1972)

- "Schoolbells"
  (Gone 5039)
  Nicky and The Nobels (1959)

- "Schooldays, Oh Schooldays"
  (Parkway 804)
  Chubby Checker (1959)

- "See You in September"
  (Climax 102)
  Tempos (1959)

- "See You in September"
  (B. T. Puppy 520)
  Happenings (1966)

- "Seventeen"
  (King 1470)
  Boyd Bennett and His Rockets (1955)

- "She Was Only Seventeen"
  (Columbia 41208)
  Marty Robbins (1958)

- "Short Fat Fannie"
  (Specialty 608)
  Larry Williams (1957)

- "Skip a Rope"
  (Monument 1041)
  Henson Cargill (1968)

- "Smokin' in the Boys' Room"
  (Big Tree 16011)
  Brownsville Station (1974)

- "So You Want to Be a Rock 'n' Roll Star"
  (Columbia 43987)
  The Byrds (1967)

- "Society's Child (Baby I've Been Thinking)"
  (Verve 5027)
  Janis Ian (1967)

- "Someone Saved My Life Tonight"
  (MCA 40421)
  Elton John (1975)

- "Son of a Preacher Man"
  (Atlantic 2580)
  Dusty Springfield (1969)

- "Son of Hickory Holler's Tramp"
  (Columbia 44425)
  O. C. Smith (1968)

- "Spiders and Snakes"
  (MGM 14648)
  Jim Stafford (1974)

- "Sticks and Stones"
  (ABC-Paramount 10118)
  Ray Charles (1960)

- "Still Crazy After All These Years"
  (Columbia 0332)
  Paul Simon (1976)

- "Stood Up"
  (Imperial 5483)
  Ricky Nelson (1958)

- "Subterranean Homesick Blues"
  (Columbia 43242)
  Bob Dylan (1965)

- "Summertime Blues"
  (Liberty 55144)
  Eddie Cochran (1958)

- "Summertime Blues"
  (Decca 32708)
  The Who (1970)

- "Summertime, Summertime"
  (Epic 9281)
  Jamies (1958)

- "Sylvia's Mother"
  (Columbia 45562)
  Dr. Hook (1972)

- "Sweet Little Sixteen"
  (Chess 1683)
  Chuck Berry (1958)

- "Swingin' on a Star"
  (Dimension 1010)
  Big Dee Irwin (1963)

- "Swingin' School"
  (Cameo 175)
  Bobby Rydell (1960)

- "Take This Job and Shove It"
  (Epic 50469)
  Johnny Paycheck (1977)

- "Talk of the School"
  (Capitol 4178)
  Sonny James (1959)

- "Taxi"
  (Elektra 45770)
  Harry Chapin (1972)

- "Teach Me Tiger"
  (Imperial 5626)
  April Stevens (1959)

- "Teach Me Tonight"
  (Epic 9504)
  George Maharis (1962)

- "Teach Your Children"
  (Atlantic 2735)
  Crosby, Stills, Nash, and Young (1970)

- "Teacher"
  (Reprise 0899)
  Jethro Tull (1970)

- "The Teacher and the Pet"
  (AGP 110)
  Johnny Christopher (1969)

- "Teacher, Teacher"
  (Columbia 41152)
  Johnny Mathis (1958)

- "Teacher's Pet"
  (Columbia 41123)
  Doris Day (1958)

- "Teenage Lament '74"
  (Warner Brothers 7762)
  Alice Cooper (1974)

- "That's Life"
  (Reprise 0531)
  Frank Sinatra (1966)

- "That's the Way I've Always Heard It Should Be"
  (Electra 45724)
  Carly Simon (1971)

- "To Be Young, Gifted, and Black"
  (RCA 0269)
  Nina Simone (1969)

- "To Sir with Love"
  (Epic 10187)
  Lulu (1967)

- "Town Without Pity"
  (Musicor 1009)
  Gene Pitney (1962)

- "2 + 2 = ?"
  (Capitol 2143)
  Bob Seger System (1968)

- "Venus in Blue Jeans"
  (Ace 8001)
  Jimmy Clanton (1962)

- "Waitin' in School"
  (Imperial 5483)
  Ricky Nelson (1958)

- "Wake Me, Shake Me"
  (Atco 6168)
  The Coasters (1960)

- "Wake Up Little Susie"
  (Cadence 1337)
  The Everly Brothers (1957)

- "We Just Disagree"
  (Columbia 10575)
  Dave Mason (1977)

- "We May Never Pass This Way (Again)"
  (Warner Brothers 7740)
  Seals and Crofts (1973)

- "Welcome Back"
  (Reprise 1349)
  John Sebastian (1976)

- "(What a) Wonderful World"
  (Columbia 10676)
  Art Garfunkel, James Taylor, and Paul Simon (1978)

- "What Did You Learn in School Today?"
  (Mercury 72257)
  Chad Mitchell Trio (1964)

- "What Good Is Graduation?"
  (Corsican 0058)
  Graduates (1959)

- "What Is a Teenage Boy?"
  (Coral 61773)
  Tom Edwards (1957)

- "What Is a Teenage Girl?"
  (Coral 61773)
  Tom Edwards (1957)

- "When the Boys Get Together"
  (Warner Brothers 5308)
  Joanie Sommers (1962)

- "When the Boys Talk About the Girls"
  (Roulette 4066)
  Valerie Carr (1958)

- "Whenever a Teenager Cries"
  (World Artists 1036)
  Reparata and The Delrons (1965)

- "Where the Boys Are"
  (MOM 12971)
  Connie Francis (1961)

- "White Sport Coat (And a Pink Carnation)"
  (Columbia 40864)
  Marty Robbins (1957)

- "Who Are You?"
  (MCA 40948)
  The Who (1978)

- "Who Will Answer?"
  (RCA 9400)
  Ed Ames (1968)

- "Why Can't My Teacher Look Like Mr. Novak?"
  (Capitol 5325)
  Jackie and Gayle (1964)

- "Why Do Kids Grow Up?"
  (Rust 5073)
  Tandy and The Rainbows (1963)

- "Why Don't They Understand?"
  (ABC-Paramount 9862)
  George Hamilton IV (1958)

- "Wonderful World"
  (Keen 2112)
  Sam Cooke (1960)

- "Wonderful World"
  (MOM 13354)
  Herman's Hermits (1965)

- "Won't Get Fooled Again"
  (Decca 32846)
  The Who (1971)

- "Woodstock"
  (Atlantic 2723)
  Crosby, Stills, Nash, and Young (1970)

- "Workin' at the Carwash Blues"
  (ABC 11447)
  Jim Croce (1974)

- "Yakety Yak"
  (Atco 6116)
  The Coasters (1958)

- "Yesterday When I Was Young"
  (Dot 17246)
  Roy Clark (1969)

- "You and Me Against the World"
  (Capitol 3897)
  Helen Reddy (1974)

- "You May Be Right"
  (Columbia 11231)
  Billy Joel (1980)

- "You Never Can Tell"
  Chuck Berry
  (Chess 1906)

- "Young School Girl"
  (Imperial 5537)
  Fats Domino (1958)

- "Your Mama Don't Dance"
  (Columbia 45719)
  Loggins & Messina (1973)

BIBLIOGRAPHY

Adams, Peter M. "Music and Youth: Sounds and Significance," *Social Education*, XXXVIII (April 1954), pp. 356-363.

Arnett, Jeffrey Jensen. *Metal Heads: Heavy Metal Music and Adolescent Alienation*. Boulder, CO: Westview Press, 1996.

Barr, Robert D. "Youth and Music," in *Values and Youth: Teaching Social Studies in an Age of Crisis*—No. 2. Washington, DC: National Council for the Social Studies, 1971, pp. 88-103.

Bennett, Tony, Simon Frith, Lawrence Grossberg, John Sheperd, and Graeme Turner (eds.). *Rock and Popular Music: Politics/Policies/Institutions*. London: Routledge, 1993.

Binda, Kenneth J. (ed.). *America's Musical Pulse: Popular Music in Twentieth-Century Society*. Westport, CT: Praeger Books, 1992.

Bloodworth, John D. "Communication in the Youth Counter Culture: Music As Expression," *Central States Speech Quarterly*, 26 (Winter 1975), pp. 304-309.

Brown, Elizabeth and William Hendee. "Adolescents and Their Music," *Journal of the American Medical Association,* 262 (September 22-29, 1989), pp. 1659-1663.

Butchart, Ronald E. and B. Lee Cooper. "Perceptions of Education in the Lyrics of American Popular Music, 1950-1980," *American Music*, 5 (Fall 1987), pp. 271-281.

Carney, George O. (ed.). *Fast Food, Stock Cars, and Rock 'n' Roll: Place and Space in American Pop Culture*. Lanham, MD: Rowman and Littlefield, 1995.

Cooper, B. Lee. "Awarding an 'A' Grade to Heavy Metal: A Review Essay," *Popular Music and Society,* 17 (Fall 1993), pp. 99-102.

Cooper, B. Lee. "Can Music Students Learn Anything of Value Investigating Popular Recordings?," *International Journal of Instructional Media*, 10, No. 3 (1993), pp. 273-284.

Cooper, B. Lee. "Education," in *A Resource Guide to Themes in Contemporary Song Lyrics*, 1950-1985. Westport, CT: Greenwood Press, 1986.

Cooper, B. Lee. "The Image of the Outsider In Contemporary Lyrics," *Journal of Popular Culture*, 12 (Summer 1978), pp. 168-178.

Cooper, B. Lee. *Images of American Society in Popular Music: A Guide to Reflective Teaching*. Chicago: Nelson-Hall, 1982.

Cooper, B. Lee. " 'It's a Wonder I Can Think at All': Vinyl Images of American Public Education, 1950-1980," *Popular Music and Society*, 9 (Winter 1984), pp. 47-65.

Cooper, B. Lee. "Lyrical Commentaries: Learning from Popular Music," *Music Educators Journal*, 77 (April 1991), pp. 56-59.

Cooper, B. Lee. *Popular Music Perspectives: Ideas Themes, and Patterns in Contemporary Lyrics*. Bowling Green, OH: Bowling Green State University Popular Press, 1991.

Cooper, B. Lee. "A Resource Guide to Studies in the Theory and Practice of Popular Culture Librarianship," in *Popular Culture and Acquisitions*, edited by Allen Ellis. Binghamton, NY: The Haworth Press, 1992, pp. 131-146.

Cooper, B. Lee. *A Resource Guide to Themes in Contemporary American Song Lyrics 1950-1985*. Westport, CT: Greenwood Press, 1986.

Cooper, B. Lee. "Rhythm 'n' Rhymes: Character and Theme Images from Children's Literature in Contemporary Recordings, 1950-1985," *Popular Music and Society,* 13 (Spring 1989), pp. 53-71.

Cooper, B. Lee. "Sounds of Schooling in Modern America: Recorded Images of Public Education, 1950-1980," *International Journal of Instructional Media*, 11, No. 3 (1983-1984), pp. 255-271.

Cooper, B. Lee and Wayne S. Haney. *Rock Music in American Culture: Rock 'n' Roll Resources.* Binghamton, NY: The Haworth Press, 1995.

Cooper, B. Lee and Wayne S. Haney. *Rock Music in American Culture II: More Rock 'n' Roll Resources.* Binghamton, NY: The Haworth Press, 1997.

Cooper, B. Lee and William L. Schurk. "From 'I Saw Mommy Kissing Santa Claus' to 'Another Brick in the Wall': Popular Recordings Featuring Pre-Teen Performers, Traditional Childhood Stories, and Contemporary Pre-Adolescent Perspectives, 1945-1985," *International Journal of Instructional Media*, 16, No. 1 (1989), pp. 83-90.

Curtis, Jim. *Rock Eras: Interpretations of Music and Society 1954-1984.* Bowling Green, OH: Bowling Green State University Popular Press, 1987.

Denisoff, R. Serge. *Inside MTV.* New Brunswick, NJ: Transaction Books, 1991. (c. 1988).

Denisoff, R. Serge and William D. Romanowski. *Risky Business: Rock in Film.* New Brunswick, NJ: Transaction Books, 1991.

Desmond, Roger Jon. "Adolescents and Music Lyrics: Implications of a Cognitive Perspective," *Communication Quarterly*, 35 (Summer 1987): 276-284.

Dotter, Daniel. "Rock and Roll Is Here to Stray: Youth Subculture, Deviance, and Social Typing in Rock's Early Years," in *Adolescents and Their Music: If It's Too Loud You're Too Old*, edited by Jonathan S. Epstein. New York: Garland Publishing, 1994, 87-114.

Dunne, Michael. *Metapop: Self-Referentiality in Contemporary American Popular Culture.* Jackson, MS: University Press of Mississippi, 1992.

Epstein, Jonathan S. (ed.). *Adolescents and Their Music: If It's Too Loud, You're Too Old.* New York: Garland Publishing, 1994.

Epstein, Jonathan S. "Misplaced Childhood: An Introduction to the Sociology of Youth and Their Music," in *Adolescents and Their Music: If It's Too Loud, You're Too Old*, edited by Jonathan S. Epstein. New York: Garland Publishing, 1994, pp. xiii-xxiv.

Epstein, Jonathan S. and David J. Pratto. "Heavy Metal Rock Music, Juvenile Delinquency, and Satanic Identification," *Popular Music and Society,* 14 (Winter 1990), pp. 67-76.

Farber, Paul, Eugene F. Provenzo Jr., and Gunilla Holm (eds.). *Schooling in the Light of Popular Culture.* Albany, NY: State University of New York Press, 1994.

Fornas, Johan, Ulf Lindber, and Ove Sernhede (translated by Jan Teeland). *In Garageland: Rock, Youth, and Modernity.* New York: Routledge, 1995.

Friedlander, Paul. *Rock and Roll: A Social History.* Boulder, CO: Westview Press, 1996.

Frith, Simon. *Sound Effects: Youth, Leisure, and the Politics of Rock 'n' Roll.* New York: Pantheon Books, 1981.

Frith, Simon and Andrew Goodwin (eds.). *On Record: Rock, Pop, and the Written Word*. New York: Pantheon Books, 1990.

Giroux, Henry A. and Roger I. Simon. *Popular Culture: Schooling and Everyday Life*. Westport, CT: Bergin and Garvey, 1989.

Goodall, H. L. Jr. *Living in the Rock 'n' Roll Mystery: Reading Context, Self, and Others As Clues*. Carbondale, IL: Southern Illinois University Press, 1991.

Gordon, Robert. *It Came from Memphis*. Boston: Faber and Faber, 1995.

Grossberg, Lawrence. "Another Boring Day in Paradise: Rock and Roll and the Empowerment of Everyday Life," in *Popular Music 4: Performers and Audiences*, edited by Richard Middleton and David Horn. Cambridge, England: Cambridge University Press, 1984, pp. 225-258.

Grossberg, Lawrence. "The Politics of Youth Culture: Some Observations on Rock and Roll in American Culture," *Social Text*, 8 (Winter 1983-84), pp. 104-126.

Hakanen, Ernest A. and Alan Wells. "Adolescent Music Marginals: Who Likes Metal, Jazz, Country, and Classical," *Popular Music and Society*, 14 (Winter 1990), pp. 57-66.

Hakanen, Ernest A. and Alan Wells. "Music Preference and Taste Cultures Among Adolescents," *Popular Music and Society*, 17 (Spring 1993), pp. 55-69.

Harris, James F. *Philosophy at $33^1/_3$ R.P.M.: Themes of Classic Rock Music* La Salle, IL: Open Court Publishing, 1993.

Hendler, Herb. *Year by Year in the Rock Era: Events and Conditions Shaping the Rock Generations That Reshaped America*. Westport, CT: Greenwood Press, 1983.

Hibbard, Don J. and Carol Kaleialoha. *The Role of Rock: A Guide to the Social and Political Consequences of Rock Music*. Englewood, NJ: Prentice-Hall, 1983.

Hilsabeck, Steven A. "The Blackboard Bumble: Popular Culture and the Recent Challenges to the American High School," *Journal of Popular Culture*, 18 (Winter 1984), pp. 25-30.

Jochem, Phil. "Some Popular Songs Rip into Teachers," *Instructor*, 85 (October 1975), pp. 40-42.

Johnson, Michael L. *Education on the Wild Side: Learning for the Twenty-First Century*. Norman, OK: University Of Oklahoma Press, 1993.

Kirschner, Tony. "The Lalapalooziation of American Youth," *Popular Culture and Society*, 18 (Spring 1994), pp. 69-90.

Kotarba, Joseph A. (ed.). "Adolescents and Rock 'n' Roll," *Youth and Society*, XVIII, No 4 (June 1987), pp. 323-432.

Lipsitz, George. *Time Passages: Collective Memory and American Popular Culture*. Minneapolis, MN: University of Minnesota Press, 1990.

Martin, Linda and Kerry Segrave. *Anti-Rock: The Opposition to Rock 'n' Roll*. Hamden, CT: Archon Books, 1988.

McClary, Susan. "Same As It Ever Was: Youth Culture and Music," In *Microphone Fiends: Youth Music and Youth Culture*, edited by Andrew Ross and Tricia Rose. New York: Routledge, 1994, pp. 29-40.

McLaurin, Melton and Richard Peterson (eds.). *You Wrote My Life: Lyrical Themes in Country Music.* New York: Gordon and Breach, 1992.

McRobbie, Angela. "Shut Up and Dance: Youth Culture and Changing Modes of Femininity," *Cultural Studies,* 8 (October 1993), pp. 406-426.

Pichaske, David R. *A Generation in Motion: Popular Music and Culture in the Sixties.* Granite Falls, MN: Ellis Press, 1989.

Pielke, Robert G. *You Say You Want a Revolution: Rock Music in American Culture.* Chicago: Nelson-Hall, 1986.

Reidelbach, Maria. *Completely Mad: A History of the Comic Book and Magazine.* Boston: Little, Brown and Company, 1991.

Rogers, Jimmie N. *The Country Music Message: All About Lovin' and Livin'.* Englewood Cliffs, NJ: Prentice Hall, 1983.

Rogers, Jimmie N. *The Country Music Message: Revisited.* Fayetteville, AR: University of Arkansas Press, 1989.

Rose, Tricia. *Black Noise: Rap Music and Black Culture in Contemporary America.* Hanover, NH: University Press of New England, 1994.

Ross, Andrew and Tricia Rose (eds.). *Microphone Fiends: Youth Music and Youth Culture.* New York: Routledge, 1994.

Roszak, Theodore. *The Making of Counter Culture: Reflections on the Technocratic Society and Its Youthful Opposition.* Garden City, NY: Doubleday Anchor Books, 1969.

Rowe, David. *Popular Cultures: Rock Music, Sport, and the Politics of Pleasure.* Thousand Oaks, CA: Sage Publications, 1995.

Scheurer, Timothy E. *Born in the U.S.A.: The Myth of America in Popular Music from Colonial Times to the Present.* Jackson, MS: University Press of Mississippi, 1991.

Schultze, Quentin J., Roy M. Anker, James D. Bratt, William D. Romanowski, John W. Worst, and Lambert Zuidervaart. *Dancing in the Dark: Youth Popular Culture, and the Electronic Media.* Grand Rapids, MI: William B. Eerdmans Publishing, 1991.

Snow, Robert P. "Youth, Rock 'n' Roll, and Electronic Media," *Youth and Society,* 18 (June 1987), pp. 326-343.

Spring, Joel. *Images of American Life: A History of Ideological Management in Schools, Movies, Radio, and Television.* Albany, NY: State University of New York Press, 1992.

Stanley, Lawrence A. (ed.). *Rap: The Lyrics.* New York: Penguin Books, 1992.

Stern, Jane and Michael. *Encyclopedia of Pop Culture: An A to Z of Who's Who and What's What, from Aerobics to Bubble Gum to Valley of the Dolls and Moon Unit Zappa.* New York: HarperCollins Publishers, 1992.

Stevenson, Gordon. "The Wayward Scholar: Resources and Research in Popular Culture," *Library Trends,* 25 (April 1977), pp. 779-818.

Verden, Paul, Kathleen Dunleavy, and Charles H. Powers. "Heavy Metal Mania and Adolescent Delinquency," *Popular Culture and Society,* 13 (Spring 1989), pp. 73-82.

Vulliamy, Graham and Ed Lee (eds.). *Pop Music in School* (Revised Edition). Cambridge, England: Cambridge University Press, 1980.

Walser, Robert. *Running with the Devil: Power, Gender, and Madness in Heavy Metal Music*. Hanover, NH: University Press of New England, 1993.

Weinstein, Deena. *Heavy Metal: A Cultural Sociology*. New York: Lexington Books, 1991.

Weinstein, Deena. "Rock Is Youth/Youth Is Rock," in *America's Musical Pulse: Popular Music in Twentieth-Century Society*, edited by Kenneth J. Binda. Westport, CT: Praeger Books, 1992, pp. 91-98.

Weinstein, Deena. "Rock: Youth and Its Music," in *Adolescents and Their Music: If It's Too Loud, You're Too Old*, edited by Jonathan S. Epstein, New York: Garland Publishing, 1994, pp. 3-23.

Whitburn, Joel (comp.). *Top Pop Album Tracks, 1955-1992*. Menomonee Falls, WI: Record Research, Inc., 1993.

Whitburn, Joel (comp.). *Top Pop Single, 1955-1993*. Menomonee Falls, WI: Record Research, Inc., 1994.

Whitburn, Joel (comp.). *Top Pop Singles CD Guide, 1955-1979*. Menomonee Falls, WI: Record Research, Inc., 1995.

Whitburn, Joel (comp.). *Top Rhythm and Blues Singles*, 1988. Menomonee Falls, WI: Record Research, Inc., 1988.

Chapter 12

Rock Songs

Fabulous Flips: Great B-Sides of the 1950s and 1960s (Ace CDCHD 444). London: Ace Records, 1993. 26 songs.

Fabulous Flips—Volume Two (Ace CDCHD 560). London: Ace Records, 1995. 26 songs.

The 45 rpm record reigned supreme during the first rock 'n' roll decade. Most youthful music enthusiasts toted their flat, black, circular vinyl treasures around in little square boxes. Since these containers held seventy-five to eighty-five records, personal collections were usually limited to that maximum number. Trading kept the number relatively stable; turntable wear and tear also created vacancies for new acquisitions. Though heresy to serious disc collectors ("Don't play that recording. You might scratch it!"), once Bill Doggett's "Honky Tonk" was worn beyond playing, it was dumped from the collection in favor of Wilbert Harrison's "Kansas City." No loss. The memory of Doggett's virtuoso saxophone was indelibly etched in the music lover's mind after more than 400 performances.

The peculiar magic of a fixed-size, rotating collection was the tendency to listen to both sides of each recording. The 1990s compact disc generation neither remembers nor understands this concept. Neither do "only-play-me-the-top-ten-tunes" 1970s and 1980s music fanatics. Despite the rise of numerous "golden oldies" radio formats, most playlist planners are reluctant

---

The material in this chapter by B. Lee Cooper was originally published as "Searching for the Most Popular Songs of the Year . . . with Menomonee Falls Joel, Big Al, Louisiana Jim, and Bayou Barry," *Popular Culture in Libraries,* I, No. 2 (1973), pp. 125-130; and "Killer B's: Two-Sided Hits from Rock's Golden Age, 1955-1963," *Popular Music and Society,* XX, No. 3 (Fall 1996), pp. 141-144. Reprint permission granted by the author, editor Frank Hoffmann, The Haworth Press, editor Gary Burns, and The Bowling Green State University Popular Press.

to schedule anything but top-charted tunes from the pre-Beatles era. Too bad. There are so many nifty, groovy, bitchin', boppin', cool, hot, wild, and def B-side songs that deserve to be reprised—along with A-side hits such as "Johnny B. Goode," "Runaround Sue," and "Queen of the Hop."

It is especially fun to recall the wealth of 45s that were remarkable no matter which side landed face up on the turntable. From 1955 to 1963, "Killer Bs" (tough B-side tunes) were amazingly common. This was especially true for Elvis Presley, Little Richard, Ray Charles, Fats Domino, and many other founding fathers of rock. Britain's Ace Records has compiled fifty-two B-side gems on two compact discs and released them under the title *Fabulous Flips.* A few of the tunes are examples of profound influence, such as Larry Williams' "Slow Down"—one of the Specialty label songs adopted by The Beatles; a few of the numbers are potent illustrations of particular musical genres, such as Sanford Clark's rockabilly classic "Lonesome for a Letter" and Jack Scott's "Leroy"; and many others are simply great tunes that happened to be paired with extremely popular A-side releases. This latter category includes "Little Queenie" (flip side of "Almost Grown") by Chuck Berry, "Over and Over" (flip side of "Rockin' Robin") by Bobby Day, "My Babe" (flip side of "Love You So") by Ron Holden, and "Miss Ann" (flip side of "Jenny, Jenny") by Little Richard.

The extended notations provided in the *Fabulous Flips* volumes will alert both vinyl veterans and CD novices to the A-sides of all featured tunes. Informative biographical sketches of the performing artists and composers are also included. The only unanswered question is: Why highlight these particular songs? Upon reflection about B-side recordings that were more influential, more stylistically relevant, and more popular than those included in the two collections, the following releases come to mind immediately:

- "Teardrops on Your Letter" and "The Twist"
  (King 5171)
  Hank Ballard and The Midnighters (1959)

- "Back in the U.S.A." and "Memphis, Tennessee"
  (Chess 1729)
  Chuck Berry (1959)

- "I Walk the Line" and "Get Rhythm"
  (Sun 241)
  Johnny Cash (1956)

- "I Can't Stop Loving You" and "Born to Lose"
  (ABC-Paramount 10330)
  Ray Charles (1962)

- "What'd I Say? (Parts 1 & 2)"
  (Atlantic 2031)
  Ray Charles (1959)
- "Searchin' " and "Young Blood"
  (ATCDO 6087)
  The Coasters (1957)
- "Oh, Boy!" and "Not Fade Away"
  (Brunswick 55009)
  The Crickets (1957)
- "That'll Be the Day" and "I'm Looking for Someone to Love"
  (Brunswick 55009)
  The Crickets (1957)
- "Bo Diddley" and "I'm a Man"
  (Checker 814)
  Bo Diddley (1955)
- "Hey! Bo Diddley" and "Mona (I Need You Baby)"
  (Checker 860)
  Bo Diddley (1956)
- "Honky Tonk Parts 1 & 2"
  (King 4950)
  Bill Doggett (1956)
- "Blueberry Hill" and "Honey Chile"
  (Imperial 5407)
  Fats Domino (1956)
- "I'm in Love Again" and "My Blue Heaven"
  (Imperial 5386)
  Fats Domino (1956)
- "All I Have to Do Is Dream" and "Claudette"
  (Cadence 1348)
  The Everly Brothers (1958)
- "Bird Dog" and "Devoted to You"
  (Cadence 1350)
  The Everly Brothers (1958)
- "Ebony Eyes" and "Walk Right Back"
  (Warner Brothers 5199)
  The Everly Brothers (1961)
- "Sea Cruise" and "Roberta"
  (Ace 554)
  Frankie Ford (1959)

- "Sixteen Tons" and "You Don't Have to Be a Baby to Cry"
  (Capitol 3262)
  Tennessee Ernie Ford
- "Oh Lonesome Me" and "I Can't Stop Lovin' You"
  (RCA 7133)
  Don Gibson (1958)
- "I Put a Spell on You" and "Little Demon"
  (Okeh 7072)
  Screamin' Jay Hawkins (1956)
- "Shout (Parts 1 & 2)"
  (RCA 7588)
  The Isley Brothers (1959)
- "It's Too Soon to Know" and "Seven-Day Fool"
  (Argo 5402)
  Etta James (1961)
- "I Like It Like That (Parts 1 & 2)"
  (Instant 3229)
  Chris Kenner (1961)
- "I'm Sorry" and "That's All You Gotta Do"
  (Decca 31093)
  Brenda Lee (1960)
- "Long Tall Sally" and "Slippin' and Slidin' (Peepin' and Hidin')"
  (Specialty 572)
  Little Richard (1956)
- "Lucille" and "Send Me Some Lovin' "
  (Specialty 598)
  Little Richard (1957)
- "Rip It Up" and "Ready Teddy"
  (Specialty 579)
  Little Richard (1956)
- "There's Something on Your Mind (Parts 1 & 2)"
  (Fire 1022)
  Bobby Marchan (1960)
- "Chances Are" and "The Twelfth of Never"
  (Columbia 40993)
  Johnny Mathis (1957)
- "Travelin' Man" and "Hello Mary Lou"
  (Imperial 5741)
  Ricky Nelson (1961)

- "Mean Woman Blues" and "Blue Bayou"
  (Monument 824)
  Roy Orbison (1963)

- "Crying" and "Candy Man"
  (Monument 447)
  Roy Orbison (1961)

- "Blue Suede Shoes" and "Honey Don't"
  (Sun 234)
  Carl Perkins (1956)

- "Boppin' the Blues" and "All Mama's Children"
  (Sun 243)
  Carl Perkins (1956)

- "Don't Be Cruel" and "Hound Dog"
  (RCA 47-6604)
  Elvis Presley (1956)

- "Heartbreak Hotel" and "I Was the One"
  (RCA 6420)
  Elvis Presley (1956)

- "I Forgot to Remember to Forget" and "Mystery Train"
  (Sun 223)
  Elvis Presley (1955)

- "Jailhouse Rock" and "Treat Me Nice"
  (RCA 47-7635)
  Elvis Presley (1957)

- "(Let Me Be Your) Teddy Bear" and "Loving You"
  (RCA 7000)
  Elvis Presley (1957)

- "Little Sister" and "(Marie's the Name) of His Latest Flame"
  (RCA 47-7903)
  Elvis Presley (1961)

- "Love Me Tender" and "Anyway You Want Me
    (That's How I Will Be)"
  (RCA 6643)
  Elvis Presley (1956)

- "One Night" and "I Got Stung"
  (RCA 47-7410)
  Elvis Presley (1958)

- "Silhouettes" and "Daddy Cool"
  (Cameo 117)
  The Rays (1957)

- "Rocking Pneumonia and the Boogie Woogie Flu" (Parts 1 & 2)
  (Ace 530)
  Huey Smith and The Clowns (1957)

- "Lipstick Traces (on a Cigarette)" and "Fortune Teller"
  (Minis 644)
  Benny Spellman (1962)

- "You Can't Sit Down (Parts 1 & 2)"
  (Boyd 3398)
  The Philip Upchurch Combo (1961)

- "Donna" and "La Bamba"
  (Del-F 4110)
  Ritchie Valens (1958)

- "Bony Moronie" and "You Bug Me Baby"
  (Specialty 615)
  Larry Williams

- "What Am I Living for?" and "Hang Up My Rock and Roll Shoes"
  (Atlantic 1179)
  Chuck Willis

- "Doggin' Around" and "Night"
  (Brunswick 55166)
  Jackie Wilson (1960)

Both *Fabulous Flip*s discs are worth owning. They reprise performances that are rare, rockin', raunchy, and revealing. Fans of The Shirelles, Gary "U.S." Bonds, Jerry Butler, Nappy Brown, Link Wray, and The Everly Brothers will enjoy hearing their heroes performing less-than-frequently-played tunes. "Whatcha Gonna Do?," the flip side of "So Tough" by The Kuf-Linx, is my favorite Killer-B on these Ace anthologies.

*   *   *

Big Al Pavlow (comp.). *Hot Charts 1957*. Providence, RI: Music House Publishing, 1991. Unpaged.

Jim Quirin and Barry Cohen (comp.). *Rock 100: An Authoritative Ranking of the 100 Most Popular Songs for Each Year, 1956 Through 1986* (Fourth Edition). Covington, LA: Chartmasters, 1986. 98 pp.

Joel Whitburn (comp.). *Pop Singles Annual, 1955-1990.* Menomonee Falls, WI: Record Research, Inc., 1991. Illustrated. 710 pp.

Retrospective analyses of commercial recordings are designed to help collectors, nostalgia buffs, American culture scholars, ethnomusicologists, and rock music fans identify the most popular songs of the 1950-1990 period. The three studies examined here represent the most authoritative resources available. Al Pavlow's *Hot Charts 1957* is the eighth volume released during the past two years in a chronological series that will eventually extend from 1950 to 1963. Jim Quirin and Barry Cohen have been statistically analyzing annual chart listings for more than a decade. The fourth edition of *Rock 100* covers 1956 through 1986. Joel Whitburn's 1991 song survey updates his 1987 volume. *Pop Singles Annual, 1955-1990* is a massive study that dwarfs all other compilations in both scope and size.

Pavlow's *Hot Charts* are divided into month-by-month listings that feature between 150 and 200 songs arranged in numerical order. A complicated definitional point system, briefly explained but totally enigmatic, allows the author to establish his commercial recording hierarchy. The 1957 volume concludes with a cumulative Top 500 song list for the entire year.

Quirin and Cohen argue that their quantitative approach to create an annual ranking avoids the skewing pitfalls of using less-than-reliable retail sales reports, radio station requests, jukebox plays, and disc jockey polls. They claim to have established "a unique system [of ranking] formulated on a firm, objective, mathematical basis" (p. 1). The system, carefully explained and reduced to a complex math formula, is truly bizarre to the average disc fan. The authors produce their lists of 100 top annual hit recordings from a cumulative analysis of *Billboard's* "Hot 100," "Top 40," "Top 10," and "No. 1" charts.

Whitburn, currently the most respected chart compiler in America, has refined his *Billboard*-based record data with minor corrective adjustments over the past two decades. The bulk of his research is drawn directly from the "Hot 100" charts. During the late 1950s, of course, four other inter-related sources—"Best Sellers in Stores," "Most Played by Jockeys," "Most Played in Juke Boxes," and "Top 100"—were tapped.

Using 1957 as an illustration year, which songs do Pavlow, Quirin/ Cohen, and Whitburn assert to be the "Top 10" (#1-#10) and the "Bottom 10" (#91-#100) of the hundred most popular songs? (See Table 12.1.)

While the Top 10 list for each chart analyst is similar, the lower level listings are clearly not consistent. So what? Lavern Baker's bouncy 1957 hit "Jim Dandy" is #101 for Pavlow, #91 for Quirin/Cohen, and #141 for

TABLE 12.1. Top Ten/Bottom Ten Most Popular Songs of 1957 According to Pavlow, Quirin/Cohen, and Whitburn

Cohen	Pavlow Whitburn	Quirin/
1. "All Shook Up"	1. "All Shook Up"	1. "All Shook Up"
2. "Love Letters in the Sand"	2. "Love Letters in the Sand"	2. "Love Letters in the Sand"
3. "Tammy"	3. "Let Me Be Your Teddy Bear"	3. "Jailhouse Rock"
4. "Bye Bye Love"	4. "Tammy"	4. "(Let Me Be Your) Teddy Bear"
5. "So Rare"	5. "So Rare"	5. "April Love"
6. "Little Darlin' "	6. "Jailhouse Rock"	6. "Young Love"
7. "Teddy Bear"	7. "Young Love"	7. "Tammy"
8. "Jailhouse Rock"	8. "Bye Bye Love"	8. "Honeycomb"
9. "Young Love"	9. "Little Darlin' "	9. "Wake Up Little Susie"
10. "Round and Round"	10. "Honeycomb"	10. "You Send Me"
---	---	---
91. "Love Me"	91. "Jim Dandy"	91. "Mangos"
92. "I'm Walkin' "	92. "Gonna Find Me a Bluebird"	92. "Love Is a Golden Ring"
93. "Just Born"	93. "Shangri-La"	93. "Silhouettes"
94. "Shangri-La"	94. "Freight Train"	94. "Raunchy"
95. "C. C. Rider"	95. "Loving You"	95. "Shish-Kebab"
96. "Just Between You and Me"	96. "I'm Stickin' with You"	96. "Love Is Strange"
97. "I Dreamed"	97. "Black Slacks"	97. "Mama Look at Bubu"
98. "Liechtensteiner Polka"	98. "He's Mine"	98. "Four Walls"
99. "Around the World"	99. "Almost Paradise"	99. "Shangri-La"
100. "Freight Train"	100. "Just Born (to Be Your Baby)"	100. "I'm Sorry"

Whitburn. Her song is still undeniably a piece of popular music, regardless of how its placement is calculated. Using all three of these volumes to identify a single record as a hit is a sure way to identify American pop tunes. If only one volume is to be contacted, though, it should be *Pop Singles Annual, 1955-1990.* Whitburn's work dominates all competition for print clarity, scope of songs covered, special supplementary features (annual "Time Capsule," "Top 20 Artists" for each year, and "Top Artist Debuts"), and specific details about each record cited (label and record number, time of play, artist, and special stylistic designations as well). In addition, Whitburn's study includes an alphabetized song title section index (pp. 563-692), "Top 100 Records of 1955-1990," and "Top 50 #1 Hits" of 1955-59, 1960-69, 1970-79, and 1980-89, plus several specialized lists including the "Christmas Singles, 1955-1990" (pp. 707-710).

Only one question remains unanswered by all of these volumes: how valid is it to rate the popularity of a given song in a single calendar year? Clearly, tunes that initially reach the pop charts in November/December and then continue to receive public approval during January/February are at a statistical disadvantage in terms of annual (January 1-December 31) chart assessments. A good example of this phenomenon is Pat Boone's "April Love" (Dot 15660). This recording debuted on the *Billboard* chart on October 28, 1957. It peaked at #1 on December 16, 1957, and remained a charted tune for a total of twenty-six weeks, well into 1958. Whitburn lists "April Love" as the #5 top song of 1957 and ignores the tune entirely in his 1958 survey. Quirin/Cohen follow the opposite approach. They list "April Love" as the #5 top hit of 1958, and do not recognize the song at all in their 1957 survey. Pavlow notes "April Love" three times in his 1957 chart survey—#40 in October, #7 in November, and #3 in December. However, for the entire year of 1957 the highly popular Pat Boone tune secures only a #30 annual rank. The problem with year-to-year rankings of songs is similar to the bias in decade-to-decade performer popularity statistics. This difficulty haunts Whitburn's efforts to define top artists of the 1950s, 1960s, 1970s, and 1980s. While Michael Jackson, Prince, and Madonna are clearly 1980s giants, their total careers vary dramatically. Jackson is a strong 1970s creature as well; Prince is largely isolated to success in the Reagan decade; Madonna enters the 1990s as a multimedia superstar of true cross-decade distinction. Aretha Franklin is the prime example of a recording superstar whose lengthy across-three-decades career (1961-1989) has never secured deserved recognition in either annual compilations or in decade-to-decade listings.

Sound recording archivists, music librarians, and record collectors can benefit from acquiring all of these volumes. While Pavlow and Quirin/Cohen are optional, Whitburn is essential.

BIBLIOGRAPHY

Albert, George and Frank Hoffmann (comps.). *The Cash Box Black Contemporary Singles Charts, 1960-1994*. Metuchen, NJ: Scarecrow Press, 1986.

Albert, George and Frank Hoffmann (comps.). *The Cash Box Singles Charts, 1958-1982*. Metuchen, NJ: Scarecrow Press, 1984.

Berry, Peter E. *". . . And the Hits Just Keep on Comin'."* Syracuse, NY: Syracuse University Press, 1977.

Bronson, Fred. *The Billboard Book of Number One Hits* (Third Edition). New York: Billboard Books, 1992.

Bronson, Fred. *Billboard's Hottest Hot 100 Hits* (revised and enlarged edition). New York: Billboard Books, 1995.

Brooks, Elston. *I've Heard Those Songs Before—Volume Two: The Weekly Top Ten Hits of the Last Six Decades.* Fort Worth, TX: The Summit Group, 1991.

Cohen, Barry and Jim Quirin (comps.). *Rock One Hundred: An Authoritative Ranking of the Most Popular Songs for Each Year, 1954 Through 1991* (Fifth Edition). Los Angeles: Chartmasters, 1992.

Coryton, Demitri and Joseph Murrells (comps.). *Million Sellers of the Sixties.* London: Batsford Press, 1989.

Downey, Pat, George Albert, and Frank Hoffmann. *Cash Box Pop Singles Charts, 1950-1993.* Englewood, CO: Libraries Unlimited, Inc., 1994.

Downey, Pat. *Top 40 Music on Compact Disc, 1955-1994.* Boulder, CO: Pat Downey Enterprises, 1996.

Edwards, Joseph (comp.). *Top 10's and Trivia of Rock and Roll and Rhythm and Blues, 1950-1980.* St. Louis, MO: Blueberry Hill Publishing Company, 1981.

Ehnert, Gunter. *Hit-Records: British Chart Singles, 1950-1965.* Hamburg, Germany: Taurus Press, 1995.

Elrod, Bruce C. (ed.). *Your Hit Parade and American Top 10 Hits: A Week-by-Week Guide to the Nation's Favorite Music, 1935-1994* (Fourth Edition). Ann Arbor, MI: Popular Culture, Ink., 1994.

Gambaccini, Paul, Tim Rice, and Jonathan Rice (comps.). *British Hit Singles* (Eighth Edition). Enfield, Middlesex, England: Guinness Publishing, Ltd., 1991.

Gambaccini, Paul, Tim Rice, and Jonathan Rice (comps.). *Hit Albums* (Fifth Edition). Enfield, Middlesex, England: Guinness Publishing, Ltd.

Gambaccini, Paul, Tim Rice, and Jonathan Rice (comps.). *U.K. Top 1,000 Singles.* Enfield, Middlesex, England: Guinness Publishing, Ltd., 1990.

George, Nelson. *Top of the Charts—The Most Complete Listing Ever: The Top 10 Records and Albums for Every Week of Every Year from 1970.* Piscataway, NJ: New Century Publishers, 1983.

Gillett, Charlie (ed.). *Rock File.* London: New English Library, 1972.

Hall, Roy. *The Chum Chart Book, 1957-1983: A Complete Listing of Every Charted Record.* Rexdale, Ontario, Canada: Stardust Productions, 1984.

Hoffmann, Frank (comp.). *The Cash Box Singles Charts, 1950-1981.* Metuchen, NJ: Scarecrow Press, 1983.

Hoffmann, Frank and George Albert (comps.). *The Cash Box Black Contemporary Album Charts, 1975-1987.* Metuchen, NJ: Scarecrow Press, 1989.

Hoffmann, Frank and George Albert. *The Cash Box Country Album Charts, 1964-1988.* Metuchen, NJ: Scarecrow Press, 1989.

Hoffmann, Frank and George Albert, with the assistance of Lee Ann Hoffmann (comps.). *The Cash Box Album Charts, 1955-1974.* Metuchen, NJ: Scarecrow Press, 1988.

Hoffmann, Frank and George Albert, with the assistance of Lee Ann Hoffmann (comps.). *The Cash Box Album Charts, 1975-1985.* Metuchen, NJ: Scarecrow Press, 1987.

Jancik, Wayne. *The Billboard Book of One-Hit Wonders.* New York: Billboard Books/Watson-Guptill Publications, 1990.

Jasper, Tony (comp.). *British Record Charts, 1955-1978.* London: MacDonald and Janes, 1979.

Jasper, Tony (ed.). *The Top Twenty Book, 1955-1990* (Fifth Edition). London: Blandford Press, 1991.

McAleer, Dave (comp.). *The All Music Book of Hit Albums: The Top 10 U.S. and U.K. Album Charts from 1960 to the Present Day.* San Francisco: Miller Freeman Books, 1995.

McAleer, Dave (comp.). *The All Music Book of Hit Singles: Top Twenty Charts from 1954 to the Present Day.* San Francisco: Miller Freeman Books, 1994.

McAleer, Dave. *The Omnibus Book of British and American Hit Singles, 1960-1990.* London: Omnibus Press, 1990.

Miles, Betty T., Daniel J. Miles, and Martin J. Miles. *The Miles Chart Display of Popular Music—Volume I: Top 100, 1955-1970.* Boulder, CO: Covex Industries, 1981 (c. 1971).

Miles, Daniel J., Betty T. Miles, and Martin J. Miles (comps.). *The Miles Chart Display of Popular Music—Volume II: 1971-1975.* New York: Arno Press, 1977.

Miron, Charles (comp.). *Rock Gold: All the Hit Charts from 1955 to 1976.* New York: Drake Publishing, 1977.

Murrells, Joseph (comp.). *Million Selling Records from the 1900s to the 1980s: An Illustrated Directory.* New York: Arco Publishing, 1984.

Nugent, Stephen and Charlie Gillett (comps.). *Rock Almanac: Top Twenty American and British Singles and Albums of the '50's, '60's and '70's.* Garden City, NY: Anchor Press/Doubleday, 1976.

Osborne, Roger (comp.). *The Complete NME Album Charts.* London: Boxtree Books, 1995.

Osborne, Roger (comp.). *Forty Years of NME Charts.* London: Boxtree Books, 1992.

Pavlow, Al (comp.). *Big Al Pavlow's The R&B Book: A Disc-History of Rhythm and Blues.* Providence, RI: Music House Publishing, 1983.

Rees, Daffyd and Barry Lazell (comps.). *The Complete NME Singles Charts.* London: Boxtree Books, 1995.

Rice, Jo, Tim Rice, Paul Gambaccini, and Mike Read (comps.). *The Guinness Book of British Hit Albums.* London: Guinness Superlatives, Ltd., 1983.

Roland, Tom. *The Billboard Book of Number One Country Hits.* New York: Billboard Books/Watson-Guptill Publications, 1991.

Rosen, Craig. *The Billboard Book of Number One Albums: The Inside Story Behind Pop Music's Blockbuster Records.* New York: Billboard Books, 1996.

Solomon, Clive (comp.). *Record Hits: The British Top 50 Charts, 1954-1976.* London: Omnibus Press, 1977.

Tanner, John F. (comp.). *Hits Through the Years: 1952.* Whitley Bay, Tyne and Wear, UK: JFT-Valid Records, 1989.

Tanner, John F. (comp.). *Hits Through the Years: 1963.* Whitley Bay, Tyne and Wear, UK: JFT-Valid Records, 1989.

Tanner, John F. (comp.). *Hits Through the Years: 1976.* Whitley Bay, Tyne and Wear, UK: JFT-Valid Records, 1989.

Tharin, Jr., Frank C. (comp.). *Chart Champions: 40 Years of Rankings and Ratings.* San Francisco: Chart Champions, 1980.

Theroux, Gary, and Bob Gilbert. *The Top Ten: 1956 to the Present.* New York: Simon and Schuster, 1982.

Whitburn, Joel (comp.). *The Billboard Book of Top 40 Albums: The Complete Chart Guide to Every Album in the Top 40 Since 1955* (revised and enlarged edition). New York: Billboard Books, 1991.

Whitburn, Joel (comp.). *The Billboard Book of Top 40 Hits* (Sixth Edition). New York: Billboard Books, 1996.

Whitburn, Joel (comp.). *Billboard Hot 100 Charts: The Sixties.* Menomonee Falls, WI: Record Research, Inc., 1990.

Whitburn, Joel (comp.). *Billboard Hot 100 Charts: The Seventies.* Menomonee Falls, WI: Record Research, Inc., 1990.

Whitburn, Joel (comp.). *Billboard Hot 100 Charts: The Eighties.* Menomonee Falls, WI: Record Research, Inc., 1991.

Whitburn, Joel (comp.). *Billboard #1s, 1950-1991.* Menomonee Falls, WI: Record Research, Inc., 1991.

Whitburn, Joel (comp.). *Billboard Pop Album Charts, 1965-1969.* Menomonee Falls, WI: Record Research, Inc., 1994.

Whitburn, Joel (comp.). *The Billboard Pop Charts, 1955-1959.* Menomonee Falls, WI: Record Research, Inc., 1992.

Whitburn, Joel (comp.). *Billboard's Top 10 Charts, 1958-1995.* Menomonee Falls, WI: Record Research, Inc., 1995.

Whitburn, Joel (comp.). *Billboard Top 1,000 Singles, 1955-1992: The 1,000 Biggest Hits of the Rock Era.* Menomonee Falls, WI: Record Research, Inc., 1993.

Whitburn, Joel (comp.). *Billboard's Top 2000, 1955-1985: The 2000 Biggest Hits of the Rock Era.* Menomonee Falls, WI: Record Research, Inc., 1986.

Whitburn, Joel (comp.). *Billboard's Top 3000+, 1955-1990.* Menomonee Falls, WI: Record Research, Inc., 1990.

Whitburn, Joel (comp.). *Bubbling Under the Hot 100, 1959-1985.* Menomonee Falls, WI: Record Research, Inc., 1992.

Whitburn, Joel (comp.). *Daily #1 Hits, 1940-1992.* Menomonee Falls, WI: Record Research, Inc., 1993.

Whitburn, Joel (comp.). *Pop Annual, 1955-1994.* Menomonee Falls, WI: Record Research, Inc., 1995.

Whitburn, Joel (comp.). *Pop Hits, 1940-1954.* Menomonee Falls, WI: Record Research, Inc., 1994.

Whitburn, Joel (comp.). *Pop Memories, 1890-1954: The History of American Popular Music.* Menomonee Falls, WI: Record Research, Inc., 1986.

Whitburn, Joel (comp.). *Pop Singles Annual, 1955-1990.* Menomonee Falls, WI: Record Research, Inc., 1991.

Whitburn, Joel (comp.). *Rock Tracks: Album Rock (1981-1995) and Modern Rock (1988-1995).* Menomonee Falls, WI: Record Research, Inc., 1995.

Whitburn, Joel (comp.). *Top Adult Contemporary 1961-1993.* Menomonee Falls, WI: Record Research, Inc., 1993.

Whitburn, Joel (comp.). *Top Country & Western Records, 1949-1971.* Menomonee Falls, WI: Record Research, Inc., 1972.

Whitburn, Joel (comp.). *Top Country Singles, 1944-1993.* Menomonee Falls, WI: Record Research, Inc., 1994.

Whitburn, Joel (comp.). *Top Easy Listening Records, 1961-1974.* Menomonee Falls, WI: Record Research, Inc., 1975.

Whitburn, Joel (comp.). *Top LP Records, 1945-1972.* Menomonee Falls, WI: Record Research, Inc., 1973.

Whitburn, Joel (comp.). *Top Pop Albums, 1955-1996.* Menomonee Falls, WI: Record Research, Inc., 1997.

Whitburn, Joel (comp.). *Top Pop Album Tracks, 1955-1992.* Menomonee Falls, WI: Record Research, Inc., 1993.

Whitburn, Joel (comp.). *Top Pop Album Tracks, 1993-1996.* Menomonee Falls, WI: Record Research, Inc., 1996.

Whitburn, Joel (comp.). *Top Pop Records, 1940-1955.* Menomonee Falls, WI: Record Research, Inc., 1973.

Whitburn, Joel (comp.). *Top Pop Singles CD Guide, 1955-1979.* Menomonee Falls, WI: Record Research, Inc., 1995.

Whitburn, Joel (comp.). *Top Pop Singles, 1955-1993.* Menomonee Falls, WI: Record Research, Inc., 1994.

Whitburn, Joel (comp.). *Top R&B Singles, 1942-1995.* Menomonee Falls, WI: Record Research, Inc., 1996.

Whitburn, Joel (comp.). *Top Rhythm and Blues Records, 1949-1971.* Menomonee Falls, WI: Record Research, Inc., 1973.

Whitburn, Joel (comp.). *Top 1000 X 5: Five Top 1000 Rankings of America's Favorite Hits.* Menomonee Falls, WI: Record Research, Inc., 1997.

White, Adam. *Billboard Book of Gold and Platinum Records.* New York: Billboard Books/Watson-Guptill Publications, 1990.

White, Adam and Fred Bronson. *The Billboard Book of Number One Rhythm and Blues Hits.* New York: Billboard Books/Watson-Guptill Publications, 1993.

Chapter 13

Scholarship

A Guide to Popular Music Reference Books: An Annotated Bibliography. Compiled by Gary Haggerty. Westport, CT: Greenwood Press, 1995. 210 pp.

Rock Music Scholarship: An Interdisciplinary Bibliography. Compiled by Jeffrey N. Gatten. Westport, CT: Greenwood Press, 1995. 294 pp.

Rock Stars/Pop Stars: A Comprehensive Bibliography, 1955-1994. Compiled by Brady J. Leyser, with additional research by Pol Gosset. Westport, CT: Greenwood Press, 1994. 302 pp.

Rock scholarship, rock journalism, rock criticism, and rock history are generally misnomers. The "scholarship" usually lacks resource citation and theoretical foundation; the "journalism" is often shallow and unperceptive; the "criticism" is too laudatory and generally lacking in comparative analysis; and the "history" is inevitably too narrowly focused and without multidecade perspective. This is not to imply that rock music lacks competent scholars (George Lewis, R. Serge Denisoff, and George Carney), journalists (Philip Norman, Robert Hilburn, and Gary Giddins), critics (Bill Flanagan, Dave Marsh, and Robert Christgau), and historians (Philip Ennis, Peter Guralnick, and Howard DeWitt). But the list of quali-

---

The material in this chapter by B. Lee Cooper was originally published as "Popular Music in Print," *Popular Music and Society,* XIX (Winter 1995), pp. 105-112; "Review of *Living in the Rock 'n' Roll Mystery* by H. L. Goodall Jr.," *Popular Culture in Libraries,* I, No. 1 (1993), pp. 158-160; and "Review of *Philosophy at 33 1/3 R.P.M.* by James R. Harris," *Popular Music and Society,* XVII (Winter 1993), pp. 144-145. Reprint permission granted by the author, editor Frank Hoffmann, The Haworth Press, managing editor Pat Browne, and the Bowling Green State University Popular Press.

fied writers in the realm of popular music is amazingly short. The field is dominated by hacks. Propaganda and publicity parade as journalism and criticism. With very few exceptions, biographical studies tend to be thumbnail sketches framed with publicity photos and concert snapshots. And much that is labeled scholarship or historical investigation is actually collectormania, trivial pursuits, and fandom in full flower.

Despite the paucity of great writing, however, students of popular music still require reference guides to locate available literary resources on performing artists, recording companies, and various rock era activities. While many authors provide limited reference sections in their books, and a few scholarly periodicals (*ARSC Journal* and *Popular Music*) feature annual book lists, comprehensive bibliographies are rare. Early compilations by Mark Booth (1983), Frank Hoffmann (1981), David Horn (1977), and others marked heroic efforts to locate limited documentation of the literary trail of rock. Later studies by Ed Hanel (1983), Frank Hoffmann and B. Lee Cooper (1986, 1995), D. W. Krummel (1987), and Paul Taylor (1985) greatly expanded the bibliographic net. While there have been a number of extensive popular culture resource studies by Jeffrey Gatten (1993), Frank Hoffmann (1995), and M. Thomas Inge (1989) and many, many sharply focused bibliographic excursions such as those of Mary L. Dimmick (1979), B. Lee Cooper and Wayne S. Haney (1990), and Stephen Wolter and Karen Kimber (1992), the three new volumes from the Greenwood Press are truly fascinating finds. Librarians should seize these studies with glee. They constitute gold mines of reference information and musical styles, present varying perspectives on the kaleidoscopic world of popular music print.

A Guide to Popular Music Reference Books (1995) explores bibliographies, biographical dictionaries, encyclopedias, discographies, glossaries, guidebooks, almanacs, and yearbooks. Author Gary Haggerty, a professional musician and assistant library director at Boston's Berklee College of Music, offers succinct yet valuable annotations for each of the 427 titles cited. This comprehensive reference highlights a plethora of contrasting musical styles—jazz, swing, Tin Pan Alley, country, blues, gospel, soul, rhythm and blues, rock, musical theater, heavy metal, rockabilly, and film music. The slim volume is essential for librarians, music scholars, students, and collectors.

Rock Music Scholarship (1995) shifts perspective from reference resources to functional academic disciplines. Author Jeffrey N. Gatten, a sociologist and librarian at Kent State University who compiled *The Rolling Stone Index* (1993), has researched ten specific fields where popular music scholars have crafted interdisciplinary studies. The scope of Gatten's inquiry includes: communication, education, ethnomusicology, history, literature and arts, music, politics, psychology, religion, and sociology. For each subject the author provides annotated entries from journal articles, anthology chapters, books, dissertations, and films or videos. The 934 citations and commentaries are remarkably thorough and detailed. No comparable scholarly resource exists.

Rock Stars/Pop Stars lists over 3,600 books and provides biographical information on performers from AREA, Paula Abdul, AC/DC, and Bryan Adams to Neil Young, Frank Zappa, The Zombies, and ZZ Top. Author Brady J. Leyser, a Canadian advertising agency manager and a rock memorabilia collector, provides bibliographic, discographic, and filmographic resources for each artist listed. No annotations are added. The international scope of the listings, however, attests to the breadth of the author's research. This magnificent resource should be on every rock reader's shelf.

While the materials cited by Haggerty, Gatten, and Leyser are pertinent and comprehensive, the presentation formats are still somewhat problematic for rock researchers. Without combining the twin elements of historical and musicological perspective, even a biographical format is less than helpful. The genius of Frank Hoffmann's immense *Literature of Rock* series (1978, 1986, 1995) is found in the continually expanding historical network he has crafted to frame the huge amount of literary information featured in his three volumes. This format has enabled him to be retrospective, stylistic, thematic, biographic, and bibliographic throughout his protracted investigative activities. No other rock reference resource has seized such high ground. Hoffmann, a librarian and historian at Sam Houston State University, is without peer as rock's print compiler and resource organizer.

The following pages offer a selected profile of recent rock bibliographies. While the field is narrow, the search for the perfect popular music reference format precedes apace. As noted above, the Greenwood Press is a leader in producing superb, creative models of music resource scholarship.

* * *

Living in the Rock 'n' Roll Mystery: Reading Context, Self, and Others As Clues. By H. L. Goodall Jr. Carbondale, IL: Southern Illinois University Press, 1991. 286 pp.

H. Lloyd Goodall Jr. describes himself as an organizational detective, an ethnographer of communication and cultural studies, and a rock musician. He pursues mysteries, challenges theories, attacks models, and enjoys the subtle (and not so subtle) complexities of his life in Utah. He seeks to answer existential questions by probing the real world rather than by focusing on theoretical or philosophical constructs. Goodall is not a touchy-feely New Age sage who ignores the rigors of scholarship. This ample bibliography (pp. 279-286) features a broad range of learned social science commentary. This author elects to forge a path to knowledge that melds theory, practice, and perception. In the latter category, Goodall is superior.

Living in the Rock 'n' Roll Mystery is too complex an investigation to describe in a brief review. This Sherlock Holmes tale deserves full reading, not just a last-page peek at who-done-it. The most fascinating part of Goodall's work, though, is found in the assumptions he operates from rather than in his ultimate conclusions. He begins by noting that ". . . rock 'n' roll is not just a musical style but also a social attitude that informs a wide variety of social and professional constructions of reality" (p. xix). Typecasting himself as researcher/participant/observer, Goodall employs this multifaceted perspective to form an interpretative thesis about twentieth-century popular music, especially blues and rock songs. After World War II, what once had been a source of entertainment and relief from daily drudgery transformed into a new form of social and political life. The American experience witnessed, or more accurately culminated in, the clash of rational/technical and emotive/sensual forces. In terms of interpretative ethnography and historical analogy, rock 'n' roll is the informative, upstart jester in the kingdom of material success. In Goodall's own words, rock 'n' roll ". . . played the fool to technology's genius, and as a fool it could sing the truth while wearing a fool's clothing. This time around, however, the king is not a nation but a dominant ideology of technological capitalism (and formula-driven research reports) that is the currency of the mixed media of the side-by-side modern and postmodern eras" (p. 19). The author even borrows an observation from the late Rolling Stone critic Lester Bangs to emphasize the ultimate power of the jester: "Rock 'n' roll is all just a joke and a mistake, just a bunch of foolishness. What's truest in it, though, is that you cannot enslave a fool" (p. 20).

There are mysteries about this volume that puzzle even the most supportive reviewer. First, the absence of a selected discography is regrettable. Second, the lack of an index in a volume this complex and fact-filled is unconscionable. Finally, the failure of the author to include seminal song-in-society studies by R. Serge Denisoff, Richard Peterson, David Pichaske, and Jerome Rodnitzky in his bibliography is inexplicable. Concerning this resource criticism, it should be noted that a thinker can both

understand and articulate a position without encountering other scholarship on the same topic. Nevertheless, the thoroughness of Goodall's academic base in regard to other cultural commentaries can be reinforced by
consulting a variety of English, history, and sociological scholars.

Living in the Rock 'n' Roll Mystery is fascinating. It is theoretical and
philosophical, objective and subjective, eminently engaging. This text is a
natural for students of anthropology, popular culture, history, literature,
contemporary music, sociology, and mass communications. Although
heavy reading at times, the autobiographical portions of most chapters
provide clarifications, illustrations, and marvelous insights. Don't miss
this volume.

* * *

Philosophy at 33 ^{1}/$_3$ R.P.M.: Themes of Classic Rock Music. By James
F. Harris. Chicago: Open Court Publishing Company, 1993. 280 pp.

James F. Harris is the Christopher Columbus of lyric analysis. Ignoring
potential scholarly scorn and public skepticism, he sets sail on stormy seas
in search of rock music themes. Standing alone at the prow of his philosophical vessel, he sites (and continually cites) the 1960s. Leaping ashore,
he claims 1962 through 1974 for God and country. Earlier musical events,
eras, and literary explorers are labeled "naive," "serendipitous," "super-
ficial," "shallow," "silly," and "meaningless." Like Columbus, Harris is
both self-assured and self-possessed. The 1960s are his magic gateway to
intellectual riches, philosophical maturity, and aesthetic truth. Unlike the
heralded Genoan navigator, though, the William and Mary philosophy
professor even reports on the future, noting that post-1974 music lost its
nerve and direction and lyrically sailed off the edge of the earth.

Harris is articulate, committed, and arrogant. *Philosophy at 33 ^{1}/$_3$
R.P.M.* forces a Yuppie perspective on selected songs that resonate with
validity to many white, middle-aged, middle-class listeners. However,
even White House-dwelling baby boomers Bill and Hillary Clinton will
recoil at the author's self-indulgence in linking Descartes, Aristotle,
Freud, Laing, and Camus to Mick Jagger, Grace Slick, Joni Mitchell, Elton
John, and Paul Simon. Country music fans and rhythm and blues (or soul)
enthusiasts won't recognize much of the musical turf that Harris thematically parcels off. Neither will listeners who enjoy either traditional pop
tunes or zany Frank Zappa renderings. Too bad. Much of what Harris has
to say is interesting, historically enlightening, and socially challenging.
But it is painfully narrow.

Where does *Philosophy at 33 ^{1}/$_3$ R.P.M.* go astray? First, the author's
assumption that albums rather than specific songs are the primary curren-

cy of American lyrical culture is wrong. Whether on a heavy, black 78 rpm record or a light, silver compact disc, individual tunes are the carriers of cultural commentary. To claim that the 45 rpm recording lost credence after 1962 is a misinterpretation of youth culture, record industry marketing, and performing artist identification. Even after the release of The Beatles' magnificent *Sgt. Pepper* in 1967, few artists had the patience, the talent, or the interest to produce thematically consistent albums. Granted, The Rolling Stones, The Who, and others occasionally succeeded. But Harris inexplicably ignores several other marvelous unified efforts, including Ray Charles' *Modern Sounds in Country and Western Music* (1962) and Marvin Gaye's *What's Going On* (1971). Somehow many black performers and most country songsmiths elude Harris's vision. Second, the author is ignorant of and blind to the role of humor in American popular lyrics. He seems blissfully unaware of the heritage of Louis Jordan and Spike Jones, and disinterested in the creative works of Homer and Jethro, Dickie Goodman, and Pinkard and Borden. Parody songs, response recordings, break-in tunes, novelty discs, and the like are condemned as meaningless, with ". . . not a scintilla of satire, iota of irony, or measure of metaphor to be found anywhere in these lyrics" (p. 5). Harris needs to reconsider Charlie Daniels' "Uneasy Rider" (1973), Jim Stafford's "Swamp Witch" (1973), Ray Stevens' "Mr. Businessman" (1968), Jim Croce's "Workin' at the Car Wash Blues" (1975), Jerry Reed's "Another Puff" (1972), and Albert King's "Born Under a Bad Sign" (1967), and "Angel of Mercy" (1972).

Finally, Harris parallels traditional Western European hubris by claiming to have "discovered" a field of study that is actually already quite well-defined and well-populated. Lyric analysis, particularly the exploration of the specific themes identified in *Philosophy At $33^{1}/_{3}$ R.P.M.*— alienation, friendship, community, hedonism, self-assertion, judgment, and redemption—is well-explored research ground. Following the ethnocentric Columbus mode, though, Harris's bibliography fails to cite many significant studies that predate his book-length beachhead. Those scholars omitted include Richard Aquila, Gary Burns, George O. Carney, Bruce L. Chipman, Norm Cohen, Don Cusic, Robin Denselow, Michael Dunne, Mary Ellison, Aaron A. Fox, H. L. Goodall Jr., Kenneth A. Fuchsman, Charles F. Gritzner, David Hatch, Herb Hendler, Frank Hoffmann, Dorothy Horstman, Hugo Keesing, George H. Lewis, George Lipsitz, Katie Letcher Lyle, Melton McLaurin, David A. Milberg, Timothy Miller, Stephen Millward, Brian Murdoch, Carol Offen, Paul Oliver, Robert Palmer, Robert G. Pielke, Bruce Pollock, Ray Pratt, Robert Reid, Walter Rimler, Jerome L. Rodnitzky, Jimmie N. Rogers, William D. Romanowski,

Bob Sarlin, John Anthony Scott, Bob Shannon, Arnold Shaw, Irwin Silber, Nicholas E. Tawa, Stephen I. Thompson, Jacques Vassal, and Peter Wicke. Beyond these omissions, the author also ignores three major lyric theme resource guides: *The Stecheson Classified Song Directory* (1961) and *Supplement* (1978) by Anthony and Anne Stecheson; *A Resource Guide to Themes in Contemporary American Song Lyrics*, 1950-1985 (1986) by B. Lee Cooper; and *The 1987 Green Book: Songs Classified by Subject* (1986) by Jeff Green. Similarly absent are references to several other valuable investigative song references: *The Great Song Thesaurus*, Second Edition (1989) by Roger Lax and Frederick Smith; *Music Master: The 45 R.P.M. Singles Directory—44 Years of Recorded Music from 1948 to 1992 Listed Alphabetically by Artist and Title* (1992) by Paul C. Mawhinney; and *Top Country Singles, 1944-1988* (1989), *Top Pop Singles 1955-1990* (1991), and *Top R&B Singles, 1942-1988* (1988) by Joel Whitburn.

Philosophy at 33$^1/_3$ R.P.M. has serious flaws. No doubt it was a labor of love for the author to unite the audio philosopher-kings of his childhood with his current literary academic heroes. But like Janell R. Duxbury's recent discographic examinations of classical music borrowings by rock-era composers, Harris severely overextends his contentions and thus undermines his credibility. Post-World War II popular music is an incredibly complex sociological enterprise. Lyric analysis is but one path to interpret the influence of the 1950s, 1960s, and 1970s rock revolutions on American society. The problem with this volume is that it ignores cultural diversity, shuns historical perspective, avoids research into previous song studies, and affirms philosophical roots that may be inferred but rarely, if ever, are claimed by those participating in the song production system. The eclectic Mr. Harris has provided a memoir of his personal voyage through adolescence into the new world of college teaching. Music is the ocean that buoyed his journey. Like Columbus, though, Harris needs to recognize that others preceded him and still more researchers will follow him. A healthy dose of humility would have been beneficial to both explorers.

* * *

All That Glitters: Country Music in America. George H. Lewis. Bowling Green, OH: State University Popular Press, 1993.

The twenty-eight essays assembled in *All That Glitters* constitute the most thorough, perceptive analysis of post-World War II country music ever assembled. The range of artists examined is impressive, ranging from Bill Monroe, Hank Williams, and Patsy Cline to George Strait, Alison

Krauss, and Rosanne Cash. But this exceptional volume is much more than a series of biographical essays. It is a cogently argued sociological survey addressing ten theoretical issues related to the impact of country music on modern American society. The themes that occur again and again throughout the investigations are: authenticity, creativity, regional influences, southernization, traditionalism, pop music adaptation, lyric meaning, ideological contradictions, socialization, and academic value.

The genius behind this multi-faceted analytical framework is editor George H. Lewis. This University of the Pacific sociology professor has been a constructive critic, lucid commentator, and productive partisan for popular culture studies since 1970. With the possible exceptions of R. Serge Denisoff and Richard A. Peterson, no other writer has demonstrated broader interests in the interactive analysis of commercial music production, artistic creativity, audience receptivity, and general cultural impact. For *All That Glitters* Lewis has gathered a scholarly writing squad that sparkles. Contributors include Bill Malone, Joli Jensen, George Lipsitz, Ken Tucker, Jimmie N. Rogers, Neil V. Rosenberg, and Michael Dunne. The editor also provides four thought-provoking essays ("Mexican Musical Influences on Country Songs and Styles," "A Tombstone Every Mile: Country Music In Maine," "The Commercial Art World of Country Music," and "Tension, Conflict, and Contradiction in Country Music"), along with an introduction and theme-defining prefaces for each of the text's eight chapters. This volume is the rarest of literary creatures—a scholarly anthology that is focused, farsighted, and fun.

What can be criticized about this compilation? Very little. The balance of original essays (twelve) to previously published studies (sixteen) is reasonable; the periodicals utilized as sources for vintage essays—*Journal of Popular Culture, JEMF Quarterly, Popular Music, Journal of Country Music, Popular Music and Society, Village Voice Rock and Roll Quarterly*, and *Studies in Popular Culture*—are diverse yet central to academic inquiries into music and American culture; and the "Works Cited" portions that follow each essay provide an array of up-to-date bibliographic information. Only three improvements might be considered. First, the editor should have recruited a first-rate country music record reviewer/sound recording archivist to compile an authoritative 700 to 800 item album discography for this study. Second, commentaries by such noted country music scholars as Charles Wolfe, Richard Peterson, Nick Tosches, Charles Gritzner, and Michael Bane should have been solicited for *All That Glitters*. Finally, the voices of country music's legion of critics—those hostile for aesthetic reasons as well as those who focus on cultural conflict issues—should have been prominently featured. This minor carping aside, though, one must admit that the book is a monument to thoughtful planning, clear organization, and fine representation of country music images, ideas, and attitudes.

BIBLIOGRAPHY

Booth, Mark W. *American Popular Music: A Reference Guide*. Westport, CT: Greenwood Press, 1983.

Booth, Mark W. "Music," in *Handbook of American Popular Culture* (Second Edition), edited by M. Thomas Inge. Westport, CT: Greenwood Press, 1989, pp. 771-790.

Burdex, Monica, Simon Frith, Stephen A. Fry, David Horn, Barbara James, Toru Mitsui, and Robert Springer (comps.). "Booklist," in *Popular Music 4*, edited by Richard Middleton and David Horn. New York: Cambridge University Press, 1984, pp. 377-406.

Cooper, B. Lee. *The Popular Music Handbook: A Resource Guide for Teachers, Libraries, and Media Specialists*. Littleton, CO: Libraries Unlimited, Inc., 1984.

Cooper, B. Lee, Simon Frith, Bernhard Hefele, Frank Hoffmann, David Horn, Toru Mitsui, Robert Springer, and Erzsebet Szeverenyi (comps.). "Booklist," *Popular Music*, V (October 1986), pp. 361-385.

Cooper, B. Lee, Simon Frith, Bernhard Hefele, Frank Hoffmann, David Horn, Toru Mitsui, Robert Springer, and Erzsebet Szeverenyi (comps.). "Booklist," *Popular Music*, VI (October 1987), pp. 361-385.

Cooper, B. Lee, Simon Frith, Bernhard Hefele, Frank Hoffmann, David Horn, Toru Mitsui, Paul Oliver, Stan Rijuen, and Robert Springer (comps.). "Booklist," *Popular Music*, VII (October 1988), pp. 357-371.

Cooper, B. Lee, Frank Hoffmann, Bernhard Hefele, Robert Springer, David Horn, and Toru Mitsui (comps.). "Booklist," *Popular Music*, VIII (October 1989), pp. 335-347.

Cooper, B. Lee, Simon Frith, Bernhard Hefele, Frank Hoffmann, David Horn, Toru Mitsui, and Robert Springer (comps.). "Booklist," *Popular Music*, IX (October 1990), pp. 389-405.

Cooper, B. Lee, Simon Frith, Bernhard Hefele, Frank Hoffmann, Toru Mitsui, Lynne Sharma, and Robert Springer (comps.). "Booklist," *Popular Music, X* (October 1991), pp. 361-378.

Cooper, B. Lee, Frank Hoffmann, Simon Frith, Bernhard Hefele, David Horn, Jaap Gerritse, Antoine Hennion, and Toru Mitsui (comps.). "Booklist," *Popular Music*, XI (October 1992), pp. 385-404.

Cooper, B. Lee, David Buckley, Simon Frith, Jaap Gerritse, Bernhard Hefele, Frank W. Hoffmann, and Toru Mitsui (comps.). "Booklist," *Popular Music*, XII (October 1993), pp. 331-352.

Cooper, B. Lee, Jaap Gerritse, Bernhard Hefele, Frank Hoffmann, Toru Mitsui, and Motti Regeu (comps.). "Booklist," *Popular Music*, XIII (October 1994), pp. 375-399.

Cooper, B. Lee, Simon Frith, Paul Hansen, Bernhard Hefele, David Horn, and Toru Mitsui (comps.). "Booklist," *Popular Music,* XIV (October 1995), pp. 391-413.

Cooper, B. Lee, Simon Frith, Paul Hansen, Bernhard Hefele, Dave Lang, and Toru Mitsui (comps.). "Booklist," *Popular Music,* XV (October 1996), pp. 391-413.

Cooper, B. Lee and Wayne S. Haney. *Rockabilly: A Bibliographic Resource Guide.* Metuchen, NJ: Scarecrow Press, 1990.

Cooper, B. Lee and Wayne S. Haney. *Rock Music in American Popular Culture: Rock 'n' Roll Resources.* Binghamton, NY: The Haworth Press, 1995.

Cooper, B. Lee and Wayne S. Haney. *Rock Music in American Popular Culture II: More Rock 'n' Roll Resources.* Binghamton, NY: The Haworth Press, 1997.

De Lerma, Dominique-Rene. *Bibliography of Black Music—Volume One: Reference Materials.* Westport, CT: Greenwood Press, 1981.

De Lerma, Dominique-Rene. *Bibliography of Black Music—Volume Two: Afro-American Idioms.* Westport, CT: Greenwood Press, 1981.

De Lerma, Dominique-Rene. *Bibliography of Black Music—Volume Three: Geographical Studies.* Westport, CT: Greenwood Press, 1982.

De Lerma, Dominique-Rene. *Bibliography of Black Music—Volume Four: Theory, Education, and Related Studies.* Westport, CT: Greenwood Press, 1984.

Denisoff, R. Serge. *American Protest Songs of War and Peace: A Selected Bibliography and Discography.* Los Angeles: Los Angeles Center for the Study of Armament and Disarmament, California State College, 1970.

Denisoff, R. Serge, "The Battered and Neglected Orphan: Popular Music Research and Books," in *Sing a Song of Social Significance.* Bowling Green, OH: Bowling Green State University Popular Press, 1983, pp. 214-233.

Dimmick, Mary Laverne. *The Rolling Stones: An Annotated Bibliography* (revised and enlarged edition). Pittsburgh: University of Pittsburgh Press, 1979.

Dr. Demento. "Everything You Ever Wanted to Read About Rock: The Complete Big Beat Reference Shelf," *Waxpaper,* 3 (April 1978), pp. 20-22, 40-41.

Duckles, Vincent (comp.). *Music Reference and Research Materials: An Annotated Bibliography* (Second Edition). New York: Free Press, 1967.

Floyd, Samuel and Marsha J. Reisser. *Black Music Biography: An Annotated Bibliography.* White Plains, NY: Krause Publications, 1987.

Frith, Simon, Stephen M. Fry, and David Horn, comps. "Booklist," *Popular Music 2,* edited by Richard Middleton and David Horn. New York: Cambridge University Press, 1982, pp. 324-341.

Frith, Simon and David Horn, with the assistance of Stephen M. Fry, Barbara James, Toru Mitsui, and Robert Springer (comps.). "Booklist," *Popular Music III,* edited by Richard Middleton and David Horn. New York: Cambridge University Press, 1983, pp. 337-363.

Gatten, Jeffrey N. (comp.). *The Rolling Stone Index: Twenty-Five Years of Popular Culture, 1967-1991.* Ann Arbor, MI: Popular Culture, Ink., 1993.

Ginsburg, David D. "State of the Art Survey of Reference Sources in Pop, Rock, and Jazz," *Reference Services Review,* VI (July/September 1978), pp. 5-16.

Grace, Stephen B. and Jonathon S. Epstein. "Recent Theory and Research in the Sociology of Popular Music: A Selected and Annotated Bibliography," in *Adolescents and Their Music: If It's Too Loud You're Too Old,* edited by Jonathon S. Epstein. New York: Garland Publishing, Inc., 1994, pp. 329-388.

Gray, Michael H. (comp.). *Bibliography of Discographies—Volume II: Popular Music.* New York: R. R. Bowker Company, 1983.

Hanel, Ed (comp.). *The Essential Guide to Rock Books.* London: Omnibus Press, 1983.

Harry, Bill. *Paperback Writers: The History of The Beatles in Print.* London: Virgin Books, 1984.

Hart, Mary L., Brenda M. Eagles, and Lisa N. Howe (comps.). *The Blues: A Bibliographic Guide.* New York: Garland Publishers, 1989.

Heintze, James. *American Music Studies: A Classified Bibliography of Master's Theses.* Detroit, MI: Information Coordinators, 1985.

Hoffmann, Frank (comp.). *The Literature of Rock, 1954-1978.* Metuchen, NJ: Scarecrow Press, Inc., 1981.

Hoffmann, Frank W. "Popular Music," in *American Popular Culture: A Guide to the Reference Literature.* Englewood, CO: Libraries Unlimited, Inc., 1995, pp. 87-113.

Hoffmann, Frank and B. Lee Cooper. *The Literature of Rock II, 1979-1983* (Two Volumes). Metuchen, NJ: Scarecrow Press, Inc., 1986.

Hoffmann, Frank W. and B. Lee Cooper. *The Literature of Rock III,* 1984-1990. Metuchen, NJ: Scarecrow Press, Inc., 1995.

Horn, David (comp.). *The Literature of American Music in Books and Folk Music Collections: A Fully Annotated Bibliography.* Metuchen, NJ: Scarecrow Press, Inc., 1977.

Horn, David, Monica Burdex, Simon Frith, Stephen M. Fry, Bernhard Hefele, Toru Mitsui, Stan Rijuen, and Robert Springer (comps.). "Booklist," *Popular Music 5: Continuity & Change,* edited by Richard Middleton and David Horn. New York: Cambridge University Press, 1985, pp. 357-391.

Horn, David with Richard Jackson (comps.). *The Literature of American Music in Books and Folk Music Collections: A Fully Annotated Bibliography—Supplement I.* Metuchen, NJ: Scarecrow Press, Inc., 1988.

Inge, M. Thomas (ed.). *Handbook of American Popular Culture, Three Volumes* (Second Edition, revised and enlarged). Westport, CT: Greenwood Press, 1989.

Iwaschkin, Roman, (comp.). *Popular Music: A Reference Guide.* New York: Garland Publishing, Inc., 1986.

Keesing, Hugo A. "Annotated Bibliography of Pop/Rock Music," in *Popular Culture Methods,* III (October 1976), pp. 4-22.

Keesing, Hugo A. (comp.). *Incomplete Bibliography of Pop/Rock Music.* Columbia, MD: H. A. Keesing, 1985.

Kendrick, Terry A. (comp.). *Rock Music (Readers Guide No. 37).* Northumberland, England: Public Libraries Group of the Library Association, 1981.

Krummel, D. W. *Bibliographical Handbook of American Music.* Urbana, IL: University of Illinois Press, 1987.

Krummel, D. W., Jean Geil, Doris J. Dyen, and Deane L. Root. *Resources of American Music History: A Directory of Source Materials from Colonial Times to World War II.* Urbana, IL: University of Illinois Press, 1981.

Lewis, George H. "The Sociology of Popular Music: A Selected and Annotated Bibliography," *Popular Music and Society,* VII, 1977, pp. 57-68.

MacLeod, Beth and David Ginsburg. "State of the Art Survey of Reference Sources in Music," *Reference Services Review,* V (January/March 1977), pp. 21-29.

MacPhail, Jessica. *Yesterday's Papers: The Rolling Stones in Print, 1963-1984.* Ann Arbor, MI: Popular Culture, Ink., 1986.

Maultsby, Portia K. "Selective Bibliography: U.S. Black Music," *Ethnomusicology,* XXIX (September 1975), pp. 421-449.

McCoy, Judy. *Rap Music in the 1980s: A Reference Guide.* Metuchen, NJ: Scarecrow Press, 1992.

Meadows, Eddie S. *Jazz Reference and Research Materials: A Bibliography.* New York: Garland Publishing, 1981.

Rodman, Gilbert B. (comp.). "Everyday I Write the Book: A Bibliography of (Mostly) Academic Work on Rock and Pop Music," *Tracking: Popular Music Studies,* II (Spring 1990), pp. 17-50.

Rodman, Gilbert B. (comp.). *Everyday I Write the Book: A Bibliography of (Mostly) Academic Work on Rock and Pop Music.* Champaign, IL: G. B. Rodman/Institute of Communications Research, 1992.

Rosenberg, Neil V. "Rock Books: An Incomplete Survey (Part I)" *JEMF Quarterly,* VIII (Spring 1972), pp. 48-56.

Rosenberg, Neil V. "Rock Books: An Incomplete Survey (Part II)" *JEMF Quarterly,* VIII (Summer 1972), pp. 109-116.

Schilling, James Von. "Records and the Recording Industry," in *Handbook of American Popular Culture* (Second Edition), edited by M. Thomas Inge. Westport, CT: Greenwood Press, 1989, pp. 1,155-1,183.

Skowronski, JoAnn (comp.). *Black Music in America: A Bibliography.* Metuchen, NJ: Scarecrow Press, 1981.

Taylor, Paul (comp.). *Popular Music Since 1955: A Critical Guide to the Literature.* New York: Mansell Publishing Ltd., 1985.

Terry, Carol D. *Here, There, and Everywhere: The First International Beatles Bibliography, 1962-1982.* Ann Arbor, MI: Popular Culture, Ink., 1985.

Terry, Carol D. *Sequins and Shades: The Michael Jackson Reference Guide.* Ann Arbor, MI: Pierian Press, 1987.

Vann, Kimberly R. *Black Music in Ebony: An Annotated Guide to the Articles on Music in Ebony Magazine, 1945-1985.* CBRM Monographs No. 2. Chicago: Center for Black Music Research, 1990.

Wolter, Stephen and Karen Kimber. *The Who in Print: An Annotated Bibliography, 1965 through 1990.* Jefferson, NC: McFarland, 1992.

Wood, Carolyn E. (comp.). *The Literature of Rock and Roll: A Special Collection.* Cambridge, MA: Charles B. Wood III Antiquarian Booksellers, 1991.

Chapter 14

Social Commentary

AMERICAN POLITICAL CONCERNS

I have no quarrel with folklorists and ethnomusicologists . . . whose chief concern is with the "purest" music of their culture. But I choose to view music as a dynamic, ever-changing art, and I see the history of music in our country as retaining a high level of energy and innovation over such a sustained period of time precisely because new vitality has been brought to it periodically by the introduction and integration of music from a succession of different cultures.

Charles Hamm, *Music in the New World,* 1983

Rock songs are pieces of oral history. Just as written accounts that attempt to communicate personal reactions to political ideas and social events are inevitably incomplete, so too, contemporary recordings contain only partial visions of United States history. The limited perspective provided by popular lyrics is magnified by several factors. First, the physical nature of sound recordings restricts the duration of a singer's commentary to an extremely brief time. The average rock song is less than three minutes long. Second, the achievement of popularity for a single recording indicates a broad level of public acceptance for a particular song. This market-oriented reality tends to limit extremes of lyrical deviance. Third, the radio-play life span for most rock songs is quite brief. A particular tune may be a frequently played, much discussed commodity for six to ten weeks, and then disappear from the music charts forever. Finally, rock

This chapter by B. Lee Cooper was originally printed as "Mick Jagger as Herodotus and Billy Joel as Thucydides? A Rock Music Perspective, 1950-1985," *Social Education,* XLIX (October 1985), pp. 596-600. Copyright © National Council for the Social Studies. Reprinted by permission. The review by B. Lee Cooper was originally published as "Review of *When the Music's Over* by Robin Denselow," *Notes: The Quarterly Journal of the Music Library Association,* XLIX (March 1992), pp. 889-890. Reprint permission granted by the author.

songs may either consciously or unconsciously address significant historical conditions or personal concerns. Various listening publics may accept,
reject, ignore, or be totally unaware of the lyrical commentary being
presented. This means that intent, content, and influence with rock music
are rarely synonymous.

Recognizing these limitations in assessing the impact of sound recording communications, why should rock songs be considered valuable oral
history resources? As a communication medium, rock lyrics do not sys-
tematically propagandize listeners. Likewise, they do not function as flaw-
less historical mirrors. Such polarized indictments of rock songs ignore the
inherent pluralism of contemporary lyrics, a pluralism that is a logical
by-product of the intellectual (and sometimes anti-intellectual) variety of
modern U.S. society. Rock songs replicate in unsystematic, segmented
fashions a multiplicity of ideas and values; in contemporary culture they
form an unpredictable, ever-changing audio collage. The oral history that
rock lyrics present resembles the historical remnants available in an Indian
burial mound. Just as an archaeologist must reconstruct cultural reality
from innumerable fragments of a former civilization—pieces of pottery,
arrowheads, tools for building, stone drawings, ancient toys and games,
eating utensils, religious tokens, death masks—the contemporary sound-
scape researcher must examine many, many recordings produced within a
defined time span in order to identify persistent social trends.

Some subjects of rock lyrics are overwhelmingly available for scrutiny.
For example, the standard courtship theme—boy meets girl, boy dates girl,
love blooms, marriage beckons, and a wedding occurs—is predominant
throughout popular music. However, there are also numerous variations to
this typical scenario. Women's liberation, birth control, social mobility,
economic independence, the sexual revolution, and dozens of other ideas,
trends, and situations in post-1950 U.S. history have dramatically altered
and complicated the previously simple courtship theme. These same social
and political activities have generated an enlarged spectrum of lyrical
commentary within many rock tunes. From 1950 to 1985, U.S. society has
been verbally photographed by innumerable itinerant tunesmiths and dis-
played in audio galleries across this continent and throughout the world.
Radios, jukeboxes, cable television (MTV), cassette recordings, motion
picture soundtracks, compact discs, and millions and millions of records
sound a clarion call to prospective oral historians. The irony is that so few
teachers have utilized these recorded history resources. But just as armies
of archaeologists have successfully reconstructed the fabric of ancient
Indian cultures by carefully examining buried relics, it is vital that modern
historians, teachers, and students of humanity and culture apply their logical

analyses and reasoned perspectives to the vinyl remnants of the U.S. music industry.

Examining Social Issues Through Songs

> Common sense tells us that sound recording—that is, records and cassettes—is a mass medium just like newspapers, film, or television. In industrialized countries, listening to records is just as much part of everyday life as reading the newspaper or listening to the radio.

> Pekka Gronow
> "The Record Industry:
> The Growth of a Mass Media" (1983)

Is rock music really a legitimate resource for investigating contemporary society? For Dick Clark, Wolfman Jack, and Casey Kasem, maybe so; but what about the thousands of teachers and millions of students in classrooms across the country? The answer should be a resounding "Yes!" This does not mean that rock music is either the only or the best resource for examining contemporary social and political events. Televised speeches, printed articles from newspapers and magazines, lectures by teachers, scholars, politicians, and businessmen, and innumerable other oral and written communication vehicles can stimulate student thought, reflection, decision making, and action. But rock lyrics are "ear candy" to many Americans, offering both audio gratification and the challenge of being "different" from the bland pabulum served in traditional textbooks and lectures.

What specific historical topics can be surveyed via rock tunes? Surprisingly, the 1950-1985 period is blanketed with significant lyrical commentary. Because so few teachers consider rock to be "serious music"—let alone "serious history"—few have explored the sociopolitical imagery contained in songs by Elvis Presley, Chuck Berry, and The Coasters. Beyond these early rockers, though, the idea of Mick Jagger, John Lennon, Burton Cummings, Pete Townshend, Carole King, Bob Dylan, Elvis Costello, and John Mellencamp making political and social statements is not nearly as unexpected. Rock music is after all the rhythmic voice of the young. Obviously love themes, dancing, partying, and other less-than-polemic ideas dominate rock's frantic media message. Yet individuals such as Bruce Springsteen, Paul Simon, David Bowie, and Billy Joel and groups such as The Beatles, The Rolling Stones, The Who, The Guess Who, and Culture Club defy traditional society, and explain modern history with statements of meaning and substance in their hit recordings.

The most productive approach to examining the past thirty-five years of U.S. history through rock music is to assemble a variety of lyrical resources that comment on specific themes and develop several units of songs that focus on persistent sociopolitical concerns. The value of using a multitune approach is that it encourages students to confront issues rather than just to debate the validity of a single song. It also allows teachers to demonstrate longitudinal concern for particular historical patterns and events. It does not indicate that single occurrences are unworthy of lyrical analysis—far from it. The assassination of John F. Kennedy, for instance, sparked immediate, sympathetic song responses as well as later, long-range lyrical analyses. The goal of historical study, aside from the pursuit of truth, is to enable individuals to evolve personal perspectives on key human issues. Music, even rock, is a valuable resource to enliven student interest in understanding the past.

The remainder of this essay presents six "Rock Music as History" teaching units. Each unit is defined by a major contemporary sociopolitical theme; a paragraph of analysis suggests several lyrical ideas and comments to flesh out the theme; finally, a series of rock recordings are provided to illustrate the theme. Although there may be minor disagreement about the "rockin'" credentials of a given singer or the "rollin'" rhythm of a particular hit tune, this format demonstrates how teachers can successfully employ rock recordings to generate historical analysts.

UNIT 1: CIVIL AUTHORITIES

Teaching Theme

From local policemen to National Guard units to FBI agents, U.S. society depends upon an intricate network of law enforcement officers to provide an adequate criminal justice system. A few songs such as "The Night Chicago Died" (1974) eulogize police heroism, but several other tunes express doubts, skepticism, cynicism, and open hostility toward civil authorities. "I Shot the Sheriff" (1974) details the harassment of a civilian by a legal official; "Smackwater Jack" (1971) portrays a sheriff condoning a pretrial lynching; and "Ohio" (1970) condemns the assassinations of several college students by National Guardsmen. The strong, honest, just lawmen praised in "High Noon" (1952), "(The Man Who Shot) Liberty Valance" (1962), "Big Iron" (1960), and other songs are often overshadowed by the specters of police brutality and oppression expressed in "Subterranean Homesick Blues" (1965), "For What It's Worth" (1967), and "Mad Dog" (1970).

Recordings

- "The Authority Song"
  (Riva 216)
  John Cougar (1984)

- "Bad Moon Rising"
  (Fantasy 622)
  Creedence Clearwater Revival (1969)

- "Chicago"
  (Atlantic 2804)
  Graham Nash (1971)

- "For What It's Worth (Stop, Hey, What's That Sound)"
  (Atco 6459)
  Buffalo Springfield (1967)

- "George Jackson"
  (Columbia 45516)
  Bob Dylan (1971)

- "I Fought the Law"
  (Mustang 3016)
  The Bobby Fuller Four (1966)

- "I Shot the Sheriff"
  (RSO 409)
  Eric Clapton (1974)

- "In the Ghetto"
  (RCA 47-9741)
  Elvis Presley (1969)

- "Indiana Wants Me"
  (Rare Earth 5013)
  R. Dean Taylor (1970)

- "Mad Dog"
  (A&M 4249)
  Lee Michaels (1970)

- "(The Man Who Shot) Liberty Valance"
  (Musicor 1020)
  Gene Pitney (1962)

- "My Crime"
  (Liberty 7541)
  Canned Heat (1968)

- "The Night Chicago Died"
  (Mercury 73492)
  Paper Lace (1974)

- "Ohio"
  (Atlantic 2740)
  Crosby, Stills, Nash, and Young (1970)

- "Smackwater Jack"
  (Ode 66019)
  Carole King (1971)

- "Subterranean Homesick Blues"
  (Columbia 43242)
  Bob Dylan (1965)

- "Who Are You"
  (MCA 40948)
  The Who (1978)

- "Won't Get Fooled Again"
  (Decca 32846)
  The Who (1971)

UNIT 2: MILITARY INVOLVEMENTS

Teaching Theme

Patriotic images of U.S. military history abound in contemporary lyrics—"The Battle of New Orleans" (1959), "Sink the Bismarck" (1960), "The Ballad of the Green Berets" (1966), "The Fightin' Side of Me" (1970), and "In America" (1980). However, a strong undercurrent of doubt is also expressed in rock songs about the legitimacy of participating in international conflict. Protest, fear, and anger are found in "Eve of Destruction" (1965), "Fortunate Son" (1969), "Military Madness" (1971), and "Undercover (of the Night)" (1983). Between these extremes of patriotism and pacifism, several songs raise fundamental issues of personal commitment, postwar trauma, civil disobedience, and the failure of wartime leadership. These feelings are featured in "America, Communicate with Me" (1970), "Still in Saigon" (1982), "Universal Soldier" (1965), "The Unknown Soldier" (1968), "Eve of Destruction" (1965), and "I Ain't Marching Anymore" (1969). Far from the battlefields, domestic problems haunt individuals who have either fought in wars themselves or who have lost friends as a result of military conflicts. These positions are communicated in "Ruby, Don't Take Your Love to Town" (1969), "2 + 2 = ?" (1968), "I Feel-Like-I'm-Fixin'-to-Die Rag" (1969), and "Home of the Brave" (1965).

Recordings

- "America, Communicate with Me"
  (Barnaby 2016)
  Ray Stevens (1970)

- "Are You Ready?"
  (Columbia 45158)
  Pacific Gas and Electric (1970)

- "The Ballad of the Green Berets"
  (RCA 8729)
  Barry Sadier (1966)

- "Battle Hymn of Lt. Calley"
  (Plantation 73)
  C. Company, featuring Terry Nelson (1971)

- "The Battle of New Orleans"
  (Columbia 41339)
  Johnny Horton (1959)

- "Billy, Don't Be a Hero"
  (ABD 11435)
  Bo Donaldson and The Heywoods (1974)

- "Eve of Destruction"
  (Dunhill 4009)
  Barry McGuire (1965)

- "The Fightin' Side of Me"
  (Capitol SSN-16278)
  Merle Haggard (1970)

- "Fortunate Son"
  (Capitol 2-19)
  Creedence Clearwater Revival (1969)

- "Give Peace a Chance"
  (Apple 1809)
  John Lennon (1969)

- "Home of the Brave"
  (Capitol 5483)
  Jody Miller (1965)

- "Imagine"
  (Apple 1840)
  John Lennon (1971)

- "In America"
  (Epic 50888)
  The Charlie Daniels Band (1980)

- "Military Madness"
  (Atlantic 2827)
  Graham Nash (1971)

- "Ruby, Don't Take Your Love to Town"
  (Reprise 0829)
  Kenny Rogers and The First Edition (1969)

- "Sink the Bismarck"
  (Columbia 41568)
  Johnny Horton (1960)

- "Still in Saigon"
  (Epic 02828)
  The Charlie Daniels Band (1982)

- "Stop the War Now"
(Gordy 7104)
Edwin Starr (1971)

- "2 + 2 = ?"
(Capitol Records Album)
Bob Seger System (1968)

- "Undercover (of the Night)"
(Rolling Stone 99813)
The Rolling Stones (1983)

- "Universal Soldier"
(Hickory 1338)
Donovan (1965)

- "The Unknown Soldier"
(Elektra 45628)
The Doors (1968)

- "War"
(Gordy 7101)
Edwin Starr (1970)

- "War Song"
(Reprise 1099)
Neil Young and Graham Nash (1972)

UNIT 3: PUBLIC EDUCATION SYSTEM

Teaching Theme

The youth-oriented nature of rock music dictates that public schools will be a center of lyrical attention. Neither truth nor reality, though, is guaranteed in the observations about education presented in popular songs. The joys of school life are depicted in "High School Dance" (1977), "Be True to Your School" (1963), and "Swingin' School" (1968). Not unexpectedly, lyrical exhilaration is reserved for escape from school, either by summer vacation—"School Is Out" (1961) and "School's Out" (1972)—or by securing a diploma—"Graduation Day" (1967), "Graduation's Here" (1959), and "Pomp and Circumstance (The Graduation Song)" (1961). A few songs praise sensitive, thoughtful teachers—"To Sir with Love" (1967) and "Welcome Back" (1976), but most tunes characterize the instructional staff as insensitive, doctrinaire, and ignorant. Not only are "School Days" (1957) viewed as grim torture, but those who participate often feel robbed of their natural good instincts and their future intellectual freedom. These viewpoints are communicated in "Another Brick in the Wall" (1980) and "The Logical Song" (1979).

Recordings

- "Abigail Beecher"
  (Warner Brothers 5409)
  Freddy Cannon (1965)

- "Another Brick in the Wall-Part II"
  (Columbia 11187)
  Pink Floyd (1980)

- "Be True to Your School"
  (Capitol 5069)
  The Beach Boys (1963)

- "Don't Be a Drop-Out"
  (King 6056)
  James Brown (1966)

- "Don't Stand So Close to Me"
  (A&M 2301)
  The Police (1981)

- "The Free Electric Band"
  (Mums 6018)
  Albert Hammond (1973)

- "Harper Valley P.T.A."
  (Plantation 3)
  Jeannie C. Riley (1968)

- "High School U.S.A."
  (Atlantic 51-78)
  Tommy Facenda (1959)

- "Kodachrome"
  (Columbia 45859)
  Paul Simon (1973)

- "The Logical Song"
  (A&M 2128)
  Supertramp (1979)

- "School Day"
  (Chess 1653)
  Chuck Berry (1957)

- "School Is Out"
  (LeGrand 1009)
  Gary "U.S." Bonds (1961)

- "School's Out"
  (Warner Brothers 7569)
  Alice Cooper (1972)

- "Smokin' in the Boys' Room"
  (Big Tree 16011)
  Brownville Station (1974)

- "To Sir with Love"
  (Epic 10187)
  Lulu (1967)

- "Welcome Back"
  (Reprise 1349)
  John Sebastian (1976)

UNIT 4: RAILROADS

Teaching Theme

The history of the United States since the mid-nineteenth century is intertwined with the development of railroading. Since 1950 songs have illustrated elements of railway construction, reports of train robberies, and denunciations of interstate toll charges—"John Henry" (1956), "Nine-

Pound Steel" (1967), "Let Jesse Rob the Train" (1979), and "Rock Island Line" (1956). In contemporary society, trains are viewed as vehicles of escape from rural poverty, nagging parents, bossy wives, or the drudgery of a boring job. These sentiments appear in "I'm Movin' On" (1963), "Johnny B. Goode" (1970), "Me and Bobby McGee" (1971), "The Promised Land" (1974) and "Train, Train" (1979). Trains are also utilized in records as metaphorical vehicles to secure freedom from either physical or spiritual captivity. Illustrations of this theme occur in "Midnight Special" (1965), "Friendship Train" (1969), "Love Train" (1973), "Peace Train" (1971), and "People Get Ready" (1965). In addition, some songs depict railroad employment functions, such as "Hey Porter" (1955).

Recordings

- "Catch a Train"
  (A&M 4349)
  Free (1972)

- "The City of New Orleans"
  (Reprise 1103)
  Arlo Guthrie (1972)

- "Folsom Prison Blues"
  (Columbia 44513)
  Johnny Cash (1968)

- "Friendship Train"
  (Soul 35068)
  Gladys Knight and The Pips (1969)

- "I'm Movin' On"
  (Smash 1813)
  Matt Lucas (1963)

- "Johnny B. Goode"
  (Columbia 45058)
  Johnny Winter (1970)

- "Keep This Train a-Rollin' "
  (Warner Brothers 49670)
  The Doobie Brothers (1981)

- "Let Jesse Rob the Train"
  (Warner Brothers 49118)
  Buck Owens (1979)

- "Long Twin Silver Line"
  (Capitol 4836)
  Bob Seger and The Silver Bullet Band (1980)

- "Love Train"
  (Philadelphia International 3524)
  The O'Jays (1973)

- "Me and Bobby McGee"
  (Mercury 73248)
  Jerry Lee Lewis (1971)

- "Midnight Special"
  (Imperial 66087)
  Johnny Rivers (1965)

- "Midnight Train to Georgia"
  (Buddha 383)
  Gladys Knight and The Pips (1973)

- "Mystery Train"
  (Sun 223)
  Elvis Presley (1955)

- "Promised Land"
  (RCA 10074)
  Elvis Presley (1974)

- "Rock Island Line"
  (London 1650)
  Lonnie Donnegan (1956)

- "Train, Train"
  (Atco 7207)
  Blackfoot (1979)

UNIT 5: REPRESENTATIVE GOVERNMENT

Teaching Theme

Our political system, from its organizational and leadership structures to its ideals of equality, liberty, and the pursuit of happiness, is a frequent subject of commentary in rock lyrics. Patriotic praise for the United States government is expressed in "America, Communicate with Me" (1970), "Battle of New Orleans" (1974), "The Declaration" (1970), "Okie from Muskogee" (1969), "The Star-Spangled Banner" (1968), "Stars and Stripes Forever" (1950), and "West of the Wall" (1962). This idealism is countered by strong doses of lyrical cynicism toward political authority featured in "Eve of Destruction" (1965), "Undercover (of the Night)" (1983), "Monster" (1969), "Fortunate Son" (1969), "Power" (1980), and "You Haven't Done Nothin' " (1974). The failure of majority rule to function in practice and the general unwillingness of the majority to defend minority rights are chronicled in "Hey Big Brother" (1971), "Won't Get Fooled Again" (1971), "What's Going On?" (1971), and "Elected" (1972). American society's problems, according to lyrical commentaries, are more often the fault of an insensitive government rather than the result of malicious individual activities.

Recordings

- "American Woman"
  (RCA 0325)
  The Guess Who (1971)

- "Elected"
  (Warner Brothers 7631)
  Alice Cooper (1972)

- "Eve of Destruction"
  (Dunhill 4009)
  Barry McGuire (1965)

- "(For God's Sake) Give More Power to the People"
  (Brunswick 55450)
  The Chi-Lites (1971)

- "Fortunate Son"
  (Fantasy 634)
  Creedence Clearwater Revival (1969)

- "Hey Big Brother"
  (Rare Earth 5038)
  Rare Earth (1971)

- "Monster"
  (Dunhill 4221)
  Steppenwolf (1969)

- "Power"
  (Gordy 7183)
  The Temptations (1980)

- "Revolution"
  (Apple 2276)
  The Beatles (1968)

- "Spirits in the Material World"
  (A&M 2390)
  The Police (1982)

- "Synchronicity II"
  (A&M 2571)
  The Police (1983)

- "Undercover (of the Night)"
  (Rolling Stone 99813)
  The Rolling Stones (1983)

- "What's Going On"
  (Tamla 54201)
  Marvin Gaye (1971)

- "Won't Get Fooled Again"
  (Decca 32846)
  The Who (1971)

- "You Haven't Done Nothin' "
  (Tamla 54252)
  Stevie Wonder (1974)

- "You're the Man"
  (Tamla 54221)
  Marvin Gaye (1972)

UNIT 6: OTHER SOCIOPOLITICAL ISSUES
IN CONTEMPORARY AMERICAN SOCIETY

Racism, Discrimination, and Prejudice

- "Choice of Colors"
  (Curtom 1943)
  The Impressions (1969)

- "Ebony and Ivory"
  (Columbia 02860)
  Paul McCartney and Stevie Wonder (1982)

- "The Family of Man"
  (Dunhill 4306)
  Three Dog Night (1972)

- "Half-Breed"
  (MCA 40102)
  Cher (1973)

- "Indian Reservation"
  (Columbia 45332)
  Paul Revere and the Raiders (1971)

- "Living for the City"
  (Crossover 981)
  Ray Charles (1975)

- "Why Can't We Live Together?"
  (Glades 1703)
  Timmy Thomas (1973)

Social Pressure for Conformity

- "Dedicated Follower of Fashion"
  (Reprise 0471)
  The Kinks (1966)

- "Harper Valley P.T.A."
  (Plantation 3)
  Jeannie C. Riley (1968)

- "Little Boxes"
  (Columbia 42940)
  Pete Seeger (1964)

- "Mr. Businessman"
  (Monument 1083)
  Ray Stevens (1968)

- "Pleasant Valley Sunday"
  (Colgems 1607)
  The Monkees (1967)

- "Signs"
  (Lionel 3213)
  The Five-Man Electrical Band (1971)

- "Society's Child (Baby, I've Been Thinking)"
  (Verve 5027)
  Janis Ian (1967)

- "The Son of Hickory Holler's Tramp"
  (Columbia 44425)
  O. C. Smith (1968)

Unemployment, Automation, and Worker Frustration

- "Allentown"
  (Columbia 03413)
  Billy Joel (1983)

- "Industrial Disease"
  (Warner Brothers 29880)
  Dire Straits (1983)

- "Mr. Roboto"
  (A&M 2525)
  Styx (1983)

- "A Natural Man"
  (MGM 14262)
  Lou Rawls (1971)

- "9 to 5"
  (RCA 12133)
  Dolly Parton (1981)

- "Sixteen Tons"
  (Atlantic 3323)
  The Don Harrison Band (1976)

- "Take This Job and Shove It"
  (Epic 50469)
  Johnny Paycheck (1977)

- "Workin' at the Car Wash Blues"
  (ABC 11447)
  Jim Croce (1974)

Urban Unrest

- "Baker Street"
  (United Artists 1192)
  Gerry Rafferty (1978)

- "Dead-End Street"
  (Capitol 5869)
  Lou Rawls (1967)

- "In the Ghetto"
  (RCA 47-9741)
  Elvis Presley (1969)

- "Inner City Blues (Make Me Wanna Holler)"
  (Tamla 54242)
  Marvin Gaye (1971)

- "Masterpiece"
  (Gordy 7126)
  The Temptations (1973)

- "Takin' It to the Streets"
  (Warner Brothers 8196)
  The Doobie Brothers (1976)

INTERNATIONAL POLITICAL CONCERNS

When the Music's Over: The Story of Political Pop. By Robin Denselow. London: Faber and Faber, 1990. Illustrated. 298 pp.

British journalist and BBC television commentator Robin Denselow presents a thorough, comprehensive examination of the interaction between popular music and political activities in the international arena since World War II. Most of the heroes (Pete Seeger, Harry Belafonte, Curtis Mayfield, Phil Ochs, Bob Marley, Harry Chapin, and Bob Geldof) and villains (Joseph McCarthy, the House Un-American Activities Committee, Richard Nixon, the all-white Pretoria government, Ronald Reagan, and Margaret Thatcher) are predictable. However, the mixed reviews on The Kingston Trio, Neil Young, Eric Clapton, Paul Simon, Bob Dylan, John Lennon, Lonnie Donegan, Bruce Springsteen, and Jim Morrison are fascinating and well-reasoned. Denselow, tackling a complex subject full of potential interpretative problems, avoids the twin traps of bald-faced fandom or ideological simplicity. His critical journalistic perspective permits clear, factual reporting with ample opportunity for thoughtful, perceptive editorial assessment.

Denselow emphasizes that musicians achieve political impact by spreading ideas—most often via lyrics, though occasionally in public addresses and interviews—and by raising money through benefit performances. His examination of the Irish band U2 and their controversial lead singer/lyricist Bono illustrates the balance and insight the author maintains. Denselow notes that while U2 has musically campaigned for worldwide nuclear disarmament, against apartheid in South Africa, for world charity (through Live Aid concerts), and against human rights violations in Central America (through Amnesty International), Bono acknowledges that his audiences are often confused about his principles of aggressive pacificism (based on admiration for Martin Luther King Jr.), and antinationalism (illustrated by hatred of state flags and other symbols of human separation). *When the Music's Over* plumbs numerous issues of artist/audience/politician misunderstandings and conflicts with genuine insight. Denselow's concluding observation is open-ended: "Mixing pop music and politics has never been easy, and the bigger the show, the bigger the pressures and contradictions can be. . . . Pop musicians have learned that they have the power to use both their music and their position, to comment, to travel, to raise vast sums of money, and to try to reflect and even alter the course of history, just like the earlier troubadours of the world's folk movements. How that power is used is up to them" (p. 282).

This study is especially valuable because of its historic breadth (1945-1990), the absence of polemical tone, the inclusion of non-Western influences and ideas and the acknowledgement that individual freedom demands vigilance, commitment, and action. From Martin Luther King Jr. to Nelson Mandela, Denselow links empowering political personalities with those singers and songwriters who emerge as more than mere celebrities. Whether challenging the censorship goals of Tipper Gore's Parents Music Resource Center or condemning the apathy of world governments toward the starving people of Ethiopia, musicians of courage and character (Ruben Blades, Stevie Wonder, Joan Baez, Billy Bragg, Hugh Masekela, Miriam Makeba, Peter Gabriel, Sweet Honey in the Rock, Gil Scott-Heron, Sting, and Bob Marley) have proven to be more than commercial ciphers or political pawns. *When the Music's Over* warrants careful reading by scholars and government officials. Hopefully, it will also alert many ahistorical teenage cassette/CD buyers that there are many issues in the 1990s worth living, and perhaps even dying, for.

BIBLIOGRAPHY

Butchart, Ronald E. and B. Lee Cooper. "Perceptions of Education in the Lyrics of American Popular Music, 1950-1980," *American Music*, V (Fall 1987), pp. 271-281.

Chapple, Steve and Reebee Garofalo, *Rock 'n' Roll is Here to Pay: The History and Politics of the Music Industry*. Chicago: Nelson-Hall, Inc., 1977.

Clee, Ken (comp.). *The Dictionary of American 45 R.P.M. Records—Volume One* (Revised Edition). Philadelphia: Stak-O-Wax Publications, 1982.

Clee, Ken (comp.). *The Dictionary of American 45 R.P.M. Records—Volume Two* (Revised Edition). Philadelphia: Stak-O-Wax Publications, 1985.

Clee, Ken (comp.). *The Dictionary of American 45 R.P.M. Records—Volume Three* (Revised Edition). Philadelphia: Stak-O-Wax Publications, 1986.

Clee, Ken (comp.). *The Dictionary of American 45 R.P.M. Records—Volume Four*. Philadelphia: Stak-O-Wax Publications, 1983.

Cooper, B. Lee. "Can Music Students Learn Anything of Value by Investigating Popular Recordings?" *International Journal of Instructional Media*, XX, No. 3 (1993), pp. 273-284.

Cooper, B. Lee. "Christmas Songs As American Cultural History: Audio Resources for Classroom Investigation, 1940-1990," *Social Education*, LIV (October 1990), pp. 374-379.

Cooper, B. Lee. "Controversial Issues in Popular Lyrics, 1960-1985: Teaching Resources for the English Classes," *Arizona English Bulletin*, XXIX (Fall 1986), pp. 174-187.

Cooper, B. Lee. "Creating an Audio Chronology: Utilizing Popular Recordings to Illustrate Ideas and Events in American History, 1965-1987," *International Journal of Instructional Media*, XVI, No. 2 (1989), pp. 167-179.

Cooper, B. Lee. "Examining Social Change Through Contemporary History: An Audio Media Proposal," *History Teacher*, VI (August 1973), pp. 523-534.

Cooper, B. Lee. "Folk History, Alternative History, and Future History," *Teaching History: A Journal of Methods*, II (Spring 1977), pp. 58-62.

Cooper, B. Lee. "I'll Fight for God, Country, and My Baby: Persistent Themes in American Wartime Songs," *Popular Music and Society*, XVI (Summer 1992), pp. 95-111.

Cooper, B. Lee. "The Image of the Outside in Contemporary Lyrics," *Journal of Popular Culture*, XII (Summer 1978), pp. 168-178.

Cooper, B. Lee. *Images of American Society in Popular Music: A Guide to Reflective Teaching.* Chicago: Nelson-Hall, Inc., 1982.

Cooper, B. Lee. "Lyrical Commentaries: Learning from Popular Music," *Music Educators Journal*, LXXVII (April 1991), pp. 56-59.

Cooper, B. Lee. "Music and the Metropolis: Lyrical Images of Life in American Cities, 1950-1980," *Teaching History: A Journal of Methods*, VI (Fall 1981), pp. 72-84.

Cooper, B. Lee. "Political Protest and Social Criticism," in *A Resource Guide to Themes in Contemporary American Song Lyrics, 1950-1985.* Westport, CT: Greenwood Press, 1986, pp. 183-199.

Cooper, B. Lee. "Political Protest Movements and Social Trends Depicted in American Popular Music, 1960-1985: A Chronological Guide to Recorded Resources," *International Journal of Instructional Media*, XIV, No. 2 (1987), pp. 147-160.

Cooper, B. Lee. "Popular Music: An Untapped Resource for Teaching Contemporary Black History," *Journal of Negro Education*, XLVIII (Winter 1979), pp. 20-36.

Cooper, B. Lee. "Popular Music and Academic Enrichment in the Residence Hall," *NASPA Journal*, XI (Winter 1974), pp. 50-57.

Cooper, B. Lee. *Popular Music in the Social Studies Classroom: Audio Resources for Teachers,* (How to Do It—Series Two, No. 13). Washington, DC: National Council for the Social Studies, 1981.

Cooper, B. Lee. *Popular Music Perspectives: Ideas, Themes, and Patterns in Contemporary Lyrics.* Bowling Green, OH: Bowling Green State University Popular Press, 1991.

Cooper, B. Lee. "Popular Records as Oral Evidence: Creating an Audio Time Line to Examine American History, 1955-1987," *Social Education*, LIII (January 1989), pp. 34-40.

Cooper, B. Lee. "Popular Songs, Military Conflicts, and Public Perceptions of the United States at War," *Social Education*, LVI (March 1992), pp. 160-168.

Cooper, B. Lee. "Promoting Social Change Through Audio Repetition: Black Musicians as Creators and Revivalists, 1953-1978," *Tracking: Popular Music Studies*, II (Winter 1989), pp. 26-46.

Cooper, B. Lee. "Record Revivals as Barometers of Social Change: The Historical Use of Contemporary Audio Resources," *JEMF Quarterly*, XIV (Spring 1978), pp. 38-44.

Cooper, B. Lee. "Review of *Born in the U.S.A.: The Myth of America in Popular Music from Colonial Times to the Present* by Timothy E. Scheurer," *Journal of American Culture,* XV (Summer 1992), pp. 91-92.

Cooper, B. Lee. "Review of *Work's Many Voices* (JEMF 110/111). Compiled by Archie Green," *Popular Music and Society,* XII (Spring 1988), pp. 77-79.

Cooper, B. Lee. "Rock Music and Religious Education: A Proposed Synthesis," *Religious Education,* LXX (May-June 1975), pp. 289-299.

Cooper, B. Lee. "Rumors of War: Lyrical Continuities, 1914-1991," in *Continuities of Popular Culture,* edited by Ray B. Browne and Ronald J. Ambrosetti. Bowling Green, OH: Bowling Green State University Popular Press, 1993, pp. 121-142.

Cooper, B. Lee. "Social Change, Popular Music, and the Teacher," *Social Education,* XXXVII (December 1973), pp. 776-781, 783.

Cooper, B. Lee. "Social Concerns, Political Protest, and Popular Music," *Social Studies,* LXXIX (March-April 1988), pp. 53-60.

Cooper, B. Lee. "Sultry Songs and Censorship: A Thematic Discography for College Teachers," *International Journal of Instructional Media,* XX, No. 2 (1993), pp. 181-194.

Cooper, B. Lee. "Sultry Songs as High Humor," *Popular Music and Society,* XXVII (Spring 1993), pp. 71-85.

Cooper, B. Lee. "Tapping a Sound Recording Archive for War Song Resources to Investigate America's Major Military Involvements, 1914-1991," *Popular Culture in Libraries,* I, No. 4 (1993), pp. 71-93.

Cooper, B. Lee and Larry S. Haverkos. "The Image of American Society in Popular Music: A Search for Identity and Values," *Social Studies,* LXIV (December 1973), pp. 319-322.

Cooper, B. Lee and William L. Schurk. "Smokin' Songs: Examining Tobacco Use as an American Cultural Phenomenon Through Contemporary Lyrics," *International Journal of Instructional Media,* XXI, No. 3 (1994), pp. 261-268.

Cooper, B. Lee and Donald E. Walker with assistance from William L. Schurk. "The Decline of Contemporary Baseball Heroes in American Popular Recordings," *Popular Music and Society,* XV (Summer 1991), pp. 49-58.

Cooper, Laura E. and B. Lee Cooper. "The Pendulum of Cultural Imperialism: Popular Music Interchanges Between the United States and Britain, 1943-1967," *Journal of Popular Culture,* XXVII (Winter 1993), pp. 61-78.

Curtis, James M. *Rock Eras: Interpretations of Music and Society, 1954-1984.* Bowling Green, OH: Bowling Green State University Popular Press, 1987.

Denisoff, R. Serge. *Sing a Song of Social Significance* (Second Edition). Bowling Green, OH: Bowling Green State University Popular Press, 1983.

Denisoff, R. Serge and Richard A. Peterson. (eds.). *The Sounds of Social Change: Studies in Popular Culture.* Chicago: Rand McNally and Company, 1972.

Denselow, Robin. *When the Music's Over: The Story of Political Pop.* London: Faber and Faber, 1990.

Ellison, Mary. *Lyrical Protest: Black Music's Struggle Against Discrimination.* New York: Praeger Books, 1989.

Finson, Jon W. *The Voices That Are Gone: Themes in 19th-Century American Popular Song.* New York: Oxford University Press, 1994.

Fogo, Fred. *I Read the News Today: The Social Drama of John Lennon's Death.* Lanham, MD: Littlefield Adams Quality Paperbacks, 1994.

Gammond, Peter. *The Oxford Companion to Popular Music.* New York: Oxford University Press, 1991.

Garofalo, Reebee (ed.). *Rockin' the Boat: Mass Music and Mass Movements.* Boston: South End Press, 1992.

Green, Jeff (comp.). *The 1987 Green Book: Songs Classified by Subject.* Smyrna, TN: Professional Desk Services, 1986.

Gronow, Pekka. "The Record Industry: The Growth of a Mass Medium," in *Popular Music 3: Producers and Markets,* edited by Richard Middleton and David Horn. Cambridge, England: Cambridge, England: Cambridge University Press, 1983, pp. 53-75

Hamm, Charles. *Music in the New World.* New York: W W. Norton and Co., 1983.

Harris, James F. *Philosophy at 33$^1/_3$ R.P.M.: Themes of Classic Rock Music.* La Salle, IL: Open Court Publishing Company, 1993.

Hatch, David and Stephen Millward. *From Blues to Rock: An Analytical History of Pop Music.* Manchester, England: Manchester University Press, 1989.

Hibbard, Don J. and Carol Kaleialoha. *The Role of Rock: A Guide to the Social and Political Consequences of Rock Music.* Englewood, NJ: Prentice-Hall, Inc., 1983.

Lax, Roger and Frederick Smith. *The Great Song Thesaurus* (Second Edition, updated and expanded). New York: Oxford University Press, 1989.

Lipsitz, George. *Class Culture in Cold War America: A Rainbow at Midnight.* Brooklyn, NY: J.F. Bergin Publishers, Inc., 1981.

Lipsitz, George. *Time Passages: Collective Memory and American Popular Culture.* Minneapolis, MN: University of Minnesota Press, 1990.

Macken, Bob, Peter Fornatale, and Bill Ayres (comps.). *The Rock Music Source Book.* Garden City, NY: Anchor Books, 1980.

Mawhinney, Paul C. (comp.). *MusicMaster: The 45 R.P.M. Record Directory, 1947-1982—Volume One: Artists.* Pittsburgh: Record-Rama, 1983.

Mawhinney, Paul C. (comp.). *MusicMaster: The 45 R.P.M. Record Directory, 1947-1982—Volume Two: Titles.* Pittsburgh Record-Rama, 1983.

Mawhinney, Paul C. (comp.). *MusicMaster: The 45 R.P.M. Singles Directory/Supplement—44 Years of Recorded Music from 1948-1992 Listed Alphabetically by Artist.* Pittsburgh: Record-Rama Sound Archives, 1992.

Mawhinney, Paul C. (comp.). *MusicMaster: The 45 R.P.M. Singles Directory/Supplement—44 Years of Recorded Music from 1948-1992 Listed Alphabetically by Title.* Pittsburgh: Record-Rama Sound Archives, 1992.

McLaurin, Melton A. and Richard A. Peterson (eds.). *You Wrote My Life: Lyrical Themes in Country Music.* Philadelphia: Gordon and Breach, 1992.

Miller, Timothy. *The Hippies and American Values.* Knoxville, TN: University of Tennessee Press, 1991.

Reeve, Andru J. *Turn Me On, Dead Man: The Complete Story of the Paul McCartney Death Hoax.* Ann Arbor, MI: Popular Culture, Ink., 1994.

Rimler, Walter. *Not Fade Away: A Comparison of Jazz Age with Rock Era Pop Song Composers.* Ann Arbor, MI: Pierian Press, 1984.

Rodnitzky, Jerome L. *Minstrels of the Dawn: The Folk-Protest Singer As a Cultural Hero.* Chicago: Nelson-Hall, Inc., 1976.

Rogers, Jimmie N. *The Country Music Message: All About Lovin' and Livin'.* Englewood Cliffs, NJ: Prentice-Hall, Inc., 1983.

Rogers, Jimmie N. *The Country Music Message: Revisited.* Fayetteville, AR: University of Arkansas Press, 1989.

Scheurer, Timothy E. *Born in the U.S.A.: The Myth of America in Popular Music from Colonial Times to the Present.* Jackson, MS: University Press of Mississippi, 1991.

Scott, John Anthony. *The Ballad of America: The History of the United States in Song and Story.* Carbondale, IL: Southern Illinois University Press, 1983.

Stecheson, Anthony and Anne Stecheson (comps.). *The Stecheson Classified Song Directory.* Hollywood, CA: The Music Industry Press, 1961.

Stecheson, Anthony and Anne Stecheson (comps.). *The Supplement to the Stecheson Classified Song Directory.* Hollywood, CA: Music Industry Press, 1978.

Tomaselli, Keyan G. and Bob Boster. "Mandela, MTV, Television, and Apartheid," *Popular Music and Society,* XVIII (Summer 1993), pp. 1-19.

Whitely, Sheila. *The Space Between the Notes: Rock and the Counter-Culture.* London: Routledge Books, 1992.

Wicke, Peter (translated by Rachel Fogg). *Rock Music: Culture, Aesthetics, and Sociology.* Cambridge, England: Cambridge University Press, 1990.

Wiener, Jon. *Professors, Politics, and Pop.* New York: Verso Books, 1991.

Chapter 15

Song Revivals

The practice of recording previous hit songs is common in American musical history. During the 1930s and 1940s, for instance, popular singers invariably incorporated several "standards" into their radio performances, their dance band shows, and their 78 rpm releases. Although very little research has been published on the standards of the first decade of the rock era (1954-1964),[1] it can easily be demonstrated that numerous contemporary artists have built significant portions of their repertoires on so-called golden oldie hits.

Why do contemporary singers record tunes that were previous hits for other performers? Commercially, the goal of scoring a second "Top 100" listing with a popularly-tested song is an understandable objective. Beyond the search for financial success, there are other logical reasons to revive former hit tunes. Here the "known commodity" theory emerges. The lyrics and melody of a familiar song may enable a young artist to successfully launch his or her career (Ricky Nelson's "I'm Walking"—1957; Marie Osmond's "Paper Roses"—1973; and Leif Garrett's "Surfin' USA"—1977, "Runaround Sue"—1978, and "The Wanderer"—1978) by tapping a well-known musical resource. Beyond the mere duplication of a previous sound, though, some artists revive traditional tunes to demonstrate their own unique singing styles. The reinterpretation of a lyric or the conversion of a rhythm pattern has served several novice (Gloria Gaynor's "Never Can Say Goodbye"—1975; Amii Stewart's "Knock on Wood"—1979; and The Marcels' "Blue Moon"—1961, "Heartaches"—1961, and "Summertime"—1961) and experienced (Marvin Gaye's "I Heard It Through the Grape-

The material in this chapter by B. Lee Cooper was originally published as "Johnny Rivers and Linda Ronstadt: Rock 'n' Roll Revivalists," *JEMF (John Edwards Memorial Foundation) Quarterly,* XVIII (Fall 1982/Winter 1983), pp. 166-177; and as essays in several issues of *Popular Music and Society.* Reprint permission granted by the author, managing editor Pat Browne, and the Bowling Green State University Popular Press.

vine"—1968; Ike and Tina Turner's "Proud Mary"—1971; and Ray Charles' "Yesterday"—1967, "I Can't Stop Loving You"—1962, and "Living for the City"—1975) performers well. Still another reason for reviving a particular song is to pay tribute to the performing artistry or creative talent of its originator. Occasionally the musical debt is openly acknowledged in the new recording (Wilson Pickett's "Everybody Needs Somebody to Love"—1967 and Dave Edmunds' "I Hear You Knocking"—1971); most of the time it is only implied (Elton John's "Lucy in the Sky with Diamonds"—1975; Ike and Tina Turner's "I've Been Loving You Too Long"—1969; and The Beatles' "Slow Down"—1964, "Roll Over Beethoven"—1964, and "Twist and Shout"—1964). A unique form of personal revival, of course, is the re-recording of a hit song by the original artist. Several fine examples of this phenomenon include Neil Sedaka's "Breaking Up Is Hard to Do"—1962 and 1976; The Ventures' "Walk—Don't Run"—1960 and 1964; Joni Mitchell's "Big Yellow Taxi"—1970 and 1975; and Shirley and Lee's "Let the Good Times Roll"—1956 and 1960.

The preceding illustrations of song revivals offer only a small sample of this fascinating musical activity. Clearly the practice is as common to new performers as it is to established artists. From Elvis Presley to The Beatles, from Ray Charles to The Rolling Stones, even the careers of popular music's most prestigious and innovative stars have been nurtured, enriched, and extended through reissuing previous hits. It is particularly fascinating to investigate in discographic detail the recording histories of two very popular, very influential artists to see how, when, and from whom they "borrowed" hit songs to spark their live performances and to fill their albums. The remainder of this section will concentrate on the activities of Johnny Rivers and Linda Ronstadt, two of the most successful rock 'n' roll revivalists of the past two decades.

Johnny Rivers (b. November 7, 1942) has been a potent force on the American popular music scene since 1964. His diversified talents as a singer, guitarist, composer, record producer, music publisher, and recording company executive are well-known. The high quality of his recorded sound—whether from live nightclub performances at the Whisky a Go Go, or on themes for television shows, or in standard studio performances— has consistently generated positive public attention. It is hardly surprising that Joel Whitburn's survey of the top 100 artists in the pop music field between 1955 and 1972 ranked Johnny Rivers at #55, just nine spots behind Chuck Berry (#46), but twenty-one spots ahead of Little Richard (#76).[2]

For the rock 'n' roll fan who continues to cherish the tunes of the pre-Beatles era (1954-1964), Johnny Rivers is a very special figure. Much of his recording career has focused on reproducing the jukebox sounds that he encountered in Baton Rouge, New York City, and Nashville during his youth. He is a master rock song revivalist. This is not to imply that he lacks creative musical talent. The numerous original pop hits that he has written—including "Poor Side of Town"—and recorded—including "Summer Rain," "Secret Agent Man," and "Swayin' to the Music (Slow Dancin')"—belie this type of shallow criticism. Instead, calling him a rock revivalist is an acknowledgment of his distinctive ability to take another person's musical creation and to breathe new vitality into it, to make it come alive again for a new generation of listeners. Johnny Rivers is not a cover-recording pirate seeking to steal profits from less well-known artists; nor is he simply a carbon copy record reissue fanatic. His recordings rank among the finest illustrations of rock 'n' roll song revivals. They demonstrate not only professional sensitivity to original recording styles, but also the genius of an artist who understands and appreciates the use of contemporary audio technology as a flexible device for re-creating former musical triumphs. Quality and character are hallmarks of Johnny Rivers' song revivals.[3]

The chart listed on the following pages (see Table 15.1) provides selected illustrations of the song revival activities of Johnny Rivers between 1964 and 1977.[4] The objective in constructing this outline is not to present all of this recording star's revival tunes. Rather, this presentation is designed to show how this talented singer's career has been dedicated to retrieving, updating, and rejuvenating, his own rock 'n' roll roots.

The significance of Johnny Rivers' efforts as a performer of both old and new rock songs cannot be underestimated. He represents a significant vocal bridge between the pre-Beatles and post-Beatles decades. Although 1950s giants such as Chuck Berry, Fats Domino, and Jerry Lee Lewis continue to defy generation gap barriers with their singing vigor, the deaths of Elvis Presley and Bill Haley have signaled that most authentic rock 'n' rollers from the 1950s and early 1960s are reaching ages where performing will probably cease to be their primary wage-earning activity. Similarly, few contemporary pop groups display the same unswerving devotion to rock's roots that originally motivated The Beatles and continues to fuel the artistic imaginations of Mick Jagger and the Rolling Stones. Of the current crop of popular male singers and musicians, the only rivals for Johnny Rivers' revivalist role are Daryl Dragon, Jacky Ward, Dave Loggins and Jim Messina, Narvel Felts, and a few others. If the sounds of 1954 through 1964 are to continue to leaven contemporary music, there must be a cadre of current performers who will either reacquaint or initiate

TABLE 15.1. The Johnny Rivers Rock 'n' Roll Revival System: Selected Examples of His Hit Tunes 1964-1967

45 rpm Releases

Date of Release by Rivers (Record Number)	Title of Song and Composer(s)	Date of Original Release (Record Number)	Name of Original Artist(s)
1964 (Imperial 66832)	"Memphis" (C. Berry)	1959 (Chess 1729)	Chuck Berry
1964 (Imperial 66056)	"Maybelline" (C. Berry)	1955 (Chess 1604)	Chuck Berry
1964 (Imperial 66075)	"Mountain of Love" (H. Dorman)	1960 (Rita 1003)	Harold Dorman
1965 (Imperial 66087)	"Midnight Special" (Adapted from Traditional American Folk Song)	1960 (Guaranteed 205)	Paul Evans
1965 (Imperial 66087)	"Cupid" (S. Cooke)	1961 (RCA Victor 47-7883)	Sam Cooke
1965 (Imperial 66133)	"Where Have All the Flowers Gone?" (P. Seeger)	1962 (Capitol 4671)	Kingston Trio
1965 (Imperial 66144)	"Under Your Spell Again" (D. Rhodes and B. Owens)	1959 (Capitol 4245)	Buck Owens
1967 (Imperial 66277)	"Baby I Need Your Lovin' " (E. Holland, B. Holland and L. Dozier)	1964 (Motown 1062)	The Four Tops
1971 (United Artists 50822)	"Sea Cruise" (H. Smith)	1959 (Ace 554)	Frankie Ford
1972 (United Artists 50960)	"Rockin' Pneumonia and the Boogie Woogie Flu" (J.Vincent and H. Smith)	1957 (Ace)	Huey "Piano" Smith and The Clowns
1973 (United Artists 198)	"Blue Suede Shoes" (C. Perkins)	1956 (Sun 234)	Carl Perkins
1977 (Big Tree 16106)	"Curious Mind (Um, Um, Um, Um, Um, Um)" (C. Mayfield)	1964 (Okeh 7187)	Major Lance

Album Releases

Date of Release by Rivers *Album Title* (Record Number)	Title of Song and Composer(s)	Date of Original Release (Record Number)	Name of Original Artist(s)
1964 *Johnny Rivers at the Whisky-A-Go-Go* (Imperial LP 9264)	"Oh Lonesome Me" (D. Gibson)	1958 (RCA VIctor 47-7133)	Don Gibson
	"Lawdy Miss Clawdy" (L. Price)	1952 (Specialty 428)	Lloyd Price
	"Walkin' the Dog" (R. Thomas)	1963 (Stax 140)	Rufus Thomas
	"You Can Have Her (I Don't Want Her)" (B. Cook)	1961 (Epic 9434)	Roy Hamilton
	"Multiplication" (B. Darin)	1961 (Atco 6214)	Bobby Darin
	"Brown-Eyed Handsome Man" (C. Berry)	1956 (Chess 1635)	Chuck Berry
1964 *Here We a Go Go Again* (Imperial LP 9274)	"Josephine" (A. Domino and D. Bartholomew)	1960 (Imperial 5704)	Fats Domino
	"High Heel Sneakers" (R. Higgenbotham)	1964 (Checker 1067)	Tommy Tucker
	"I've Got a Woman" (R. Charles)	1965 (Atlantic 1050)	Ray Charles
	"Bobby What You Want Me to Do" (J. Reed)	1960 (Vee-Jay 333)	Jimmy Reed
	"Roll Over Beethoven" (C. Berry)	1956 (Chess 1626)	Chuck Berry
	"Johnny B. Goode" (C. Berry)	1958 (Chess 1691)	Chuck Berry
	"Whole Lotta Shakin' Goin' On" (D. Williams and S. David)	1957 (Sun 267)	Jerry Lee Lewis
	"Dang Me" (R. Miller)	1964 (Smash 1881)	Roger Miller

TABLE 15.1 *(continued)*
Album Releases

Date of Release by Rivers *Album Title* (Record Number)	Title of Song and Composer(s)	Date of Original Release (Record Number)	Name of Original Artist(s)
1964 *Go, Johnny Go!* (United Artists UAL 3386)	"To Be Loved" (T. Carlo, B. Gordy Jr., and G. Gordy)	1958 (Brunswick 55052)	Jackie Wilson
1965 *In Action!* (ImperialLP 9280)	"Promised Land" (C. Berry)	1964 (Chess 1916)	Chuck Berry
	"I'm in Love Again" (A. Domino and D. Bartholomew)	1956 (Imperial 5386)	Fats Domino
	"Rhythm of the Rain" (J. Gummoe)	1963 (Valiant 6026)	The Cascades
	"Oh, Pretty Woman" (R. Orbison and B. Dees)	1964 (Monument 851)	Roy Orbison
	"Moody River" (G. D. Bruce)	1961 (Dot 16209)	Pat Boone
	"Keep A-Knockin' " (R. Penniman)	1957 (Specialty 611)	Little Richard
1965 *Meanwhile Back at the Whisky A Go Go* (Imperial 9284)	"Silver Threads and Golden Needles" (D. Rhodes and J. Reynolds)	1962 Philips 40038)	The Springfields
	"Land of 1,000 Dances" (C. Kenner)	1963 (Instant 3252)	Chris Kenner
	"Break Up" (C. Rich)	1958 (Sun 303)	Jerry Lee Lewis
	"Stagger Lee" (H. Logan and L. Price)	1958 (ABC-Paramount 9972)	Lloyd Price
	"Susie Q" (D. Hawkins, S. J. Lewis, and E. Broadwater)	1957 (Checker 863)	Dale Hawkins
	"Greenback Dollar" (Traditional)	1963 (CAP 4898)	The Kingston Trio

Album Releases

Date of Release by Rivers *Album Title* (Record Number)	Title of Song and Composer(s)	Date of Original Release (Record Number)	Name of Original Artist(s)
1965 *Johnny Rivers Rocks the Folk* (Imperial LP 9293)	"Tom Dooley" (Traditional)	1958 (Capitol 4049)	The Kingston Trio
	"Michael (Row the Boat Ashore)" (Traditional)	1961 (United Artists 258)	The Highwaymen
	"Blowin' in the Wind" (B. Dylan)	1963 (Warner Brothers 5268)	Peter, Paul, and Mary
	"Green, Green" (B. McGuire and R. Sparks)	1963 (Columbia 42805)	The New Christy Minstrels
	"If I Had a Hammer" (L. Hays and P. Seeger)	1962 (Warner Brothers 5296)	Peter, Paul, and Mary
	"Tall Oak Tree" (D. Burnette)	1960 (Era 3012)	Dorsey Brothers
	"500 Miles" (B. Bare and H. West)	1963 (RCA 8238)	Bobby Bare
1966 *And I Know You Wanna Dance* (Imperial LP 9307)	"You've Lost That Lovin' Feelin'" (P. Spector, B. Mann, and B. Weil)	1964 (Philles 124)	The Righteous Brothers
1970 *Johnny Rivers' Golden Hits* (Imperial LP 12324)	"La Bamba" (W. Clauson)	1959 (Del-Fi 4110)	Ritchie Valens

modern listeners to the potent songs of Chuck Berry, Wlillie Dixon, Otis-Blackwell, Jimmy Reed, Jerry Leiber and Mike Stoller, Huey Smith, Berry Gordy, and Chris Kenner.

Within the past twenty years several female singers have successfully revived a number of classic rock 'n' roll tunes. Dolly Parton cut "Great Balls of Fire" (RCA 11705); Tanya Tucker issued a version of "Not Fade Away" (MCA 40976); Linda Ronstadt recorded "Just One Look" (Asylum 46011); Rita Coolidge released "One Fine Day" (A&M 2169); and Amii Stewart produced a disco-oriented approach to "Knock on Wood" (Ariola

7736). The recording activities of these five popular female artists illustrate a dominant trend in contemporary popular music. During the last decade numerous singing stars female and male, new and veteran performers, representing such diverse singing styles as country, jazz, pop, soul, rock, and disco, have been raiding rock's musical attic to uncover usable tunes from previous decades. Obviously, the original hits of Jerry Lee Lewis, Buddy Holly and The Crickets, Doris Troy, The Chiffons, and Eddie Floyd served the five ladies mentioned above very well. Similarly, the works of rhythm and blues giants such as The Drifters, Charles Brown, Chuck Berry, and Maurice Williams and the Zodiacs have recently provided suitable lyrical material for George Benson ("On Broadway"—Warner Brothers 8542), The Eagles ("Please Come Home for Christmas"—Asylum 45555), Elton John ("Johnny B. Goode"—MCA 41159), and Jackson Browne ("Stay"—Asylum 45485).

Occasional reliance on reissuing "oldies but goldies" is understandable and has been a relatively common recording practice. However, some artists have been indelibly wedded to sponsoring record revivals throughout their careers. As illustrated in previous paragraphs, Johnny Rivers is the primary male proponent of this recording tactic. On the distaff side, the foremost female figure in the rock song recycling sweepstakes is Linda Ronstadt (b. July 15, 1946).[5] The fact that the management of Miss Ronstadt's career has been extremely complex since she emerged as lead singer with The Stone Poneys in 1967 means that the selection of her recording material may or may not represent her own choices. Even if she exercises total artistic control over her repertoire, though, the power of suggestion by producers, arrangers, friends, or other sources surely contributes to the musical collage that emerges. Whatever the reason, Linda Ronstadt is the unchallenged queen of rock's revivalists.[6]

Throughout her long and successful career, Linda Ronstadt has demonstrated superior skill in interpreting, updating, and revitalizing several classic rock tunes. She became the gorgeous embodiment of rock's evolution from the 1950s and 1960s into the 1970s, 1980s, and 1990s. She has not forgotten the simplicity of her medium and is an extremely talented song stylist. She is physically attractive, vocally powerful, able to interpret lyrics with great skill, gifted in responding to and manipulating concert audiences, and a proven industry powerhouse who knows herself and the professionals with whom she works. What Linda Ronstadt has apparently always understood is that good popular music can frequently be discovered in the hit tunes of previous years. That's a very simple statement. Obviously, it is only the extraordinary performer who can translate this elementary revival theory into successful artistic practice. Linda Ronstadt can.

One dramatic way to illustrate the impact of song revivals on Linda Ronstadt's career is to examine her 45 rpm hit production during the 1967-1979 period. During that time she reached *Billboard*'s Top 100 chart with twenty-three songs. More than half of these tunes were revivals of previous *Billboard*-charted songs. Beyond the realm of 45s in the world of albums, the revival pattern in Linda Ronstadt's tune selection is once again obvious. The selected discography in Table 15.2 presents eleven years of single and LP record-making success by this highly talented female singer.

The song revival pattern depicted in the preceding chart has been acknowledged by one of Linda Ronstadt's perceptive biographers. In 1978 Vivian Claire noted, "*Heart Like a Wheel* was a phenomenon. It established a pattern of success that Linda has been able to repeat over and over. The formula depends largely on Peter Asher, on brilliant and creative production, and on encouraging and supporting Linda's own taste in music rather than forcing musical ideas onto her." Claire concludes her observations by declaring, "Asher helped to make Linda more marketable by encouraging her to include two or three oldies on each album. Oldies like 'You're No Good' and 'When Will I Be Loved' sold *Heart Like a Wheel,* creating a much larger audience for her more subtle work with talented but not as well known songwriters like Jackson Browne, Warren Zevon, J. D. Souther, Anna McGarrigle, and Karla Bonoff, to name a few. This is not to imply that Linda's approach to oldies is anything other than brilliant. A solid part of her creativity is how sweetly—and with what apparent ease—she is able to remake, and improve, songs like Smokey Robinson's "Tracks of My Tears."[7]

What general conclusions can be drawn from the commercial success and celebrity status that Johnny Rivers and Linda Ronstadt have achieved through their record revival activities? Speculation is possible, but certainty is not. By age and cultural exposure, both Johnny Rivers and Linda Ronstadt are children of the rock era (1954-1964). Their own musical roots—in terms of songs, singing, styles, and favorite artists—probably reinforced their willingness to record tunes from that time. Granted, their decision to continue a record revival pattern is undoubtedly founded more in their chart-topping economic success than on either personal preference or nostalgia. But as younger generations emerge, it is interesting to note that their collective receptivity to songs from the 1950s and 1960s seem to demonstrate that new "standards" of popular music are being established each year. For the parents of the post World War II baby boomers this means that "Stardust," "Some Enchanted Evening," and "Deep Purple" are being either joined or supplanted by a variety of new numbers such

TABLE 15.2. The Linda Ronstadt Rock 'n' Roll Revival System: Selected Examples of Her Hit Tunes, 1967-1979

45 rpm Releases

Date of Release by Ronstadt (Record Number)	Title of Song and Composer(s)	Date of Original Release (Record Number)	Name of Original Artist(s)
1974 (Capitol 3990)	"You're No Good" (C. Ballard Jr.)	1963 (Vee-Jay 566)	Betty Everett
1975 (Capitol 4050)	"When Will I Be Loved?" (P. Everly)	1960 (Cadence 1380)	The Everly Brothers
1975 (Capitol 4050)	"It Doesn't Matter Anymore" (P. Anka)	1959 (Coral 62074)	Buddy Holly
1975 (Asylum 45282)	"Heat Wave" (B. Holland L. Dozier, and E. Holland)	1963 (Gordy 7022)	Martha and the Vandellas
1976 (Asylum 45340)	"That'll Be the Day" (J. Allison, B. Holly, and N. Petty)	1957 (Brunswick 55009)	The Crickets
1977 (Asylum 45431)	"Blue Bayou" (R. Orbison and J. Melson)	1963 (Monument 824)	Roy Orbison
1978 (Asylum 45519	"Back in the U.S.A." (C. Berry)	1959 (Chess 1729)	Chuck Berry
1979 (Asylum 46011)	"Just One Look" (G. Carroll and D. Payne)	1963 (Atlantic 2188)	Doris Troy
1979 (Asylum 46011)	"Love Me Tender" (E. Presley and V. Matson)	1956 (RCA Victor 47-6643)	Elvis Presley

Album Releases

Date of Release by Ronstadt *Album Title* (Record Number)	Title of Song and Composer(s)	Date of Original Release (Record Number)	Name of Original Artist(s)
1969 *Hand Sown, Home Grown* (Capitol ST 202)	"Silver Threads and Golden Needles" (J. Rhodes and D. Reynolds)	1962 (Philips 40038)	The Springfields
1970 *Silk Purse* (Capitol ST 407)	"Lovesick Blues" (I. Miles and C. Friend)	1962) (RCA Victor 47-8013) (Vee-Jay 477)	Floyd Cramer Frank Ifield

Album Releases

Date of Release by Ronstadt *Album Title* (Record Number)	Title of Song and Composer(s)	Date of Original Release (Record Number)	Name of Original Artist(s)
	"Will You Still Love Me Tomorrow?" (G. Goffin and C. King	1960 (Scepter 1211)	The Shirelles
	"I'm Leavin' It All Up to You" (D. Terry and D. Harris)	1963 (Montel 921)	Dale and Grace
1970 *Linda Ronstadt* (Capitol SMAS 635)	"I Fall to Pieces" (H. Cochran and H. Howard)	1961 (Decca 31205)	Patsy Cline
	"Crazy Arms" (R. Mooney and C. Seals)	1956 (Columbia 21510)	Ray Price
1974 *Heart Like a Wheel* (Asylum ST 11358)	"I Can't Help It (If I'm Still in Love with You)" (H. Williams)	1958 (Dot 15680)	Margaret Whiting
1976 *Hasten Down the Wind* (Asylum 7E-1072)	"Crazy" (W. Nelson)	1961 (Decca 31317)	Patsy Cline
1978 *Living in the USA* (Asylum 6E-155)	"When I Grow Too Old to Dream" (O. Hammerstein and S. Romberg)	1958 (Capitol 4048)	Ed Townsend

as "Memphis," "Blue Suede Shoes," "Silver Threads and Golden Needles," and "You've Lost That Loving Feelin'." Johnny Rivers and Linda Ronstadt are in the vanguard of a legion of contemporary rock revivalists. They have followed the advice of Edgar Winter when he sang, "Keep Playin' That Rock 'n' Roll!"[8]

* * *

The Best of The Crew Cuts: The Mercury Years (Mercury CD 314 534 731-2) By The Crew Cuts. New York: Mercury/PolyGram Records, 1996. 22 songs.

A grotesque misconception appears time and again in music criticism. It is fostered by artistic (literary) tradition and defended by legal (copyright/patent) practice. Yet it is a flawed idea when applied to popular music. Hit songs are invariably public domain critters. They elude branding; they transcend ownership. Only by hoarding, by not sharing, can a composer guarantee personal control over a particular lyric or melody. The beauty of popular songs arises from the multiple translations of words and instrumentation by numerous artists in a variety of musical genres.

The exploitation of black songwriters and black singers via cover recording practices during the 1953-1959 period has been widely documented. However, White-on-White covers of the 1930s and 1940s and black-on-white covers of the 1960s and 1970s have received very little research attention or critical commentary. Similarly, labeling Paul Simon a cultural imperialist because of his dedication to integrating African and Latin American rhythms in his music is farcical.

The Crew Cuts, a Toronto quartet consisting of Johnnie Perkins, Rudi Maugeri, Pat Barrett, and Ray Barrett, pursued a commercial career with Mercury Records as unabashed cover artists. Between 1954 and 1957 they released song after song that had originally been written, arranged, recorded, and issued by other performers. The tight, crisp vocal styling that was illustrated on their own first Mercury hit, "Crazy 'Bout Ya Baby" (1954), was subsequently applied to many other borrowed tunes. The Crew Cuts melded tight harmony, articulate lyrics, and bouncy orchestration in their versions of "Sh-Boom" (Life Could Be a Dream)" (1954), "Earth Angel (Will You Be Mine)" (1955), "Out of the Picture" (1956), and "I Like It Like That" (1957). The fact that these songs were originally recorded by The Chords, The Penguins, The Robins, and The Spaniels is musically irrelevant. The Crew Cuts demonstrated distinctive group harmony skills in adapting these four songs, along with others by Otis Williams and The Charms, Nappy Brown, Shirley Gunther and The Queens, and Gene and Eunice, to the American record buying scene.

Like The Diamonds, The Hilltoppers, The Gaylords, The Four Lads, and other White male vocal groups of the 1950s, The Crew Cuts were . . . just popular songsters. They represented no revolution in style or substance—just straight-ahead pop vocalization. *The Best of the Crew Cuts: The Mercury Years* is nostalgic, melodic, and fun. It highlights a group worthy of a retrospective disc, especially on cuts such as "Mostly Martha" (1955) and "Angels in the Sky" (1955). Their translation or transfiguration of numerous R&B songs is also enlightening since it demonstrates how musical acculturation works. One shouldn't forget what Bill Haley did to Joe Turner's "Shake, Rattle, and Roll" or how Elvis Presley boarded Junior Parker's "Mystery Train."

* * *

The Best of The Diamonds: The Mercury Years (Mercury CD 314 532 734-2). New York: Mercury/Polygram Records, 1996. 22 songs.

The Diamonds Collection (Stardust CD 1010). Etobiocoke, Ontario, Canada: Stardust Productions, 1993. 25 songs.

Sophisticated orchestration, clear diction, consistent harmonies, enhanced technical facilities, and well-coordinated marketing and distribution enabled The Diamonds to thrive as white R&B song stylists. Between 1956 and 1961 this Ontario, Canada, quartet—initially consisting of Dave Somerville (lead), Bill Reed (bass), Ted Kowalski (tenor), and Phil Leavitt (baritone)—placed sixteen "Hot 100" pop songs and seven "Hot R&B Sides" on the *Billboard* charts. The Diamonds covered tunes by Frankie Lymon and The Teenagers ("Why Do Fools Fall in Love"), The Willows ("Church Bells May Ring"), The Clovers ("Love, Love, Love"), The G-Clefs ("Ka-King Dong"), The Gladiolas (Little Darlin' "), and The Rays ("Silhouettes" and "Daddy Cool"). They also reprised songs by Buddy Holly ("Words of Love"), Neil Sedaka ("Oh! Carol"), and The Danleers ("One Summer Night"). Among The Diamonds' most entertaining original releases are "The Stroll" and three crafty novelty tunes—"Black Denim Trousers and Motorcycle Boots," "Sneaky Alligator," and "Dracula."

Not unlike The Crew Cuts, this group moved from Canada to upstate New York to Cleveland as cabaret vocalists before being transformed into pop recording stars by Bill Randle, Dick Clark, and Mercury label management. Lead singer Dave Somerville bragged, "We were to R&B what The Kingston Trio was to folk." They were, too! As popularizers, translators, and transformers of rhythm and blues tunes, they made reasonable incomes and broadened the R&B listening audience. *The Best of The Diamonds: The Mercury Years* is a fine assemblage of tunes with nice historical liner notes; however, *The Diamonds Collection* features more quirky, interesting songs in addition to standard Diamonds' hits.

If you like Pat Boone doing "Tutti Frutti" and "At My Front Door (Crazy Little Mama)," you'll love these two anthologies.

* * *

Dot's Cover to Cover . . . Hit Upon Hit (ACE CDCHD 609). Compiled by Rob Finnis and John Broven. London: Ace Records, 1995. 30 songs.

Creativity and commercialism make strange bedfellows. When regionalism, racism, and stylistic variation are added to the mix, there is bound to be misunderstanding and misinterpretation. The long-running journalistic and scholarly discussions concerning practices of "cover recording" within the commercial music industry illustrate the degree of dissension that can accompany aesthetic and economic interplay. The release of *Dot's Cover to Cover . . . Hit Upon Hit* provides a number of factual illustrations that might take some of the caustic edge off of the ongoing debate.

Cover recording is ostensibly the action of one artist performing a song recently released by another artist. The chronological proximity of the second recording to the original is usually defined maliciously as either stealing potential sales from or misappropriating the aesthetic style of the initial artist. The motive is invariably assumed to be negative and the economic result is similarly deemed to be harmful. Thus, when Dot Records' performers Pat Boone, Gale Storm, The Fontane Sisters, and The Hilltoppers issued covers of songs originally released by Otis Williams and The Charms ("Two Hearts"), Smiley Lewis ("I Hear You Knocking"), Fats Domino ("I'm in Love Again"), and The Platters ("Only You"), it was alleged that racism was robbing these R&B stars of both popular recognition and enhanced revenue. This may be partially true. However, cover recording practices preceded the mid-1950s rock era and involved far more white-to-white confrontations than interracial spats. During the 1940s, for instance, major recording labels (Capitol, Columbia, Decca, and RCA Victor) routinely issued covers for nearly every song that gained public attention. Tunes such as the 1942 hit "Deep in the Heart of Texas," for example, were commercially released by Alvino Rey on Bluebird, Bing Crosby on Decca, Horace Heidt on Columbia, The Merry Macs on Decca, and Ted Weems on Decca. Notable female singers such as Doris Day, Dinah Shore, Jo Stafford, and Connee Boswell regularly produced covers of their competitors' tunes. Notwithstanding white covers of black songs during the mid-1950s, country performers constantly faced stiff challenges from pop artists during the same period. Joni James of MOM and Frankie Laine of Columbia bested gifted singer/songwriter Hank Williams of MOM in pop sales on "Your Cheatin' Heart" in 1953. It is even more interesting to note how the Disney-driven "Ballad of Davy Crockett" spawned 1955 revenue for Bill Hayes on Cadence, Tennessee Ernie Ford on Capitol, Fess Parker on Columbia, and The Voices of Walter Schumann on RCA.

Although Dot Records, the 1950 creation of Randy Wood in Gallatin, Tennessee, is notable for producing cover recordings, the company also spawned a variety of original tunes. "The Fool" by Sanford Clark, "Green Door" by Jim Lowe, "Confidential" by Sonny Knight, and "Come Go with Me" by the Dell-Vikings were undeniably distinctive contributions to the rock era. Nevertheless, *Dot's Cover to Cover . . . Hit upon Hit* constitutes a magnificent opportunity to encounter several different perspectives on the cover recording issue. First, the improved diction and skilled instrumentation used in transcribing rough-hewn R&B performances into white-bread pop is particularly well-illustrated on tunes originally released by The Marigolds, The Charms, and Smiley Lewis. Second, the vocal quality and dexterity of Pat Boone is amply illustrated in his cover versions of hits by Little Richard ("Long Tall Sally"), Otis Williams and The Charms ("Two Hearts"), The El Dorados ("At My Front Door [Crazy Little Mama]"), Joe Turner ("Chains of Love"), and The Flamingos ("I'll Be Home"). Third, the unsuccessful attempt to launch a synergistic singing career for the nonmusical Tab Hunter via Sonny James' 1957 hit "Young Love" provides an example of white-on-white cover failure. Fourth, the inability to revive The Mills Brothers' fading commercial image with a cover of The Silhouettes' 1958 novelty number "Get a Job" demonstrates a black-on-black cover fiasco. Fifth, the example of Gale Storm (of "My Little Margie" TV fame) translating her small-screen acting talent into vocal success through the hit songs of Frankie Lymon and The Teenagers ("Why Do Fools Fall in Love"), The Charms ("Ivory Tower"), and Ruth Brown ("Lucky Lips") offers hints of future pursuits by David Cassidy and others. Finally, the numerous white-on-white covers—Nick Todd doing "At the Hop" after Danny and The Juniors (1957), The Hilltoppers copying "Marianne" from Terry Gilkyson and The Easy Riders (1957), The Fontane sisters performing "Seventeen" after Boyd Bennett and His Rockers (1955), and Billy Vaughn remaking "Raunchy" from Bill Justis (1957) suggest that the 1940s practice was never forgotten, and certainly not limited to racial bias.

The thirty tunes on this compact disc are accompanied by a fascinating explanatory booklet by Rob Finnis and a detailed discography listing both Dot performers and the original artists for all tunes featured on the compilation.

* * *

Borrowed Tales (American Harvest CD 57703-2). By Don Williams. Las Vegas, NM: American Harvest Recording Society, 1995. 13 songs.

Texas tunesmith Don Williams illustrates the richness and diversity of late-twentieth-century pop music throughout *Borrowed Tales*. Utilizing sparse but distinctive orchestration and his own marvelous country/folk vocal talent, Williams revisits thirteen classic songs. Music genres including R&B, country, pop, rock, folk, and even show tunes are melded sensitively. Little

Willie John, The Everly Brothers, Gordon Lightfoot, James Taylor, Ray Price, The Box Tops, and Eric Clapton inform this set. The themes of lost love ("Crying in the Rain"), hope ("Peace Train"), and mutual support ("You've Got a Friend") dominate this lyric-rich collection. A superb retrospective.

* * *

Run for Cover (Scott Brothers CD 72392 75499-2). By The Nylons. Santa Monica, CA: Scotti Brothers Records, 1996. 11 songs.

Originally assembled in 1979 and drastically reorganized in the early 1990s, Toronto's Nylons continue to produce stellar vocal harmony. Veterans Claude Morrison and Arnold Robinson are joined by newcomers Gavin Hope and Garth Mosbaugh on *Run for Cover*. The group features thoughtfully arranged, skillfully sung a cappella renditions of several well-known ("Lady Madonna," "My Cherie Amour," and "The Shoop Shoop Song ["It's in Her Kiss"]) and some more obscure ("Maybe," "Stranded in the Jungle," and "The Girl Can't Help It") tunes. They handle humorous lyrics especially well, but are overmatched by their doo-wop predecessors—The Flamingos—on the classic "Lovers Never Say Goodbye." This is a superb contribution to The Nylons' portfolio of albums.

NOTES

1. Cooper, B. Lee and Verdan D. Traylor. "Establishing Rock Standards—The Practice of Record Revivals in Contemporary Music, 1953-1977," *Goldmine*, No. 36 (May1979), pp. 37-38; and Cooper, B. Lee. "The Song Revival Revolution of the Seventies: Tapping the Musical Roots of Rock," *Goldmine*, No. 42 (November 1979), p. 126.

2. This ranking system, which is quantitatively based upon the number of weeks that a performer's songs were listed on *Billboard*'s "Hot 100" chart, is presented in *Top Pop Records, 1955-1972*. Menomonee Falls, WI: Record Research, Inc., 1973, pp. 398-400.

3. One might also note the eclectic nature of Johnny Rivers' song selections throughout his career. Although this discussion focuses on music of 1954-1964 vintage, it should not go unnoted that Rivers also recorded Irving Berlin's "Blue Skies" (*Go, Johnny, Go!*—United Artists UAL 3386), The World War II classic "(There'll Be Bluebirds Over) The White Cliffs of Dover" (*Go, Johnny, Go!*), and at least two Frank Sinatra tunes—"Softly As I Leave You" and "Strangers in the Night" (*Changes*—Imperial LP 9334). He has also recorded several Beatles' tunes including: "I Should Have Known Better" (*In Action*—Imperial LP 9280), "I'll

Cry Instead" (*Meanwhile Back at the Whisky a Go Go*—Imperial LP 9284), "Can't Buy Me Love (*Here We a Go Go Again!*—Imperial LP 9274, and "Run for Your Life" (*And I Know You Wanna Dance*—Imperial LP 9307).

4. The author wishes to express his gratitude to William L. Schurk, Sound Recordings Archivist at Bowling Green (Ohio) State University's Audio Center, for providing much of the discographic information used in this study.

5. A variety of books and articles chronicle the career of Linda Ronstadt. Among these are: Carl Arrington, "A Heart to Heart with Linda Ronstadt," *Creem;* VIII (December 1976), pp. 44-47ff; Vivian Claire, *Linda Ronstadt.* New York: *Flash Books*, 1978; Noel Coppage, "Linda Ronstadt Linda Ronstadt," *Stereo Review*, XXXVII (November 1976), pp. 78-82; Cameron Crowe, "Linda Ronstadt: The Million Dollar Woman," *Rolling Stone* (December 2, 1976), pp. 111-117; Stephen Holder, "Linda Ronstadt Breaks Training," *High Fidelity*, XXVIII (November 1977), pp. 150-151; Stephen Holden, "Linda Ronstadt Punks Out," *Rolling Stone* (April 3, 1980), p. 63; Susan Katz, "Linda Ronstadt," in *Superwoman of Rock.* New York: Grosset and Dunlap, 1978, pp. 59-84; Leibovitz, Annie, "Linda Ronstadt: More Than Just One Look," *Rolling Stone* (April 3, 1980), pp. 10-13; "Linda Down the Wind," *Time,* CIX (February 28, 1977), pp. 58-32; Maury Ellen Moore, *The Linda Ronstadt Scrapbook.* New York: Sunridge Publishers, 1978; Katherine Orloff, "Linda Ronstadt," in *Rock 'n' Roll Woman.* Los Angeles: Nash Publishing, 1975, pp. 121-138; John Rockwell, "Living in the U.S.A." in *Stranded: Rock and Roll for a Desert Island,* edited by Greil Marcus. New York: Alfred A. Knopf, 1979, pp. 188-218; Steve Sirnels, "Linda Ronstadt: Toughening Up," *Stereo Review*, XLI (December 1978), p. 122; Jean Vallely and Linda Ronstadt, "Playboy Interview: Linda Ronstadt," *Playboy*, XXVII (April 1980), pp. 85-118; and "Who Is Really the Most Popular Female Singer?" *Record Digest*, I (March 15, 1978), pp. 3-7.

6. No reference is made here to the following early albums: *The Stone Poneys* (Capitol ST 11382), *Evergreen* (Capitol ST 2763), and *Stone Poneys and Friends* (Capitol ST 2863).

7. Claire, Vivian. *Linda Ronstadt.* New York: Flash Books, 1978, pp. 55-56.

8. Epic 10788 (released in 1972).

BIBLIOGRAPHY

Ackerman, Paul. "R&B Tunes Boom Relegates Pop Field to Cover Activity," *Billboard*, LXVII (March 26, 1955), pp. 18, 22.

Bane, Michael. *White Boy Singin' the Blues: The Black Roots of White Rock.* New York: Penguin Books, 1982.

Banke, Lars M. "Various Artists Sing Bob Dylan: An Annotated Discography of Albums Featuring Dylan Songs," *Goldmine*, No. 91 (December 1983), pp. 173-176, 178.

Belz, Carl. "Early Rock: Crossovers and Covers," in *The Story of Rock* (Second Edition) New York: Harper and Row, 1972, pp. 425-430.

Castleman, Harry and Walter J. Podrazik. "The Beatles from Others," in *All Together Now: The First Complete Beatles Discography, 1961-1975.* New York: Ballantine books, 1975, pp. 225-242.

Castleman, Harry and Walter J. Podrazik. "The Beatles from Others," in *The Beatles Again?* Ann Arbor, MI:Pierian Press, 1977, pp. 76-83.

Chapple, Steve and Reebee Garofalo. "Black Roots, White Fruits: Racism in the Music Industry," in *Rock 'n' Roll Is Here to Pay: The History and Politics of the Music Industry.* Chicago: Nelson-Hall, 1977, pp. 231-267.

Cooper, B. Lee. "The Black Roots of Popular Music," in *Images of American Society in Popular Music.* Chicago: Nelson-Hall, 1982, pp. 111-123.

Cooper, B. Lee. "Cover Recordings and Song Revivals," in *Popular Music Perspectives.* Bowling Green, OH: Bowling Green State University Popular Press, 1991, pp. 140-154.

Cooper, B. Lee. "Promoting Social Change Through Audio Repetition: Black Musicians as Creators and Revivalists, 1953-1978," *Tracking: Popular Music Studios,* II (Winter 1989), pp. 26-46.

Cooper, B. Lee. "Repeating Hit Tunes A Cappella Style: The Persuasions as Song Revivalists, 1967-1982," *Popular Music and Society,* XIII (Fall 1989), pp. 17-27.

Cooper, Laura E. and B. Lee Cooper. "From American Forces Network to Chuck Berry, from Larry Parnes to George Martin: The Rise of Rock Music Culture in Great Britain, 1943 to 1967 and Beyond—A Biblio-Historical Study," *Popular Culture in Libraries,* I (Summer 1993), pp. 33-64.

Cooper, Laura E. and B. Lee Cooper. "The Pendulum of Cultural Imperialism: Popular Music Interchanges Between the United States and Britain, 1943-1967," *Journal of Popular Culture,* XXVII (Winter 1993), pp. 61-78.

Cooper, B. Lee and Wayne S. Haney. *Response Recordings: An Answer Song Discography, 1950-1990.* Metuchen, NJ: Scarecrow Press, 1990.

Cotten, Lee. "Introduction," in *Shake, Rattle and Roll—The Golden Age of American Rock 'n' Roll: Volume One, 1952-1955.* Ann Arbor, MI: Pierian Press, 1989, pp. xvii-xxx.

Cummings, Gordon. "Rock 'n' Roll Crossover," *Now Dig This,* No. 39 (June 1986), pp. 12.

Curtis, Jim. "Cover Records," in *Rock Eras: Interpretations of Music and Society, 1954-1984.* Bowling Green, OH: Bowling Green State University Popular Press, 1987, pp. 63-67.

Daniels, Bill. "Dusty Charts—A Concise Summary of R&B Records to Penetrate the Pop Charts [1950-1955]," *Record Exchanger,* IV (Summer 1975), pp. 16-17.

DeWitt, Howard A. "Chuck Berry's Songs: Some Sources" and "Cover Records," in *Chuck Berry: Rock 'n' Roll Music* (Second Edition). Ann Arbor, MI: Pierian Press, 1985, pp. 249-264.

Driver, Dave. "Under the Covers," *Now Dig This,* No. 102 (September 1991) pp. 5-6.

Duxbury, Janel R. (comp.). *Rockin' the Classics and Classicizin' the Rock: A Selectively Annotated Discography—First Supplement.* Westport, CT: Greenwood Press, 1991.

Ferrandino, Joe. "Rock Culture and the Development of Social Consciousness," in *Side-Saddle on the Golden Calf: Social Structure and Popular Culture in America*, edited by George H. Lewis. Pacific Palisades, CA: Goodyear Publishing Company, 1972, pp. 263-290.

Gillett, Charles. "The Black Market Roots of Rock," in *The Sounds of Social Change: Studies in Popular Culture*, edited by R. Serge Denisoff and Richard A. Peterson. Chicago: Rand McNally and Company, 1972, pp. 274-281.

Griggs, Bill. "Spotlight on Cover Songs: What Were They and Why Did We Have Them?" *Rockin' 50s*, No. 20 (October 1989), pp. 8-14.

Kamin, Jonathon. "Taking the Roll Out of Rock 'n' Roll: Reverse Acculturation," *Popular Music and Society*, II (Fall 1972), pp. 1-17.

Kirby, Kip. "Country Charts Reflecting Pop, Rock, R&B Revivals: Hits In '79 Come from Odd Sources," *Billboard*, XCI (March 17, 1979), pp. 50, 55.

Komorowski, Adam, Bill Miller, and Ray Topping. "Elvis: The Original Versions and Other Notes," *New Kommotion*, No. 17 (Autumn 1977), pp. 4-9. (Also see Addenda in No. 19 (Spring 1978), p. 15 and No. 22 (Spring 1979), p. 64.)

Lonz, Rich. " '50's Covers," *Record Exchanger*, IV (Summer 1975), pp. 18-22.

Marinello, Nick. "What's Under the Covers? Playing Cover Songs Gives a New Band a Chance to Know Itself and Its Audience," *Wavelength*, No. 60 (October 1985), pp. 10-11.

McFarlin, Jim. "Recycled Gold," *Detroit [Michigan] News* (November 2, 1986), pp. 1J, 8J.

McNutt, Randy. "Go, Cats, Go! But Please Don't Cover My Cover," In *We Wanna Boogie: An Illustrated History of the American Rockabilly Movement* (Fairfield, OH: Hamilton Hobby Press, 1987), pp. 76-77.

Michlig, John. "Dot Records: Varese Vintage—Preserving the Sounds of Dot Records," *DISCoveries*, No. 80 (January 1995), pp. 29-33.

Millar, Bill. "Rockin' 'n' Drifting," in *The Drifters: The Rise and Fall of the Black Vocal Group*. New York: Collier Books, 1971: pp. 65-92.

Moonoogian, George. "Elvis and the Originals," *Record Exchanger*, III (February 1973), p. 16.

Morris, Edward. "To Publishers' Glee, Acts Mine Golden Country Songs," *Billboard*, XCIX (December 26, 1987), pp. 3, 93.

Paikos, Mike (comp.). *R&B Covers and Re-Recordings*. Moraga, CA: M. Paikos, 1993.

Panigrosso, Mike. "Cover Records in the 1950's," *Record Collectors Monthly* (December 1984), pp. 1, 3.

Pavlow, Big Al (comp.). *The R&B Book: A Disc-History of Rhythm and Blues*. Providence, RI: Music House Publishing, 1983.

Reed, John. "Under the Covers," *Record Collector*, No. 161 (January 1993), pp. 98-100.

Reed, John. "Under the Covers," *Record Collector*, No. 167 (July 1993), p. 131.

Reed, John. "Under the Covers," *Record Collector*, No. 168 (August 1993), p. 134.

Rypens, Arnold. *The Originals: You Can't Judge a Song by the Cover*. Brussels, Belgium: BRT Vitgrave, 1987.

Sandmel, Ben. "Whose Toot-Toot?" *Wavelength,* No. 56 (June 1985), pp. 24-28.

Sarlin, Bob. "Rock-and-Roll!" in *Turn It Up (I Can't Hear The Words): The Best of the New Singer/Songwriters.* New York: Simon and Schuster, 1973, pp. 29-37.

Schery, Allen C. (comp.). "Cover Him: A Discography of Springsteen Songs Recorded by Other Artists," *Goldmine,* No. 208 (July 15, 1988), pp. 7-8.

Seroff, Doug. "Open the Door Richard!" *Record Exchanger,* No. 20 (Summer 1975), pp. 10-11.

Shawl, Arnold. "Interview with Randy Wood," in *Honkers and Shouters: The Golden Years of Rhythm and Blues.* New York: Collier Books, 1978, pp. 327-340.

Snyder, Robert. "Cover Records: What? When? and Why?" *Record Digest,* I (July 1, 1978), pp. 3-18.

Stierle, Wayne. "Let Us Count the Elvis Cover Records (Wait a Minute! There Aren't Any!)," *DISCoveries,* II (January 1989), pp. 38-39.

Stuessy, Joe. "The Emergence of Rock and Roll" in *Rock and Roll: Its History and Stylistic Development.* Englewood Cliffs, NJ: Prentice-Hall, Inc., 1990, pp. 31-45.

Szatmary, David P. "The 1980s: The Age of Revivalism and the Future of Rock," in *Rockin' in Time: A Social History of Rock and Roll* (Second Edition). Englewood Cliffs, NJ: Prentice Hall, Inc., 1991, pp. 195-214.

Tosches, Nick. *Unsung Heroes of Rock 'n' Roll: The Birth of Rock in the Wild Years Before Elvis* (Revised Edition). New York: Harmony Books, 1991.

Tucker, Ken. "The Top Fifty Country Crossovers," in *Country: The Music and the Musicians,* edited by Paul Kingsbury and Alan Axelrod. New York: Abbeville Press, 1988, pp. 396-397.

Whitburn, Joel (comp.). *Top R&B Singles, 1942-1995.* Menomonee Falls, WI: Record Research, 1996.

Wood, Gerry. "Country—R&B Swap Songs," *Billboard,* LXXXIX (December 17, 1977), pp. 1, 62, 67.

Woodford, Chris. "Don't Mess with My Toot Toot'" *Now Dig This,* No. 31 (October 1985), p. 25.

Chapter 16

Tobacco

Social studies students should be encouraged to thoughtfully investigate tobacco use. Sound judgment and behavior consistent with such judgment is the goal of social studies instruction. Yet on controversial issues such as cigarette smoking, teachers are often tempted to align their classroom positions with statistical health data, legal mandates, regional political pressure groups, and the social stigma that fuels antismoking crusades. Clearly, such predispositions generate propaganda, not education. The responsibility of a teacher is to present evidence, to demonstrate debatable positions, and to engage students in active exploratory roles. The American Cancer Society and the North Carolina Tobacco Growers Association are obviously at opposite poles as information sources. But arguments from both camps should be considered. Democratic citizenship without the tension of public policy debate is a misnomer. And the preparation of young people for citizenship remains a primary reason for sustaining the social studies curriculum in American public education.

American popular culture features many valuable teaching resources. From nursery rhymes to patriotic hymns, from science fiction tales to postage stamps, significant images and themes resonate in the minds of the general public as they parade across the media landscape. Skillful teachers take notice. They seize ideas from comic strips, television programs, motion pictures, and even games. Awakening young minds is always a challenge. Sole reliance on traditional textbooks and daily lectures no longer suffice in the age of MTV, multiplex cinemas, and monster-size malls. By pursuing the popular culture perspectives suggested by Ray B. Browne, John Cawelti, Roger B. Rollin, and Timothy Scheurer, though, social studies teachers can avoid the twin intellectual dangers of value neutrality and single-minded propaganda.

This chapter recommends a novel approach for examining the smoking issue. Rather than simply positioning C. Everett Koop versus Jesse Helms,

This chapter by B. Lee Cooper and William L. Schurk was originally titled "Cigarettes, Song Lyrics, and Social Studies Students: Examining Smoking Imagery Through Popular Music." It was developed for publication in this anthology.

the teaching strategy developed below hinges on a broader historic perspective: How has tobacco use been depicted in American song lyrics since World War II? This question challenges students to think beyond black-and-white, good-and-bad polarity and to consider differing social and personal meanings inherent in the ongoing tobacco use debate. Sophistication of understanding demands active confrontation with complexity. However, the learning resources used to develop flexible, thorough, inclusive thought patterns can be amazingly simple. Like molecules in science, single recordings can function as unitary building blocks to greater understanding. The information presented in several songs can stimulate students to create more than one hypothesis about the reasons for smoking popularity. For instance, rather than just relaxation or reverie (as illustrated in tunes such as "My Cigarette and I" and "Smoke Rings"), the act of smoking may symbolize active rebellion against adult authority. Recordings by The Coasters ("Charlie Brown") and Brownsville Station ("Smokin' in the Boys' Room") demonstrate this position in respect to public school rules. Beyond youthful experimentation within an educational setting, though, songs about cigarettes may also define behavior in specific subcultures ("The Jet Song" from *West Side Story*), illustrate personal economic status ("King of the Road"), provide justification for acceptance of brotherhood ("Get Off of My Cloud"), or feature elements borrowed from an entirely different culture ("Black Smoke from the Calumet," "Pass That Peace Pipe," and "Smoke My Peace Pipe (Smoke It Right)").

The heritage of cigarette imagery and tobacco themes in American music is long-standing. Long before Joe Camel and the Marlboro Man appeared on 1990s billboards, there were televised chants ("Call for Phillip Morris!"), dancing girls garbed in Old Gold cigarette packs, catchy radio acronyms ("L.S.M.F.T.—Lucky Strike means fine tobacco!"), and often repeated advertising phrases ("So round, so firm, so fully packed— so free and easy on the draw"). Just as Old Gold sponsored *Your Hit Parade,* the *Camel Caravan of Musical Stars* was led by Vaughn Monroe and His Royal Canadians. The pre-World War II period featured a variety of tobacco tunes as well. Song hits included "Let's Have Another Cigarette" by The Benny Goodman Orchestra, "Love Is Like a Cigarette" by Duke Ellington, "One Cigarette for Two" by Freddy Martin and His Orchestra, "Two Cigarettes in the Dark" by Bing Crosby, "Weed Smoker's Dream" by The Harlem Hamfats, and "While a Cigarette Was Burning" by Paul Whiteman and His Orchestra. But it was after World War II that songsmiths and recording artists promulgated the most remarkable spectrum of audio images concerning cigarette smoking. It is the 1945-1995 period that offers social studies teachers and their students an abundance of lyrical commentaries to hear, analyze, categorize, and judge.

SELECTED SONGS FEATURING CIGARETTE REFERENCES
AND TOBACCO IMAGES AND THEMES, 1945-1995

- "Cigareetes, Whuskey, and Wild, Wild Women"
  (Victor 202199)
  Sons of the Pioneers (1947)

- "Smoke! Smoke! Smoke! (That Cigarette)"
  (Capitol Americana 40001)
  Tex Williams (1947)

- "Cigarette Song (Always Grabbing Someone's Butt)"
  (Pearl 74)
  Larry Vincent (1948)

- "Don't Smoke in Bed"
  (Capitol 10120)
  Peggy Lee (1948)

- "Coffee, Cigarettes, and Tears"
  (Apollo 1177)
  Larks (1948)

- "Coffee and Cigarettes"
  (Columbia CL 6199)
  Johnnie Ray (1952)

- "Smoke Rings"
  (Capitol 2123)
  Les Paul and Mary Ford (1952)

- "Smoking My Sad Cigarette"
  (Columbia 39951)
  Jo Stafford (1953)

- "Smoke from Your Cigarette"
  (Coral 61363)
  Billy Williams Quartet (1955)

- "Smoke Another Cigarette"
  (Mercury MG 20179)
  Harry Revel (1956)

- "While a Cigarette Was Burning"
  (Mercury MD 20098)
  Patti Page (1956)

- "Ashtrays for Two"
  (Coral CRL 57060)
  Bob Crosby (1957)

- "Share with Me a Lonely Cigarette"
  (Decca DL 8452)
  Daniel DeCarlo (1957)

- "Three Cigarettes in an Ashtray"
  (Decca 30406)
  Patsy Cline (1957)

- "A Cigarette, Sweet Music, and You"
  (Capitol SW 845)
  Fred Waring and The Pennsylvanians (1957)

- "Cigarettes and Coffee Blues"
  (Columbia 41268)
  Lefty Frizzell (1958)

- "Got a Match?"
  (ABC-Paramount 9931)
  Frank Gallop (1958)

- "Let's Have a Cigarette Together"
  (RCA Victor LSP 1799)
  Vaughn Monroe (1958)

- "Charlie Brown"
  (ATCO 6132)
  The Coasters (1959)

- "Don't Smoke in Bed"
  (Bethlehem 11055)
  Nina Simone (1960)

- "Cigarettes"
  (Columbia CS 8480)
  Yaffa Yarkoni (1961)

- "Jet Song" from *West Side Story*
  (Columbia 2070)
  Russ Tamblyn and The Jets (1961)

- "Saved"
  (Atlantic 2099)
  LaVerne Baker (1961)

- "Smoke! Smoke! Smoke! (That Cigarette)"
  (Columbia 8535)
  Jimmy Dean (1961)

- "Smoky Places"
  (Tuff 1808)
  Corsairs (1961)

- "Cigarette Girl"
  (Jubilee JGM 1035)
  Bob Peck (1962)

- "Lipstick Traces (on a Cigarette)"
  (Minis 644)
  Benny Spellman (1962)

- "Twenty Cigarettes"
  (Columbia CS 8687)
  Little Jimmy Dickens (1962)

- "When You Smoke Tobacco"
  (Mercury MG 20781)
  Ernie Sheldon (1962)

- "Cigarette"
  (Original Sound 32)
  Visions (1963)

- "Cigarettes and Coffee Blues"
  (Columbia 42701)
  Marty Robbins (1963)

- "Cigareetes, Whuskey, and Wild, Wild Women"
  (Warner Brothers 5336)
  Johnny Nash (1963)

- "Smoke Rings"
  (RCA Victor LSP 2673)
  Sam Cooke (1963)

- "Down to My Last Cigarette"
  (Columbia 43120)
  Billy Walker (1964)

- "My Cigarette and I"
  (Columbia CL 2149)
  J's with Jamie (1964)

- "Smoke from Your Cigarette"
  (Chattahoochie 649)
  Drake Sisters (1964)

- "Cigarettes and Whiskey"
  (Arvee A-434)
  Sammy Jackson (1965)

- "Get Off of My Cloud"
  (London 9792)
  The Rolling Stones (1965)

- "King of the Road"
  (Smash 1965)
  Roger Miller (1965)

- "Lipstick Traces (on a Cigarette)"
  (Imperial 66102)
  O'Jays (1965)

- "Smoke, Drink, Play 21"
  (Dot 16806)
  Tony Williams (1965)

- "Cigarettes and Coffee"
  (Volt 413)
  Otis Redding (1966)

- "I Can't Quit Cigarettes"
  (Decca 31931)
  Jimmy Martin (1966)

- "Tobacco"
  (RCA Victor LSP 3601)
  George Hamilton IV (1966)

- "Cigarette Ashes"
  (Epic LN 24249)
  Ed Henry (1967)

- "One Little Packet of Cigarettes"
  (MOM SE 4478)
  Herman's Hermits (1967)

- "Cigarette"
  (Adelphi AD 1001)
  Mike Stewart (1968)

- "May I Light Your Cigarette?"
  (MOM SE 4568)
  Beacon Street Union (1968)

- "Smoke, Smoke, Smoke—'68"
  (Boone 1069)
  Tex Williams (1968)

- "Cigarette Smoking"
  (Liberty 56128)
  Brother Sammy Shore (1969)

- "The Cigarette Song" from *Promenade*
  (RCA Victor LSO 1161)
  Gilbert Price, Ty Connell, and Sandra Schaeffer (1969)

- "Smoke Smoke Smoke (But Not Around Me)"
  (Monument 1108)
  Grandpa Jones (1969)

- "Cigarette Grubber"
  (GRT 22)
  Sam Taylor Jr. (1970)

- "Blue Money"
  (Warner Brothers 7462)
  Van Morrison (1971)

- "Cigarette Blues"
  (Blue Goose BG 2005)
  Roger Hubbard (1971)

- "I Love Them Nasty Cigarettes"
  (Chart 5112)
  Jim Nesbitt (1971)

- "Another Puff"
  (RCA 0613)
  Jerry Reed (1972)

- "Tobacco, White Lightning, and Women Blues, No. 2"
  (Capitol SW 874)
  Buck Owens (1972)

- "Smoke"
  (Kama Sutra KSBS 2069)
  Roger Cook (1973)

- "Smoke! Smoke! Smoke! (That Cigarette)"
  (Paramount 0216)
  Commander Cody and His Lost Planet Airmen (1973)

- "Smokin' in the Boys' Room"
  (Big Tree 16011)
  Brownsville Station (1973)

- "Cigarettes and Muskatel Wine"
  (Prince 1008)
  Little Joe Cale (1974)

- "Fool for a Cigarette"
  (Reprise MS 2179)
  Ry Cooder (1974)

- "Should I Smoke"
  (Warner Brothers BS 2827)
  Badfinger (1974)

- "Smokin' Room"
  (ABC 11427)
  Rufus (1974)

- "Smoking Cigarettes"
  (Capitol ST 2823)
  Golden Earring (1974)

- "Workin' at the Car Wash Blues"
  (ABC 11447)
  Jim Croce (1974)

- "Candy, Brandy, and a Carton of Cigarettes"
  (Golden Crest CR 3044)
  Lou Carter (1975)

- "Smokin' "
  (Virgin V2056)
  Keith Hudson (1976)

- "Flick the Bic"
  (RSO RS 13-017)
  Rick Dees (1977)

- "Lipstick Traces"
  (Mercury 55005)
  Jimmie Peters (1977)

- "A Beer and a Cigarette"
  (Stiff 940573)
  Terraplane (1978)

- "Cigarettes"
  (Mercury 3737)
  City Boy (1978)

- "The Gambler"
  (United Artists 1250)
  Kenny Rogers (1978)

- "Smoke Rings and Wine"
  (Marlin 2210)
  Ralph MacDonald (1979)

- "You Burn Me Up—I'm a Cigarette"
  (EG LP 101)
  Robert Fripp (1981)

- "Caffeine, Nicotine, Benzedrine (and Wish Me Luck)"
  (RCA 12157)
  Jerry Reed (1981)

- "Smokin' and Drinkin' "
  (TC 1042)
  James Brown (1981)

- "Tryin' to Live My Life Without You"
  (Capitol 5042)
  Bob Seger (1983)

- "A Beer and a Cigarette"
  (Johanna JHN 3008)
  Hanoi Rocks (1983)

- "Reasons to Quit"
  (Epic 03494)
  Merle Haggard and Willie Nelson (1984)

- "Cigarette Head"
  (Reuben Kincade RKP 001)
  Hype (1985)

- "Cigarettes"
  (Flat Black Music FN 1002)
  Full Nelson (1985)

- "Smokin' in the Boys' Room"
  (Elektra 69625)
  Mötley Crüe (1986)

- "Cigarette"
  (Enigma 73208)
  Smithereens (1986)

- "Smoke Rings"
  (Warner Brothers 25400)
  Laurie Anderson (1986)

- "Cigarettes of a Single Man"
  (A&M SP 5161)
  Squeeze (1987)

- "No Smokin' "
  (Enigma SV 73276)
  Todd Rundgren (1988)

- "I'm Down to My Last Cigarette"
  (Sire 27919)
  k. d. lang (1988)

- "Love Is Like a Cigarette"
  (Pangaea Pan 42137)
  Kip Hanrahan (1988)

- "Smoke Another Cigarette"
  (Geffen GHS 24201)
  Toll (1989)

- "Cigarette"
  (Mammoth 9663)
  Sidewinders (1989)

- "Cigarette in the Rain"
  (Warner Brothers 26002)
  Randy Crawford (1989)

- "Opposites Attract"
  (Virgin 99158)
  Paula Abdul (1989)

- "Pack o' Smokes"
  (Scot 2)
  Prisonshake (1990)

- "Cigarette Breath"
  (Elektra 60890)
  Shinehead (1990)

- "Smoking Lounge"
  (Horton/Reflex HR 008)
  Helltrout (1992)

- "Ashtray"
  (Lookout 62)
  Screeching Weasel (1992)

- "Cigarette Ashes on the Floor"
  (Giant 24452)
  Miki Howard (1992)

- "Smokers"
  (Munstor MR 0230)
  Cancer Moon (1993)

- "Three on a Match"
  (Big Money Inc. BMI 039)
  Mickey Finn (1993)

IMAGES AND THEMES

The following sections of this chapter define a variety of teaching themes and topics featured in tobacco-related songs. The previous list of recordings is designed to illustrate in chronological fashion the wealth of recordings released during the past five decades. The tunes listed constitute only a small portion of the total array of songs containing comments about cigarette use, smoking situations, or personal observations about tobacco. The following thematic teaching suggestions are not structured by year; rather, they are arranged in three general subject categories: (a) individual cigarette-smoking behavior; (b) social settings and accompanying smoking elements; and (c) humor, cultures, and tobacco products. Each category features several song illustrations that can be adapted for classroom use. A brief bibliography highlighting popular culture interpretations of health care practices, medicine, and tobacco use concludes this chapter.

Individual Cigarette-Smoking Behavior

Since smoking is a personal habit, it is hardly surprising that many songs depict the activity as a time of individual relaxation and private reverie. Comfortable memories glow like embers on a cigarette ash. Whether alone blowing "Smoke Rings" and contemplating "My Cigarette and I," or waiting impatiently in "Smoky Places" for someone who may say "Let's Have a Cigarette Together," a smoker tries to be at ease. The Fred Waring recording of "A Cigarette, Sweet Music, and You" captures the romantic theme perfectly. Still positive, but much more assertive and challenging, are youthful smokers such as "Charlie Brown" who vent their cynicism about school rules and adult authority figures by "Smokin' in the Boys' Room."

The most frequently illustrated feelings of individuals who smoke alone are attitudes of melancholy and sadness. "Cigarettes of a Single Man," "Share with Me a Lonely Cigarette," and "Smoking My Sad Cigarette" are laments for better times. The same sentiments of despair pervade "Cigarettes and Coffee Blues," "Coffee, Cigarettes, and Tears," and "I'm Down to My Last Cigarette." The rolled tobacco tube is imaged as a consoling companion, the same way that one's own reflection is treated in songs such as "My Echo, My Shadow, and Me" and "Me and My Shadow." The recent loss of a loved one is visually symbolized in Benny Spellman's haunting "Lipstick Traces (On a Cigarette)."

More difficult problems facing an individual smoker appear to stem from social stigma, self-deception, and self-ridicule. Addiction to nicotine is usually not understood by nonsmoking friends or family members. Excessive use of tobacco and the corollary compulsion to interrupt on-going conversations, card games, or even romantic encounters is often puzzling, frustrating, and annoying. Although Paula Abdul maintains that "Opposites Attract," the reality is that former smokers and nonsmokers often find chain-smoking habits to be incomprehensible. Heartfelt and humorous commentaries on cigarette use are found in "Smoke! Smoke! Smoke! (That Cigarette)," "Trying to Live My Life Without You," and "Smoke Smoke Smoke (But Not Around Me)." Social studies students may find this latter 1960s song to be a precursor of the passive smoking or secondhand smoke arguments that gained prominence during the late 1980s and early 1990s.

The frustration of a smoker who genuinely wants to terminate association with the so-called evil weed is revealed in many, many songs. Once again, solitary reflection is usually the setting, with lyrics that feature hostility born of a genuine love/hate relationship. Jimmy Martin concedes "I Can't Quit Cigarettes." Jerry Reed takes "Another Puff" while debating when to stop. Merle Haggard and Willie Nelson look for "Reasons to Quit." And Jim Nesbitt finally acknowledges "I Love Them Nasty Cigarettes." Helplessness abounds. The only advice that seems reasonable is to never start smoking in the first place!

Social Settings and Accompanying Elements

While most students will have previously encountered the range of prosmoking and antismoking arguments depicted above, few will have considered tobacco use as a cultural phenomenon. The notion of being trapped in an isolated, single-crop-economy American town has provided lyrical material for such diverse artists as Roy Clark and Jamul. The Nashville Teens' "Tobacco Road" is a challenge to the freedom and individual spirit more than to the addictive nature of cigarettes. Location and setting are also defined by poor air quality in many tunes. Bars, saloons, juke joints, and basement cabarets are illustrated in "Dim Lights, Thick Smoke, and Loud, Loud Music," "Hangin' Out in Smoky Places," and "Smoky Places." The Corsairs' 1961 version of the latter song depicts a secret affair that can only be carried on in a dark, cloudy venue. A more humorous acknowledgment of enforced tobacco isolation is Helltrout's 1990 recording "Smoking Lounge."

Social settings blend easily into workplaces. Occupational associations may be either voluntary or involuntary. Billy Joel's "Piano Man" cannot control the smoky atmosphere he encounters during a club's happy hours. But many workers treasure the opportunity to take a smoke break, such as the young female model in "Blue Money." The western image of casual, roll-your-own tobacco use is featured in "The Cowboy's Serenade (While Smoking My Last Cigarette)" and "The Gambler." For the long-distance trucker, however, nicotine is just one of several over-the-counter drugs used to sustain lengthy periods of boring highway coverage. Jerry Reed pleads this case in "Caffeine, Nicotine, and Benzedrine (And Wish Me Luck)." Finally, Jim Croce lionizes a southern racetrack hero known for rolling his pack of cigarettes into his T-shirt sleeve. This hard-driving man is "Rapid Roy the Stockcar Boy." From bartenders to those behind bars, there are numerous settings where cigarettes are so ubiquitous that notions of "smoke-free" environments are laughable.

One might consider a match, or a lighter, and an ashtray to be the most logical accompanying elements to cigarette use. Lyrically, this assumption is only partially accurate. Songs highlighting smoking equipment include "Ashtray," "Ashtrays for Two," "Flick the Bic" "Got a Match?" "Three Cigarettes in an Ashtray" and "Three on a Match." But the items most frequently linked with a smoker's activity tend to be coffee and alcohol. The failure to note that addiction to nicotine is often associated with surrender to other nonprescription drugs is a frequent error of many tobacco apologists. Lyricists are not so gullible. The chain smoker/alcoholic personality is depicted, often tongue-in-cheek, in the following tunes: "A Beer and a Cigarette," "Candy, Brandy, and a Carton of Cigarettes," "Cigareetes, Whuskey, and Wild, Wild Women," "Cigarettes and Coffee," "Cigarettes and Muskatel Wine," "Cigarettes and Whiskey," "Smoke, Drink, and Play 21," "Smoke Rings and Wine," "Smokin' and Drinkin'," and "Tobacco, White Lightning, and Women Blues, No. 2." Two more extreme tobacco and drug use songs are "Dope Smokin' Moron" by The Replacements and "My Mom Smokes Pot" by The Lookouts.

Humor Cultures and Tobacco Products

The seemingly endless list of pejorative slang terms that relate to smoking provide a roomful of gallows humor. From butt, cancer stick, and evil weed to fag, gasper, and coffin nail, the cigarette is an object of linguistic condemnation and ridicule. Comedians have jumped on the lyrical bandwagon to satirize, mock, and degrade the smoking habit. Bob Peck threatens to put his "Cigarette Girl" into a flip-top box (coffin) if she doesn't stop smoking. Larry Vincent's "Cigarette Song" condemns a cheap colleague who is described as always grabbing someone's butt. Mooching behavior is also chided by Sam Taylor Jr. in "Cigarette Grubber." Phil Harris attacks compulsive nicotine pursuit in "Smoke! Smoke! Smoke! (That Cigarette)" and Tex Williams extends this same joke in "Smokey, Smoke, Smoke—'68." Short comedy sketches by Steve Martin ("Smokin' ") and Brother Sammy Shore ("Cigarette Smokin' ") attack the society that permits self-inflicted vaporous suicide. Other less caustic, more offbeat jabs at cigarette use include "Got a Match?," "Nick Teen and Al K. Hall," "Smokin' in Bed," and "You Burn Me Up—I'm a Cigarette."

As mentioned earlier, many smoking terms have been borrowed from the Native American culture and adapted to popular songs. Beyond calumets, though, numerous illustrations of cultural and socioeconomic distinctions are lodged in smoking songs. From poverty ("King of the Road") to prison life ("Twenty Cigarettes"), from social posturing ("The Cigarette Song" from *Promenade*) to daydreaming ("Workin' at the Car Wash Blues"), and from urban gangs ("The Jet Song") to The Salvation Army ("Saved"), lyrics depict cigarette use as a code that identifies stratified rank in society.

Finally, it should be noted that tobacco products other than cigarettes are featured in popular lyrics. "Chew Tobacco Rag" by Arthur Smith honors chewing tobacco. But the dominant option in recordings is not smokeless tobacco, but the cigar. Although once the comic trademark of Groucho Marx, the honor of singing about "A Real Good Cigar" was reserved for George Burns. It is interesting to note that cigar songs are few in number, unencumbered by associated addictions, and generally upbeat. In addition to "Workin' at the Carwash Blues," songs that laud cigars include "Cigar Eddie," "Have a Cigar," "A Man Smoking a Cigar," and "Here Goes a Cigar Smoking Man."

CONCLUSIONS

Teachers should avoid functioning as propaganda merchants and strive to achieve the goals of stimulating active classroom investigation and motivating personal decision making on the issue of tobacco use. Song lyrics are valuable resources to help promote these instructional objectives. Once social studies students have listened to fifteen to twenty recordings featuring cigarette imagery, a teacher should initiate the following educational challenges. Have the class:

1. Define common circumstances and social settings where smoking seems to be both encouraged and acceptable.
2. Analyze differing perceptions of smoking behavior.
3. Assess varying self-images of smokers.
4. Determine the broad range of responses articulated by nonsmokers to the use of cigarettes.
5. List the benefits of smoking.
6. List the detriments of smoking.
7. Predict future patterns of cigarette use in the United States.
8. Speculate on nonsmoking activities that can promote relaxation, ease tension, or otherwise substitute for cigarette use in public and private settings.
9. Describe incidents of youthful rebellion in public school settings that do not involve smoking; cite circumstances of isolation, loneliness, and depression that are unrelated to smoking behavior.
10. React to the personal frustration and self-ridicule of smokers compared to similar feelings found among chronically overweight people.
11. Identify workplaces where smoking cannot be effectively controlled or totally eliminated.
12. Explain the use of humor and satire to define or bring attention to potential health hazards other than smoking.
13. Comment on examples of cultural borrowing to illustrate, justify, or condemn individual smoking activities.
14. Identify notable social class distinctions in smoking song imagery or magazine-based cigarette advertising.
15. Identify several specific words and phrases that relate positively or negatively to smoking behavior.

Clearly, contemporary lyrics can provide a rich resource field of terms, ideas, social situations, personal observations, and general cultural contexts to support classroom examinations of cigarette use in American society.

BIBLIOGRAPHY

Altman, David G., Michael D. Slater, Cheryl L. Albright, and Nathan Maccoby. "How An Unhealthy Product Is Sold: Cigarette Advertising in Magazines, 1960-1985," *Journal of Communication,* 37 (Autumn, 1987): pp. 95-106.

Breed, Warren and James R. DeFoe. "Drinking and Smoking on Television, 1950-1982," *Journal of Public Health Policy,* 5 (June, 1984): pp. 257-270.

Browne, Ray B. and Ronald J. Ambrosetti (eds.). *Continuities of Popular Culture: The Present in the Past and the Past in the Present and Future.* Bowling Green, OH: Bowling Green State University Popular Press, 1993.

Burnham, John C. *Bad Habits: Drinking, Smoking, Taking Drugs, Gambling, Sexual Misbehavior, and Swearing in American History.* New York: New York University Press, 1993.

Cawelti, John. *Adventure, Mystery, and Romance: Formula Stories As Art and Popular Culture.* Chicago: University of Chicago Press, 1976.

Cooper, B. Lee. "Christmas Songs As American Cultural History: Audio Resources for Classroom Investigation, 1940-1990," *Social Education,* 54 (October 1990): pp. 374-379.

Cooper, B. Lee. "Lyrical Commentaries: Learning from Popular Music," *Music Educators Journal,* 77 (April 1991): pp. 56-59.

Cooper, B. Lee. *Popular Music Perspectives: Ideas, Themes, and Patterns in Contemporary Lyrics.* Bowling Green, OH: Bowling Green State University Popular Press, 1991.

Cooper, B. Lee. "Popular Songs, Military Conflicts, and Public Perceptions of the United States at War," *Social Education,* 56 (March 1992): pp. 160-168.

Cooper, B. Lee. "Processing Health Care Images from Popular Culture Resources: Physicians, Cigarettes, and Medical Metaphors in Contemporary Recordings," *Popular Music and Society,* 17 (Winter 1993): pp. 105-124.

Cooper, B. Lee. *A Resource Guide to Themes in Contemporary American Song Lyrics, 1950-1985.* Westport, CT: Greenwood Press, 1986.

Cooper, B. Lee and Wayne S. Haney. *Rock Music in American Popular Culture: Rock 'n' Roll Resources.* Binghamton, NY: The Haworth Press, 1994.

Cooper, B. Lee. "Smokin' Songs: Examining Tobacco Use As An American Cultural Phenomenon Through Contemporary Lyrics," *International Journal of Instructional Media,* 21, No. 3 (1994): pp. 261-168.

Cooper, B. Lee and Wayne S. Haney. *Rock Music in American Popular Culture II: More Rock 'n' Roll Resources.* Binghamton, New York: The Haworth Press, 1997.

Cruz, Jon and Lawrence Wallack. "Trends in Tobacco Use on Television," *American Journal of Public Health,* 76 (June 1986): pp. 698-699.

Fiore, Michael, Thomas E. Novotny, John P. Pierce, Euridki J. Hatziandreu, Kantilal M. Patel, and Ronald M. Davis. "Trends in Cigarette Smoking in the United States: The Changing Influence of Gender and Race," *Journal of the American Medical Association,* 261 (January 6, 1989): pp. 49-55.

Fritschler, A. Lee. *Smoking and Politics: Policymaking and the Federal Bureaucracy* (Second Edition). Englewood Cliffs, NJ: Prentice-Hall, Inc., 1975.

Goodman, Jordon. *Tobacco in History: The Cultures of Dependence.* New York: Routledge, 1993.

Greenberg, Bradley S. "Smoking, Drugging, and Drinking in Top-Rated TV Series," *Journal of Drug Education*, 11 (1981): pp. 227-234.

Heart, Spenser R. "Learning How to Study Images As Potent Forces in our History," *Chronicle of Higher Education*, 35 (March 8, 1989.): p. A44.

Hendler, Herb. *Year by Year in the Rock Era: Events and Conditions Shaping the Rock Generations That Reshaped America.* Westport, CT: Greenwood Press, 1983.

Hibbard, Don J., and Carol Kaleialoha. *The Roll of Rock: A Guide to the Social and Political Consequences of Rock Music.* Englewood, NJ: Prentice-Hall Inc., 1983.

Inge, Thomas M. (ed.). *Handbook of American Culture*—Three Volumes (Second Edition). Westport, CT: Greenwood Press, 1989.

Klein, Richard. *Cigarettes Are Sublime.* Durham, NC: Duke University Press, 1993.

Koop, C. Everett.. "Foreword," in *Merchants of Death: The American Tobacco Industry*, by Larry C. White. New York: Beech Tree Books/William Morrow and Company, 1988, pp. 9-11.

National Commission on Smoking and Public Policy. *A National Dilemma: Cigarette Smoking or the Health of Americans.* New York: American Cancer Society, 1978.

Pierce, John P. "International Comparisons of Trends in Cigarette Smoking Prevalence," *American Journal of Public Health*, 79 (February, 1989): 152-157.

Robert, Joseph C. *The Story of Tobacco in America.* Chapel Hill, NC: University of North Carolina Press, 1967.

Rollin, Roger (ed.). *The Americanization of the Global Village: Essays in Comparative Popular Culture.* Bowling Green, OH: Bowling Green State University Popular Press, 1989.

Scheurer, Timothy E. *Born in the U.S.A.: The Myth of America in Popular Music from Colonial Times to the Present.* Jackson, MS: University Press of Mississippi, 1991.

Sobel, Robert. *They Satisfy: The Cigarette in American Life.* New York: Anchor Books, 1978.

Sontag, Susan. *Illness as Metaphor.* New York: Farrar, Straus, and Giroux, 1977.

Troyer, Ronald J., and Gerald E. Markle. *Cigarettes: The Battle Over Smoking.* New Brunswick, NJ: Rutgers University Press, 1983.

Trudeau, Gary B. *You're Smokin' Now, Mr. Butts!* A Doonesbury Book. Kansas City, MO: Andrews and McMeel, 1990.

Turow, Joseph. *Playing Doctor: Television, Storytelling, and Medical Power.* New York: Oxford University Press, 1989.

Wagner, Susan. *Cigarette Country: Tobacco in American History and Politics.* New York: Praeger Books, 1971.

Whitburn, Joel (comp.). *Pop Hits 1940-1954.* Menomonee Falls, WI: Record Research, Inc., 1994.

Whitburn, Joel (comp.). *Pop Memories, 1890-1954: The History of American Popular Music*. Menomonee Falls, WI: Record Research, Inc., 1986.

Whitburn, Joel (comp.). *Top Country Singles, 1944-1993*. Menomonee Falls, WI: Record Research, Inc., 1994.

Whitburn, Joel (comp.). *Top Pop Albums, 1955-1996*. Menomonee Falls, WI: Record Research, Inc., 1997.

Whitburn, Joel (comp.). *Top Pop Singles 1955-1993*. Menomonee Falls, WI: Record Research, Inc., 1994.

Whitburn, Joel (comp.). *Top Rhythm and Blues Singles 1942-1995*. Menomonee Falls, WI: Record Research, Inc., 1996.

White, Larry C. *Merchants of Death: The American Tobacco Industry*. New York: Beech Tree Books/William Morrow and Company, 1988.

Wilson, Charles R., and William Ferris (eds.). *Encyclopedia of Southern Culture*. Chapel Hill, NC: University of North Carolina Press, 1989.

Yankauer, Alfred. "Smoking and Health: A 25-Year Perspective," *American Journal of Public Health,* 79 (February 1989.): 141-143.

Chapter 17

Western Images

Songs of the West (Rhino CD R2-71263). Los Angeles, CA: Rhino Records, 1993. Four compact discs, seventy-three selections, with illustrated booklet.

We live in an age of media-packaged history. Nowhere is this phenomenon more visible than in song reissue anthologies. Time-Life Music Inc. alone reconstructs recent musical history in twelve formats: "Your Hit Parade" (1945-1954), "Contemporary Country" (1970-1989), "Big Bands" (1940s), "Guitar Rock" (1960s through 1980s), "Classic Rock" (1964-1969), "Rhythm and Blues" (1950s through 1960s), "The Rock 'n' Roll Era" (1954-1964), "Sounds of the Seventies" (1970-1979), "Country USA" (1950s through 1970s), "The Time-Life History of Rock 'n' Roll" (1950s through 1970s), "Superhits" (1960-1973), and "The Rolling Stone Collection" (1967-1992). The technological shift from black vinyl to silver compact discs has undeniably stimulated the surge to define post-World War II popular music via preassembled nostalgia packets. Sound quality is vastly improved; but musical variety is significantly diminished. Treasured tunes are preserved; but minor hits, novelty songs, B-side surprises, and sub-Top 40 releases from prior decades vanish as if they had never graced any turntables. The rebellious James Dean has been transformed into the lovable Arthur Fonzarelli of *Happy Days* fame.

Rhino Records, unlike its conservative Time-Life Music counterpart, has maintained a distinctive mode of irreverence, unpredictability, experimentation, and creativity in its song compilation activities. This philosophy of providing the unexpected continues in *Songs of the West*. Producers James Austin and Randy Poe are sly dogs. They resurrect "The West" from the

---

This chapter by B. Lee Cooper was originally published as "Songs of the West," *Popular Music and Society,* XVIII, No. 3 (Fall 1994), pp. 97-99. Reprint permission granted by the author, editor Gary Burns, and the Bowling Green State University Popular Press. The book review was developed for this anthology.

perspective of a mid-century urban kid. Rather than being either a historical period or a defined geographical territory, these four compact discs harken to the 1950s state of mind about horses, guns, cactus-dotted deserts, rugged canyons, and (most important of all) cowboys. Utilizing a fascinating collage of traditional country and western favorites—"Tumbling Tumbleweeds," "Cool Water," "The Strawberry Roan," and "Home on the Range"—along with more contemporary nostalgia tunes such as "Hoppy, Gene, and Me" and "Last of the Silver Screen Cowboys," Rhino's Wild West compilers successfully ignore all pretensions of folk song seriousness. Instead, they highlight the talents and perspectives of America's favorite singing cowboy heroes: Gene Autry, Tex Ritter, and Roy Rogers. Through numerous vocal flashbacks the feature films and weekly television series that made Western imagery an all-American fantasy are masterfully recalled. Bob Wills salutes the "New San Antonio Rose"; Walter Brennan mourns the passing of "Old Rivers"; and The Sons of the Pioneers declare "I'm an Old Cowhand (From the Rio Grande)." Thanks to week-to-week repetition on the small home screen, program theme recordings such as "Bonanza," "Gunsmoke," "The Lone Ranger (William Tell Overture)," and "Maverick" still sound like old, comfortable friends.

Are there any shortcomings in this delightful Rhino romp through the mythical West? You betcha, Pardner! The singing cowgirl image is limited to Patsy Montana and Dale Evans. Why not include additional C&W tunes by Rosalie Allen, Patsy Cline, Lynn Anderson, Crystal Gayle, or even that wild child Tanya Tucker? A far more serious omission is the lack of blood-spilling sagas about reckless gunslingers and mean-spirited outlaws. Where are the recordings of "Billy the Kid," "Desperado," "Don't Take Your Guns to Town," "Folsom Prison Blues," "Jesse James," "(The Man Who Shot) Liberty Valance," and the "Midnight Special"? Even more unexplainable is the absence of several honorific C&W classics: "Bob Wills Is Still the King," "I Dreamed of a Hill-Billy Heaven," and "My Heroes Have Always Been Cowboys." Beyond Waylon Jennings, Tex Ritter, and Willie Nelson, though, there are a couple of offbeat, yet haunting images of living hell in the West that deserve mention. "Riders in the Sky (A Cowboy Legend)" and "Indian Reservation (The Lament of the Cherokee Reservation Indian)" would seem to be solid candidates for inclusion. But the strangest omissions of all, especially in a Rhino anthology, are the irreverent, off-the-wall Western image discs. Where are "Along Came Jones" and "Western Movies," two songs that skillfully parody 1940s cowboy serials and 1950s gunfighter TV programs? Where are "Coca-Cola Cowboy," "The Cowboy in a Continental Suit," "Cowboy in a Three-Piece Business Suit," and "Rhinestone Cowboy," with wry commentaries about urban life in $400 Justin boots and a $300 Stetson hat? And where oh where is Larry Verne's cackling eulogy for that egotistical yellow-haired cavalry commander from "The Battle of the Little Big Horn?"

Minor carping aside, *Songs of the West* is as neat a packaged audio history as one could hope to lasso. The fact-filled booklet that accompanies this four-CD set justifies the selections of songs, artists, and themes in an articulate, sensitive fashion. Most of these complaints are ill-founded. But from the personal perspective of a Great Falls-based reviewer, I am distressed that the Rhino compilers shortchanged the Treasure State. For humor, sensitivity, and Big Sky splendor, this collection should have included "Beaus from Butte," "Mr. Custer," "Tanya Montana," and "Wild Montana Skies."

* * *

Wanted Dead or Alive: The American West in Popular Culture. Edited by Richard Aquila. Urbana, IL: University of Illinois Press, 1996. 313 pp. Illustrated.

Ball State University historian Richard Aquila has assembled a fascinating, informative profile of the American West. Although his approach is neither historical nor geographical, it nonetheless features both traditional characters (Buffalo Bill Cody, George Armstrong Custer, Annie Oakley, and Crazy Horse) and scenes of sagebrush, Rocky Mountain peaks, and desert cactus. Aquila uses novels, Wild West shows, motion pictures, television programs, popular music, and commercial art to probe the "popular culture West" that fostered a distinctive state of mind and monumentally mythic ideas about the region. The perceptive contributors to this unique anthology detail the foundations of America's love affair with cowboys, wide open spaces, personal freedom, and the simplicity of frontier justice.

The ten chapters in *Wanted Dead or Alive* are provocative and fact-filled. Coverage of feature films and TV Westerns by John H. Lenihan, Ray White, and Gary A. Yoggy is especially intriguing. All contributors provide meticulous citations within their essays and each section also features a full bibliography. The essays on music by Kenneth J. Bindas ("Cool Water, Rye Whiskey, and Cowboys: Images of the West in Country Music") and Aquila ("A Blaze of Glory: The Mythic West in Pop and Rock Music") feature thoroughly illustrated discussions of the non-Western roots of country music, the creation of media-derived cowboy singers (Gene Autry and Roy Rogers), and the universal honky-tonk themes of broken loves, hard living, and infidelity championed by Hank Williams and The Drifting Cowboys.

This superb study recounts prior regional interpretations (from Frederick Jackson Turner to Peter Thorpe) with critical care and suggests new ideas on a variety of visual, aural, and intellectual fronts. The editor's genius in balancing rationales and resources is the determining strength of this volume. The wisdom in claiming a third path, different from either romanticism or realism toward the Old West, makes Aquila's quest invaluable as a research model to all popular culture analysts.

BIBLIOGRAPHY

Ackerman, Paul. "The Poetry and Imagery of Cowboy Songs," *Billboard: The World of Country Music*, LXXVIII (1966), pp. 14-16.

Aquila, Richard. "A Blaze of Glory: The Mythic West in Pop and Rock Music," in *Wanted Dead or Alive: The West in Popular Cultur.e*. Urbana, IL: University of Illinois Press, 1996, pp. 191-215.

Aquila, Richard. "Images of the American West in Rock Music," *Western Historical Quarterly*, XI (October 1980), pp. 415-432.

Axelrod, Alan. *Songs of the Wild West*. New York: Metropolitan Museum of Art, Simon and Schuster, 1991.

Bindas, Kenneth J. "Cool Water, Rye Whiskey, and Cowboys: Images of the West in Country Music," in *Wanted Dead or Alive: The West in Popular Culture*, edited by Richard Aquila. Urbana, IL: University of Illinois Press, 1996, pp. 216-240.

Cawelti, John G. *The Six-Gun Mystique*. Bowling Green, OH: Bowling Green State University Popular Press, 1972.

Cusic, Don. *Cowboys and the Wild West: An A-Z Guide from the Chisholm Trail to the Silver Screen*. New York: Facts on File, 1994.

Dunne, Michael. "Romantic Narcissism in 'Outlaw' Cowboy Music," in *All That Glitters: Country Music in America,* edited by George H. Lewis. Bowling Green, OH: Bowling Green State University Popular Press, 1993, pp. 226-238.

Edwards, Don. *Classic Cowboy Songs*. Salt Lake City, UT: Gibbs-Smith, 1994.

Everson, William K. *The Hollywood Western: 90 Years of Cowboys, Indians, Train Robbers, Sheriffs and Gunslingers and Assorted Heroes and Desperados*. New York: Citadel Press, 1992.

Green, Douglas B. "The Singing Cowboy: An American Dream," *Journal of Country Music*, VII (May 1978), pp. 4-61.

Green, Douglas B. "Tumbling Tumbleweeds: Gene Autry, Bob Wills, and the Dream of the West," in *Country: The Music and the Musicians—From the Beginnings to the '90s* (Revised and Updated Edition), edited by Paul Kingsbury and the Country Music Foundation. New York: Abbeville Publishing Group, 1994, pp. 79-103.

Harris, Charles W. and Buck Rainey. *The Cowboy: Six-Shooters, Songs, and Sex*. Norman, OK: University of Oklahoma Press, 1976.

Heide, Robert and John Gilman. *Box-Office Buckaroos: The Cowboy Hero from the Wild West Show to the Silver Screen*. New York: Abbeville Press, 1989.

Johnson, Michael L. "Garth and Friends: Resinging the West, Dancing to the Cowboy Beat," in *New Westers: The West in Contemporary American Culture.* Lawrence, KS: University Press of Kansas, 1996, pp. 260-302.

Krishef, Robert K. and Bonnie Lake. *Western Stars of Country Music.* Minneapolis, MN: Lerner Publishing Company, 1978.

Lingenfelter, Richard E., Richard A. Dwyer, and David Cohen. *Songs of the American West.* Berkeley, CA: University of California Press, 1968.

Logsdon, Guy (ed.). *"The Whorehouse Bells Were Ringing" and Other Songs Cowboys Sing.* Urbana, IL: University of Illinois Press, 1995 (c. 1989).

Logsdon, Guy, Mary Rogers, and William Jacobson. *Saddle Serenaders: Biographies of a Complete Range of Western Musicians.* Salt Lake City, UT: Gibbs-Smith, 1995.

MacDonald, J. Fred. *Who Shot the Sheriff? The Rise and Fall of the Television Western.* New York: Praeger, 1987.

Malone, Bill C. *Singing Cowboys and Musical Mountaineers: Southern Culture and the Roots of Country Music.* Atlanta: University of Georgia Press, 1993.

Moore, Ethel, and Chauncey O. Moore. *Ballads and Folk Songs of the Southwest.* Norman, OK: University of Oklahoma Press, 1964.

Morrow, Patrick. "The West As Idea in Recent Rock Music," *Indiana Social Studies Quarterly,* XXVI (1973/1974), pp. 52-64.

Oermann, Robert K., with Douglas B. Green. "Singing Cowboys," in *The Listener's Guide to Country Music.* New York: Facts on File, 1983, pp. 40-50.

Ohrlin, Glenn. *The Hell-Bound Train: A Cowboy Songbook.* Urbana, IL: University of Illinois Press, 1973.

Parks, Jack. "Hollywood's Singing Cowboys: They Packed Guitars As Well As Six-Shooters," *Country Music,* I (July 1973), pp. 34-38.

Rainey, Buck. *The Reel Cowboy: Essays On the Myth in Movies and Literature.* Jefferson, NC: McFarland and Company, Inc., 1996.

Rothel, David. *The Singing Cowboys.* Cranbury, NJ: A.S. Barnes, 1978.

Savage Jr., William W. *Singing Cowboys and All That Jazz: A Short History of Popular Music in Oklahoma.* Norman, OK: University of Oklahoma Press, 1983.

Silber, Irwin (ed.) *Songs of the Great American West.* New York: Dover Books, 1995.

Thorp, N. Howard ("Jack"). *Songs of the Cowboys.* Lincoln, NE: University of Nebraska Press, 1984 (c. 1908).

Tinsley, Bob. *For a Cowboy Has to Sing.* Orlando, FL: University of Central Florida Press, 1991.

Tinsley, Bob. *He Was Singin' His Song.* Orlando, FL: University of Central Florida Press, 1981.

Weissman, Dick. "The Life and Music of the American Cowboy," in *Music Making in America.* New York: Frederick Ungar, 1982, pp. 49-67.

White, John I. *Git Along, Little Dogies: Songs and Songmakers of the American West.* Urbana, IL: University of Illinois Press, 1976.

Bibliography

Books

Aquila, Richard (ed.). *Wanted Dead or Alive: The American West in Popular Culture.* Urbana, IL: University of Illinois Press, 1996.

Arnett, Jeffrey Jensen. *Metal Heads: Heavy Metal Music and Adolescent Alienation.* Boulder, CO:: Westview Press, 1996.

Bacon, Tony (ed.). *Classic Guitars of the '50s: The Electric Guitar and the Musical Revolution of the '50s.* San Francisco: Miller Freeman Books, 1996.

Bindas, Kenneth J. (ed.). *America's Musical Pulse: Popular Music in Twentieth-Century Society.* Westport, CT: Praeger Books, 1992.

Brackett, David. *Interpreting Popular Music.* Cambridge, England: Cambridge University Press, 1995.

Brunning, Bob. *Blues in Britain: The History—1950s to the Present.* London: Blandford Press, 1995.

Buckley, Jonathan and Mark Ellingham (eds.). *The Rough Guide to Rock.* London: Rough Guides, Ltd, 1996.

Carney, George O. (ed.). *The Sounds of People and Places: A Geography of American Folk and Popular Music* (Third Edition). Lanham, MD: Rowman and Littlefield, Inc, 1994.

Clarke, Donald. *The Rise and Fall of Popular Music: A Narrative History from the Renaissance to Rock 'n' Roll.* New York: St. Martin's Press, 1995.

Clayson, Alan. *Beat Merchants: The Origins, History, Impact, and Rock Legacy of the 1960s British Pop Groups.* London: Blandford Books, 1996.

Cohn, Nik. *A Wop Bop A Loo Bop A Lop Bam Boom: The Golden Age of Rock.* New York: Da Capo Press, 1996 (c. 1969).

Cooper, B. Lee. *Images of American Society in Popular Music: A Guide to Reflective Teaching.* Chicago: Nelson-Hall, Inc, 1982.

Cooper, B. Lee. *The Popular Music Handbook: A Resource Guide for Teachers, Librarians, and Media Specialists.* Littleton, CO: Libraries Unlimited, Inc, 1984.

Cooper, B. Lee. *Popular Music Perspectives: Ideas, Themes, and Patterns in Contemporary Lyrics.* Bowling Green, OH: Bowling Green State University Popular Press, 1991.

Cooper, B. Lee. *A Resource Guide to Themes in Contemporary American Song Lyrics, 1950-1985.* Westport CT: Greenwood Press, 1986.

Cooper, B. Lee and Wayne S. Haney. *Response Recordings: An Answer Song Discography, 1950-1990.* Metuchen, NJ: Scarecrow Press, 1990.

Cooper, B. Lee and Wayne S. Haney. *Rockabilly: A Bibliographic Resource Guide.* Metuchen, NJ: Scarecrow Press, 1990.

Cooper, B. Lee and Wayne S. Haney. *Rock Music in American Popular Culture: Rock 'n' Roll Resources*. Binghamton, NY: The Haworth Press, Inc., 1995.

Cooper, B. Lee and Wayne S. Haney. *Rock Music in American Popular Culture II: More Rock 'n' Roll Resources*. Binghamton, NY: The Haworth Press, Inc., 1997.

Cotten, Lee. *Reelin' and Rockin'—The Golden Age of American Rock 'n' Roll: Volume Two, 1956-1959*. Ann Arbor, MI: Popular Culture, Ink., 1995.

Cotten, Lee. *Shake, Rattle, and Roll—The Golden Age of American Rock 'n' Roll: Volume One, 1952-1955*. Ann Arbor, MI: Pierian Press, 1989.

Davis, Francis. *The History of the Blues: The Roots, the Music, the People from Charley Patton to Robert Cray*. New York: Hyperion Books, 1995.

Dean, John and Jean-Paul Gabilliet (eds.). *European Readings of American Popular Culture*. Westport, CT: Greenwood Press, 1996.

DeCurtis, Anthony (ed.). *Present Tense: Rock and Roll and Culture*. Durham, NC: Duke University Press, 1992.

DeCurtis, Anthony and James Henke, with Holly George-Warren (eds.). *The Rolling Stone Illustrated History of Rock and Roll* (Fully Revised and Updated). New York: Random House, 1992.

Denisoff, R. Serge. *Inside MTV*. New Brunswick, NJ: Transaction Books, 1991 (c. 1988).

Denisoff, R. Serge and William D. Romanowski. *Risky Business: Rock in Film*. New Brunswick, NJ: Transaction Books, 1991.

Denselow, Robin. *When the Music's Over: The Story of Political Pop*. London: Faber and Faber, 1990 (c. 1989).

DiMartino, Dave. *Singer-Songwriters: Pop Music's Performer-Composers, From A to Zevon*. New York: Billboard Books, 1994.

Ellison, Mary. *Lyrical Protest: Black Music's Struggle Against Discrimination*. New York: Praeger Books, 1989.

Ennis, Philip H. *The Seventh Stream: The Emergence of Rocknroll in American Popular Music*. Hanover, NH: Wesleyan University Press, 1992.

Erlewine, Michael, Vladimir Bogdanov, Chris Woodstra, and Stephen Thomas Erlewine (eds.). *All Music Guide: The Experts' Guide to the Best CDs, Albums and Tapes* (Third Edition). San Francisco: Miller Freeman Books, 1997.

Erlewine, Michael, Vladimir Bogdanov, and Chris Woodstra (eds.). *All Music Guide to Rock*. San Francisco: Miller Freeman Books, 1995.

Erlewine, Michael, Vladimir Bogdanov, Chris Woodstra, and Cub Koda (eds.). *All Music Guide to the Blues*. San Francisco, CA: Miller Freeman Books, 1996.

Escott, Colin. *Tattooed on Their Tongues: A Journey Through the Backrooms of American Music*. New York: Schirmer Books, 1996.

Ewbank, Alison J. and Fouli T. Papageorgiou (eds.). *Whose Master's Voice? The Development of Popular Music in Thirteen Cultures*. Westport, CT: Greenwood Press, 1997.

Fornas, Johan, Ulf Lindberg, and Ove Sernhede (translated by Jan Teeland). *In Garageland: Rock, Youth, and Modernity*. New York: Routledge, 1995.

Forte, Allen. *The American Popular Ballad of the Golden Era, 1924-1950.* Princeton, NJ: Princeton University Press, 1995.

Friedlander, Paul. *Rock and Roll: A Social History.* Boulder, CO: Westview Press, 1996.

Frith, Simon (ed.). *Facing the Music.* New York: Pantheon Books, 1988.

Frith, Simon. *Music for Pleasure: Essays in the Sociology of Pop.* New York: Routledge, Chapman, and Hall, 1988.

Frith, Simon. *Performing Rites: On the Value of Popular Music.* Cambridge, MA: Harvard University Press, 1996.

Frith, Simon. *Sound Effects: Youth, Leisure, and the Politics of Rock 'n' Roll.* New York: Pantheon Books, 1981.

Frith, Simon and Andrew Goodwin (eds.). *On Record: Rock, Pop, and the Written Word.* New York: Pantheon Books, 1990.

Frith, Simon, Andrew Goodwin, and Lawrence Grossberg (eds.). *Sound and Vision: The Music Video Reader.* New York: Routledge, 1993.

Furia, Philip. *The Poets of Tin Pan Alley: A History of America's Great Lyricists.* New York: Oxford University Press, 1990.

Gabbard, Krim. *Jammin' at the Margins: Jazz in the American Cinema.* Chicago: University of Chicago Press, 1996.

Gammond, Peter. *The Oxford Companion to Popular Music.* New York: Oxford University Press, 1993.

Garofalo, Reebee. *Rockin' Out: Popular Music in the USA.* Boston: Allyn and Bacon, 1997.

Gatten, Jeffrey N. *Rock Music Scholarship: An Interdisciplinary Bibliography.* Westport, CT: Greenwood Press, 1995.

Gillett, Charlie. *The Sound of the City: The Rise of Rock and Roll* (Second Edition). New York: Da Capo Press, 1996 (c. 1983).

Gracyk, Theodore. *Rhythm and Noise: An Aesthetics of Rock.* Durham, NC: Duke University Press, 1996.

Graff, Gary (ed.). *MusicHound Rock: The Essential Album Guide.* Detroit, MI: Visible Ink Press, 1996.

Green, Jeff (comp.). *The Green Book of Songs by Subject: The Thematic Guide to Popular Music* (Fourth Edition, Updated and Expanded). Nashville, TN: Professional Desk Services, 1995.

Gribin, Anthony J. and Matthew M. Schiff. *Doo-Wop: The Forgotten Third of Rock 'n' Roll.* Iola, WI: Krause Publications, 1992.

Griggs, Bill. *The Evolution and Decline of 1950s Rock and Roll Music.* Lubbock, TX: William F. Griggs/Rockin' 50s Magazine, 1996.

Guralnick, Peter. *Sweet Soul Music: Rhythm and Blues and the Southern Dream of Freedom.* New York: Harper and Row, 1986.

Haggerty, Gary. *A Guide to Popular Music Reference Books: An Annotated Bibliography.* Westport, CT: Greenwood Press, 1995.

Hamm, Charles. *Music in the New World.* New York: W. W. Norton and Co., 1983.

Hannusch, Jeff (a.k.a. Almost Slim). *I Hear You Knockin': The Sound of New Orleans Rhythm and Blues.* Ville Platte, LA: Swallow Press, 1985.

Hardy, Phil, and Dave Laing. *The Da Capo Companion to 20th-Century Popular Music*. New York: Da Capo Press, 1995 (c. 1990).

Hatch, David and Stephen Millward. *From Blues to Rock: An Analytical History of Pop Music*. Manchester, England: Manchester University Press, 1989 (c. 1987).

Hendler, Herb. *Year by Year in the Rock Era: Events and Conditions Shaping the Rock Generations that Reshaped America*. Westport, CT: Greenwood Press, 1983.

Henke, James (ed.). *Rock Facts: Rock and Roll Hall of Fame and Museum*. New York: Universe Publishing, 1996.

Hildebrand, Lee. *Stars of Soul and Rhythm and Blues: Top Recording Artists and Showstopping Performers, from Memphis and Motown to Now*. New York: Billboard Books, 1994.

Hoffmann, Frank. *American Popular Culture: A Guide to the Reference Literature*. Englewood, CO: Libraries Unlimited, Inc., 1995.

Hoffmann, Frank (comp.). *The Literature of Rock, 1954-1978*. Metuchen, NJ: Scarecrow Press, Inc., 1981.

Hoffmann, Frank and B. Lee Cooper (comps.). *The Literature of Rock II, 1979-1983* (Two Volumes). Metuchen, NJ: Scarecrow Press, Inc., 1986.

Hoffmann, Frank and B. Lee Cooper (comps.). *The Literature of Rock III, 1984-1990*. Metuchen, NJ: Scarecrow Press, Inc., 1995.

Horstman, Dorothy (comp.) *Sing Your Heart Out, Country Boy: Classic Country Songs and Their Inside Stories, by the Men and Women Who Wrote Them* (Third Edition). Nashville, TN: Vanderbilt University Press/Country Music Foundation Press, 1995.

Jancik, Wayne and Tad Lathrop. *Cult Rockers: 150 of the Most Controversial, Distinctive, Offbeat, Intriguing, Outrageous, and Championed Rock Musicians of All Time*. New York: Fireside Books, 1995.

Joynson, Vernon. *The Tapestry of Delights: The Comprehensive Guide to British Music of the Beat, R&B, Psychedelic, and Progressive Eras, 1963-1976*. Telford, England: Borderline Publications, 1995.

Kick, Brent E. *The Ultimate Musician's Reference Handbook: The Most Complete Guide to Who's Who in Popular Music*. Anaheim Hills, CA: Centerstream Publishing, 1996.

Kingsbury, Paul (ed.). *The Country Reader: Twenty-Five Years of the Journal of Country Music*. Nashville, TN: Country Music Foundation Press/Vanderbilt University Press, 1996.

Krebs, Gary M. *The Rock and Roll Reader's Guide: A Comprehensive Guide to Books by and About Musicians and Their Music*. New York: Billboard Books, 1997.

Larkin, Colin (ed.). *The Guinness Encyclopedia of Popular Music* (Concise Edition). Enfield, Middlesex, England: Guinness Books, 1993.

Lavine, Michael and Pat Blashill. *Noise from the Underground: A Secret History of Alternative Rock*. New York: Fireside/Simon and Schuster, 1996.

Lazell, Barry with Dafydd Rees and Luke Crampton (eds.) *Rock Movers and Shakers: An A to Z of the People Who Made Rock Happen*. New York: Billboard Publications, Inc., 1989.

Lewis, George H. (ed.). *All That Glitters: Country Music in America*. Bowling Green, OH: Bowling Green State University Popular Press, 1993.

Leyser, Brady J. with additional research by Pol Gosset (comps.). *Rock Stars/Pop Stars: A Comprehensive Bibliography, 1955-1994*. Westport, CT: Greenwood Press, 1994.

Lichtenstein, Grace and Laura Dankner. *Musical Gumbo: The Music of New Orleans*. New York: W. W. Norton and Company, 1993.

Lipsitz, George. *Dangerous Crossroads: Popular Music, Postmodernism, and the Poetics of Place*. New York: Verso Books, 1994.

Lipsitz, George. *Time Passages: Collective Memory and American Popular Culture*. Minneapolis, MI: University of Minnesota Press, 1990.

Macan, Edward. *Rocking the Classics: English Progressive Rock and the Counterculture*. New York: Oxford University Press, 1997.

Marcus, Greil (ed.). *Stranded: Rock and Roll for a Desert Island*. New York: Da Capo Press, 1996 (c. 1979).

McCloud, Barry, et al. *Definitive Country: The Ultimate Encyclopedia of Country Music and Its Performers*. New York: Perigee Books, 1995.

Morrison, Craig. *Go Cat Go! Rockabilly Music and Its Makers*. Champaign, IL: University of Illinois Press, 1996.

Ochs, Michael. *1000 Record Covers*. New York: Taschen, 1995.

Oermann, Robert K. *America's Music: The Roots of Country*. Atlanta, GA: Turner Publishing, Inc., 1996.

Palmer, Robert. *Rock and Roll: An Unruly History*. New York: Harmony Books, 1995.

Peretti, Burton W. *The Creation of Jazz: Music, Race, and Culture in Urban America*. Urbana, IL: University of Illinois Press, 1992.

Pichaske, David R. *A Generation in Motion: Popular Music and Culture in the Sixties*. Granite Falls, Minnesota: Ellis Press, 1989.

Pielke, Robert G. *You Say You Want a Revolution: Rock Music in American Culture*. Chicago: Nelson-Hall, Inc., 1986.

Pratt, Ray. *Rhythm and Resistance: Explorations in the Political Uses of Popular Music*. New York: Praeger Books, 1990.

Pruter, Robert. *Chicago Soul*. Urbana, IL: University of Illinois Press, 1991.

Pruter, Robert. *Doowop: The Chicago Scene*. Urbana, IL: University of Illinois Press. 1996.

Rees, Dafydd and Luke Crampton. *Encyclopedia of Rock Stars*. New York: D. K. Publishing, 1996.

Rimler, Walter. *Not Fade Away: A Comparison of Jazz Age with Rock Era Pop Song Composers*. Ann Arbor, MI: Pierian Press, 1984.

Rodnitzky, Jerome L. *Minstrels of the Dawn: The Folk-Protest Singer As a Cultural Hero*. Chicago: Nelson Hall, Inc., 1976.

Rogers, Jimmie N. *The Country Music Message: All About Lovin' and Livin'*. Englewood Cliffs, NJ: Prentice-Hall, Inc., 1983.

Rogers, Jimmie N. *The Country Music Message: Revisited*. Fayetteville, AR: University of Arkansas Press, 1989.

Romanowski, Patricia and Holly George-Warren, with Jon Pareles (eds.). *The New Rolling Stone Encyclopedia of Rock and Roll* (Revised and Updated). New York: Fireside/Rolling Stone Press Book, 1995.

Ruppli, Michel (comp.). *The Aladdin/Imperial Labels: A Discography.* Westport, CT: Greenwood Press, 1991.

Ruppli, Michel (comp.). *Atlantic Records: A Discography* (Four Volumes). Westport, CT: Greenwood Press, 1979.

Ruppli, Michel (comp.). *The Chess Labels: A Discography* (Two Volumes). Westport, CT: Greenwood Press, 1983.

Ruppli, Michel (comp.).*The Decca Labels: A Discography* (Six Volumes). Westport, CT: Greenwood Press, 1996.

Ruppli, Michel, with the assistance of Bill Daniels (comps.). *The King Labels: A Discography* (Two Volumes). Westport, CT: Greenwood Press, 1985.

Sanjek, Russell (updated by David Sanjek). *Pennies from Heaven: The American Popular Music Business in the Twentieth Century.* New York: Da Capo Press, 1996 (c. 1988).

Santelli, Robert. *The Big Book of the Blues: A Biographical Encyclopedia.* New York: Penguin Books, 1993.

Santino, Jack (ed.). *Halloween and Other Festivals of Death and Life.* Knoxville, TN: University of Tennessee Press, 1994.

Santino, Jack. *New Old-Fashioned Ways: Holidays and Popular Culture.* Knoxville, TN: University of Tennessee Press, 1996.

Scheurer, Timothy E. (ed.). *American Popular Music—Volume One: The 19th Century and Tin Pan Alley.* Bowling Green, OH: Bowling Green State University Popular Press, 1989.

Scheurer, Timothy E. (ed.). *American Popular Music—Volume Two: The Age of Rock.* Bowling Green, OH: Bowling Green State University Popular Press, 1989.

Scheurer, Timothy E. *Born in the U.S.A.: The Myth of America in Popular Music from Colonial Times to the Present.* Jackson, MS: University Press of Mississippi, 1991.

Schultze, Quentin J., Roy M. Anker, James D. Bratt, William D. Romanowski, John W. Worst, and Lambert Zuidervaart. *Dancing in the Dark: Youth, Popular Culture, and the Electronic Media.* Grand Rapids, MI: William B. Eerdmans Publishing Company, 1991.

Scott, Frank, Al Ennis, and the Staff of Roots and Rhythm. *The Roots and Rhythm Guide to Rock.* Pennington, NJ: A Cappella Books, 1993.

Scott, Frank, and the Staff of Down Home Music. *The Down Home Guide to the Blues.* Pennington, NJ: A Cappella Books, 1991.

Scott, John Anthony. *The Ballad of America: The History of the United States in Song and Story.* Carbondale, IL: Southern Illinois University Press, 1983 (1996).

Segrave, Kerry. *Payola in the Music Industry: A History, 1880-1991.* Jefferson, NC: McFarland and Company, Inc., 1994.

Seidenberg, Steven, Maurice Sellar, and Lou Jones. *You Must Remember This: Songs at the Heart of the War.* London: Boxtree, Ltd., 1995.

Shaw, Arnold. *Honkers and Shouters: The Golden Years of Rhythm and Blues.* New York: Collier Books, 1978.

Shaw, Arnold. *The Rockin' '50s: The Decade That Transformed the Pop Music Scene.* New York: Hawthorn Books, 1974.

Southern, Eileen. *The Music of Black Americans: A History* (Third Edition). New York: W. W. Norton and Company, 1997.

Stambler, Irwin. *The Encyclopedia of Pop, Rock and Soul* (Revised Edition). New York: St. Martin's Press, 1989.

Straw, Will, Stacey Johnson, Rebecca Sullivan, and Paul Friedlander (eds.). *Popular Music: Style and Identity.* Montreal, Canada: Centre for Research on Canadian Cultural Industries and Institutions, 1995.

Sumrall, Harry. *Pioneers of Rock and Roll: 100 Artists Who Changed the Face of Rock.* New York: Billboard Books, 1994.

Szatmary, David. *A Time to Rock: A Social History of Rock 'n' Roll.* New York: Schirmer Books, 1996.

Tosches, Nick. *Country: The Twisted Roots of Rock 'n' Roll.* New York: Da Capo Press, 1996 (c. 1977).

Tyler, Sean (ed.). *International Who's Who in Music—Volume Two: Popular Music.* Cambridge, England: Melrose Press, Ltd./International Who's Who in Music, 1996.

Walker, Donald E. and B. Lee Cooper. *Baseball and American Culture: A Thematic Bibliography of Over 4,500 Works.* Jefferson, NC: McFarland and Company, Inc., 1995.

Ward, Ed, Geoffrey Stokes, and Ken Tucker. *Rock of Ages: The Rolling Stone History of Rock and Roll.* New York: Rolling Stone Press/Summit Books, 1986.

Warner, Jay. *Billboard's American Rock 'n' Roll in Review.* New York: Schirmer Books, 1997.

Warner, Jay. *The Billboard Book of American Singing Groups: A History, 1940-1990.* New York: Billboard Books, 1992.

Welding, Pete and Toby Byron (eds.). *Bluesland: Portraits of Twelve Major American Blues Masters.* New York: Dutton/Penguin Books, 1991.

Whitburn, Joel (comp.). *1996 Music Yearbook.* Menomonee Falls, WI: Record Research, Inc., 1997.

Whitburn, Joel (comp.). *Pop Hits, 1940-1954.* Menomonee Falls, WI: Record Research, Inc., 1994.

Whitburn, Joel (comp.). *Pop Memories, 1890-1954: The History of American Popular Music.* Menomonee Falls, WI: Record Research, Inc., 1986.

Whitburn, Joel (comp.). *Rock Tracks: Album Rock (1981-1995) and Modern Rock (1988-1995).* Menomonee Falls, WI: Record Research, Inc., 1995.

Whitburn, Joel (comp.). *Top Country Singles, 1944-1993.* Menomonee Falls, WI: Record Research, Inc., 1994.

Whitburn, Joel (comp.). *Top 1000 X 5: Five Top 1000 Rankings of America's Favorite Hits* (1996 Edition). Menomonee Falls, WI: Record Research, Inc., 1997.

Whitburn, Joel (comp.). *Top Pop Albums, 1955-1996.* Menomonee Falls, WI: Record Research, Inc., 1997.

Whitburn, Joel (comp.). *Top Pop Album Tracks, 1955-1992.* Menomonee Falls, WI: Record Research, Inc., 1993.

Whitburn, Joel (comp.). *Top Pop Album Tracks, 1993-1996.* Menomonee Falls, WI: Record Research, Inc., 1996.

Whitburn, Joel (comp.). *Top Pop Singles CD Guide, 1955-1979.* Menomonee Falls, WI: Record Research, Inc., 1995.

Whitburn, Joel (comp.). *Top Pop Singles, 1955-1993.* Menomonee Falls, WI: Record Research, Inc., 1994.

Whitburn, Joel (comp.). *Top R&B Singles, 1942-1995.* Menomonee Falls, WI: Record Research, Inc., 1996.

White, Timothy. *Music to My Ears: The Billboard Essays—Profiles of Popular Music in the '90s.* New York: Henry Holt and Company, 1996.

Wicke, Peter (translated by Rachel Fogg). *Rock Music: Culture, Aesthetics, and Sociology.* Cambridge, England: Cambridge University Press, 1990 (c. 1987).

Wynn, Ron, with Michael Erlewine and Vladimir Bogdanov (eds.). *All Music Guide to Jazz: The Best CDs, Albums, and Tapes.* San Francisco: Miller Freeman Books, 1994.

Articles

Aquila, Richard. "The Homogenization of Early Rock and Roll,." in *America's Musical Pulse,* edited by Kenneth J. Bindas. Westport, CT: Praeger Books, 1992. pp. 269-280.

Bernard-Donals, Michael. "Jazz, Rock 'n' Roll, Rap, and Politics." *Journal of Popular Culture,* XXV, (Fall 1994), pp. 127-138.

Bowman, Rob. "Stax Records: A Lyrical Analysis." *Popular Music and Society,* XX, No. 1, (Spring 1996), pp. 71-92.

Cafarelli, Carl. "An Informal History of Bubblegum Music." *Goldmine,* No. 437, (April 25 1997), pp. 16-19, 32, 38, 60, 66-76.

Chastagner, Claude. 1996."Here, There, and Everywhere: Rock Music, Mass Culture, and the Counterculture," in *European Readings of American Popular Culture,* edited by John Dean and Jean-Paul Gabilliet. Westport, CT: Greenwood Press, 1996, pp. 69-77.

Christianen, Michael. "Cycles of Symbol Production? A New Model to Explain Concentration, Diversity, and Innovation in the Music Industry." *Popular Music,* XIV, No. 1, (January 1995), pp. 55-93.

Cooper, B. Lee. "Examining the Medical Profession Through Musical Metaphors." *International Journal of Instructional Media,* XXI, No. 2, 1994, pp. 155-163.

Cooper, B. Lee. "For the Record: The Popular Music Contributions of Jerry Leiber and Mike Stoller." *Popular Music and Society,* XXI, No. 4 (Winter 1997), pp. 128-131.

Cooper, B. Lee. "From Johnny Ace to Frank Zappa: Debating the Meaning of Death in Rock Music—a Review Essay." *Popular Culture in Libraries,* III, No. 1 (1995), pp. 51-75.

Cooper, B. Lee. "From 'Love Letters' to 'Miss You': Popular Recordings, Epistolary Imagery, and Romance During War Time, 1941-1945." *Journal of American Culture,* XIX, No. 4 (Winter 1996), pp. 15-27.

Cooper, B. Lee. "It's Still Rock 'n' Roll to Me: Reflections on the Evolution of Popular Music and Rock Scholarship." *Popular Music and Society,* XXI, No. 1 (Spring 1997), pp. 101-108.

Cooper, B. Lee. "Killer B's: Two-Sided Hits from Rock's Golden Age, 1955-1963." *Popular Music and Society,* XX, No. 3 (Fall 1996), pp. 141-144.

Cooper, B. Lee. "Popular Music in Print." *Popular Music and Society,* XIX, No. 4, (Winter 1995), pp. 105-112.

Cooper, B. Lee. "Please Mr. Postman: Images of Written Communication in Contemporary Lyrics." *International Journal of Instructional Media,* XXIII, No. 1 (1996), pp. 79-89.

Cooper, B. Lee. "Reveille, Riveting, and Romance Remembered: Popular Recordings of the World War II Era," in *Proceedings of the University of Great Falls Symposium,* edited by William Furdell. Great Falls, MT: University of Great Falls Press, (1995) October 2-6, pp. 43-73.

Cooper, B. Lee. "A Taxonomy of Tributes on Compact Disc: A Review Essay." *Popular Music and Society,* XX, No. 2 (Summer 1996), pp. 204-217.

Cooper, B. Lee. "Terror Translated Into Comedy: The Popular Music Metamorphosis of Film and Television Horror, 1956-1991." *Journal of Popular Film and Television,* XX, No. 3 (Fall 1997), pp. 31-42.

Cooper, B. Lee. "What Kind of Fool Am I? Audio Imagery, Personal Identity, and Social Relationships." *International Journal of Instructional Media,* XXIV, No. 3 (1997), pp. 253-267.

Cooper, B. Lee. "Wise Men Never Try: A Discography of Fool Songs, 1945-1995." *Popular Music and Society,* XXI, No. 2 (Summer 1997), pp. 115-131.

Cooper, B. Lee, Simon Frith, Paul Hansen, Bernhard Hefele, David Horn, and Toru Mitsui. "Book List." *Popular Music,* XIV, No. 3, (October 1995), pp. 391-413.

Cooper, B. Lee, Simon Frith, Bernhard Hefele, Dave Lang, and Toru Mitsui. "Book List." *Popular Music,* XV, No. 3, (October 1996), pp. 371-396.

Cooper, B. Lee and William L. Schurk. "Smokin' Songs: Examining Tobacco Use As an American Cultural Phenomenon through Contemporary Lyrics." *International Journal of Instructional Media,* XXI, No. 3, (1994), pp. 261-268.

Eberhart, George M. "Stack Lee: The Man, the Music, the Myth." *Popular Music and Society,* XX, No. 1, (Spring 1996), pp. 1-70.

Fitzgerald, Jon. "When the Brill Building Met Lennon-McCartney: Continuity and Change in the Early Evolution of the Mainstream Pop Song." *Popular Music and Society,* XIX, No. 1, (Spring 1995), pp. 59-77.

Gronow, Pekka. "The Record Industry: The Growth of a Mass Medium," in *Popular Music 3: Producers and Markets,* edited by Richard Middleton and David Horn. Cambridge, England: Cambridge University Press, 1983, pp. 53-75.

Hay, Fred J. " 'Blues What I Am': Blues Consciousness and Social Protest." in *America's Musical Pulse,* edited by Kenneth J. Bindas. Westport, CT: Praeger Books, 1992, pp. 13-21.

Jarrett, Michael. "Concerning the Progress of Rock and Roll." *South Atlantic Quarterly,* XC, No. 4, (Fall 1991), pp. 803-817.

Johnson, Michael L. "Garth and Friends: Resinging the West, Dancing to the Cowboy Beat." *New Westers: The West in Contemporary American Culture.* Lawrence, KS: University Press of Kansas, 1996, pp. 260-302.

Keil, Charles. " 'Ethnic' Music Traditions in the USA (Black Music; Country Music; Other; All)." *Popular Music,* XIII, No. 2, (May 1994), pp. 175-178.

Lewis, George H. "Taste Cultures and Musical Stereotypes: Mirrors of Identity?" *Popular Music and Society,* XIX, No. 1, (Spring 1995), pp. 37-58.

Mahabir, Cynthia. "Wit and Popular Music: The Calypso and the Blues." *Popular Music,* XV, No. 1, (January 1996), pp. 55-81.

North, Adrian C. and David J. Hargreaves. "Eminence in Pop Music." *Popular Music and Society,* XIX, No. 4, (Winter 1995), pp. 41-66.

Peterson, Richard A. "The Dialectic of Hard-Core and Soft-Shell Country Music," in *Readin' Country Music: Steel Guitars, Opry Stars, and Honky Tonk Bars,* edited by Cecelia Tichi. Durham, NC: Duke University Press, 1995, pp. 273-300.

Peterson, Richard A. "Five Constraints on the Production of Culture: Law, Technology, Market, Organizational Structure, and Occupational Careers," in *American Popular Music—Volume One: The 19th Century and Tin Pan Alley,* edited by Timothy E. Scheurer. Bowling Green, OH: Bowling Green State University Popular Press, 1989, pp. 16-27.

Peterson, Richard A. and David G. Berger. "Cycles in Symbol Production: The Case of Popular Music," in *On Record: Rock, Pop, and the Written Word,* edited by Simon Frith and Andrew Goodwin. New York: Pantheon Books, 1990, pp. 140-159.

Powers, Jim. "Mondo Melodica Exotica: The Unexpected, Thoroughly Thrilling Return of Incredibly Strange Space-Age Bachelor Pad Music." *Goldmine,* No. 411, (April 26, 1996), pp. 20-34, 184.

Roberts, Robin. "Independence Day: Feminist Country Music Videos." *Popular Music and Society,* XX, No. 1, (Spring 1996), pp. 135-154.

Rodnitzky, Jerome. "Popular Music As Politics and Protest," in *America's Musical Pulse,* edited by Kenneth J. Bindas. Westport, CT: Praeger Books, 1992, pp. 3-11.

Rothenbuhler, Eric W. and John W. Dimmick. "Popular Music: Concentration and Diversity in the Industry, 1974-1980." *Journal of Communication,* XXXII, (Winter 1982), pp. 143-149.

Sanjek, David. "Blue Moon of Kentucky Rising Over the Mystery Train: The Complete Construction of Country Music," in *Readin' Country Music: Steel Guitars, Opry Stars, and Honky Tonk Bars,* edited by Cecelia Tichi. Durham, NC: Duke University Press, 1995, pp. 29-55.

Sanjek, David. "Pleasure and Principles: Issues of Authenticity in the Analysis of Rock 'n' Roll." *Tracking: Popular Music Studies*, IV, (Spring 1992), pp. 12-21.

Shepherd, John. "Music, Culture, and Interdisciplinarity: Reflections on Relationships." *Popular Music*, XIII, No. 2, (May 1994), pp. 127-141.

Shumway, David R. "Rock and Roll as a Cultural Practice." *South Atlantic Quarterly*, XC, (Fall 1991), pp. 753-769.

Stilwell, Robynn J. "In the Air Tonight: Text, Intertextuality, and the Construction of Meaning." *Popular Music and Society*, XIX, No. 4, (Winter 1995), pp. 67-103.

Tamarkin, Jeff. "Five Hundred Points of Contention: The Hall of Fame Lists Its Favorite Songs." *Goldmine*, No. 397, (October 13, 1995), pp. 8-12.

Tucker, Bruce. " 'Tell Tchaikovsky the News': Postmodernism, Popular Culture, and the Emergence of Rock 'n' Roll." *Black Music Research Journal*, IX, (Fall 1989), pp. 271-295.

Wilson, Janelle L. and Gerald E. Markle. "Justify My Ideology: Madonna and Traditional Values." *Popular Music and Society*, XVI, (Summer 1992), pp. 75-84.

Index

Order Your Own Copy of
This Important Book for Your Personal Library!

ROCK MUSIC IN AMERICAN POPULAR CULTURE III
More Rock 'n' Roll Resources

_____ in hardbound at $59.95 (ISBN: 0-7890-0489-5)

_____ in softbound at $29.95 (ISBN: 0-7890-0490-9)

COST OF BOOKS _____

OUTSIDE USA/CANADA/
MEXICO: ADD 20%_____

POSTAGE & HANDLING_____
*(US: $3.00 for first book & $1.25
for each additional book)
Outside US: $4.75 for first book
& $1.75 for each additional book)*

SUBTOTAL_____

IN CANADA: ADD 7% GST_____

STATE TAX_____
*(NY, OH & MN residents, please
add appropriate local sales tax)*

FINAL TOTAL_____
*(If paying in Canadian funds,
convert using the current
exchange rate. UNESCO
coupons welcome.)*

☐ **BILL ME LATER:** ($5 service charge will be added)
(Bill-me option is good on US/Canada/Mexico orders only;
not good to jobbers, wholesalers, or subscription agencies.)

☐ Check here if billing address is different from
shipping address and attach purchase order and
billing address information.

Signature_____

☐ **PAYMENT ENCLOSED: $**_____

☐ **PLEASE CHARGE TO MY CREDIT CARD.**

☐ Visa   ☐ MasterCard   ☐ AmEx   ☐ Discover
☐ Diners Club
Account # _____

Exp. Date _____

Signature _____

Prices in US dollars and subject to change without notice.

NAME _____

INSTITUTION _____

ADDRESS _____

CITY _____

STATE/ZIP _____

COUNTRY _____ COUNTY (NY residents only) _____

TEL _____ FAX _____

E-MAIL_____
May we use your e-mail address for confirmations and other types of information? ☐ Yes   ☐ No

Order From Your Local Bookstore or Directly From
The Haworth Press, Inc.
10 Alice Street, Binghamton, New York 13904-1580 • USA
TELEPHONE: 1-800-HAWORTH (1-800-429-6784) / Outside US/Canada: (607) 722-5857
FAX: 1-800-895-0582 / Outside US/Canada: (607) 772-6362
E-mail: getinfo@haworthpressinc.com
PLEASE PHOTOCOPY THIS FORM FOR YOUR PERSONAL USE.

BOF96